D1527787

THE SCOTTISH PEOPLE AND THE FRENCH REVOLUTION

The Enlightenment World:
Political and Intellectual History of the
Long Eighteenth Century

Series Editor: Michael T. Davis
Series Co-Editors: Jack Fruchtman, Jr
   Iain McCalman
   Paul Pickering
Advisory Editor: Hideo Tanaka

Titles In This Series

Harlequin Empire: Race, Ethnicity and the Drama of the Popular Enlightenment
David Worrall

The Cosmopolitan Ideal in the Age of Revolution and Reaction, 1776–1832
Michael Scrivener

Writing the Empire: Robert Southey and Romantic Colonialism
Carol Bolton

Adam Ferguson: History, Progress and Human Nature
Eugene Heath and Vincenzo Merolle (eds)

Charlotte Smith in British Romanticism
Jacqueline Labbe (ed)

Forthcoming Titles

Adam Ferguson: Philosophy, Politics and Society
Eugene Heath and Vincenzo Merolle (eds)

The Evolution of Sympathy in the Long Eighteenth Century
Jonathan Lamb

John Thelwall: Radical Romantic and Acquitted Felon
Steve Poole

Rhyming Reason: The Poetry of Romantic-Era Psychologists
Michelle Faubert

William Wickham, Master Spy: The Secret War against the French Revolution
Michael Durey

www.pickeringchatto.com/enlightenmentworld

THE SCOTTISH PEOPLE AND THE FRENCH REVOLUTION

BY

Bob Harris

LONDON
PICKERING & CHATTO
2008

Published by Pickering & Chatto (Publishers) Limited
21 Bloomsbury Way, London WC1A 2TH

2252 Ridge Road, Brookfield, Vermont 05036-9704, USA

www.pickeringchatto.com

BRITISH LIBRARY CATALOGUING IN PUBLICATION DATA

Harris, Bob, 1964–
The Scottish people and the French Revolution. – (The
Enlightenment world)
1. Political culture – Scotland – History – 18th century 2. Scotland – Politics
and government – 18th century 3. France – History – Revolution, 1789–1799
– Influence
I. Title
320.9'411'09033

ISBN-13: 9781851968848

This publication is printed on acid-free paper that conforms to the American
National Standard for the Permanence of Paper for Printed Library Materials.

Typeset by Pickering & Chatto (Publishers) Limited
Printed in the United Kingdom at the University Press, Cambridge

CONTENTS

PREFACE

This book is designed to help readers better understand Scottish politics in the 1790s, and hopefully to stimulate its fuller integration into eighteenth-century British history. Even where general texts include some consideration of Scottish developments, which is all too rarely, they are frequently inaccurate and ill informed. Anyone who reads about the history of the British Isles in this period cannot but be struck by the relative wealth of scholarship on England and Ireland, and the paucity of material on Scotland. There is a gap to be filled, therefore, and this book is a contribution towards this.

To some the subject and the approach which I have adopted may seem a bit old fashioned. For reasons that are all too obvious, the 1790s has not in recent years attracted the sort of attention from British historians it did several decades ago, although this is beginning to change. Ireland is in this, as in so many things, very different. More could be said about ideology and rhetoric, and hopefully this book may stimulate others to do this, if perhaps only out of irritation at my relative neglect of these things. However, it seemed to me that we needed to establish a fuller picture of what happened, of some of the basic structures of politics and contours of political debate in this period, as an essential preliminary to more narrowly focused investigations. The threads that are pursued are, in any case, ones explicitly designed to aid thinking about British experience in this decade, both in terms of interaction and connection between Scottish and predominantly English politics and in a comparative sense. For an English-born and educated individual writing on Scotland, this is a natural perspective to adopt; but it is also one which helps to illuminate central features of the politics of the 1790s in Scotland.

This book has taken considerably longer to write than was originally envisaged, although there is probably very little that is unusual in this. It was, nevertheless, started in Scotland and finished in Oxford. It is a book rooted in relationships and enthusiasms which I developed in Scotland, and that I have written it at all owes a great deal to the encouragement of colleagues working in a number of the Scottish universities and other institutions. I am especially grateful to Chris Smout for inviting me to give a paper to a British Academy conference on Anglo-Scottish relations in 2004, which allowed me to develop my thinking on 'union' as a theme in radical politics in this period. Alan Langlands, Principal of the University of Dundee, allowed me a year's research leave in 2005–6, when the bulk of it was written. This followed a period as head of the Department of History at Dundee, and his support for me and for history in the University is something which I look back to with enormous gratitude. Chris Whatley will recognize elements of the book, and Chapter 6 in particular owes a great deal to insights which he has brought to the understanding of eighteenth-century Scottish society. I hope that it is a book he will enjoy, but I would be surprised if he agreed with all of it. Alex Murdoch has offered supportive comment at various points for a 'British' approach, and I would like to record here my thanks to him for this. David Brown of the National Archives of Scotland has very generously shared information on various sets of papers in the Archives, and offered suggestions about other material that might prove useful. I would like to thank Vivienne Dunstan, Rhona Fiest, Karen Cullen and David Barrie for help with some of the research which underpins this book. In most cases, this was research for other projects, but it has happily proved very useful to this one. Vivienne was a model researcher on an investigation into the Angus burghs in the later Georgian period, and in the course of doing this turned up several archival nuggets. Considerable thanks are due to archivists and librarians in several places, especially the National Archives of Scotland; the National Library of Scotland; Edinburgh Central Library; Edinburgh City Archives; the Mitchell Library, Glasgow; Edinburgh University Special Collection; Angus Archives; and the Perth and Kinross County Archives. I am extremely grateful to Sir William Macpherson for allowing me access to his family archive at Newton Castle, Blairgowrie; to Major Graham of Fintry for permission to consult the microfilm copies of the papers of his ancestor, Robert Graham of Fintry; the permission of the Duke of Buccleuch and Queensberry, KT, to cite material from the Buccleuch Papers; and for the great help provided by Jane Anderson in making accessible material in the Atholl Papers from Blair Castle.

Properly among the dedicatees of this book is Max, whose requests for a walk when I was living in the Angus glens were always easy to cave in to. He has adapted to life in Oxford, but dogs are pragmatic beasts. Families can be less so, but the most important dedicatees of this book are Tess and the boys. It is no easy thing to move school at any stage, and if it has not always been smooth to date then I hope that for Sam, Tom and Matthew it will prove in the end to have been a positive experience. The last word should be for Tess: she has shouldered the only really important burdens in the last eighteen months, and for that and much else she has my unstinting love.

Bob Harris
February 2008

INTRODUCTION

Modern historians have portrayed the impact of the French Revolution on Scottish politics and society as limited, especially when compared to other parts of the British Isles. Scots, it is argued, were strongly loyal to the political and social status quo, and the populace largely quiescent in the face of the political excitements and strains of the 1790s. As Louis Cullen wrote in 1989, in words which fully reflect this orthodoxy: 'The French Revolution ... passed over Scotland not quite unnoticed but with little sign of a likelihood of upheaval'.[1] Cullen was comparing Scotland to Ireland, a comparison which inevitably tends to emphasize what did not happen in the former. Nevertheless, the implication remains the same; that what needs explanation is the country's political stability in the 1790s and, in T. C. Smout's phrase, the 'uninflammability' of its population.[2]

Scotland's *relative* stability in this period is undeniable, and it is a theme which will feature at various points in this book. Edinburgh was not London or Dublin, and Glasgow, or Dundee or Paisley, to take two of the country's fastest growing manufacturing towns of the later eighteenth century, were not, say, Sheffield, Norwich or Belfast, all sites of strong and tenacious radical political organizations and traditions. Compared to Ireland and some parts of England, radicalism as an open force was quickly suppressed, although this was due in no small part to a uniquely (in a British context) repressive legal system. Edinburgh became a stronghold of political reaction, which, given the strategic importance of the capital in political culture in this period, including radical politics, was another fact of major importance in explaining the course and outcome of the radicals' campaign. An embattled opposition Whig element led by Henry Erskine, until 1796 the Dean of the Faculty of Advocates, did manage to retain a foothold in public life in the capital and, on occasion, such as in late 1795, mobilize a significant amount of opposition to policies of political repression and the conduct of the war; but their influence was episodic and limited. Glasgow seems to have been only marginally different, although the Professor of Civil Law, John Millar, and his coterie provided a focus for opposition Whig opinion in the university. The Glasgow mercantile classes were, however, for the most part strong supporters of Pitt and Dundas, with whom they had multiple and usually very open lines of communication.[3]

The predominant impact of the Irish Rebellion of 1798 seems, meanwhile, to have been to produce a reassuring sense of distance, psychological if not geographical, from the unhappy conflagration across the St George's Channel.[4] While Scotland's opposition Whigs, as in the rest of Britain, used the convulsion further to condemn policies of official repression and the conduct of the military in Ireland, what impressed more people was the brutality and savage violence unleashed by the Irish 'rebels'. That the British military were at least as vicious was not ignored, but seen as justified by circumstances. As the editor of the *Dumfries Weekly Journal* declared on 5 June 1798, 'At such a mode of warfare humanity shudders; but, relying on the wisdom of his Majesty's councils, we persuade ourselves that dire necessity will be found to justify their severity'. There was a Scottish insurrectionary body, the Society of the United Scotsmen, which was linked, in ways and to an extent which remain obscure, to the revolutionary conspiracies of the Society of the United Irishmen – rightly described by Devine as the 'most formidable revolutionary body in the British Isles'[5] – and through them to revolutionary France, but its numbers appear to have been small. A wave of arrests in November 1797 had, moreover, decapitated it of much of its leadership, most notably the Dundee weaver George Mealmaker. In January 1798, Mealmaker was sentenced to fourteen years' transportation. At the end of the decade, very high food prices and economic depression between 1799 and 1801 led to considerable, periodically intense suffering, and several waves of disturbances, but produced relatively little disaffection, passive or active. By this point, keeping faith with revolutionary France and radicalism was very much the preoccupation of a tiny minority, a minority which barely registers in the historical record. As Hamish Fraser has noted elsewhere, neither the Despard conspiracy of 1802 nor the failed Emmet rising in Dublin in the following year had any Scottish dimension.[6]

When confronted with the rise of republicanism and violence in France from the summer of 1792, the efflorescence of domestic popular radicalism during that autumn, and from February 1793 war with revolutionary France, the Scottish elites closed ranks in defence of the political and social status quo. Unity at the top of society in opposition to radicalism was one of many reasons why radical societies found it hard to survive after their initial flourishing.

The political division which opened up in 1792 was also a social one, however. The battle between radicals and the authorities and their supporters became, at least until 1794, one for the hearts and minds of the labouring classes. The difference with other parts of the British Isles was obviously one of degree, but it was notable for all that. Henry Dundas declared on 12 November 1792, in the course of a visit to Scotland which convinced him of the gravity of the challenge posed by developments north of the border:

Everybody of Character, Respect and Property are so much of one mind here on all the great Principles of real Government, that there is no occasion to write to them. *The contest here is with the lower orders of People, whose minds are poisoned up to the Point of Liberty, Equality, and an Agrarian Law* [my emphasis].[7]

Weavers were very strongly represented among the rank and file of the radical societies which sprang into life in late 1792. Their numbers had grown rapidly in the previous decade, and they often comprised the largest proportion of the male population of Scotland's rapidly growing towns and industrial villages.[8] Scottish popular radicalism, apart from in Edinburgh, emerged from these multiplying and burgeoning weaving communities, a pattern which was to be repeated in 1816–20. It was in the industrial parishes of Renfrewshire, Ayrshire and Dumbartonshire in the west and Fife and Angus in the east, as well as in several of the larger manufacturing towns – Paisley, Perth, Stirling, Dundee, Glasgow – that radicalism, albeit briefly, took a strong hold. Contemporaries were much more equivocal and hesitant in their judgements than some historians have been about the loyalties and views of this section of the population, even, in some cases, after open radicalism had been finally suppressed and cowed in the early months of 1794. As Henry Mackenzie acknowledged to the Prime Minister, William Pitt, at the end of 1793: 'It must be confessed, that the public mind of the country has not got into such a state as to be much more easily agitated & disturbed than formerly; *the lowest of the people talk & read, & think of Politics*'.[9]

Scotland's underlying stability is, therefore, a main theme, but it is not the only one. Equally significant, and overlooked by most historians, were the limitations of the loyalist counter-reaction in Scotland to the rise of radicalism in late 1792. The loyalists' success in mobilizing opinion to combat the threat of radicalism was neither quickly nor easily achieved. Nor were the significance and meanings of any loyalist victory (if it can be so called) unambiguous; there was no uniform loyalist ideological consensus, but rather a strong commitment to order and stability in the fraught, perilous conditions of the decade. If something distinctive needs explaining here it may be why the Scottish elite was so quick in and intent on supporting social and political stability. Here it is that the socio-economic and structural explanations emphasized by Professor Devine are most compelling.[10] On the other hand, such approaches tend to downplay situational factors – in this case the conjunction of events which accompanied and stimulated both the radical campaign and the loyalist counter-reaction in the final months of 1792, the self-defeating posturing of the radicals at the British convention in late 1793, and the discovery of the so-called Watt or Pike Plot early in the following year – and take for granted the success of loyalism, without examining how this was achieved and where it failed as well as succeeded.[11] They also accord relatively little importance to ideology, although clearly there was some relationship between this and social and economic factors. It is worthy

of note in this context that several Scots were to the fore in producing histori-
cally-minded, empirical defences of the British state at the end of the eighteenth
and in the early nineteenth centuries which emphasized progress since 1688
or 1707.[12] This modernizing narrative, which identified Britain's distinctive
achievement as one of political stability, liberty and economic and commercial
progress, was nurtured and systematized by Scottish Enlightenment writers, and
may, given Scotland's recent experience of rapid economic growth, have been
one which the elites found it difficult to resist. It may also, perhaps less obviously, have produced a climate of opinion more than usually inclined to value
order, as well as liberty, as a precondition of social and economic progress. It was
precisely in such terms that the political constitution or 'sett' of Edinburgh was
defended in 1777 against those seeking to make it more directly representative
of the capital's population. What it ensured, one writer declared, was the 'equal
distribution of power' throughout the 'whole community', the maintenance of
'peace' and 'to prevent, as far as possible, the many abuses that would otherwise
ensue'.[13] Given the nature of Edinburgh's constitution, the very narrow oligarchy
which it served to entrench in power, what might seem striking is that such an
argument could be made at all.

In the later 1790s, the main threat to political and social stability came not
from domestic disaffection, although it continued to cast a sinewy shadow, but
from an expansionist France under the Directory and then Napoleon, a threat
which called forth a patriotic response from across the political and social spec-
trum, and for the suspension of differences to 'bid defiance to the threat of
France'.[14] Defensive patriotism was a broader, more pervasive phenomenon than
loyalism; it stretched to include, for example, groups of religious dissenters and
the lower ranks who, by and large, had remained outside the loyalist reaction of
the earlier 1790s. Nevertheless, because of this elasticity, it lacked even the limited degree of ideological coherence displayed by loyalism.[15]

The principal purpose of this book is to examine the rise, trajectory and
nature of radical, loyalist and patriotic politics in Scotland in the 1790s from
the perspectives of those who took part in them. This is partly done out of a
conviction that we need to return to the evidence before seeking to explain in
structural terms what did or did not happen; that we need, in short, to pay more
attention to the contemporary experiences of radicals and those who sought to
defeat them and their ambitions. We also need to map more carefully than has
occurred hitherto the opportunities for participation in public and political life
and debate to which the developments of the 1790s gave rise. Some of the fas-
cination of this aspect lies in the fact that for most individuals and groups such
opportunities had fewer precedents than in many places in England or in Ireland. For those who became the rank and file of the new radical societies formed
in the final third of 1792, the unprecedented explosion of political debate in this

period meant, for probably the first time, there was a powerful incentive to read about events in newspapers, to discuss them with others, and to seek to construct a new type of politics. The fact that this resulted in failure does not mean that we should relate this story primarily or only with this in view. The full story of Scottish loyalism in this period has, in any case, not been told elsewhere.[16]

This book, then, focuses on the varieties of political experience which were created by the unusual conditions of political life in the 1790s. The sources for doing this are, however, limited in several important ways. This is particularly true of radicalism. Scottish radicalism in the 1790s produced few pamphlets of note and only two short-lived newspapers. In the case of one of the latter, moreover, the *Caledonian Chronicle*, just two issues survive.[17] Of the few pamphlets, the most notable is James Thomson Callender's *The Political Progress of Britain*, which first appeared in 1792 in serial form in James Anderson's periodical, *The Bee*. It has been described by Callender's modern biographer as 'the only lengthy treatise attacking British political institutions to be published in Scotland during the era of the French Revolution'.[18] Almost the only other work which might fall into this category is George Mealmaker's *The Moral and Political Catechism of Mankind* (1797), the existence of which has led to his being described, with little further evidence to support the proposition, as the 'chief ideologue' of the United Scotsmen.[19] It is not hard to think of reasons which might explain why so few Scottish radical pamphlets emerged in the 1790s. First, it reflected London's role throughout the eighteenth century as a magnet to aspirant Scottish writers and journalists. Once there, these individuals tended to adopt a metropolitan perspective on debates, albeit their works were shaped by distinctively Scottish intellectual currents and formations. The full title of James Mackintosh's riposte to Edmund Burke's *Reflections on the Revolution in France – Vindicae Gallicae; a Defence of the French Revolution and its English Admirers* (1791) – is significant and representative in this context. Second, a combination of repression and shortage of funds can only have deterred further efforts at putting pen to paper following a series of prosecutions of Scottish radical writers and publishers in early 1793. It is probably significant in this context that the Paisley weaver James Kennedy's verse collection *Treason!!! Or, Not Treason!!!* (1795) was published not in Scotland but in London by that 'pugnaciously persistent' radical publisher Daniel Isaac Eaton.[20] (It was also Eaton who published a second edition of Callender's *The Political Progress* in 1795.) Third, the Scottish intelligentsia were, for the most part, conformist by habit, conviction or circumstance – or some combination of these – and the few that were not were largely, although not entirely, silent on reform issues in the 1790s. What Scotland singularly lacked was anything comparable to the extensive culture and institutions of rational dissent out of which came so many of the English reform voices of the 1790s. Fourth, partly because of the repressive climate and the loyalist bias of most of the Scottish press, Scottish radicals and reformers came to depend heavily on English reform and radical newspapers and propaganda, a dependency which only increased as the decade went on.

The voices of Scottish artisan radicals of the 1790s are equally, if not more, elusive, even where they played a notable role in radicalism locally and nationally. It was on these men that the fortunes of radicalism in Scotland came to rest in the second half of 1793 as their propertied, opposition Whig and burgh reformer allies fell away, but they have left little mark in the historical record, partly because they were defeated so quickly and completely at the end of 1793 and then cowed or driven underground. Their contributions to the debates at the general conventions of Scottish radicals were limited. Rather, these were dominated by a small number of leading delegates, who were from the professional or educated classes, although on occasion the discussions hint at a much broader hinterland of opinion only weakly reflected in the national deliberations. Political talk amongst Scottish radicals more often than not took place in private spaces – weaving shops, rooms in tenement or cottages – rarely accessible to the historian's scrutiny. Subscription coffee rooms, by the later eighteenth century increasingly the most common and certainly the most visible type of coffee room present in Scottish towns, were not haunts of Scottish radicals, something which reflected, in the first place, the relatively high cost of subscription. Nor were the ranks of merchants who tended to frequent them generally sympathetic to the radical cause. An anonymous report on Perth radicalism dating from late 1792 noted: 'A list of subscribers to the Guild Coffee House has been seen but there does not seem to be many Friends of the People among them'.[21] Towards the end of 1793, Walter Hart, one of the city's delegates to the British convention, was hissed from the Glasgow tontine coffee room; in the spring of the same year, the subscribers to the Dundee coffee room terminated the subscription to the *Edinburgh Gazetteer*, mouthpiece of the Scottish Friends of the People.[22] Radicals met in taverns and tap rooms, but such gatherings have produced few records.[23] Sympathetic booksellers' shops were almost certainly common radical haunts. George Galloway, the Glasgow agent of the *Gazetteer*, appears to have set up a reading room in his new shop in 1793, but we have only a single, very brief, mention of this.[24]

The best published account of Scottish political life in this period remains that of Henry W. Meikle, which appeared as long ago as 1912.[25] His narrative was largely based on sources from the national and French archives; and he was not greatly interested in reconstructing viewpoints from beyond Edinburgh. This book seeks to balance a national perspective with a shift in focus to events beyond the capital, although again this is not easily done. There are no equivalents of the provincial radical papers which have proved such a rich source for the study of provincial radicalism in England, and very few papers of any kind other than those published in Edinburgh and Glasgow. Only a tiny number of the radical societies formed in the early 1790s have left any record of their existence other than a solitary notice in a newspaper or a note that they sent a delegate to one of the national conventions of the Scottish Friends of the People held in Edinburgh in 1792–3. What follows, therefore, is not exhaustive, and some places are better represented than others. There is scope for more work on Renfrewshire, Dumbartonshire and Ayrshire, especially in the early 1790s. This book does draw, however, on private manuscript collections and local archival sources which take us a deal further into local and regional conditions than other historians have yet managed. Of particular note in this context are the Atholl Papers, held at Blair Castle. These papers contain a wealth of correspondence between the fourth Duke of Atholl, from 1794 the new Lord Lieutenant of Perthshire, and his deputy lieutenants and other members of the Perthshire and Angus gentry.

A further major aim is to examine how Scotland fits into a broader British and to a lesser extent Irish pattern of politics in this period. There are two elements to this. First, Scottish politics in this period – radical, loyalist and patriotic – in somewhat different ways was or increasingly became a dimension of British politics, in terms of identity, strategy and relationships. Just as a local, regional and national context is helpful in illuminating developments, crucial also is a British one. Linda Colley emphasized the British nature and identity of radical politics in the 1790s some years ago.[26] What this meant and how it was achieved are questions which have never been fully explored, although important work has been done on Scottish radical identities and their national outlook.[27] Perhaps the oddity is that we know rather more about Scottish-Irish connections in light of the influence of the Society of United Irishmen on the Society of United Scotsmen. Prior to 1796, however, connections to England were much more important in influencing the paths taken by Scottish radical politics; and even after 1796 they remained significant.[28]

This book pays close attention, therefore, to the role which individuals and personal relationships played in creating connections between radical politics in Scotland and England from the summer of 1792. This, in turn, serves to bring into new prominence the role in the opening phase of Scottish radical politics of several politicians who are best described as *British* reformers, including most notably Lord Daer, the eldest son of the Earl of Selkirk, and Norman Macleod, until 1796 opposition Whig MP for Invernesshire. Paradoxically, Daer, who remains a somewhat shadowy presence, would appear to have been a Scottish nationalist, at least from the contents of a remarkable letter which he wrote in early 1793 to Charles Grey; in practice and tactically, however, he was a British politician.[29] A member of the Scottish Friends of the People, he was also a member of the London body of the same name and the London Corresponding Society (LCS). He was in addition a very active member of the Society for Constitutional Information, which together with the LCS played a coordinating role in English radicalism in the early 1790s, and which took him to the very heart of metropolitan radical politics.[30] Macleod's connections in London were with the opposition Whigs, and to some extent, therefore, his role represents a natural extension of the increasing integration of Scottish and English opposition politics from the 1780s, as indeed does the initially close connection between the Scottish Friends of the People and the Whig Association of the Friends of the People. Macleod's enthusiasm for parliamentary reform seems to have gone beyond most opposition Whigs and certainly most Scottish opposition Whigs. Another important figure in this context was the staunchly independent-minded Earl of Lauderdale, and his hand can be detected behind the renewed momentum of the Scottish opposition Whigs in the later 1790s. The presence of Scots in metropolitan radical circles – Thomas Hardy, the founder and first secretary of the LCS, being only the most famous – was equally crucial to this process of forging connections between groups north and south of the border. 'Union' as a strategy and goal among radicals was undoubtedly impelled in part by the common experience of repression, but it was also a natural extension of the radicals' outlook and search for unanimity as a means of achieving reform. The pattern of relationships across the national border established in 1792–3 was replicated, to differing degrees and in somewhat different ways, by others in the mid to later 1790s, including the Edinburgh 'bookseller to the people' and agent for the London Corresponding Society, Alexander Leslie. The British thread in the Scottish politics of this period is a major theme in this book.

There is also a comparative aspect which runs throughout much of this book, in that another recurrent theme is Scottish similarity and difference with developments south of the border. To date, where comparison has been made this is with Ireland, with the effect of underlining, or seeming to, the relative placidity of Scottish society and opinion. But conditions in Ireland were uniquely combustible; there was dynamic towards violence and instability there which was not present elsewhere in the British Isles, certainly not to the same degree.[31] Given the diversity of conditions and experiences in England and indeed Scotland, it may be that sub-national comparisons are a more meaningful exercise. Nevertheless, if we wish to construct fuller, more complete narratives of British politics in the 1790s, the approach adopted here provides one way of positioning Scottish experience within a British framework. Much of the existing work on Scotland in the 1790s is, in any case, implicitly comparative on a national basis. Here this aspect is made explicit in the belief that this is a natural perspective to adopt; but it is also done to encourage further debate about Scottish experience among historians of eighteenth-century Britain.

The book is divided into six chapters. The first searches for the eighteenth-century roots of the rise of popular radicalism in the Scotland of the early 1790s. Here Scotland fits awkwardly into the standard narratives of politicization in

eighteenth-century Britain, which has led some historians to miss several important continuities spanning the second half of the century. To a considerable
degree, the causes of the stark social and political fissure which opened up in
Scottish society in late 1792 are to be found in cultural, intellectual and religious
developments in previous decades. If the Scottish Enlightenment was, ultimately,
a moderate and conservative phenomenon, popular Calvinist orthodoxy provided a well-spring of emotion, commitment and a tradition of 'liberty' which
prepared, if no more than this, sections of the labouring classes for the democratic message of liberty created by the French Revolution and Thomas Paine
in 1792. Chapter 2 traces the course of political debate and opinion as reflected
in the newspapers of the decade. They possess obvious limitations as sources for
doing this, but their influence was a growing one in the 1790s as the habit of
newspaper readership was powerfully stimulated, and at the same time broad-
ened and deepened socially, by the French Revolution. They have the advantage
of allowing us to sketch the broad outlines and contours of opinion, especially
among the propertied classes. Reflecting their unique capacity to form circuits
of political communication, and their authority as disseminators of news about
international events, newspapers were also active and influential agencies in the
politics of the period, and for this reason alone their role merits close attention.

Chapters 3 and 4 look, respectively, at the rise and decline of radical politics
and the mobilization of loyalist feeling and demonstrations during the period
1792 to 1794. These chapters should be read closely alongside one another;
together they help us see the strengths and limitations of both radicalism and
loyalism at different moments. They also focus on what radicalism and loyalism
meant at specific points. As with English radicalism, Scottish radicalism in the
early 1790s was diverse; it also changed over time in response to new opportunities and new constraints and pressures. From a national, British perspective H.
T. Dickinson has emphasized radical weakness and its limited support as important factors in its failure.[32] Scotland fits this picture well. Support flourished
briefly and then decline set in very quickly as the initial optimism and expectation which surrounded its rise were not sustained. Yet if numbers of radicals
were not overwhelming, loyalists in Scotland did not carry all before them. In
many places in England in the early 1790s a noisy, vocal loyalist reaction, which
seems to have reached far into society, cowed radicals from late 1792;[33] north
of the border, loyalism was probably confined in this period to rural and urban
elite uncertain about the views of many of the 'middling' and 'lower' sort. It was
led from 'above' and directed, to a significant extent, by the authorities in Edinburgh. Significant sections of society resisted pressures to subscribe to a loyalist
consensus, mostly obviously religious dissenters, while others viewed loyalist
initiatives with apathy if not downright hostility. As we will see, opinions and
emotions also shifted abruptly according to circumstance and context.

Chapter 5 focuses on the years 1797–8, which yielded starkly contradictory images of Scottish loyalty and discontent. An underlying theme is how we might reconcile these images and what, together, they tell us about the limitations of any patriotic consensus on Scotland in this period in reaction to the threat of invasion from revolutionary France, rendered only too clear by the arrival of a French fleet off Bantry Bay in Ireland in late 1796. George Ramsay, a director of the Royal Bank of Scotland, recorded tersely in his diary for 9 February: 'dreadful apprehensions of invasion'.[34] In 1796, a visitor to the lowlands identified the volunteer forces first raised in the spring of 1794 as the salvation of places like Ayr, Dumfries, Perth and Dundee, by which he presumably meant that they had successfully intimidated and cowed radicals or those inclined to disorderly conduct.[35] This was before the further marked expansion of volunteering in 1797–8. The account of what motivated those who joined their ranks in these years, or sought to do so, provides further support to those historians who have tended to emphasize the pragmatic reasons for membership on the part of lesser tradesmen, artisans and labourers.[36] One of the causes of the anger which burst out over the implementation of the Militia Act in 1797, a wave of protest which profoundly unsettled the ruling elites in the late summer of that year, albeit only relatively briefly, was the fact that many offers to join volunteer companies earlier in the spring had been rejected. James Wodrow, a minister in an Ayrshire parish, noted in mid April 1797:

> The military spirit had begun to rouse & if properly fanned, we woud [sic] soon have had near that number [5,000] of trained men in most counties. In the towns of Saltcoats and Stevenston after a little effort, which I heartily seconded, even from the Pulpit, we had three companies of 60 men each drilling themselves with much spirit. Their offers of service have been to their great mortification now rejected by the Gov. t and a Militia is said to be about to be forced upon us.[37]

Service in the militia was altogether more onerous and disruptive to labouring families than volunteering, and, therefore, resented. The obligation of service also fell on only a small section of the population, and was further resented for that fact. At one level, the stark contrast between the effusion of patriotic spirit in the spring and the violent resistance to the implementation of the Militia Act in the late summer of 1797 emphasizes again the pronounced mutability of popular opinion in this decade. It also indicates very clearly the limitations of patriotism as a socially integrative force.

The subject of Chapter 6 is responses to two periods of shortages of grain and high food prices, 1795–6 and 1799–1801, the second of which was accompanied by an economic and trade depression. In England, the former was linked to, although not caused by, a revival of radical politics in London and elsewhere, which took the form of large, open-air meetings, while the latter was accompanied by a deep undercurrent of political alienation and disaffection. In Scotland, a radical revival was almost entirely absent in 1795, although the opposition Whigs did manage to mobilize considerable support for petitions for peace and against the so-called Gagging Acts, the latest round of repression passed by the Pitt ministry. The groundswell of opinion in support of peace was fuelled by a perception that the dearth was linked to the war. In the later crisis, any political content to the disturbances (whatever its significance) was very rare and confined to a few places in the west. In both periods, there were also a relatively small number of protests, certainly when compared to England, and those that did take place were generally quite orderly and peaceful. Among the factors which have been put forward to explain this is the proposition that paternalism was a more active and pervasive force in Scottish society than south of the border. Related is the view that economic progress, despite accelerating and broadening from the final third of the eighteenth century, created relatively few tensions and stress points in society, which might have led to alienation and disaffection. Nor did it weaken the hegemony of a small, very powerful landed class. One of the main themes of this chapter is to explore the different faces of paternalism in this period, and to examine more systematically than has been done hitherto their possible role in explaining Scottish *difference* during the period 1799–1801. A further aim here is to examine how far the regulation of the bread market in Scotland was similar to or different from the practices and habits of intervention in England. In an English context, this period has been represented as a critical phase in the repudiation of 'moral economy', although it is an idea which has not gained universal acceptance.[38] Scottish conditions and experience have to date not formed any part of this debate.

A brief word, finally, is required about political terminology. Political labels, in this decade more than most, could be very slippery things. When in 1796 a highland minister called Robert Burns a 'staunch republican', what he really meant by this is a moot point.[39] Did he mean an opponent of monarchy and the balanced constitution of King, Lords and Commons? Or, did he simply mean a reformer and opponent of war against revolutionary France? Republican, like its near relation in the 1790s 'Jacobin', was a much-employed term in the loyalist lexicon of abuse and as such tended to be loosely applied; subtle distinctions between varieties of radicalism and reform were not to the purpose of opponents of any sort or measure of reform. Reformers, meanwhile, tended to speak in different voices in different contexts, by turns revealing or concealing aspects of their motivations and inspirations for basically prudential or tactical reasons.[40] Radical politics was also at moments infused with an excitement and intensity which bred a rhetorical violence which was often no more than that, or a gesture of defiance in the face of loyalist misrepresentation. The Scottish parliamentary reform movement as it emerged in 1792 was also a notably broad alliance comprising moderate reformers as well as individuals with a wider and deeper commitment to change. Nevertheless, as we will see in Chapter 3, reform of parliamentary representation was, in line with radical movements and agitations elsewhere in this period, for a growing number of people a beginning rather than an end; the 'cause of liberty' was a campaign of social and individual, as well as political and even moral, recreation, a call to eradicate privilege and aristocratic government in Britain and its attendant ills in the name of humanity and equality. It is this facet of reform politics in this period which above all seems to justify the use of the label 'radical' even though it was not a contemporary usage. Or, to put this another way, Professor John Millar was a reformer who sought principally the dismantling of the Pittite system of government and an end to the war against France: the radicals, taking their lead from Paine and the French Revolution, saw in the cause of political reform the potential for a much more far-reaching transformation of British politics *and* society.

1 THE EIGHTEENTH-CENTURY ROOTS OF SCOTTISH 'JACOBIN' POLITICS

The extent to which popular radicalism in the 1790s should be seen as a new departure in the political culture of the British Isles has long been a topic of lively debate among historians. The current consensus seems to be that in England the lines of continuity with preceding decades were strong ones, although, as John Stevenson cautioned some years ago, considerable gaps exist in our knowledge.[1] Stevenson noted that the artisan world of tavern clubs and dissenting congregations between the era of Wilkes and the 1790s had only been dimly illuminated by research, while relatively few studies had been forthcoming of the worlds out of which sprang many of the provincial radical societies of the 1790s. Since he wrote this (in the late 1980s), little in this regard has changed.[2] Nor, even where it can be shown to have taken place, did the participation of lesser tradesmen and artisans in political debate and activity in an earlier period guarantee that a strong radical presence would emerge in the 1790s. Birmingham saw a lively popular politics develop in the 1760s and '70s under a Wilkite-inspired platform of 'independence', but radicals in the city in the 1790s appear to have been an isolated, tiny minority with only a flickering existence as an organized body.[3] It is the development of political life in the large unrepresented towns such as Manchester, Sheffield and Leeds in the later eighteenth century which, by and large, remains least well understood. Such places did not produce petitions in support of parliamentary reform in 1783 or indeed 1785, a fact which raises difficult questions about attempts to trace lines of development back from the 1790s into the previous decade or indeed earlier. More generally in explaining the rise of popular radical societies in the 1790s, much seems to have depended on particular, local configurations of political forces and conditions, and, in the early phases, on the existence of leadership drawn from among the middling sorts and, on occasion, the landed classes.[4]

Ireland presents, at first glance, a more straightforward picture; this at least is true of Protestant Ireland. A significant number of the early members of the United Irishmen cut their political teeth in the volunteer and parliamentary reform agitations of the late 1770s and early 1780s.[5] These agitations created traditions, habits and an extensive repertoire of political rhetoric and argument which Wolfe Tone and his political allies were able to draw on in the 1790s. In Dublin and parts of Ulster, these traditions and habits go back even further to the later 1740s and 1750s, when first Charles Lucas and then the Money Bill crisis produced a Patriot politics and platform which elicited a strong popular response.[6] Looked at more deeply, the politics of 1779–84 show a tendency towards alienation and extremism, certainly at the level of rhetoric and political argument, which may better help to explain the trajectory of Irish reform politics in the subsequent decade.[7] To put this in more precise terms, the political and imaginative leap which Presbyterian and Anglican reformers had to make in the 1790s to embrace the politics of republican separatism may not have been quite so great as it is sometimes represented.

In the case of Scotland, the continuities between the 1790s and earlier decades are less apparent, and the roots of popular politicization more obscure. This has led a number of historians, following Henry Meikle at the beginning of the last century, to argue that the foundations of Scottish radical politics in the 1790s were notably shallow.[8] As we will see below, there are strong reasons for adopting this position. Scottish eighteenth-century political culture cannot readily be subsumed within the sorts of explanatory frameworks which have been used to characterize developments in popular politics in the rest of the 'Atlantic World' in this period.[9] Yet it may be that we need to adjust our angle of vision in the Scottish case, and move away somewhat from these frameworks. There was a developing popular political consciousness in Scotland in the later eighteenth century, but it can largely escape our view if we mainly or only look for similarity with the rest of the British Isles. The impact of the French Revolution and the writings of Paine were, as we will see in the next chapter, crucial factors in the emergence of a popular reform movement in Scotland in the final third of 1792. It is unlikely, however, that they would have been decisive without the prior existence of this political awareness, albeit its manifestations were fitful and diverse, and its extent and depth are impossible to establish with anything like the precision which has been managed by John Phillips in the case of England in the 1770s.[10]

Political Structures and Political Subordination

Political structures and the nature of political culture in eighteenth-century Scotland left, at first glance, very little space for the development of 'public opinion' as an independent force in society and politics. In the first place, and most notoriously, Scottish electorates were small and, in the burghs, markedly and often flagrantly venal.[11] They also had special features – in counties the fact that votes (so-called 'fictitious' votes) could be manufactured or conveyed through a variety of legal devices, in the burghs that the vote resided in self-electing councils and for all but Edinburgh in a system of delegates from a number of burghs grouped together for electoral purposes – which made them very susceptible to control and manipulation by 'shady tricks' of a kind which readily provoked the indignation of a growing number of electoral reformers in the later eighteenth century.[12] 'A mere mockery upon the name or idea' was Thomas Oldfield's verdict on the Scottish 'system of representation'.[13] Whether the conduct of elections was more corrupt than in closed boroughs or some counties in England and Wales, or indeed in Ireland after 1768, is debateable, although burgh elections did undoubtedly produce a succession of episodes of petty skulduggery, involving, for example, the detention of councillors to prevent their voting.[14] Attempts, meanwhile, to curtail the creation of fictitious votes in the counties were made by Parliament in 1714, 1734 and again in 1743. These were, however, ineffective, in the last case because insufficient powers of regulation were conferred on the Court of Session and because a judgement by Lord Mansfield in the House of Lords in 1770 undermined on appeal an attempt by this body to impose some order and restriction on who could vote. The result was the continued growth of fictitious votes, especially after 1774, continued attempts in shires, at times politically motivated, to purge their rolls of these votes, and a growing impulse to seek reform of county elections.[15]

Despite these features, however, Scottish electorates were far from always or even normally easily managed.[16] Reflecting a long national tradition of literal representation, which did not disappear at the Union, electors expected their MPs to defend and promote their personal and collective interests in London; they also expected access to patronage.[17] It was this, and the pressure it placed on MPs to secure jobs and favour for their constituents, which as much as anything else lay behind the eighteenth-century stereotype of the patronage-hunting Scot. Nor did the individuals who governed the royal burghs lack a pronounced sense of their own importance. As William Ferguson emphasized in the 1950s in what remains probably the best introduction to Scottish burgh elections in the eighteenth century:

> The small men who sat upon the town councils ... although overshadowed by the parliamentary politicians, and for the most part manipulated by them, emphatically were not ciphers. Their greed, ambitions, vanities, hopes and fears had all to be catered for.[18]

George Dempster, MP for Perth Burghs between 1774 and 1790, advised on the eve of the general election of 1790: 'The Baillie is such a card in Forfar both now & afterwards that he cannot be too much attended to'.[19] The rulers of Scotland's royal burghs were easily offended if their requests were denied, although few wrote in such peremptory and unembarrassed terms as Alexander Riddoch, the long-time Provost of Dundee, to Robert Graham of Fintry, the Scottish Commissioner of Excise, in 1793:

... his Grace [the Duke of Atholl] does not think the recommendation of the Chief Magistrate & Town Council of Dundee as of sufficient consequence to be attended to, and, of course, I must add, that both they and I will in future act accordingly.

As Atholl wrote to Graham, 'a more extraordinary one [i.e. letter] I never read', but more significant were his protests that he and the MP for Perthshire, his uncle Captain George Murray, had always treated Riddoch and Dundee with the 'utmost attention'.[20] If there was a direct obligation on Scottish MPs to be representatives in Parliament and London, rather than acting as independent agents, and the burghs were not simply subservient to magnate interests, Scottish elections in this period cannot, nevertheless, normally be described as participatory affairs, even at the level of ritual, of which much has made in an English context in recent years.[21] Poll elections were relatively rare events – there were just four in 1754, eight in 1761 and thirteen in 1768.[22] To a degree that was unusual in the British Isles in this period, electoral politics in Scotland relied on personal relations and communication between a very small number of individuals and on present and presumed future access to patronage.[23] It was the latter which conferred on the leading Scottish political managers – the second and third dukes of Argyll between 1725 and 1761 and during the final decades of the century Henry Dundas – such formidable influence in the electoral sphere, especially when they built alliances with regional magnate interests, for example, Queensberry in the south-west, Hamilton in Lanarkshire, Atholl in Perthshire and Angus, and Fife and Gordon in the north-east.

Second, for most of the eighteenth century the Scottish press lacked the vigour and political maturity of its English and Irish counterparts. A crude indicator of this is its relatively slow growth. This was in part caused by the strength of competition from English newspapers, which, in turn, reflected quickening and multiplying communication links between London, Edinburgh and other towns north and west of Edinburgh, as well as the spread of booksellers, who acted as agents for newspapers, across much of lowland Scotland by the 1770s. By 1789, there were ten Scottish newspapers in existence, just three of which were published outside of Glasgow and Edinburgh. In 1790, twenty-three papers were published in London, and by 1800 over a hundred in the English provinces.[24] Glasgow papers circulated throughout the west of the country, while Edinburgh papers were, in effect, national ones, having a readership that extended throughout most of Scotland. The *Aberdeen Journal*, which served the north of Scotland, was produced in Aberdeen from 1748 by the remarkable James Chalmers and subsequently by his sons, but attempts to develop a competitor to it in the 1750s and again in the 1780s failed.[25] There were two similarly abortive attempts in the 1790s.[26] In the south-west, Dumfries had a short-lived paper in 1721, which was followed half a century later by the development of, first, a weekly magazine (in

1773) and then, from 1788, a newspaper, the *Dumfries Weekly Journal*. In Kelso in the Borders, beginning in 1783, James Palmer published the weekly *Kelso Chronicle*, renamed the *British Chronicle; or Union Gazette* in the following year. The rapidly growing town of Dundee appears to have had a very short-lived newspaper in 1755, and enterprising local printer Thomas Colville experimented with several magazine-type publications which included news from the 1770s, but it was only in 1801 that a newspaper of any significant duration was established.[27] One could argue of course that a growing volume of English papers in circulation in Scotland compensated for this small number, and there is something in this view. As we will see in a later chapter, English radical and pro-reform papers found a Scottish readership throughout the 1790s, as did loyalist ones. English newspapers could not, however, and did not represent Scottish opinion and views in the same way as those produced in Scotland.

Third, urban government seems to have given rise to relatively few tensions and conflicts which might have interacted with national political issues, and thereby helped to stimulate and invigorate a tradition of urban political independence. Many Scottish towns were, in British and even European terms, very small, and as such part of a rural or at least semi-rural world in which they were deeply enmeshed, economically, socially and culturally.[28] It may also be that the landed classes had greater influence in many towns than was typically the case in England, although such differences are hard to assess in anything other than somewhat impressionistic terms.[29] The main importance of speculative freemasonry, probably the fastest growing form of association among the Scottish elites and upper middling ranks in this period, could well have been in terms of it helping to form a social bridge between local gentry and urban professionals and merchants.[30] Nevertheless, as Alexander Murdoch has shown, there is evidence from the central decades of the eighteenth century of several urban areas acting as 'centres of opposition to landed oligarchy'.[31] This is the case for Edinburgh and Glasgow, but also Dumfries, and Irvine on the Ayrshire coast, the latter a beneficiary in the eighteenth century of expanding trade with Ireland, especially in coal and textiles. There may well be other, similar examples which have yet to come to light in the archives. All of these episodes of resistance had their origins in inter-elite rivalries, which provoked one party to seek to exploit older conflicts between the merchant guilds and the trades incorporations.[32] Trades incorporations, which represented the interests of skilled tradesmen and artisans, were not entirely denuded of political weight or significance after 1700, although we lack detailed modern work on Scottish urban society which might shed more thorough light on this.[33] What we can point to is that they were periodically mobilized across different towns in pursuit of common interests – for example, in the sphere of economic lobbying or, as occurred during the War of American Independence in the north-east, in opposition to arbitrary recruitment practices by the military.[34] They also maintained a strong institutional identity and role within burgh society and urban ceremonial culture. Conflicts, meanwhile, over the exercise of jurisdiction and rights in the civic arena, including those of the trades, regularly led to cases being brought before the Court of Session in Edinburgh. At issue on occasion was the nature of the 'sett', or civic constitution, as occurred with regard to Stirling in 1773.[35] Other cases might involve encroachment by local landowners on a town's common-land, in which concepts of a separate 'civic identity' were invoked.[36] Hard to assess, however, is how strong the resistance to landed oligarchy was, and the vitality (or otherwise) of the traditions and precedents which carried it. As we will see below in the case of Edinburgh, the autonomy of such developments can be questioned, and they might better be seen mainly as extensions of elite rivalry rather than autonomous political currents; or at the very least as largely subordinate to these rivalries. More intriguingly, and in some ways at odds with the above point, there were connections and an ideological affinity between opposition to oligarchy in the political sphere and opposition to patronage in the Church of Scotland, the latter of which, as we will see later, certainly had the potential to galvanize popular opinion in the second half of the eighteenth century. Archibald Fletcher, the opposition Whig Advocate and notable burgh reformer, wrote a tract in support of the abolition of patronage in which, his widow recalled:

> He proved ... that the exercise of their rights in the choice of their religious teachers would accustom the people to reflection, and raise them in their own esteem, and thus prepare them for a due estimation of all the civil and political rights that belonged to them as a nation of free men.[37]

An important participant in the Dumfries events of 1759–60 investigated by Murdoch was Andrew Crosbie, author of another influential pamphlet published in 1769 attacking patronage.[38] It may be, however, that the relationship worked at least as much the other way round, in that it was the groundswell of opposition to patronage in the early 1780s which fed into, and provided much of the momentum behind, the burgh reform agitation which emerged in Edinburgh and Aberdeen and came to embrace most of the other royal burghs, and within them the trades incorporations and merchant guilds, from 1783.

Fourth, while in England and Ireland the era of the American Revolution saw the emergence of parliamentary reform as a major focus for public and press debate and popular political agitation, the noisy battles of the 1760s to early 1780s had only weak echoes in Scotland.[39] In 1776, as discussion in London and many other places in England raged about the outbreak and opening shots of the War of American Independence, an Edinburgh correspondent, finding nowhere near the same intensity of debate in the Scottish capital, wrote to the *London Chronicle*: 'Scotland at present seems to consist of greedy individuals. It is like a kennel of hounds, where each looks no farther than his own supply.'[40] Even allowing for what by then were thoroughly conventional terms of denigration of Scottish national character, the perception that society north of the border was less sharply divided by the conflict was almost certainly correct. Writing to his regular correspondent, the English dissenter William Kenrick, James Wodrow, minister of the parish of Stevenston in Ayrshire, declared in September 1775: 'We look upon the cry raised about Liberty to be chiefly the cry of disappointed faction joined by a few worthy & many worthless men ...'. A few weeks later, he asserted: 'In Scotland I am sure nineteen twentieth parts ... are on the side of Gov.t in the present unhappy Quarrel'. It would be the same message three years later when he wrote (in 1778) that people were 'almost universally on the side of government'.[41] In Edinburgh, a debating club established in 1773, the Pantheon Society, discussed the conduct of the war against the colonies on at least two occasions. In the spring of 1778, the authorities were accused of bribing 'Pantheonites' attending a debate on the question 'Ought the present ministry to be removed from his Majesty's councils?' to ensure that supporters of the war prevailed.[42] A club also emerged as a focus of opposition to the war in the capital, the Orange Club. It was almost certainly this same body, describing itself as 'one of the first Patriotic clubs instituted for free discussion of Political sentiment', which in 1782 voted its thanks to the Earl of Buchan for his efforts to reform the Scottish peerage elections.[43] At least two future Edinburgh radicals were members of the club, which was described by one of them as 'a Liberty Society'. The same individual recalled how it had met weekly during the American war, but following the Peace of Paris (1783) had begun to meet monthly, and afterwards quarterly, half-yearly and then annually until collapsing entirely at a date which was not specified.[44]

The divisions created by the War of American Independence did not run so deep as in England or indeed Ireland, or carry the same political or ideological charge. Consistent with this, Scots played only a minor role in the reform campaigns which unfolded in the rest of the British Isles in the later stages of the war and its immediate aftermath. During 1782–3, the emerging burgh reform agitation and the English association movement appeared to be on converging paths, a development which did not go uncriticized in Scotland, reflecting, no doubt, the novelty of what was occurring. As a letter published in the *Caledonian Mercury* complained: 'What relates to Scotland ought to be cared for by Scotland'.[45] Scotland featured in the reform proposals agreed by the committee of the Yorkshire association in late 1782, while Christopher Wyvill and the Yorkshire committee were in communication with Scots reformers in several places, including Edinburgh and Stirling.[46] The immediate practical significance of this was minimal, however, although it does anticipate the much stronger process of convergence in reform politics which took place in the following decade, and which forms a major theme of subsequent chapters. Scottish burgh reformers placed little importance on coordinating their activities with those of Wyvill's Yorkshire committee or indeed other English reformers, and, following the defeat of Pitt's reform proposals of 1785, sought to distance themselves from the broader cause of parliamentary reform. Instead, they emphasized the fundamentally conservative nature of their goals, which were from 1785 focused on reform of the internal government of the burghs.[47] Similarly, the growing appeal of county reform from 1774 was located amongst the traditional country gentry and cut across any developing partisan allegiances.[48]

In a recent general survey of eighteenth-century Scottish politics, John Shaw, reiterating an earlier judgement of William Ferguson's, has written about the 'trivializing' of politics in this era.[49] He was referring to its narrow preoccupation with issues of personal and factional interest, something which, in turn, he attributes to, first, Scotland's politically subordinate condition after 1707 – the degree to which its destiny was ultimately determined in London – and, second, the crucial importance of patronage and connection in the construction of political interests and influence. In the present context, at issue is how far this, and the unusual power and influence of its landed classes, effectively prevented displays of political vitality below the level of a tiny political elite in Scotland in this period. Given its size and status as the country's political and administrative capital, its inherited traditions of political and religious activism, and the large and diverse body of artisans and tradesmen to be found among its population, Edinburgh provides an important lens through which to examine this question in more detail.

A striking feature of Edinburgh politics in the eighteenth century is how, particularly from the mid 1720s, control exerted by Scotland's political managers smothered a robust, popular political culture which had begun to develop in the later seventeenth century and flourished during the passage of the Union.[50] In some ways, this comes as little surprise given the ways in which the London and Dublin parliaments acted to catalyse and energize popular politics in both cities; in the absence of a parliament after 1707 to act as a stage and focus for interventions of the 'people', politically-motivated crowds largely disappeared from Edinburgh's streets. Their rare appearances – the Porteous riots of 1736, which may have had a Jacobite dimension, and the unruly anti-Catholic protests of 1779 – only bring the general pattern into sharper relief.[51] When the capital's streets witnessed a new political crowd collecting together on the nights of 4–6 June 1792, during the so-called King's birthday riots, it is striking that memories of the distant events of 1736 seem to have played a role;[52] for the most part and for most of the eighteenth century Edinburgh's populace were politically invisible. A lively political press which had flourished between the 1690s and during the time of the union debates, and for some years thereafter, similarly faded away under the Argathelian supremacy.[53] There were cases of political libel which were brought to the city authorities' attention, but they appear to have been very few in number. In 1734, William Cheyne, the printer of the *Thistle* (1734–6), a Squadrone-Patriot journal published under the direction of James Erskine of Grange, was fined for printing a series of protests occasioned by the peerage elections of that year. Significantly perhaps, in taking this action the Council were responding to a complaint made by the Earl of Caithness rather than acting on their own behalf.[54] In 1747, printed copies of a Jacobite handbill entitled 'The King of Prussia's Letter to this Royal Highness Prince Charles' were seized by local magistrates, and several coffee-house keepers examined about their provenance.[55] Political pamphlets written and published in London, quite a few of them written by Scots making their way as journalists and writers south of the border, were republished in Edinburgh. In 1733–4, the Squadrone opposition to Argyll was distributing propaganda, including the famous weekly essay paper the *Craftsman*, in Scotland, and a press was established in Edinburgh to reprint anti-government pamphlets sent up from London.[56] The opposition Whigs and those in the ministerial interest did somewhat similar things in the 1780s. Overall, however, only a relatively small proportion of the vast number of political pamphlets published every year in London seem to have found their way into the hands of Edinburgh's citizens.[57]

We do get occasional glimpses of political consciousness among the Edinburgh populace. In July 1747, following the arrival of news that Britain and its allies had been defeated in Flanders, a Catherine Beg went through the fish market cursing the government and those who took its side. A few days later, her husband, Andrew Miller, his apprentice, Thomas Miller, and Beg were outside the house of a glazier in Fish Market Close. Thomas 'called openly into said house Was the Hanoverian Club gathered yet w[i]th several other insulting expressions', causing a hostile crowd to gather. Stones were thrown into the house, and the glazier was called a 'Hanoverian Bougar' and his wife a 'damned Hanoverian bitch'.[58] Political divisions between Whigs and Jacobites, and between Argyll supporters and the Squadrone, had been sharpened by the Jacobite Rebellion of 1745–6 and seem to have had an important public dimension, as is also demonstrated by, for example, official concern about planned popular celebrations to mark the acquittal for treason of the Provost at the time of the rebellion, Archibald Stewart.[59] Politics, at least national (meaning after 1707 British) politics, was, nevertheless, far from the consuming interest of Edinburgh's professional, merchant and indeed artisan classes in the eighteenth century. Scottish visitors to London in the eighteenth century were astonished by the mania for political talk which they discovered in its many taverns. In September 1745, a young Adam Ferguson wrote from the British capital that 'every fellow reads the publick papers and talks his mind concerning them with all the vehemence imaginable'.[60]

With the establishment of Argathelian rule after 1725, the Edinburgh Town Council and other important local institutions – the two banks, the Board of

Trustees for the Improvement of Manufactures and Fisheries, the Customs and Excise Boards – became firmly entangled in the webs of patronage which were the essential sinews of political management in the eighteenth century. Control of Edinburgh was vital to control of the Convention of Royal Burghs and the General Assembly of the Church of Scotland, which only further tightened the bonds of political management.[61] William Robertson, canvassing for the principalship of the University in 1762, wrote to an ally: 'The office is in the gift of the Town Council, but that you know alters the matter only one remove ... I need not say to you, that a letter from Ld Bute to Baron Mure or Ld Milton fixes the Elections infallibly'.[62] Milton had been the third Duke of Argyll's *sous-ministre* in Edinburgh, while the third Earl of Bute, whose political star waxed very brightly in 1762, was briefly looked to as a political patron in Edinburgh following Argyll's death in 1761. When George Drummond, several times Lord Provost and most famous as the founder of the Edinburgh Royal Infirmary, experimented with an independent political opinion in the later 1730s, he was quickly brought back into line by Lord Ilay (later the third Duke of Argyll) by dismissal from the Customs Board and transfer to the Excise Board with the loss of half his salary.[63] Throughout his career in Edinburgh government and politics, Drummond repeatedly sought to put distance between himself and the dukes of Argyll and their agents, but on each occasion he was made to realize his dependent and subordinate status.[64]

For much of the eighteenth century, therefore, the strong grip of the political managers stifled tendencies to independence among Edinburgh's civic elites and citizenry. There were, however, at least two periods when factional rivalry created the conditions for manifestations of more populist politics, in a manner which seems, at first glance, to mirror the effects of elite conflicts in colonial urban America or indeed in several towns south of the border.[65] The first of these occurred in the final years of Walpole's administration, when the second Duke of Argyll moved into opposition to Walpole in 1740, and sought to wrest political control of the city and its MP away from the ministry and his former close ally, Lord Milton. In prosecuting this fight, Argyll and his allies joined forces with old opponents from the Squadrone and other discontented elements. They also aligned themselves with the English Patriot opposition to Walpole. During 1740–1, Argyll or his lieutenants were responsible for the publication of a flurry of pamphlets, handbills and even a weekly periodical entitled the *Patriot*. In 1742, Thomas Hay, writing from Edinburgh, noted: 'People here have been of late a little mobbish in different ways the better sort in sowing malicious clamour ... We have sometimes little poetical satires or comical and satirical pamphlets ... from London.'[66] Around the same time, it was observed that, 'At present every tailor here is turned politician'.[67] There was a concerted effort to engage the support of the trades incorporations and the guildry, which involved several of these bodies issuing and publishing addresses in support of Argyll and liberty.[68] Argyll's opponents also portrayed the battle in terms of political independence, but in this case civic independence and resisting the control of Scotland's first city by a peer.[69] It was a line of argument which resurfaced in the 1761 general election, which suggests that it drew on a sense of civic identity which survived the effects of political management.[70] On the other hand, it is hard not to believe that most contemporaries would have seen this struggle for what it was – a battle for power.

The second period was in the 1770s when Henry Dundas, on one side, in alliance with the Duke of Buccleuch, and Lawrence Dundas, the 'nabob of the north', on the other, wrestled for political superiority in the Scottish capital as part of a wider battle for political supremacy in Scotland.[71] Membership of the Town Council became a key battleground in this struggle, a contest which saw the revival of long-standing arguments about the nature of the city's 'sett' and the political influence of the incorporated trades.[72] The rivalry became intertwined also with debates arising from the contemporary conflict with America. In August 1777, the trades sent delegates to a congress which issued a declaration which was subsequently published.[73] At this congress, delegates adopted the names of leading American Patriot leaders. James Stoddart, who as Lord Provost began as the lynchpin of the Lawrence Dundas interest on the council, but who joined Buccleuch's and the Lord Advocate's party in 1777, was described in one pamphlet as the 'The Wilkes of the North' because of his populist tactics.[74] One of Stoddart's pamphleteering allies, writing in support of a greater role for the trades' deacons in council affairs, did so under the title *Common Sense*, almost certainly a deliberate echo of Thomas Paine's revolutionary manifesto.[75] There may well also have been efforts on both sides to engage the populace through the manufacture of stories and rumour about the impact of the outcome of the conflict on the 'cheapness of meal', an issue always calculated to stir the anxieties of the Scottish urban populace in this period.[76] Genuine social tensions were exploited in the course of the rivalry, with both parties seeking support from among the prosperous middling sort who found themselves excluded from the charmed circle. The 1780 general election, at which Lawrence Dundas, the city's MP, was opposed by Thomas Miller, a candidate backed by Dundas and Buccleuch, was fought on similar grounds, although with the added ingredients of attempts to label Dundas as the friend of the Catholics in the wake of the anti-Catholic agitation of 1779 and, in response, a new emphasis on Lawrence Dundas's having moved into opposition to the North ministry.[77]

At bottom, however, this was another struggle about power and the disposal of patronage, a fact which emerges, first, in the disputes which surrounded the raising of a volunteer regiment in the capital in 1778. Dundas's opposition to this, exercised through the Faculty of Advocates, of which he was then dean, appears to have been motivated purely by his opposition to Lawrence Dundas, who had given his support, as the city MP, to the initiative.[78] Second, it is disclosed even more clearly in several letters written by Thomas Dundas to Sir Lawrence, his father, during the disputes. In one of these, written in November 1777, the trades deacons were described as 'looking for a new market'. Thomas went on the detail the appointments necessary to demonstrate their influence, to show, as he put it, 'that both you and I are able and willing to serve those who have stood forth to serve you'.[79] A month earlier, he had written: 'I did not intend to have writ to you till tomorrow's post, but on my arrival here [Edinburgh] I find all our Friends are up in arms about provost Dalrymple's succeeding to one of the vacancies of Commissioner of the Customs ... all our principal People are so very anxious, that I am obliged to write'.[80] Without the capacity to bestow patronage on his supporters, Sir Lawrence's interest would wither. That Henry Dundas, the arch string-puller in later eighteenth-century Scottish politics, was happy to sponsor populist tactics in Edinburgh in the 1770s only further clarifies the underlying reality of political conflict in Edinburgh in this period. The Court of Session would declare in 1778 that reform of the burgh's sett could only be obtained by application to Parliament. Dundas as Lord Advocate made no attempt to do so, while Stoddart was, as Murdoch has wryly noted, appointed a Commissioner of Excise.[81]

The effects of this rivalry were temporary, and the activism of the trades subsided quickly once Henry Dundas emerged as the clear victor after 1781. More generally, the structure and traditions of local government in Edinburgh provided nothing like the sustained basis for popular political involvement that they did in Dublin or London. Except in 1689 and 1746, when poll elections were necessitated by particular circumstances, membership of the Council was by co-option, and civic politics rarely spilled out from the council chamber.[82] The 'public sphere' in Edinburgh did not become politicized, although there were signs of change in the later eighteenth century, as indicated by the case of the Pantheon debating society, referred to above.[83] Few clubs or societies emerged, however, which were narrowly political in purpose or identity. An exception was the Orange Club, also referred to earlier, although the most enduring was the Revolution Club, a Whig-loyalist society established in 1744, which boasted a sizeable membership of resident gentry, lawyers and professionals. Its role, however, seems to have largely been a ceremonial and convivial one.[84] Nothing emerged of the nature of Dublin's Society of Free Citizens, formed in 1750, which mounted a sustained challenge to oligarchical politics in the Irish capital over several decades.[85] Nor is it a coincidence that Edinburgh failed to produce any civic politicians in the mould of Dublin's Charles Lucas in the 1740s or James Napper Tandy, one of several figures who served to connect civic and Patriot politics at the national level in Ireland in the later 1770s and early 1780s, or the City of London's Humphrey Parsons, Sir John Barnard, William Beckford and their later successors, including at the turn of the nineteenth century the radical alderman Robert Waithman.[86]

Enlightenment, Presbyterianism and Conformity

Given, therefore, the nature of the country's political structures, and the close control on political life exerted 'from above', it is doubtful whether a politics characterized by independence and popular involvement of any real depth and resilience could ever have emerged in eighteenth-century Scotland. Its absence also reflected, however, the attitudes and outlook of the elites and the influence of another key institution in Scottish society – the church.

Scottish 'high culture' in this period did not lack radical or at least reform-ist voices, although we currently know little about the influence of more than a handful of these.[87] The one with the most obvious links to the reform politics of the 1790s was John Millar's, the Professor of Civil Law at the University of Glasgow between 1761 and 1801. A key influence on several radical politicians of this period, including Thomas Muir and in Ireland William Steel Dickson, and several leading opposition Whig reformers, the earls of Lauderdale and Buchan, Millar was to be accused of leading a 'democratical' faction at the University of Glasgow after 1789, although, in reality, this was opposition or Foxite Whig.[88] Other prominent figures in this group were Thomas Reid, George Jardine, James Millar, Robert Cleghorn and perhaps more famously John Anderson, founder of Anderson's Institution which would much later transmute into Strathclyde University. Jardine and Reid, together with Millar, were present at a meeting held in Glasgow on 14 July 1791 to celebrate the second anniversary of the fall of the Bastille.[89] Cleghorn's political sympathies were to prevent his preferment to chairs of natural philosophy and medicine in 1795–6, while Anderson's initial support for the French Revolution was to lead him to Paris in 1791, where he presented the French National Convention with a canon of his own design.[90] Millar's 'repub-lican' sympathies undoubtedly predated 1789. In 1784, he was compelled to write a letter to Edmund Burke, then Lord Rector of the university, defending himself against the charge of using his lectures on government to inculcate such views.[91] In March 1778, James Wodrow observed of 'American partisans in Scotland':

> At Glasgow there are fewer [than at Edinburgh] among the Literate & scarce a man among the Merch.s. Mess.rs Millar and Richardson in the Colledge are keen Amer-icans & a man equal to any of them in parts & Learning Mr A[da]m Mather Dr Craig's Assistant & the Dr himself.[92]

William Richardson was the Professor of Humanity, while Craig was later to write an account of life and writings of Millar. The criticism of 1784 was almost certainly prompted by Millar's efforts to persuade a public meeting in Glasgow not to issue an address in support of Pitt the Younger.[93]

At a much less elevated level, a leading figure in the establishment of Dundee's only eighteenth-century Enlightenment club, the Speculative Society, was the surgeon Dr Robert Stewart.[94] Together with local minister, Dr Robert Small, a Moderate and author of a work on astronomy (*Kepler's Discoveries*), Stewart was influential in the formation of a dispensary in the town in 1782 and later an infirmary in 1794.[95] He also played a role in the formation of the Dundee Public Library (in 1796), which quickly built up a collection which included many Enlightenment classics.[96] Stewart's political outlook was opposition Whig, and he was almost certainly a signatory to the address to the French National Assembly issued by the Dundee Whig Club in 1790. Other signatories included a significant number of local linen merchants, who, along with Stewart and Small, appear to have formed the core of an opposition Whig interest in the town in the final decades of the eighteenth century.[97] One of these merchants, David Jobson, chaired a meeting in the town in early January 1793 which included pro-reform clauses in a loyal address; he also appears to have provided funds to aid in the establishment of the *Scots Chronicle* in 1796, the voice of the opposition Whig interest in Scotland in the later 1790s.[98] There is no evidence that Stewart, Jobson or indeed any of these merchants joined either of the two local radical societies in the early 1790s. These individuals represent, nevertheless, a significant liberal, reformist element in Scottish urban society in the later eighteenth century, which emerged more visibly in the early 1780s in support of the English opposition Whigs and various reformist causes, and which was also a product of the Enlightenment. There was a culture of popular enlightenment, about which we know very little, but which, as we will see in a later chapter, became more visible in the 1790s with the establishment of a significant number of popular reading societies, mostly in the west and central lowlands, which often seem to have been aligned with radical politics.[99] The Encyclopaedia Club of Paisley, so called because its small collection of books included a set of the *Encyclopaedia Britannica*, may have existed as early as 1770. As John Crawford has noted, its presidents included a blacksmith, and its members a barber and a handloom weaver.[100] James Tytler, best remembered today for his ballooning exploits, might just represent another dimension to this same culture. Taught at Edinburgh University by the great chemist and friend of Millar's, William Cullen, Tytler was to become the editor of the second edition of William Smellie's *Encyclopedia Britannica*. His was a life stamped by serial disappointment and difficulty, as well as great ingenuity and literary activity. His radicalism, which saw him in early 1793 flee, under threat of prosecution for seditious libel, first to Belfast and later to Philadelphia, may simply have been one born of a sense of cumulative frustration.[101]

Despite the existence of various reformist currents, therefore, the dominant political character of the Enlightenment in Scotland was strongly conservative. The Enlightenment of Smith and David Hume produced a commercial and unionist defence of the Whig establishment at same time that it debunked many of the central myths of 'vulgar' Whiggism (to use Hume's terminology) – notably the notion of the 'ancient constitution' – myths which would form a major element of the radicals' political platform in the 1790s.[102] In his histories, William Robertson, that other pillar of the Moderate Enlightenment, and Principal of Edinburgh University between 1762 and 1793, promulgated a similar outlook – cosmopolitan, optimistic and deeply respectful of the political and religious status quo in Britain. Through his histories, Robertson strove to re-knit Scotland's divergent traditions, and, at the same time, to create a strong sense of separation between Scotland's pre-1707 past and the 'improved' and 'improving' Scotland of the present.[103] The endorsement of present progress and improvement was one of the most common tropes of Scottish Enlightenment writing in its different forms.

No single factor can fully explain the politically conformist character of the Scottish Enlightenment; although it needs to seen, as with the Enlightenment in England, as a reaction to the disruptions and traumas of the previous century, and, related to this, as a process of reconciling religion and civil society.[104] More obviously, it reflected the very close connections which existed between many Enlightenment writers and members of the social and political elite. The majority of the leading figures of the Scottish Enlightenment wrote, if not exactly within, then with the close support and encouragement of the establishment. Thanks to the work of Roger Emerson, the crucial importance to the Enlightenment in Scotland of the patronage of writers and scientists by the third Duke of Argyll and the third Earl of Bute can now be fully appreciated.[105] Landed notables on occasion gave more direct patronage to Enlightenment writers, engaging them as family tutors, as occurred with the Duke of Buccleuch and Adam Smith, Lord Cathcart and William Richardson, or the Duke of Hamilton and John Moore. Robertson's early career, to cite a further example, owed a great deal to the support of Robert Dundas of Arniston. The material as well as psychological rewards of Enlightenment could be considerable. As Richard Sher has recently emphasized, aided by a remarkable nexus of Scottish booksellers and publishers in London and Edinburgh, the sums which could be earned through publication rose sharply in the eighteenth century.[106] Widely seen and accepted as a national and patriotic enterprise, for its leading exponents, as well as for quite a few of its lesser lights, the business of enlightenment brought recognition and status, as well as profit. Circumstances such as these were unlikely to promote alienation and disaffection. On the other hand, those who failed to do well might have been expected to feel even greater frustration about the denial of success. If this happened, it seems to have done so only to very few individuals, however, for example, James Tytler, referred to above, and possibly James Thomson Callender, who emerged from a similar world of popular Enlightenment publishing.[107]

Scotland's Enlightenment writers and thinkers were not opposed to change, although they sought the 'general principles' of politics not the perfection of British politics. Their characteristic stance was a sceptical, detached one; progress, they believed, was often unwilled and unintended. If anything, they tended to express anxieties about the populist tendencies within the English (after 1707 British) system of government. 'Civil liberty' was what concerned them primarily, not 'political liberty', and its protection meant striking a careful balance between order and liberty. As Adam Ferguson declared in 1776, liberty without 'restraint' existed only on the periphery of Europe; it was not a feature of the European civilization of which commercial societies like Britain were a part.[108] In 1792, he warned that in a representative system such as Britain's:

> ... liberty depends more upon the character of the representative, than upon the form of proceeding, or the number of persons who are admitted to vote at elections, and when the matter is settled upon any footing that is safe, stability is of more consequence than any advantage to be gained by change.[109]

Where reform was necessary, this should be led from above and of a type which reflected the benign prospects of eighteenth-century Scotland. It was Ferguson again who advised, clearly with an eye on the reform debates which exploded into life in Scotland in 1792:

> Grievances, nevertheless, under the fairest government, may take place, and must be redressed; and whoever has a grievance to plead must be heard; whilst he who, without any complaint of grievance, has gone forth in search of speculative melioration, or improvement, not absolutely required to the safety of his country, is to be dreaded as a most dangerous enemy to the peace of mankind.[110]

The gap in this context between the Edinburgh illuminati and Millar and his fellow Glasgow reformers was not as great as it might appear. What divided them was, first, partisan allegiance and attitudes towards the current political leadership of Britain; where they would also disagree in the 1790s was over the desirability of pursuing reform in the febrile atmosphere that overtook political life from around 1792 and the conduct and aims of the war against revolutionary France.[111] The radical mentality in eighteenth-century Britain was, by contrast, often haunted by acute fears about the present.[112]

What of Scotland's Presbyterian religious tradition and inheritance? On the face of it, this provides a much more promising place to uncover latent radical tendencies. Yet here too there are solid reasons for scepticism. It might be argued, as indeed it was sporadically in the eighteenth century, that the self governing, representative organization of the Kirk would naturally encourage the development of a critical stance towards the oligarchical structures of the Hanoverian state. Yet this did not happen. The Moderates, who in the middle of the century came to control the General Assembly, were, guided by Robertson and his allies, firm supporters of the political and social status quo. This was to be demonstrated very clearly during both the American war and the 1790s.[113] As Colin Kidd has emphasized, 'The Kirk was a willing bastion of loyalism'.[114] Indeed what stands out is the keenness of this loyalism, a reflex which led them far from their inherited, national traditions and outlook and into a posture of deep complicity with the political and social status quo and the Anglo-Britishness which went with it. In 1797 Hugh Mitchell, explaining a recent decision to leave the ministry, would complain that he 'could not force himself to preach the old fashioned doctrines of passive obedience, which, of late, have profaned the pulpit ... in this part of the united Kingdom'.[115]

The case of the Popular clergy, who predominated in Glasgow and the west and central parts of the lowlands, is more ambiguous, as we will see further below, and they produced several vocal critics of the American war, including, most famously, the Edinburgh minister John Erskine and William Thom of Govan.[116] In Montrose, which had a persistent 'republican' element in the 1790s, Charles Nisbet preached against the war to the consternation of the burgh authorities.[117] These pro-American ministers often had strong links to the colonies, which may have played a significant role in stimulating this opposition to ministerial policy.[118] John McIntosh has, nevertheless, argued strongly that they did not push their opposition to the war very far, a view which is certainly consistent with contemporary observations about Glasgow's reaction to the conflict.[119] James Wodrow, who was a regular visitor to the city, emphasized in 1778 the lack of strong local opposition to the war, while the correspondence of the bookseller and former resident of Virginia Alexander Wilson registers the strength of local pro-ministerial opinion, but has almost nothing to say about anti-war sentiment.[120] The main concern of the Popular ministers seems to have been to demonstrate their fundamental loyalty to the state. They did not support American independence, one reason being their concern about the Americans' alliance with a 'popish' France in 1778. In the 1790s, Popular clergymen would join their Moderate counterparts in seeking to repel the contagion of French Jacobinism. Erskine was one such, publishing an alarmist, anti-French fast sermon in 1793.[121] For these ministers, their priority, unsurprisingly, was always religious rather than political principles, and the atheism of the French revolutionaries was deeply repugnant to them.

If the radical tendencies in the Presbyterian tradition were carefully emasculated by the Moderate and most Popular clergy of eighteenth-century Scotland, a genuinely popular tradition of dissent was maintained and nurtured by the Covenanters and the growing numbers of Seceders from the established church. The importance of this tradition has recently been demonstrated by Kidd, and his case does not need rehearsing in detail here.[122] Two points are, however, worth making. First, as he emphasizes, both the Secession churches and the reformed presbytery 'openly repudiated' any connection between their radicalism and that which emerged in the 1790s.[123] This was true even of ministers who clearly had a great deal of sympathy for the radical cause, such as the anti-burgher Archibald Bruce. Bruce was an articulate and vehement critic of the Pitt ministry's policy of political repression and of Britain's entry in February 1793 into the war against revolutionary France.[124] His stance and writings are, however, characterized by a great deal of equivocation and evasiveness. Bruce's prolix style – rooted, as Kidd notes, in his immersion in an older world of 'Calvinist scholasticism' – involved (from Bruce's point of view) a helpfully distracting plenitude of often contradictory comments and meanings as he sought to steer a careful path between the politics of reaction, towards which he was strongly opposed, and a politics of reform, for which he sought to offer implicit support but no explicit endorsement.[125] At the same time, he protested the political loyalty of his church, and its members' indifference to political reform when viewed as a church.[126] He also appears to have resisted joining any radical societies in the early 1790s, although, as we will see in a later chapter, this was not true of a small number of Secession ministers. Bruce saw himself as a strict adherent to the traditional teachings of his church, and his rigidity would lead him to separate from the associate synod in 1806.[127] His case highlights how tangled the threads are which might potentially link religious dissent and political dissent in the 1790s.

The fundamental source of the Secessionists' and reform presbytery's alienation from the British state was their view of its religious, not civil, shortcomings. Their aim was to secure the true religion as defined in the first National Covenant (1638) and Solemn League and Covenant (1643). They tended to view the world and current events through an apocalyptic framework, although this was a tendency which had deep roots in Presbyterian thought.[128] Where the Seceders and Covenanters seem to have differed from most ministers in the established church was how they applied this tradition to current events. Bruce saw the French Revolution as a key moment in the defeat of popery and victory of the true Protestant religion.[129] To fight a war to extinguish the Revolution was to oppose God's purpose. To dissenters like Bruce, the seventeenth-century covenanting past continued to illuminate vividly the present. Bruce and his fellow anti-burghers stood as witnesses to and agents of a continuing struggle against 'papistical and Jacobitical' forces.

Second, during the eighteenth century, Scots dissenters, despite what has just been said above, in practice retreated from the seventeenth-century vision and engagements which nourished their dissidence. Their intransigence weakened, and as it did so they tended to retreat also from the militant contractarianism of the Covenanting tradition as defined in the works of George Buchanan and Samuel Rutherford. In the case of the Seceders, it was a process which gathered momentum during the central decades of the century, with key moments being the decisions to congratulate George III on his assumption of the throne in 1760 and even more significantly to hold a day of thanksgiving to mark the centenary of the Glorious Revolution in 1788.[130] The issue of the allegiance owed to the civil power had been extensively debated at the time of the decision to renew the Covenants in 1742. At issue was, first, how far the religious views of rulers were a matter of indifference in this context, and, second, the 'lawfulness of propagating religion by offensive arms'. The synod declared that subjection to the civil power in all that was lawful was consistent with the word of God and the Covenants.[131] During the Jacobite Rebellion of 1745–6, Seceders came forward, and at an early stage, to defend the Hanoverian and Protestant succession, although they refused to be incorporated with bodies of men who 'refused to testify to corruptions in church and state'.[132]

What lay behind this accommodating tendency was primarily their reaction to the experience of religious freedom after the Glorious Revolution. There is a sharp contrast here with the increasing political restiveness after 1760 of English dissenters, especially rational dissenters.[133] Where this left the Seceders' concept of political allegiance was in outline very clear – strict obedience was owed to the established government – but in its detail it presented something of a muddle and was full of ambiguities, if not contradictions.[134] Such matters were to press very strongly on the Seceders in the 1790s, when they were forced to respond to the rise of organized loyalism and pervasive, frequently insistent suspicion about their political principles. The problem they faced was to remain true to their religious testimony and principles, while at the same time distancing themselves from those who sought political reform. In 1795, the Associate Synod supported the view that they could not subscribe to loyalist oaths which implied unqualified acceptance of the British constitution.[135] This was impossible for religious reasons. It was the anxiety of John Young, the anti-burgher minister for Hawick, to rebuff suspicions of Seceder disloyalty which led him to publish his *Essays on Government* in 1794. In this case, in his eagerness to demonstrate his and his church's loyalty, he fell off the tightrope of passive political quiescence along which the Seceders were seeking to travel, with the result that he faced investigation by the Synod.[136]

The view, therefore, that prevailing political structures, together with the main ideological and theological currents in eighteenth-century Scottish society, acted as powerful constraints on, if not in significant measure prevented, the development of a reform or radical tradition before 1789, and helped to create an enervated public political culture, is not to be lightly dismissed. This is not the whole story, however, and there are a number of facts which might serve to give us pause for thought. First, Scottish Presbyterianism did produce some highly articulate radical voices, albeit that many of them had to leave Scotland to discover this voice. Thus, Presbyterianism in Ulster proved fertile soil for political radicalism in the later eighteenth century, and the Scots-born Seceders in North America strongly supported the American Revolution.[137] In England, the Newcastle pro-Wilkite and pro-American dissenting minister James Murray and radical writer and educationalist James Burgh were both Scots Presbyterians by birth. What these individuals tended to share was a facility for fusing their Presbyterian outlook with a 'real Whig' ideology, a process which could lead them in some notably radical directions. This was not a new phenomenon – the 'real Whig' tradition was, after all, in inception British – but it further illustrates the potential for radicalism latent within traditional Presbyterianism. Murray, a native of Roxburghshire, was an orthodox Calvinist, and, as James Bradley notes, he and his family were steeped in the Scottish libertarian Covenanting inheritance.[138] Such phenomena point also to the need to identify ways in which new languages of liberty entered (or re-entered) public debate in Scotland in the later eighteenth century. Very suggestive in this context is the work of Ned Landsman and others on patronage disputes in the Church of Scotland. Landsman has argued that, in fighting patronage, popular ministers in and around Glasgow from the 1760s tended increasingly to exploit new, political languages of liberty.[139] Hearers and readers of this message would have included the rapidly growing number of weavers and other tradesmen and artisans in the west and central lowlands, and we need to reconstruct some of the main elements of the highly literate culture which they developed during this period. We will also need to revisit the role of the press and public politics as they developed in the later eighteenth century. While less impressive and certainly less striking than the political interventions of the press in English and Irish politics in the same period, the Scottish press from the 1770s did help to structure a re-emerging public sphere of debate about issues of political and public importance, a sphere which reached quite far down the social scale, and certainly encompassed many artisans and lesser tradesmen. The foundations for political developments in the 1790s may not have been as deep as in England and Ireland, but they were not as negligible as some historians have implied.

Patronage and Liberty

Patronage in the Church of Scotland had a unique capacity to excite debate and emotions in eighteenth-century Scotland. It was the major factor behind a series of secessions from the established church from 1733, which led by 1800 to around a quarter of lowland Scots adhering to different forms of Presbyterian dissent. The issue divided members of the established church, being the subject of periodically heated debate, while the imposition of unpopular ministers on parishes was resisted fiercely and on occasion violently in parts of the country by the populace in the later eighteenth century.[140] In Edinburgh and Glasgow, attempts by their respective town councils to impose ministers on churches without reference to the general sessions led to major disputes in the early 1760s.[141] Even where such protests did not occur, this was often because of recognition by patrons, including the Crown, of the need to consider popular views in presenting ministers to parishes. In Dundee this appears to have been the policy of the Town Council for most of the eighteenth century, while one pamphleteer from Glasgow referred in the early 1760s to the 'universal practice of a popular plan of election ... in all the other royal boroughs'.[142] Ministers of the Crown were similarly alert to the need not to alienate local opinion. In March 1742, the Marquess of Tweeddale, newly installed in the revived post of Scottish Secretary, wrote to Robert Craigie, the Lord Advocate:

> I desire you will consider and advise me, who are the properest persons among the clergy to consult with about Church Affairs, and in order to avoid as much as possible all Disputes between the Crown and the People great care should be taken when the Right of Patronage is in the Crown that the vacancies may be supplied in such a manner as to give satisfaction to the People and prevent the Right of the Crown from being called in question.[143]

Just who were 'the People' in Tweeddale's eyes is a debateable point; he may well have been simply referring to heritors. From the mid 1780s, the Moderates adopted a stance of prudent conciliation and delay in respect of patronage disputes, a tactic which contributed strongly to a lowering of the heat in debates about patronage after 1785.[144]

The General Assembly of the Church of Scotland remained after 1760 the main site of the argument and campaigning about patronage, with opponents increasingly seeking to commit the Church to a policy of seeking redress from the Westminster Parliament. As McIntosh and others have noted, this effort was accompanied by a growing secular emphasis in argument.[145] This was driven in part by pragmatic considerations in that Popular ministers were actively seeking to cultivate the support of the landed classes for their objective. What has been less often emphasized is how from the early 1770s and especially in the early 1780s opponents of patronage moved to embrace new styles of public lobbying. This again is partly explained by the main goal of the campaign – to pressurize parliament into repealing the Patronage Act of 1712. But it was a response also to a series of decisions in the early 1780s by the General Assembly to support the settlement of ministers in parishes without a proper call.[146] There was a striking exploitation of the press as a vehicle for debate on the issue.[147] The 1770s and early 1780s also saw the formation of anti-patronage societies in Edinburgh and Glasgow.

Little is known unfortunately about the Edinburgh body, but in Glasgow two such societies emerged, the first of which, the Glasgow Constitutional Society, was established in 1771. A key figure in this society appears to have been John Gillies, the influential minister of Glasgow (Blackfriars; 1742–96) and leader of the Popular party in the west. Its lobbying style was discreet, which is perhaps why it has remained largely hidden from the historian's scrutiny.[148] Its chosen mode of action was correspondence with ministers and elders. In 1771 it distributed the pamphlet *An Effectual Method for Recovering our Religious Liberties, Addressed to the Elders of the Church of Scotland* (Glasgow, 1770) to parishes throughout Scotland. This called on them carefully to select elders as delegates to the General Assembly with the aim of their supporting the repeal of the Patronage Act. The second society, which called itself the New Constitutional Society to distinguish itself from the existing one, emerged in the spring of 1782, the product of division among the opponents of patronage in Glasgow. While the old society sought a return to the status quo ante 1690, members of this new body were supporters of popular election. They also adopted a very different style of lobbying and a much higher degree of public visibility. They portrayed themselves as a democratic body, seeking to subject themselves to popular control through public meetings. They called on other bodies to correspond with them, indicating that they 'would be glad to know the sentiments of *men of all rank*' (my emphasis) on the issue.[149] A similar body was established in Greenock from among 'a number of merchants, shop-keepers and other inhabitants.'[150] In 1783, it was the new society which was behind a major petitioning campaign, which involved it publishing resolutions throughout the Scottish press, and sending copies of these to every parish in Scotland.[151] A connection between this body and the radical politics of the 1790s exists in the person of William Muir, Thomas's father, who was secretary to the Glasgow body.[152] The main inspiration behind the new mode of campaigning was almost certainly the campaign against Catholic Relief from 1778, a campaign which had involved many of the same groups in society, and which Robert Kent Donovan has portrayed as representing a key episode in the political awakening of the popular classes in many parts of lowland Scotland.[153] Scots were familiar also, through the press, with contemporaneous political reform campaigns in Ireland and England.[154]

Much of the debate about patronage in the later eighteenth century was conducted, as it had been earlier in the century, in narrowly scriptural, legal and historical terms, or in terms of the personal qualities requisite for an effective ministry and whether these were best secured by patronage or election.[155] This last issue was at, or never far from, the heart of exchanges between opponents and supporters of patronage. To be effective, ministers needed to command the respect of their congregations; more than that they needed to be able to communicate effectively with them. Its opponents argued that patronage prevented this. The consequences were political as well as religious, acting, as the Nine Incorporated Trades of Dundee put it in early February 1783 'to alienate their [the people's] affections from their native country, and fill them with bitterness and aversion to government'.[156]

Anti-patronage opinion should not be seen either as necessarily or even mainly democratic in inspiration or indeed meaning. Sher and Murdoch have portrayed the Popular party as seeking to restore the influence of the landed classes in the selection of ministers.[157] Andrew Crosbie wanted to vest the power of choice in the 'middle rank', declaring:

> The middle rank of people are best qualified to judge of the talents of pastors; because, possessing some knowledge of their own, they are also able to feel those powers of instruction which are apt to produce the greatest effects on the lower class.[158]

Among members of synods and in the press, there was much support for the restoration of the act of 1690, which provided for choice of ministers by elders and heritors in parishes, the preferred choice of the Glasgow Constitutional Society, as referred to above.[159] This was seen as avoiding the dangers associated with tyranny, on the one hand, and too much democracy, on the other. But more radical sentiments, if we can call them that, were regularly heard, even if their expression could be somewhat tentative. One writer in the *Caledonian Mercury* remarked in relation to popular election:

> Again, from the dependence of one part of the community upon the other, elections, especially in country parishes, would often be influenced still by people in higher life. Nor can it be denied, that in many places the people are very unfit to make a proper use of this right, though they had it.

The corollary of this was not, however, what some argued. As this writer declared, 'as a friend to mankind, I must give my voice in favour of popular election'.[160] In 1766, John, Lord Maclaurin observed that the 'end of settling a minister in a parish is the comfort and instruction, not of the rich ... but of the poor, that is tenants, labouring people, &c'. He expressed doubts about whether this objective would be obtained if the right of election was confined to the heritors.[161] Support among some ministers for popular election existed beyond Glasgow and the west, as is indicated by a proposal at a meeting of the Synod of Angus and Mearns in October 1783 of an overture supportive of investing 'the power of the Election of Ministers, in the Body of the Christian People'.[162] In the event, this was defeated in favour of one calling for the restoration of 1690 dispensation. As referred to above, the New Constitutional Society in Glasgow advocated popular election.

Popular election was defended on a range of grounds, but ultimately on the basis of the equality of the soul. Yet at the same time notions of 'natural' or 'inalienable' rights were infiltrated into public debate in this context, as were links between payment of tithes and the right to a say in the choice of minister, and the popular capacity for moral and rational judgement. The congruence here with debates about political reform hardly needs to be spelled out.

Opponents of patronage also regularly invoked notions of liberty which either drew directly on or which had much in common with real Whig conceptions and ideology. This in part reflected how easily a religious, Presbyterian language of liberty shared elements and concepts with an essentially secular one. Patronage was identified with popery and despotism, or, as in the case of the Patronage Act (1712), the spawn of Jacobite opposition to the Protestant and Hanoverian succession.[163] The fight against patronage was a fight for liberty and the restoration of the true constitution. The Patronage Act was also depicted as directly contrary to the terms of the Treaty of Union, and as such lacking any legitimacy or, even on occasion, as imperilling the Union itself.[164] Such views depended on contractual ideas of political sovereignty, and explicit rejection, in common with political radicals in England and Ireland, of the omnipotence of the Westminster Parliament.

The rhetoric deployed by opponents of patronage frequently echoed that used in battles for political liberty elsewhere in the British Isles. John Snodgrass, minister of the South Church in Dundee, declared:

> Many laudable attempts have been made of late, by the friends of liberty, to rescue us from the wretched thraldom of patronage, under which we have long been groaning. Some have bravely stood up in our ecclesiastical courts against the arbitrary measures of a prevailing faction, and contended for those sacred privileges which they have from time to time been wresting from; others, again, have employed their pens in explaining our excellent constitution ...[165]

The fight against patronage was portrayed as an extension of the struggle against popery and despotism. Another writer quoted approvingly from the patriotic works of the Deist Lord Bolingbroke in support of resisting patronage, emphasizing the degree to which religious and secular languages of liberty were mutually reinforcing.[166]

The political notes struck by some opponents of patronage were more clamorous still. Patronage was commonly portrayed as an instrument, potential as much as actual, of ministerial corruption and political enslavement. Crosbie was one of these, asking: 'If it is once supposed a possible matter, that the exercise of the right of presentation may be perverted, so as to answer political purposes, what a fund of corruption in election matters may be found in patronage ...?' He continued:

> When it appears that the great weight of this influence over the election of members of the House of Commons is in the hands of the crown and of the nobility, the idea of settlements by presentations alone lays open to our view a political evil of a very serious nature.[167]

The anti-burgher Archibald Bruce, referred to earlier, painted a more lurid picture of the patron as an agent of tyranny and landed oppression, but the underlying message was similar.[168] Another anti-patronage writer asserted that what was at stake was 'the rights of the people' as opposed to the interests of the 'rich and the great'. Patronage, they declared, was a 'yoke' of slavery which neither 'we nor our fathers were able to bear'.[169] William Thom of Govan portrayed it as subverting the 'democratical power' of the people in the church and enhancing ministerial power in church and state.[170]

Defeating patronage was, however, a matter of much more than potential electoral corruption. Patronage, it was repeatedly urged, sapped the spirit of liberty at the same time that it threatened the spiritual health of the church and society. In a very real sense, the proponents of the repeal of the 1712 act were arguing, liberty in Scotland resided in the free election of ministers. As Crosbie argued, it was 'chiefly' because of settlement by calls that 'we owe those ideas of liberty that the lower class of mankind in Scotland feel'. Only through returning to this system would the 'people' be able to 'feel their own weight' and ideas of liberty be preserved. This case was reinforced through reference to Scotland's past. 'Every struggle for liberty', Crosbie declared, 'since the Reformation has been by Presbyterians'.[171] The author of another pamphlet developed the same case at greater length, at one point warning: 'If the impressions of liberty are, by any means, worn off, or impaired, upon the minds of the people, the very source of liberty is corrupted or exhausted, and it is impossible that the state can be safe. Despotism may erect its standard.'[172] The inhabitants of Callender in Stirlingshire urged that patronage 'enervates those generous principles, which are the birthright of Britons: it prepares the soul for bondage, and the neck for the yoke of arbitrary power'.[173] Patronage meant servility, as well as oppression. 'Parishes', exclaimed another writer, 'are now considered in no other view that such a particular tract of land, and the people, whom the law calls the congregation, as so many trees upon it; for they must not pretend to either conscience or sentiments of their own, much less privileges or rights'.[174] Others embellished the point differently, but the underlying argument was the same. Popular calls nurtured liberty, and without liberty prosperity and industry would wither. For Glasgow's New Constitutional Society, what was at issue was:

> Whether Scotland shall continue to thrive in cultivation, manufactures, and commerce: or whether its inhabitants shall be enslaved, and enslaved in what of all things is most dear to them, their religion, they may be provoked in multitudes to emigrate

to other regions, where they may enjoy their privileges civil and sacred, leaving their native country to be a wilderness?[175]

Religious liberty was being identified, in short, with virtue, national prosperity, independence, civil and political freedom and the dignity of the individual.

If what mattered, therefore, was removing patronage and reviving the spirit of liberty, from where in society did this message gain most support? Callum Brown has noted that in the burghs it was merchants and tradesmen who led patronage disputes, while in rural parishes it tended to be tenant farmers, merchants or craftsmen.[176] In other words, opposition to patronage was the cause of the 'industrious classes', precisely the social constituency invoked in so much radical propaganda in the 1790s. The strength of support for the Popular Party, which led the anti-patronage cause within the established church, lay in the mercantile and trading classes, but also, especially (but certainly not exclusively), in the rapidly growing urban-industrial parishes in the west, among the weavers and other artisan groups. Supporters of the Moderates recognized this popularity, in some cases if only through their attacks on what they saw as the dangerous populism of Popular ministers. Hugo Arnot, the historian of Edinburgh, talked of the Popular party in the church 'always endeavouring by arts suitable to the end, to insinuate themselves with the rabble'.[177] One minister declared before the Synod of Glasgow and Ayr in 1784: 'There is so great a prejudice and clamour raised among many of the common people of this country against the law of patronage, that it is certainly unpopular at present, and perhaps dangerous, for any one to open his mouth in favour of it'.[178] It was from areas where the Popular party was well entrenched that petitions against patronage tended to be forthcoming in the early 1780s. These same areas were also well to the fore in the campaign against Catholic relief in 1778–82.[179]

The independence of weavers and other tradesmen and lesser tenants had been strongly evident in the religious sphere some decades earlier in the evangelical awakening of the early 1740s, when popular ministers in parishes around Glasgow had struggled to exert control over the religious responses of their flocks, and was an important element in the rise of dissenting religion in the later eighteenth century.[180] The culture of the weavers was shaped by high levels of literacy, a literacy nurtured not so much in school, but from a very young age in the home through reading the Bible and other religious works.[181] Although not a weaver, in a personal memoir John Scot of the Old Monkland parish, who participated as a thirteen-year-old in the Cambuslang revival, described being taught to read by his mother and father from the Bible and subsequently from religious works owned by his father before the age of twelve. He was taught to write aged eight by means of his father getting him to copy out the psalms. His appetite for reading grew as he moved into adolescence. He describes himself reading mostly books of divinity, but he also 'had a considerable taste for history'. With the help of his brother, who was at school, and through reading books, he taught himself arithmetic. Crucial to his religious odyssey as described in his memoir was the reading of specific popular works of devotion. In the mid 1750s he joined a religious society, and owing to his skills as a writer he would be asked to pen an account of it.[182] Ownership of works of divinity was very widespread among weavers and other artisans and tradesmen in the west and south-west, as indicated by, among other things, subscription lists for the popular devotional works published in Glasgow by evangelical publisher John Bryce.[183] Covenanting classics continued to circulate, with new editions appeared periodically throughout the century.[184] Evidence of wills can reinforce and extend this picture, although their study in a Scottish eighteenth-century context remains in its infancy. In 1777, the widow of a Dundee weaver left fourteen books, the vast majority of which were devotional or religious works, and included two bibles and the collected sermons of John Erskine.[185] Analysis of subscribers to the *Family Expositor*, a family bible and commentary published in 1763 by the Dundee printer Henry Galbraith, provides further evidence for readership of religious works among tradesmen, craftsmen and labourers in industrial areas in the north-east.[186] From Auchterderran in Fife, it was reported in the early 1790s:

> In common with the rest of Scotland, the vulgar are, for their station, literate, perhaps, beyond all other nations. Puritanic and abstruse divinity come in for a sufficient share in their little stock of books; and it is perhaps peculiar to them, as a people, that they endeavour to form opinions, by reading, as well as by frequent conversation ... They likewise read, occasionally, a variety of books unconnected with such subjects.[187]

It was from a similar cultural milieu that the weaver poets of Paisley and Renfrewshire emerged towards the end of the century, among their number several notable radicals.[188]

Through their reading, therefore, weavers and other groups kept alive memories of Covenanting resistance and struggles against Stuart tyranny. One of the works which Bryce published by subscription, first in 1775 and then in an enlarged edition in 1781, was John Howie's *Scots Worthies*, a compilation of Covenanting biographies (328 weavers subscribed to the 1781 edition[189]). Other popular biographies of Covenanters circulated widely. As Kidd notes, 'a vigorous – and far from depoliticized – Covenanting identity continued to prevail within the sphere of popular culture'.[190]

The independence of the weavers, and of other groups of artisans, was exhibited in other ways – in the formation of friendly societies and occupational associations from the 1730s, and the capacity and resourcefulness with which they fought industrial disputes and took direct action to police the marketing of grain during periods of shortage and high prices.[191] Viewed more broadly, the rise of religious dissent, together with explosive growth in semi-independent manufacturing villages in many parts of lowland Scotland, served to weaken traditional social controls in Scottish society.[192] This did not make the sudden rise of popular radical politics in 1792 inevitable, but it does help to explain why it became possible in the later eighteenth century.

The Press and Public Debate

A political (or at least sub-political) consciousness among weavers and other artisan groups was evident in other spheres by the later eighteenth century. Legislation affecting the textile industries could bring crowds of weavers onto the streets, as occurred in Anderston, near Glasgow, for example, in 1779, where weavers and master weavers burnt an effigy of Lord North in protest against the lifting of a long-standing prohibition on the importation of French cambrics.[193] In the previous year, North's attempts to relax trade restrictions with Ireland led to a major agitation against this focused in Scotland on Glasgow and Paisley. While this was led by merchants, it also drew in the local trades incorporations and weavers. In 1784, Pitt's cotton tax drew ten thousand weavers onto Glasgow Green in protest, where a committee of twenty was elected and a remonstrance drawn up. Paisley seems to have seen similar sorts of activity.[194]

These episodes were part of a broader development of public politics and public debate in later eighteenth-century Scotland, which embraced, as well as a growing body of local and national parliamentary legislation, the anti-Catholic outcry of 1778–81, the anti-patronage campaign of the early 1780s, the burgh and county reform campaigns, and from 1787 the campaign to abolish the slave trade. In 1792, Scotland would contribute a disproportionately high number, relative to population size, of petitions calling for immediate abolition of the slave trade.[195] In this case, the inspiration came in significant measure from London and the London Committee for Abolition, which sent William Dickson to Scotland in 1792 to encourage support for their latest petitioning campaign.[196] Yet, as with the other campaigns, its scope and success were dependent on the existence of a rapidly expanding public sphere of debate and engagement in urban Scotland in the later eighteenth century and on a press which was, by the final decades of the eighteenth century, beginning to be exploited much more systematically for its publicity and lobbying potential by a growing range of bodies and individuals.

The existence of this new type of public politics can be illustrated briefly by examining the impact of debates about the Corn Laws from the 1770s. As south of the border, one of the distinctive features of these debates was their potential to drive a wedge between the 'landed interest' (producers of grain in this context) and the growing urban and semi-urban population which was dependent on purchasing foodstuffs for their survival. Proposed changes to the Corn

Laws also, more importantly from our point of view, were capable of mobilizing a broad cross-section of the manufacturing population.

This last feature was evident from events in 1773, when, according to one contemporary account, an attempt by Scottish MPs to exclude Scotland from a new Corn Act was defeated 'on account of the great discontent shewn by their constituents'.[197] On hearing of the MPs' actions, Glasgow merchants had sent circular letters to all the burghs to instruct their MPs to have the clause excepting Scotland from the legislation removed. There was a major demonstration in Glasgow amongst the manufacturing population involving an effigy of a Scottish MP which was carried to the common place of execution and hanged. There is a hint of class anger in the protest in that the effigy was of 'a portly well dressed man'.[198] Four years later (in 1777), it was again Glasgow that provided the lead to Scottish opposition to proposed changes to the Corn Laws contained in a bill introduced into Parliament by the MP for Ayrshire, Sir Adam Fergusson. News of the bill appears to have reached the city in late April by means of a letter to the Provost.[199] This triggered a series of meetings of the Trades House, Merchants House and Town Council, as well as a general meeting of traders and manufacturers called by the Provost. A joint committee was formed to oppose the bill which it was widely believed would have the effect of raising the price of grain. The Glasgow merchants and manufacturers issued a detailed memorial against the measure, which was sent to the other royal burghs, and printed in several Scottish papers.[200] Of this document, one critic complained: 'It is filled with the vulgar opinions upon the subject, and probably contains all the objections made against the present law, as well as the proposed bill'.[201] In May, the annual committee of the royal burghs meeting in Edinburgh, directed by the Provost of Glasgow, resolved to oppose the bill. On 1 May the Commons ordered the bill to be printed, postponing further consideration of it for six months. An abstract of the bill duly appeared in the Scottish press.[202] In Dundee, the appearance of the bill appears to have provoked a street demonstration involving a crowd carrying an effigy through the town with a paper in one hand with the words 'Corn Bill' on it and one in the other hand with the words 'Destruction of Scotland'. The effigy was carried to the market cross at the heart of the burgh, where it was burnt.[203] In November, on the eve of the new parliamentary session, the Glasgow committee, formed in the previous spring, went to Edinburgh, where it held meetings with the Lord Advocate and 'some of the landed interest', as well as attending meetings of the annual committee of the Convention of Royal Burghs, a general meeting of the 'landed gentlemen of the most of the countys' of Scotland, and a committee appointed by this meeting.[204] No consensus could be found at these meetings. As a result, the Glasgow committee determined to continue to oppose Fergusson's bill, an opposition in which it was joined by representatives of the trades from several other burghs. In January 1778, 'Agricola', writing in the *Caledonian Mercury*, called on ministers and kirk sessions to explain the bill in an attempt to defuse the popular opposition.[205] No such initiative was forthcoming, and the opposition was sufficiently strong for the measure to be dropped.

Later changes, and proposed changes, to the Corn Laws, for example in 1786, 1790 and 1791, provoked similarly strong public reactions and intense public and press debates. The Glasgow petition to the Commons against the Corn bill in 1791 was supposedly signed by around 10,000 people.[206] The breadth of the debate – in pamphlets and newspapers – was symptomatic of a growing political maturity in the Scottish press in the final decades of the eighteenth century.[207] Through the press, and aided by an expanding postal service, circuits of communication were being created which were indispensable to the new modes of political lobbying. The commercial and manufacturing classes were the most persistent and creative exploiters of these new political possibilities. In 1790 and 1791, for example, a key role in the campaign against the new Corn Laws was played by the Glasgow and Edinburgh Chambers of Commerce. Much of the lobbying activity remained within well-established conventions and channels – the Convention of Royal Burghs, county freeholders meetings, town meetings called by local magistrates, merchant bodies and trades incorporations. Or rather, it represented a revitalization of these traditional mechanisms, with a new emphasis on publicity and transparency.

Thus, through the press and lobbying activities of various kinds by the later eighteenth century discussion about public issues was reaching down into and across a much broader cross-section of the urban and semi-urban population than had been the case earlier in the century. One further small piece of evidence which points in the same direction is three annotated lists of subscribers to a burgh reform petition of 1788 from Perth which survive in the Perth and Kinross County Archives.[208] Drawn up by the local authorities at the behest of the Convention of Royal Burghs as part of a campaign to discredit burgh reform, they show how the campaign drew support from a wide cross-section of society, including weavers, tailors and shoemakers as well as the merchants more usually associated with the cause. (This evidence must qualify the commonly expressed view that the cause of burgh reform was essentially that of the respectable middle classes.[209]) By the 1770s, groups among the skilled labouring classes were also beginning to use the press to defend their occupational interests, such as the Edinburgh journeymen masons who sponsored a series of articles in the *Caledonian Mercury* in the course of a labour dispute in 1778.[210] Journeymen masons were one of several trades well represented in the capital's reform societies in the early 1790s.[211]

The developing public sphere in Scotland in the later eighteenth century provided more influential models of political action and habits on which the reformers and radicals of the 1790s were able to build than some historians have supposed. Much of the politics which shaped and filled this sphere had a further dimension which was to be of fundamental importance for the Scottish radicals of the 1790s. This is the fact that it was British – British in the sense that it was often focused on Westminster, and British or at least Anglo-British in identity and meaning. The inhabitants of Kirkintilloch, in opposing patronage in the church, spoke of the 'free genius of the British constitution'. They also declared that 'regard for the reasonable wishes, and equal liberty of all its subjects, is a principle known to lye at the bottom of our happy civil constitution'. The inhabitants of Greenock appealed to 'British principles' in attacking patronage.[212] Opposition to patronage had, in fact, the happy facility for enabling a reconciliation of this new British identity with older, distinctively Presbyterian conceptions of nationhood. Thus, opponents of patronage could also talk of recovering the nation's 'antient independency' or 'what we have lost'. They meant not sovereignty, but independence of the church; but it was an ambiguity out of which could be built ideological bridges. Similarly proponents of burgh reform represented their cause as one of completing the Union, of fuller assimilation with British liberties, while abolitionism sought its justification in moral terms but also in terms of vindicating the British claim to be, uniquely and historically, the guardians of liberty.[213] The nation in each case was Britain, and the tradition of political liberty being appealed to English. Even economic and mercantile lobbying was British, albeit driven by pragmatic as much as ideological reasons; to achieve success the broadest possible range of support for an issue or demand needed to be shown. Campaigns against, say, Irish trade liberalization in 1778 joined Glasgow and Manchester in opposition to the North ministry. In 1785, the Glasgow Chamber of Commerce joined the newly formed, if short-lived, British Chamber of Manufactures in opposing Pitt's new taxes.[214]

Finally, the press itself was increasingly a powerful force for integration and the creation of a British outlook. This was, in the first place, because, as was noted towards the beginning of this chapter, English newspapers circulated in ever greater numbers north of the border in the later eighteenth century. But it was also a function of the ability of the press from the early 1770s to report openly on parliamentary proceedings. In so doing, the press helped to provide a common vocabulary and framework within which discussion of political developments and events could take place. The American war intensified this development as the Scottish press came to reflect more closely divisions at Westminster on its conduct and progress. In the 1780s, it was only further reinforced by the growing alignment of political rivalries in Scotland with those at Westminster, with Dundas joining Pitt in 1783 and his opponents supporting Fox and the opposition Whigs.[215] The constitutional crisis of 1783–4 and the Regency crisis of 1789 represented climacterics in this context, as reflected not only in the contents of the press, but also the holding of public meetings to discuss the propriety of issuing addresses in support of Pitt. The press helped, in short, to give substance and form to the idea of a common, national (meaning in this case British) political discussion. The practice which many Scottish papers adopted of employing London correspondents in the later eighteenth century can only have further strengthened the perception that national political life was defined in terms of a series of relationships flowing from, and centred on, the British capital. It was a perception which, as we will see in subsequent chapters, radicals in the 1790s appear fully to have shared.

2 NEWSPAPERS, THE FRENCH REVOLUTION AND PUBLIC OPINION

During the 1790s, newspapers gained unprecedented prominence in political debate throughout the British Isles.[1] In part this derived from the particular strengths of the newspaper as a means of political communication. Newspapers were, a contemporary declared, 'so much better adapted to the time, capacity and circumstances' of people than 'books and pamphlets'.[2] They would, another remarked, continue to be read 'when the pamphlet and its subject are buried in oblivion'.[3] More importantly, their serial nature and regularity of appearance enabled them to build relationships with and between readers quite unlike other forms of print, with the possible exception of some periodicals. For radicals of the period especially, being linked to these circuits of communication helped to shore up their political resolve by giving them a sense of belonging to a wider movement or body of opinion. This was the reason why placing resolutions and notices in the press was so important to radical societies; and conversely why being prevented from so doing was potentially very damaging to their cause. For many radicals newspapers had an additional, ideological meaning as the pre-eminent vehicles for the political instruction of the 'people'. Through the press, radicals might, quite literally, write and print into being a new sort of political order based on the principles of openness, transparency and reason. The irony was of course that newspapers might just as easily become instruments of political reaction, as indeed would prove to be the case in Britain, and especially Scotland, in this period.

Newspapers were also very widely available in British society by the 1790s. This was despite their not being especially cheap, and their print runs typically being quite small, especially in comparison to the final third of the nineteenth century, which saw the emergence of a genuinely popular press.[4] Their costs, in fact, rose quite sharply under the impact of successive increases in stamp duty in 1789, 1794 and 1797. On the last of these occasions, the rise was particularly marked, typically from 4 to 6d. for a single issue, an increase which seems to have depressed demand for newspapers appreciably. While most eighteenth-century increases in duty were motivated by the Treasury's frequently desperate search in wartime for revenue, the scale of the rise in 1797 undoubtedly signalled that it was a measure also aimed at reining in the influence of the press amongst the lower orders. It reflected the strength of the recognition that readership of newspapers included many skilled artisans, lesser tradesmen and shopkeepers, in other words precisely the groups from which the radicals drew their strength. As the Portland Whig, Secretary at War and bitter opponent of the French Revolution and domestic radicals William Windham complained in 1798: 'They [newspapers] were ... carried everywhere, read everywhere, by persons of very inferior capacities ....'[5] In Scotland the existence of this lower-class readership may well have been a very recent phenomenon; certainly comment by contemporaries appears to indicate a significant widening of newspaper readership coincident with the political excitement created by the French Revolution.[6] On the other hand, it is possible that it was taking place earlier but that nobody saw fit to comment on it because it was uncontroversial. Whichever was the case, what enabled the effects of the price rises to be absorbed, to the extent that they were, was, first, the practice of collective purchase. Weavers and other artisans clubbed together to buy papers in what was, from one perspective, simply an extension of a habit of collective subscription for printed material which had been strongly present in sections of the Scottish labouring classes for several decades, and which seems to have deepened under the impact of radical politics in the 1790s.[7] Newspapers were to be found also in tap rooms, coffee rooms, barbers' shops and other urban establishments. They were present too in a growing number of workplaces, including the multiplying weaving shops of urban and semi-urban society.

The combination, meanwhile, of war and political instability was conducive to growth in the press throughout the eighteenth century.[8] What was different, however, about the 1790s, compared to, say, the 1770s and early '80s, was the injection of new ideological urgency and division as a result of the impact of the French Revolution and the dramatic social widening of political debate after 1791–2. Together these developments gave newspapers a heightened visibility and influence in political conflict and debate. Under these new conditions, news itself became more than usually freighted with ideological meaning and political significance. As the Revolution from the middle of 1791 took an increasingly radical and violent turn, so public opinion became polarized around a series of issues which ultimately hinged on perceptions of the Revolution and the nature of the threat which it posed to the existing social and political orders in Europe. This point requires stressing since it is often passed over fairly quickly by historians keen to demonstrate the deep indigenous roots of contemporary radical ideologies and the limited impact, or so it is argued, of Thomas Paine's revolutionary republicanism.[9] Portraying the Revolution, nevertheless, very quickly became a central aspect of political and ideological conflict, even if it sometimes remained just below the surface of debate. Radicals and their opponents fought over the meanings of key phrases and political terms, striving to fix their own and destabilize their opponent's political lexicon. But they did so against the pressing background of shifting perceptions of and attitudes towards political conditions and developments across the Channel.[10] In the battle to shape and ultimately control perceptions and attitudes, to impose meaning on the often fast-moving, frequently confusing events of the period, newspapers had an influential role to play.

This chapter examines the impact of the French Revolution and French revolutionary wars on the Scottish press as a way, first, of tracing the main shifts and contours of Scottish public opinion in this period. It would be wrong, clearly, to assume a perfect or even a very direct correlation between the views expressed in the press and public opinion (however defined).[11] Nor can the press enable the historian to delineate the full range of shades and colourings of public opinion in any period in the past, and certainly not for the later eighteenth century. Recognizing, however, the importance in this period of newspapers as vehicles of opinion and in forming opinion and views, the competitive marketplace in which they operated, and, on the loyalist side, the generally low levels of official support or intervention in the press, they can, nonetheless, provide unparalleled insights into the outlines and main shifts in public opinion. Second, this chapter seeks to describe the role of the press in the political battles of this period, and in particular, with reference to the first half of the decade, the struggles between radicals and their loyalist opponents. Throughout the chapter, in keeping with the rest of the book, an underlying theme is the comparison and contrast with developments elsewhere in the British Isles, especially in England.

We need to begin, however, with a brief word about the relationships between the Scottish and English press in the eighteenth century, which, as emphasized in the previous chapter, were very close. Not only was the development of the former, in many ways, dependent on the latter, but Scotland's newspapers had to survive in a marketplace for newsprint which was British as much as it was Scottish. Newspapermen – journalists and publishers – crossed the border in pursuit of work and prosperity, although in this period the traffic was normally from north to south.[12] The existence of this Scottish element in the London newspaper world facilitated connections between London and Scottish papers. In other cases, as we will see below, these might derive from political relationships. More broadly, throughout the eighteenth century, the press was a powerful force for Scottish integration into a British sphere of identity, a role which in political terms strengthened appreciably from the 1780s, and further deepened in the 1790s.

This integrative role, however, also reflected the widespread availability of English papers north of the border. From at least the later seventeenth century, newsletters and newspapers from London had been sent regularly to Edinburgh and other parts of Scotland.[13] In the final third of the eighteenth century, the volume of London newspapers circulating north of the border increased markedly. Putting numbers on the rise is impossible – what figures do exist refer only to numbers being sent out from London to the rest of the British Isles through the Post Office[14] – but there is plenty of evidence for their circulation. English newspapers were available through agents in most towns, usually booksellers but sometimes printers; subscription coffee rooms, which by the end of the century existed in most sizeable towns;[15] and a growing number of commercial reading rooms, such as the Wilson Street Coffee Room in Glasgow, which, on opening in 1794, boasted of its taking several London papers, as well as the current Edinburgh and Glasgow papers.[16] At the end of the decade a visitor to Perth commented on the 'London and provincial newspapers and literary journals' available at the town's 'principal taverns, hotels, and coffee rooms'.[17]

English reformist and radical papers had a significant Scottish readership in the 1790s. One of the most keenly read of these was the press mouthpiece of the Foxite Whigs, the *Morning Chronicle*, edited by James Perry (born Pirrie), a native Aberdonian.[18] Robert Burns was a regular reader of this paper, contributing several poems to it.[19] The *Edinburgh Herald*, the most vehement of the Scots loyalist papers of the early 1790s, regularly devoted a significant amount of space to refuting claims and paragraphs in the *Morning Chronicle*, a paper it referred to as the 'seditious Chronicle'.[20] As well as its sizeable Scottish readership, this tendency probably reflected the fact that the main Scottish radical paper of this period, the *Edinburgh Gazetteer*, regularly reprinted material from the paper. The *Morning Chronicle* was unusual among London papers in that it regularly reported on events in Scotland, including the activities of the Scottish Friends of the People. In early December 1793 it reprinted, for example, minutes from the British convention of radicals held in Edinburgh.[21] Norman Macleod's two letters to the main Scottish radical organization in the early 1790s, the Scottish Friends of the People, also appeared in the paper.[22] This, in turn, almost certainly reflected the strength of the links which existed in the early 1790s between opposition Whig reformers in London and the Scottish Friends of the People. Macleod was a member of both.[23] Thomas Muir, who visited the members of the Whig Association of the Friends of the People in London in early 1793 as a self-appointed Scottish martyr of liberty, prior his to embarking on an ill-judged mission to Paris to intercede for the life of Louis XVI, used the paper as his main means of communicating his intention to return to Scotland to face trial for sedition.[24] When the *London Gazette* failed to print a copy of the Glasgow peace petition presented to the King by the Earl of Lauderdale in the summer of 1793, Lauderdale promptly turned to the *Morning Chronicle* to publish it.[25] During 1793–4, letters from Scottish reformers in Glasgow and Edinburgh frequently appeared in its pages.[26] In the later 1790s, close links existed between the *Morning Chronicle* and the Scottish opposition Whig paper launched in 1796, the *Scots Chronicle*.[27] As was the case with the *Edinburgh Gazetteer*, items from the

Morning Chronicle frequently reappeared in its Scottish relation. In 1799, Lord King was to express the opinion that the only town in Scotland where the *Morning Chronicle* was still openly available in coffee houses was Glasgow.[28] This view seems to have been incorrect, overestimating the repressive climate in Scotland at the end of the decade.[29] Throughout the decade, the *Morning Chronicle* was the Scottish reformers' English paper of choice.

It was, however, far from the only English reformist or radical paper to gain a significant Scottish readership in this period. In September 1794, the Duke of Atholl received a report that copies of Benjamin Flowers's *Cambridge Intelligencer* were being sent to two Seceders in Perthshire and then being circulated among cotton workers in a local village.[30] Seven years later Flowers claimed that a hundred copies of the paper were being sent each week to Edinburgh, Aberdeen and Glasgow.[31] With a significant elite readership in England, which included the Liverpool abolitionist coterie of William Roscoe, William Rathbone and Edward Rushton, the *Cambridge Intelligencer's* politics were of a moderate kind, one reason why Flowers escaped prosecution, at least until intervention by the House of Lords in 1799, and why the paper survived until 1803.[32] Other much more short-lived, but altogether less cautious, English radical papers which had Scottish readers included Joseph Gales's *Sheffield Register* and the *Manchester Herald*.[33] On 24 November 1792, the latter published a letter from Glasgow which declared that it was being read 'with avidity and attention' in the city and surrounding towns. A 'Paper of the People', and boasting a correspondent in Paris, the *Manchester Herald* was one of very few British radical papers of the early 1790s openly to espouse a Paineite viewpoint and to call for manhood suffrage and annual parliaments. Not surprisingly, because of this and its close links with the Manchester Reformation Society (the popular outgrowth of the Manchester Constitutional Society), it quickly became the target of loyalist hostility and was forced to close in March 1793.[34] Several copies of the *Courier*, another extreme radical paper, were being sent to taverns and coffee houses in the Scottish capital in 1793.[35] In the later 1790s, the *Chester Chronicle* and the *Sheffield Iris*, the more moderate successor to the *Sheffield Register*, were all circulating north of the border. The editor, and from June 1795 sole proprietor, of the second of these was James Montgomery, who had been born in Irvine. In early July 1795 Montgomery, who had two agents responsible for the paper's distribution in Scotland, boasted of his 'numerous subscribers' north of the border.[36] In the later 1790s, the *Manchester Gazette* printed numerous letters from Scottish correspondents, including from Glasgow, Hamilton and Stirling.[37] As Martin Smith has emphasized, from 1796, and more especially after 1798, the political line adopted by these papers moderated, their radicalism largely erased by official repression and growing disenchantment with events in France and Europe.[38] Their hatred of Pitt and opposition to the war softened in the face of the obvious French threat to British interests and the French invasion of Switzerland in 1798, a country long viewed as a beacon of republican liberty in Europe. An exception to this trend was the London evening daily paper the *Albion*, which was circulating in Glasgow in 1800.[39] Uniquely among London's papers, the *Albion* responded positively to Napoleon's coup of 18 Brumaire. Launched in September 1799, its editor was the Scotsman Allan Macleod.[40]

The circulation of these various English radical and reformist papers has considerable significance, not just in terms of how we view Scottish radicalism and reform opinion in this period, but also when placed alongside the weakness of the Scottish radical press in the 1790s and its total suppression after early 1794. This was yet one more way in which Scottish radicals and reformers were dependent on individuals and developments elsewhere in the British Isles for direction, although after 1796 the *Scots Chronicle*, and perhaps one other paper, as we will see below, continued to give voice to opposition opinion in the Scottish press.

To look at the Scottish press in isolation may, therefore, be misleading. It is, nevertheless, a defensible approach given the focus of interest in this chapter. Despite fierce competition from their English counterparts, Scottish papers survived and eventually flourished, and they did so in part because they could get news to readers in more timely and economical fashion than London papers, but also because they reflected distinctively local or more usually regional, Scottish priorities and viewpoints. As a father wrote from Edinburgh in 1790 to his son who was in England for his education, 'I like to see you Remember Auld Reekie, the place of your Birth and Rudiments of Learning, But the best way to know every thing passing there weekly is our Edinr Papers'.[41]

The Rise of a Loyal Press

Looked at from a British perspective, Scottish newspapers were relatively slow to polarize in respect of their responses to the French Revolution and domestic political reform. One reason for this was almost certainly a pronounced tendency within the eighteenth-century Scottish press to eschew partisan allegiances or divisive issues. Scottish papers were, for example, rarely vehicles for pursuing religious or personal disputes.[42] It also reflected, however, the existence of widespread complacency about the domestic and international repercussions of the French Revolution, a mood bred of buoyant economic conditions before the spring of 1793, confidence in the political leadership of Pitt the Younger, and, prior to the spring and summer of 1792, the absence of a Scottish dimension to the reawakening of the domestic campaign for parliamentary reform. Not that complacency was the peculiar preserve of Scots in relation to the early stages of the French Revolution. As has been emphasized by many historians, before 1791 many people in Britain seem to have viewed events in France in terms of the 'Glorious Revolution' of a century before, or, less commonly, and more loosely, and ambiguously, in terms of the march of reason and the quickening diffusion of the spirit of liberty.[43] What may, nevertheless, have been specific to Scotland was the strength of the sense of progress and movement in society at the beginning of the 1790s, a feeling which derived from the unexampled speed of economic development in the previous decade, together with the degree of consensus which enveloped elite opinion about 'improvement' as *the* national goal.[44] With the possible exception of the Corn Laws, and this cut across emergent party identities, no major issues existed to divide Scottish political opinion in this period, in contrast to the dissenters' campaign of 1790 to repeal of the Test and Corporation Acts south of the border.

Between, however, the summer and end of 1792 the climate of opinion changed very abruptly. Beginning with the King's birthday riot in Edinburgh on the nights of 4–6 June 1792, the country saw a succession of popular riots and protests between the summer and late autumn, which, while not in most cases linked to an upsurge of popular radical feeling, in combination with the widespread dissemination from early July of cheap editions of Paine's *Rights of Man*, the startling rise of reform societies from the autumn, the shocking events in Paris following the declaration of a republic and Austrian and Prussian military intervention against the revolution, and the edict of fraternity issued by the French national assembly in November, produced a spasm of panic among the propertied classes.[45] A somewhat different, but overlapping confluence of events produced a similar sense of crisis south of the border in the final months of 1792.[46] The alarm felt in London and Edinburgh, which was fully reflected in the press, quickly became mutually reinforcing. Against this background, from late 1792, a much more visible, distinctly loyalist voice emerged in the press; for the rest of decade it was a voice that was overwhelmingly to be the dominant one in the Scottish newspapers.

The extent and timing of the transformation in mood are clearly illustrated by examining the editorial direction of two of the more successful papers of the early 1790s – the *Glasgow Courier* and the *Edinburgh Advertiser*. Launched at the beginning of September 1791, the appearance of the *Glasgow Courier* was itself a symptom of the marked quickening of public interest in events in France and Europe over the previous few months. In its first issue (1 September), the paper forthrightly proclaimed its political 'impartiality', and with reasonable grounds for at least the first twelve months of its existence. During this period, its political stance is probably best described as moderate reformist, an outlook readily compatible with strong support for Pitt the Younger and his ministry. It regularly gave over space to both the burgh and county reformers, while other 'progressive' causes which won its approval included Fox's Libel Act of 1792 – although this was not a partisan measure – and the Polish Revolution of 1791, which even more than the French Revolution was seen as a re-enactment of the principles of 1688.[47] In the opening months of 1792, it published a veritable deluge of letters on both sides of the argument surrounding the abolition of the slave trade, reflecting the intense interest north of the border in the abolitionists' petitioning campaign of 1792.[48]

Its coverage, meanwhile, of the early phases of the French Revolution was characterized by careful neutrality, a stance which persisted, albeit in weakening form, even after the summer of 1792, by which time the menace of mob rule in France was a theme which featured with metronomic regularity throughout much of the British press. In its issues for 5 and 16 June 1792 appeared lengthy articles from André Chenier's *Journal de Paris* which sought to anatomize and warn against the threat which Jacobin clubs and populist politics posed to political stability and order in France. Chenier went on to become an influential counter-revolutionary journalist, a role for which he was to lose his life at the end of the Terror, and his articles contained several of the tropes which were to become a recurrent and insistent feature of press coverage of the Revolution from late 1792 – most obviously, the frenzied mob and the 'unnatural' role of the women who formed a very visible component of the French revolutionary crowd. Yet the inclusion of these items did not signal a major change in editorial policy. Even Louis XVI's dethronement (10 August) and the declaration of the republic (22 September) failed to bring to an end the paper's studied impartiality. The issue for 6 September, for example, saw the reprinting of a celebratory account by Louis-Marie Prudhomme of the events of 10 August, taken from his radical weekly *Révolutions de Paris*. About a month later was reprinted the Marquis de Cordorcet's vindication of the same events, in which he defended the overthrow of the French monarchy by means of comparison with the Glorious Revolution in Britain.[49] Even in mid-October 1792, the paper published paragraphs drawn from the London press which expressed the hope that the French would vindicate themselves and their revolution and show that the atrocities of early September – the so-called September massacres – were the work of a venal minority.[50]

Prior to the final months of 1792, the *Glasgow Courier* also showed limited interest in or indeed hostility towards domestic parliamentary reformers. During May 1792, it printed a series of brief anti-Paineite items, but, with hindsight, what is notable is the relative lack of attention to Paine and the *Rights of Man*, something which probably reflected how restricted the circulation of this work was in Scotland until later that summer.[51] The royal proclamation against seditious writings and publications (21 May), provoked the paper's London correspondent to write a series of paragraphs critical of the government's response to the supposed domestic radical threat.[52] Moreover, as late as 1 December, it reprinted a call for a coalition of parties – not that this was particularly unusual – but also for moderate reform as the best means to immunize Britain against the threat of domestic disaffection or revolution, precisely the line of argument being used by opposition Whig reformers, who in the previous April had formed themselves into the Whig Association of the Friends of the People. Along with many other papers in Scotland and indeed Britain during 1791–2, the paper admitted – although presumably for a price – notices and resolutions from moderate reform bodies.[53] Only in late November and December 1792 did it shift decisively its stance to an overtly anti-radical, anti-reform one.

The *Edinburgh Advertiser* was a successful biweekly, but of considerably longer standing than the *Courier*. Following its establishment in 1764, and early success, it began already in the 1770s to overshadow the long-established *Caledonian Mercury* and *Edinburgh Evening Courant*.[54] At the beginning of the 1790s, it advertised its political stance as 'independent'.[55] In practice, this came down to something very similar to the political line adopted by the *Glasgow Courier* – generally enthusiastic support for the Pitt ministry and moderate, reformist causes. Its initial response to the French Revolution was, in common with most other newspapers in Scotland and across Britain, strongly favourable, portraying it as demonstration that the 'spirit of liberty' was spreading fast throughout Europe. Early episodes of revolutionary violence, which might have produced a change in this outlook, were usually attributed to the 'fanaticism of priests', a theme echoed in other papers between 1790–1.[56] Edmund Burke's extreme warnings about the Revolution, contained in his *Reflections on the Revolution in France* – first published in London in October 1790, and which quickly appeared in the Scottish capital[57] – were met with hostility.[58] By the summer of 1791 there was, nevertheless, a growing ambivalence in the paper's reporting of the Revolution. Positive comment was matched increasingly by negative portrayals of the impact of the political changes in France. The latter typically dwelt on episodes of disorder, the poor state of national finances, commercial and economic stagnation, and on the violence associated with the opposition of clergy to the imposition of the civil oath, especially in the south-west of the country.[59] The contrast, sometimes implicit but frequently explicitly drawn, was with a prospering, peaceful Britain under the skilful guidance of Pitt and his fellow ministers.[60]

As with the *Glasgow Courier*, what served to transform the political contents of the *Edinburgh Advertiser* were the events in France of August and September 1792. Louis XVI's dethronement, the ensuing declaration of the republic, the September massacres and the trial of the King undermined any lingering regard that the conductors of the paper were prepared to show for the cause of liberty across the Channel. The dominant theme in the reporting of events in France very quickly became the 'intoxicated multitude' and the 'tyranny of the mob'.[61] Before the final months of 1792, the paper had struggled to draw a distinction between the principles of the Revolution and the conduct of the French populace; in late 1792, in the face of the spectacle of death and violence in Paris, this effort broke down completely.[62]

Most Scottish papers pursued courses very similar to those of the *Glasgow Courier* and *Edinburgh Advertiser* between 1789 and 1792.[63] The one exception was the *Edinburgh Herald*, which was established in March 1790.[64] The *Herald*'s conductor was James Sibbald, an Edinburgh bookseller-publisher with strong literary interests. His motives in founding the paper appear to have been partly patriotic – he portrayed it as a bold effort at producing a Scottish rival to the growing volume of English papers circulating in Scotland; partly opportunistic – he acknowledged the increased levels of interest in public affairs created by events in France and Europe; and partly related to his literary connections. With respect to the last of these, readers were promised the regular inclusion of 'lighter and less serious subjects', including literary intelligence. The latter received considerable and, for newspapers of this period, unusual emphasis in the first six months or so of the paper's life, comprising book news, reviews and a considerable amount of verse, including the first publication of Robert Burns's 'Tam O'Shanter' and several poems by the Paisley weaver-poet Alexander Wilson.[65] This devotion to literary and other 'lighter' subject-matter does not appear to have lasted much beyond 1791, although definitive judgement on this is impossible because issues of the paper for 1792 have gone astray.[66]

Sibbald also initially made great play of the paper's political impartiality, even juxtaposing in the first few issues items from ministerial and opposition papers to satirize the effects of partisanship in the contemporary metropolitan press. By 1791, however, its strong pro-ministerial leanings would have been increasingly apparent to readers. One indication of this was the lively support it showed for the Pitt ministry's aggressive stance towards Russian expansionism in the Black Sea region from the spring of 1791, a stance which was much criticized by the opposition Whigs and which seems to have caused considerable concern in Scotland, where peace since 1783 had delivered such rapid economic progress.[67] Early items on the French Revolution were broadly positive. Especially revealing in this context is the reaction to Burke's *Reflections on the Revolution in France*. Initially strongly supportive – extracts from the work being reprinted over three successive issues in early November[68] – space was also found for critical responses, one of which was came from the pen of the paper's regular correspondent on political affairs, the sentimental novelist Henry Mackenzie, writing under the pseudonym of 'Brutus'.[69] As we will see in Chapter 4, from late 1792 Mackenzie was to assume an influential position as a coordinator of loyal propaganda in the Scottish capital.

From the autumn of 1790, therefore, coverage of the Revolution in the *Edinburgh Herald* was beginning to be characterized by ambivalence. Some of the most negative appraisals took the form of letters purporting to be from Paris, a form of reportage which became a prominent feature in some newspapers in the 1790s, reflecting the special interest and immediacy of eyewitness reports.

The author of one of these letters, which appeared in the issue for 26 November 1790, declared:

> Every description of this country, however just, must appear exaggerated to those who are not witness to our distress; but be assured that even Mr Burke's painting is infinitely short of the real situation of France. There is no law existing; what little government there is, is in the hands of madmen. Not only commerce, but every branch of professional business is ruined. Insomuch, that in the evening, people wonder how they have subsisted through the day, and scarce reckon on a certain subsistence for to-morrow.

Positive commentary and items did not disappear, however, and they included a review in early January 1791 of the former French minister Charles-Alexandre de Calonne's *The Present and Future State of France*, the author of which compared Calonne's moderate critique of the Revolution favourably with Burke's unalloyed hostility, and also sought, adopting a line of argument much used by defenders of the Revolution in this period, to excuse the violence and disorder increasingly prevalent in France in terms of the magnitude of the political transformation underway.[70] On 18 February 1791, a similarly friendly review appeared of the rational dissenter Joseph Priestley's *Letter to the Right Hon Edmund Burke; occasioned by his Reflections*. In April, the paper even printed extracts from Part 1 of Paine's *Rights of Man*.[71] From May–June 1791, however, the volume of negative material began to grow again, in response to the French royal family's flight to Varennes and the subsequent events in France and Europe. At the end of May, a summary was printed of Burke's *Letter to a Member of the National Assembly* in which Burke sought to vindicate his earlier assessment of the Revolution.[72] By the autumn of 1791, the tone of commentary in the paper on the Revolution was unremittingly critical and frequently very hostile, with the dominant themes being the rule of the mob and consequent anarchy and chaos in France.

From the spring of 1791, the *Edinburgh Herald* also developed a much stronger anti-reform platform. In the issue for 18 May 1791, Mackenzie attacked the opposition, depicting Paine as their malign inspiration. On 27 June, an item entitled 'Democratic Candour' launched an assault on Mary Wollstonecraft, while in July, an article written by Edward Tatham, the Rector of Lincoln College, Oxford, denounced the celebrations which had taken place across much of Britain and Ireland on the anniversary of the fall of the Bastille.[73] In August 1791 the paper reprinted extracts from Burke's *Appeal from the New to the Old Whigs* and from the Scot and Treasury official George Chalmers's viciously denigratory *Life of Paine*.[74] A near-constant stream of anti-Paineite verse appeared. Conditions in Britain were increasingly directly compared to those in France, in ways that were explicitly designed to emphasize the support owed by the Scottish people, as a consequence, to the constitution and current ministry. 'There has been no period in our remembrance', the paper urged in August 1791, 'when the people of this country had more reason to be satisfied with the Constitution and the Administration of the Affairs of the Country than at present'.[75]

Scotland's Loyal Press, 1793–4

Scotland's loyal press was, therefore, with the exception of the *Edinburgh Herald*, a product of the political crisis of late 1792. Similar patterns are discernable in respect of many English papers, although what was striking and unusual was the near-total uniformity of the line taken by papers north of the border. To a significant extent, it was circumstances, not underlying attitudes, which shifted in Scotland in the early 1790s, although one might argue that the former drew out ever more clearly the fundamental conservatism of much Scottish opinion, a conservatism to a degree masked by a widely shared enthusiasm for economic improvement and cautious reform in the 1780s – including reform of burgh government and the county franchise. Whatever the case, from the end of 1792 until 1794, all but a small minority of Scottish newspapers showed strong support for the political status quo, together with equally strong hostility to the French Revolution and its leaders.

Unsurprisingly in light of its earlier editorial line, it was the *Edinburgh Herald* which led the way in these developments. Between 1793 and 1794, its hostility to the Revolution was vehement and highly ideological, and it lost no opportunity in editorial paragraphs arranged under the 'Edinburgh' heading, and in its selection of paragraphs and comment drawn from the *Star* and the *Sun*, two London loyalist papers, to demonize the Revolution and its leaders and to reject calls for reform in Britain. Its editorial voice was declamatory and intrusive, and alongside the radical newspaper the *Edinburgh Gazetteer*, it was the most overtly political of the Scottish papers of the early 1790s. It was joined in its aggressively anti-radical line by the *Glasgow Courier*, which from the end of 1792 became the main press vehicle of Glasgow's loyalists and ruling elites. From the south-west, the editor of the *Dumfries Weekly Journal* took a similarly strong anti-radical line, as reflected most obviously in the editorial paragraphs which frequently appeared in the paper under the 'Dumfries' heading. Typical of these was the following, which appeared on 2 April 1793:

> France is at present party to all the horrors of civil war. The Convention are at a loss what do in order to quiet the people, who have hitherto been deluded by false hopes – Their eyes are now beginning to be opened: and, instead of the gilded prospects which were held up to their view, they see nothing but anarchy and confusion. They have discovered their mistake, alas, too late; and their land may be deluged with blood before tranquillity can be restored. It is to be hoped that the people of this country will take warning from their fatal error, and extirpate from among them those pernicious principles which have produced such a dreadful catastrophe in that country.

The *Edinburgh Advertiser* declared in 1793 that it was seeking to steer a middle course between 'democratic infatuation' and 'ministerial influence', but it too contained, albeit less frequently, anti-reform editorials in 1793–4.[76] In early April 1793, an editorial paragraph depicted the anarchy and bloodshed, the economic chaos, prevalent in France, before declaring pointedly and in terms which made abundantly clear their relevance to domestic politics: 'Equality! Rights of Man!, Regeneration of Society! Conventions!, Reforming Associations! New Organization of Constitutions! Metaphysical Politics! –These are your Triumphs!'[77] In several other papers, the *Aberdeen Weekly Journal*, the *Glasgow Mercury*, the *Caledonian Mercury* and the *Edinburgh Evening Courant*, the editorial voice was much less intrusive. The coverage, nevertheless, of the Revolution can have left readers in no uncertainty about the underlying political message: the bloody events in France in 1793–4 were an awful lesson in the consequences of subverting and overturning natural, landed political leadership and of pursuing speculative political reform.[78]

Nor did the majority of the Scottish press provide any support to domestic radicals and radicalism in this period. Before late 1792, as we saw earlier, the newspapers had been prepared to open their pages to the resolutions of radical and reform societies. From the end of 1792, apart from the radical press, the *Glasgow Advertiser* and possibly James Palmer's *British Chronicle; or Union Gazette*,[79] the admission of such resolutions appears to have been uniformly refused. The *Edinburgh Evening Courant* announced a newly-cautious policy in this regard in its issue of 24 December 1792. Several papers published notable anti-radical items, including on one occasion a series of letters purporting to be written by a member of the Scottish Friends of the People. Allegedly authenticated by judicial authority, these were designed to give the lie to the protestations of the radicals that their goals were limited to moderate political reform.[80] In late 1792, the *Glasgow Courier* printed a succession of anti-radical items aimed explicitly at the labouring classes, some of which purported to be written by men of their rank, while in 1793 its main political correspondent, who wrote under the pseudonym 'Asmodeus', contributed a series of letters attacking local radicals.[81] Otherwise, radicalism was ignored, its activities simply erased from the pages of most papers. Almost the only direct reference to the second general convention of Scottish radicals, held in Edinburgh in April 1793, was a sneering letter in the *Glasgow Courier* mocking the pretensions of the lower orders in assuming the expertise necessary to making laws and constitutions: 'A man may shine in his profession of a shoemaker, weaver &c; he may even learn agriculture, so far as to be proficient in planting, reading and housing a potatoe – but who made him a giver of laws – who taught him to govern?'[82] Radicalism's omission may well have been a product of deliberate, politically-inspired editorial policy, but it also probably reflected a growing sense by the spring of 1793 that the radical threat, at least as organized in societies, had been successfully repelled and was in sharp decline.[83]

What most papers did report at length, however, was the suppression by the authorities of the British convention of radicals in early December 1793, and the subsequent legal and ministerial action against British radicals in the first half of 1794. In doing so, the newspapers rehearsed and endorsed ministers' portrayal of radicals as 'Jacobins' scheming to import violent revolution into Britain. Summaries of the findings of the 1794 Commons secret committee reports on treasonable activities – which ministers had used, through domination of the composition of the committee, to demonstrate the supposed substance of this view – were printed in most papers, with particular attention being given, not surprisingly, to the Scottish dimension to the alleged conspiracy.[84] The discovery of the so-called Watt ot Pike Plot in the spring of 1794, and subsequent searches for arms in different parts of Britain were reported in ways that can only have seemed to confirm the substance of the radicals' bloody designs. In late May the *Edinburgh Advertiser* declared that the 'affair of the French pikes' was a 'concerted plan' and that several such pikes had been found in London.[85] Much significance was attributed to Robert Watt's membership of the Scottish Friends of the People and his confession, given before his execution, in which he appeared to acknowledge the reality of his designs to force political change on Britain. The *Dumfries Weekly Journal* reprinted an account of Watt's execution, drawn from the Edinburgh press, which included the following observation:

> R Watt has left behind him a full confession written and subscribed by himself the evening before his execution, in which he solemnly declares as a dying man, that the plan for insurrection, rebellion, and revolution, was seriously intended by him and his accomplices, and in great forwardness, when he was apprehended.[86]

Watt's confession appeared in full in the *Edinburgh Herald*, while the *Glasgow Courier* printed a summary of its main points.[87] Meanwhile, the sedition and treason trials of Scottish and English radicals in the Scottish High Court in 1793–4 and at the Old Bailey in 1794 were reported in ways which were designed to emphasize the alleged guilt of the defendants, irrespective of the outcome of the trial.[88] Attempts by Maurice Margarot, who had attended the British convention on behalf of the London Corresponding Society, and others to use the courts as a platform for their political views were met with the omission of their often very lengthy speeches; by contrast, the addresses to the court of the prosecuting officials were usually reprinted in full.[89]

At the same time, most papers were staunchly supportive of ministerial and official efforts to suppress radicalism. The *Dumfries Weekly Journal* printed several letters in the spring of 1794 defending the suspension of habeas corpus.[90]

'Fidius', a regular correspondent in the *Glasgow Courier*, declared in a letter published on 27 May:

> There have been some later commitments in London for treasonable practices. The Ministers of the Crown have, in this instance, shown themselves the faithful guardians of the public. Whatever has the most remote tendency to disturb our mild Government, or to introduce French anarchy, are fit subjects for Parliamentary Investigation. The business in question has been brought before Parliament, and the Report of the Committee opens up a deep laid and digested scheme, not for a reform in the Government, or a correction of abuses that may have crept into it, but for the total extinction and overthrow of all Order and all Government.

There was also no echo in their pages of opposition Whig attacks on the Scottish bench following the trials and sentencing of Thomas Muir and Thomas Fyshe Palmer. In this context, it may be significant that the main press vehicle for such attacks was the London-based *Morning Chronicle*, which, as emphasized earlier, had a significant Scottish readership.[91]

During 1793–4, the majority of Scottish newspapers lent their support to the loyalist and ministerial cause in a number of other important ways. As with many of their English counterparts, several reprinted extracts from influential loyalist pamphlets. The *Dumfries Weekly Journal* carried extracts from several loyal sermons delivered by local ministers, as well as a loyal letter to the Provost of Dumfries by one of these ministers, while the *Glasgow Courier* reprinted passages from Thomas Hardy's influential pamphlet *The Patriot*, Chief Justice Ashurst's 'Charge to the Grand Jury of Middlesex' of 1793, Sir Roger Mainwaring's 'Address to the Westminster Quarter Sessions' of the spring of 1794, and from local author Dr William Taylor's *French Irreligion and Impiety Alarming to Christians. An Address to the People of Scotland* (1794).[92] Another piece of loyal propaganda widely reprinted was the speech in the Irish House of Commons of Sir Hercules Langrishe opposing Ponsonby's motion for parliamentary reform.[93] More importantly, however, these newspapers provided the main vehicles for publicizing loyalist demonstrations and initiatives of various kinds; and in doing so helped to construct a vivid picture of localities, regions and the nation as firmly united in their commitment to the existing political order and hostility to domestic and foreign enemies of this order.

Loyal subscriptions and spectacle, which burgeoned in this period, provided voluminous press copy. Lengthy lists of subscribers to patriotic causes became a prominent and very visible feature of most newspapers during the 1790s. In two issues in June and July 1793 the *Edinburgh Advertiser* printed lists detailing individual donations to the Edinburgh ladies' subscription for the widows and children of soldiers and seamen lost in battle, while throughout the autumn of 1793, details of donations to the nationwide subscription to buy flannel waistcoats for the British troops wintering on the continent appeared in issue after issue of more than one paper.[94] Loyal addresses and notices of subscriptions by burghs and counties to pay for bounties to encourage recruitment to the armed forces were regularly inserted. In 1793 and 1794, burghs and other communities inundated papers with paragraphs describing local celebrations of the King's birthday (4 June). On 10 June 1794, the *Edinburgh Advertiser* declared that the accounts it had been sent of such celebrations would fill two or three newspapers. In the same issue, it listed twenty-two places which had seen festivities. In the next issue (13 June), a further fifteen such places were listed. On 7 June, the *Glasgow Courier* declared:

> From every quarter of the country, the most grateful accounts of the uncommon festivity with which the Anniversary of his Majesty's birthday have been commemorated, have poured in upon us; a few of these, exhibiting the most unequivocal proofs of undisguised loyalty, and sincere attachment to our envied constitution, our readers will find in the sequel of this Department of our Paper.

Celebrations duly described included those at the Anderston ropeworks; Beith; the village of Straiton in Ayrshire; Greenock; Port Glasgow; Stewarton; Kilsyth; Fullarton, where an effigy of Robespierre had been burnt; and Strathblane. The descriptions of such celebrations were, as earlier in the century, often very formulaic; nevertheless, in their range and volume, they provide evidence not just of the anxiety of towns and other communities to publicize their loyalty, but also the perceived importance of the press as a means for achieving this. In 1794–5, ceremonies involving the presentation of colours to volunteer regiments regularly took up a full page of what were only four-page newspapers.[95]

The same papers also presented a view of the war against revolutionary France, which Britain entered in February 1793, which was strongly supportive of ministerial conduct of the war and its aims. British and Allied victories, especially the capture of French Caribbean colonies in 1794, were noisily proclaimed as bringing important accessions of wealth and power to Britain, while often at the same time heralding the imminent military collapse of Revolutionary France.[96] On 28 March 1793, the unswervingly loyal *Glasgow Courier* printed a letter sent by the MP for Renfrewshire, William McDowall, to the Lord Provost of Glasgow describing an Austrian victory over Dumouriez and the French revolutionary army, declaring: 'This is considered a decisive blow, and must produce the most happy effects'. Failures and setbacks, by contrast – for example, the evacuation of Toulon – were downplayed or passed over quickly. The damaging effects of the outbreak of war on credit and manufacturing were either ignored or denied.[97] This was particularly relevant in Glasgow, Paisley and the west, where manufacturing was especially adversely affected in 1793, but also in several other places.[98] The obvious bias in the coverage of the war led the Dundee Relief clergyman and radical Neil Douglas to observe:

With respect to the operation and effects of the war, and the internal state and resources of our enemies, we are continually amused with such a detail, as appears from a variety of circumstances to consist of little else than falsehoods or exaggerations; while our own situation and losses, are carefully concealed or misrepresented. The longer this artifice succeeds, the more terrible the consequence.[99]

Douglas must have known that this was to complain in vain. No opportunity was lost in most papers to draw readers' attention to the atrocities allegedly committed by the French revolutionary armies, to puff supposed Allied strength and spirit, even in the face of evidence to the contrary, and to support ministerial conduct of the war. 'Fidius', in the *Glasgow Courier*, repeatedly stressed the necessity of fighting the French. It was a war of 'law & liberty versus Anarchy & licentiousness', 'Religion versus Atheism', and 'Virtue versus Vice'. French successes were depicted as limited in their consequences and allied victory merely a matter of time.[100] If there were hints of criticism of ministerial conduct of the war, these were couched in terms of a stated preference for a 'blue-water strategy', precisely the one pushed in cabinet by Henry Dundas, who in so doing was, it seems, faithfully reflecting the wishes of the Scottish mercantile elites, especially those in the west. By the second half of 1794, there were signs too of a growing war-weariness, and rising dissatisfaction with the results of the continental campaigns, with the *Glasgow Courier* acknowledging at the end of the December 1794 that the 'prospect of a speedy peace must be highly gratifying'.[101]

Several questions arise from this very striking dominance of loyalist views and perspectives in the Scottish press in the early 1790s. Perhaps the most important in the present context is how far newspapers were leading and how far they were simply reflecting public opinion. A related question is how far loyal comment and editorial selection were a consequence of financial subvention by the authorities or of other sources and forms of support.

There is no way of answering definitively the first of these questions. To begin with, we know too little about the political views of the personnel behind the newspapers. In the case of one of them – Robert Allan, the printer of the *Caledonian Mercury* – owing to the chance survival of a letter in the Reeves Papers in the British Library, we know that his politics were, in fact, strongly loyalist. In early December 1792, Allan informed John Moore, secretary to the newly-formed Association for the Preservation of Liberty and Property Against Republicans and Levellers, that he had, on his own initiative, copied into his paper the notice announcing the Society's formation and purpose from the *Star* newspaper, and that he intended doing so again in order to 'induce similar ones to be formed in this country'. He also expressed the hope that Moore might favour him with 'further communications where appropriate'.[102] Whatever the specific political views of printers and publishers, it seems probable, however, that commercial motivations loomed at least as large as political ones with most of them in deciding editorial policy. Papers such as the *Aberdeen Weekly Journal* and the *Dumfries Weekly Journal* found their readership in whole regions, not simply within the immediate environs of their host towns. To this extent, they needed to maintain a broad appeal to survive and flourish. There seems little reason to doubt, therefore, that they both reflected and reinforced the strength of loyal opinion in these regions. Equally Edinburgh and Glasgow papers had a broad circulation, which was far from restricted to these two cities, and as such editorial policy had a natural tendency to be designed to attract as broad a readership as possible. Before the early 1790s, this usually meant, as we have seen, assuming a posture of political 'impartiality', and an avoidance of overly divisive or partisan editorial policies. In the peculiar conditions of the early 1790s, however, it meant adopting an overtly loyalist identity and content. The evidence of the *Edinburgh Advertiser* is very suggestive in this context, in that it sought to maintain a degree of political independence in the starkly polarized political climate of 1793–4, but this became, in effect, support for the constitution and opposition to domestic radicalism. It is perhaps significant too in the same context that most Scottish periodicals (as opposed to newspapers) either ignored politics in this period or adopted a generally loyalist line. A major exception was James Anderson's *The Bee, or Literary Weekly Intelligencer*, in which first appeared the articles which comprised James Thomson Callender's *The Political Progress of Britain*, a work for which the author was forced into exile in the United States rather than face a trial for sedition in the Edinburgh High Court in early 1793. *The Bee* collapsed in 1794, seemingly owing to the failure of subscribers to pay up their arrears.[103]

Nor can official intervention and support readily explain the strength and depth of loyalism in the press in this period. Prior to 1794, the only paper to receive such support was the *Edinburgh Herald*. Contact between Sibbald and Robert Dundas was made through Henry Mackenzie in 1791, but it was only in late 1792 that financial support for the paper was forthcoming.[104] This took the form of an initial payment of around £400 to the principal proprietors and an annual pension for Sibbald of £100.[105] Given that the paper was already pursuing a strongly loyal line from the middle of 1791, this probably only served to confirm it in its political stance. A sum of £134 was also spent in late 1792 from secret service accounts to insert material, of an unspecified nature, in Allan's *Caledonian Mercury*.[106] Again, given his strong loyalism, it is doubtful whether this was in any way decisive in influencing the paper's political line; before the end of 1792 Allan also accepted payment from the Scottish Friends of the People for the insertion of notices.[107] Limited official support was in line with the policy towards the London press of the Pitt ministry; subventions were generally modest in amount and the current consensus amongst historians is that they had only very modest impact on the contents of newspapers.[108] Otherwise, support for helpful English provincial papers involved not money but the regular dispatch to them of loyal London papers from which to draw information and items.[109] It is possible that the *Edinburgh Herald* and perhaps one or two other papers were the beneficiaries of similar support, but there is currently no evidence to prove this one way or the other.

Given the extent of the support for ministers and loyalism in the press, it is, therefore, perhaps surprising that in early 1794 Robert Dundas took steps to strengthen the loyalist position in the press. This involved arranging and paying for William Brown, a Dundee bookseller, to move to the capital where he assumed responsibility for editing a new newspaper, the *Patriot's Weekly Chronicle*, launched in April 1794.[110] While in Dundee, Brown had edited a fortnightly loyal publication for the local printer Thomas Colville; he was also the author in 1793 of a loyal pamphlet written (very unusually) in Scots dialect which was distributed by the Edinburgh Goldsmiths' Hall Association, the main Scottish loyalist society of the early 1790s.[111] It is likely that it is this pamphlet which brought Brown to Dundas's notice. The money to fund the establishment of the *Patriot's Weekly Chronicle* was raised by a subscription of over 500 guineas, seemingly from leading Scottish loyalists, or those whom Dundas called 'a great number of respectable Persons in Scotland'.[112] (Unfortunately there are no details about the identity of these individuals.) In 1796, the paper was merged with the *Edinburgh Herald* to form the *Herald and Chronicle*. Brown received a quarter share of the paper, and was allowed an annual salary of £50.[113] The merger may well have been a cost-cutting measure, with the original subscribers to the *Chronicle* being increasingly unwilling to underwrite its costs, and Brown struggling to turn the *Chronicle* to profit, a circumstance that he attributed mainly to want of advertisers.[114]

This is the sum total of evidence of official attempts to support a loyal press in Scotland in the 1790s, although other types of pressure were no doubt applied, and inducements provided, to editors and printers which have left only faint traces in the historical record, if indeed they have left any imprint at all. In 1797 the printer of at least one newspaper in Scotland was 'instructed' to exclude reports of anti-militia disturbances with the aim of preventing their spread to hitherto unaffected areas and communities.[115] The inclusion of a fair number of individual loyal items was no doubt paid for, as was the case with radical notices and resolutions before the end of 1792. The Edinburgh Goldsmiths' Hall Association, for example, produced a series of paragraphs for the press, including a riposte to radical complaints about the burden of taxation on the labouring classes, which duly found their way into a number of papers.[116] The anti-radical items in the *Glasgow Courier* may well have been part of a wider loyalist propaganda campaign led by the Lord Provost, who was, in turn, responding to direction from Edinburgh.[117] Such efforts, however, only account for a relatively small part of the contents of the newspapers. They do not explain the remarkable and unswerving consistency of the editorial selection of news and other items.

Scotland's Radical Press 1792–4

Dissenting and radical voices struggled, therefore, to find a place in the Scottish press from the end of 1792, and as such were squeezed to the margins of public debate. Apart from the radical press which emerged in late 1792, only John Mennons' *Glasgow Advertiser* continued to open its pages to the Friends of the People from this date. This was despite the arrest in late 1792 of Mennons and the paper's publisher, James Smith, for printing what was deemed to be a seditious resolution from a Partick radical society.[118] This prosecution had been determined on when Henry Dundas was visiting Scotland in the autumn of 1792, and was part of a package of measures put in place at that time to defeat the radical cause.[119] It also heralded a small wave of prosecutions of radical printers, publishers and authors in early 1793.[120] Another paper which may have continued to admit radical notices was James Palmer's *British Chronicle, or Union Gazette*, although insufficient issues of this paper survive for this period to confirm or refute this.[121] In the later 1790s, Palmer was distributing radical propaganda, which suggests that he was at the very least sympathetic to reform. There are also hints from 1797 that his paper had a reputation for adopting unhelpfully independent positions.[122] The *Glasgow Advertiser*, meanwhile, gave space to anti-war views in the early 1790s. The only other Scottish paper to do likewise, apart from the radical papers, was the *Edinburgh Advertiser*.[123]

Scotland's radical press in the early 1790s, meanwhile, comprised two papers, both founded in September 1792 – the *Caledonian Chronicle* and the *Edinburgh Gazetteer*. About the former we know very little, since only two issues of it survive.[124] It was closely linked, through its printer and publisher, respectively the booksellers James Robertson and Walter Berry, to the Scottish Friends of the People. Robertson printed handbills and minutes for the Friends of the People, while Berry's political activism included a visit to the London Corresponding Society in 1792.[125] The minutes of a meeting of the Edinburgh societies in late November 1792 and of the second general convention of the Scottish Friends of the People, which met in Edinburgh in late April of 1793, appeared in the *Caledonian Chronicle*.[126] According to a hostile pamphleteer, the issue for 9 November 1792 included an extract from Paine's *Letter Addressed to the Addressors in the Late Proclamation*, in which Paine developed most clearly his ideas about a convention as a revolutionary vehicle for achieving political reform.[127] This same pamphleteer was arguing that the principles of Paine and the Scottish reformers were one and the same, but whether the *Chronicle* gave further publicity to Paine and his ideology we simply cannot say. What we can say is that the paper seems to have lasted only until July 1793. In its short existence, it was hardly unusual amongst radical papers in Britain in this period, and the probable reasons for its failure were also common ones. Radical papers were normally forced to survive with very few advertisers in a period when advertising revenue was the main source of profit in newspaper publishing. The number of advertisements in the *Caledonian Chronicle* would appear to have quickly declined, a result without doubt of loyalist pressure on actual and potential advertisers. Robertson and Berry were successfully prosecuted in the spring of 1793 for the publication of Thomson Callender's *The Political Progress of Britain*, which may have caused them to show greater caution afterwards. In February 1793, their partnership was formally dissolved, although they both continued to distribute opposition and radical propaganda throughout the 1790s.[128] It is, however, also likely that it was recognized that persisting with two radical papers supported by the Scottish Friends of the People in this period was impractical. Certainly, the difficulties involved in maintaining just one in existence in 1793 – the *Edinburgh Gazetteer* – lend weight to this proposition.

The *Edinburgh Gazetteer*, meanwhile, quickly arrogated to itself the role of mouthpiece of the Scottish radicals. This no doubt partly reflected the fairly quick disappearance of the *Caledonian Chronicle*, but it also reflected its proprietorship. The paper was the initiative of Captain William Johnston, a half-pay officer who lived in the New Town. It was Johnston who chaired the meeting held in Edinburgh in July 1792 at which the Edinburgh Friends of the People came into being, and he went on to play a key role in Edinburgh radical circles during the final months of 1792 and at the first general convention of the Scottish Friends of the People held in the capital in early December. The *Edinburgh Gazetteer* reflected his own moderate and cautious political instincts, refusing items which were either overly personal in nature or, on one occasion, openly republican.[129] At the end of November, it pointedly excluded Paine's letter to the national convention in France from its pages.[130] Notwithstanding such caution, however, from its inception it attracted the close vigilance of Robert Dundas and his colleagues. Johnston was one of several radicals whose letters were regularly intercepted at the Post Office from late 1792, while his paper was, along with copies of the *Caledonian Chronicle*, regularly forwarded by Robert Dundas to his uncle in London, who as Home Secretary was directing the national ministerial (meaning British) response to the radical threat.[131] In early 1793, in what was almost certainly a politically opportunistic prosecution, Johnston was found guilty of contempt of court because of a report carried in the paper on a trial in the High Court of three journeyman printers for allegedly attempting to suborn the loyalties of soldiers in Edinburgh Castle.[132] The outcome – three months' imprisonment for Johnston and the printer, while Johnston also had to find sureties of £500 for three years for good behaviour on his release – served to reinforce the paper's cautious stance. In March 1793, Johnston refused to print some anti-war resolutions drawn up by the Dundee Unitarian minister and radical Thomas Fyshe Palmer after submitting them to a lawyer 'who rejected them in toto'.[133] By this stage he was also looking to divest himself of the paper, meeting William Skirving, secretary to the Edinburgh Friends of the People, and other radicals on 28 March to discuss how this might be brought about. These discussions quickly led to his relinquishing responsibility for the paper, and from 2 April it was conducted by Alexander Scott, formerly a clerk to the radical Edinburgh bookseller Alexander Guthrie.

The change in editorship brought no alteration in the cautious, moderate tone and content of the paper. As Scott declared in the first issue for which he was responsible (2 April):

> We are anxious not to be regarded as the organ of faction, or the trumpet of sedition. To foster the spirit of Patriotism, to encourage the virtue of good citizens, to afford a just delineation of public measures, to stimulate and encourage a taste for political enquiry, and to contribute to the extension of political knowledge, are the purposes of the present undertaking.

Nor was there any upturn in the paper's financial condition, which seems to have been parlous by the spring of 1793. Johnston agreed to hand over the types and printing apparatus upon payment of simple interest on the sum he had invested at the paper's foundation; the principal sum was only to be paid back after three years; and £500 was to be raised by subscription to finance the running costs of the paper. These were relatively generous terms. Nevertheless, in July, Scott was forced to increase the price of the paper from 3½ to 4*d*. By October, he was declaring that no new subscriptions would be allowed unless paid in advance.[134] Several issues later, he told readers that he would either soon resume twice-weekly publication or drop the paper entirely. He also informed them that he would soon be sending someone to the principal towns across Scotland to collect money owing, and would discontinue papers not paid in advance.[135] Apart from a lack of revenue from advertising,[136] it is likely that the fortunes of the paper were, like Scottish radicalism in general, hard hit by the downturn in manufacturing, and consequent unemployment, caused by the credit squeeze which followed Britain's entry into the war against France in February 1793.[137]

Meanwhile in October Scott turned to the Friends of the People for further financial support. Some time in that month he appealed to Maurice Margarot, who had arrived in Edinburgh as a delegate from the London Corresponding Society for the forthcoming British convention, for a loan to continue the paper. The issue was discussed at both the third and British conventions, with the latter appointing a committee to discuss the matter.[138] Oddly, Scott proved uncooperative, refusing to answer questions put to him by the committee, and the only result was a recommendation to the convention, which was accepted, that radical societies should support the paper and that efforts should be made to pay subscriptions in advance. On 5 December Norman Macleod withdrew his franking privilege from the paper, almost certainly because of his opposition to events at the British convention. By this stage, circulation of the paper also seems to have been being obstructed by the Post Office, again a common fate of radical newspapers in Britain in this period.[139] In early 1794, the paper collapsed when Scott and his clerks were charged with sedition for the minutes of the British convention which were published in the paper and an item which appeared to justify violent resistance on the part of the radicals.[140] Scott fled to London rather than face the High Court, arguing that he would never receive justice there.[141] Efforts to revive the paper were unavailing.

The loss of the *Edinburgh Gazetteer* was a heavy blow to an already disintegrating radical cause in Scotland. During 1793 it had provided a signal voice in the Scottish press sympathetic to reform and combating the deeply anti-radical and pro-war stance of the bulk of the Scottish press. It had also worked to deflect widespread hostility towards the Revolution in France, although there are signs that this was a role that caused it, like many other radical papers during the Terror, some awkwardness.[142] In September 1793, recognizing the importance of the paper to the Scottish radical movement, Scott had refused to print in its pages resolutions drawn up by Skirving in response to the trial of Thomas Muir on the grounds that to include them would simply give the authorities a 'handle to suppress' the paper. Apparently, several 'warm friends' to the cause had been present in the printing office when Scott took the decision. These individuals had expressed the view that 'Mr Scott [was] an enemy to the Gazetteer if he admitted them [the resolutions] as they considered the loss of the Gazetteer at this time as the filling up our misfortunes'.[143] The Perth radical Alexander Aitchison, the deputy secretary to the British convention, declared at the trial of Skirving in January 1794 that, although the convention had not supported the paper as a body, 'As individuals, all of us approved of it, and did all in our power to encourage it; as we judged it to be not only highly beneficial to the cause of Parliamentary Reform, but to the interests of civil liberty, and of the whole of the human species'.[144] As referred to earlier, the paper's demise left Scotland's demoralized radicals dependent in the mid 1790s on the English press for alternative views and perspectives to those available in the rest of the Scottish press, a situation that was only to change, as we will see further below, with the foundation in 1796 of the opposition Whig *Scots Chronicle*.

The Later 1790s

The short-lived nature of the radical presence in the Scottish press in the early 1790s underlines the extent of the victory of loyalism in the press in Scotland at this time, although it also reflects a lack of financial resources within what was, from mid-1793, a popular radical movement and the destructive pressures

which the authorities and loyalists were able to bring to bear on radical printers, publishers and readers. In the mid to later 1790s, the overall balance (or
imbalance) of political opinion in the Scottish press remained fundamentally
unchanged, with most papers continuing to give strong support to ministers
and their conduct of the war. War-weariness and growing doubts about the conduct of the war, especially in the winter of 1795–6, were echoed only faintly
in the pages of most papers.[145] During 1796–7, while the *Edinburgh Advertiser*
tended to bemoan the continuation of the war, responsibility for this was laid
squarely at the feet of the French. Indeed the conviction that the French held
the key to peace or war was a near continuous theme in the paper from the
final third of 1796 and the breakdown of the Malmesbury negotiation with the
French.[146] At the same time, the tone of comment about the war was optimistic,
emphasizing allied achievements and strength and French weaknesses, despite
Bonaparte's striking successes in Italy, and calling for unanimity in opposition
to the French at home. In 1797–8, the defensive patriotic reaction to, first, the
arrival of a French fleet off Bantry Bay in Ireland in December 1796 and then
the mobilization of a further French invasion force in the French Channel ports
received fulsome support from most Scottish newspapers. From St Andrews, Dr
George Hill observed in March 1797, when this reaction was in full flood: 'It is
delightful to any person who recollected the state of the public mind in 1792,
to observe the spirit which the present alarm has called forth in all parts of Scotland. *I trust the manifestation of that spirit in the Newspapers, which are filled with
offers to the Government*, will do much good at home' (my emphasis).[147] In 1798,
contributions to Pitt's voluntary donation filled page after page of the newspapers, as landowners and communities across Scotland competed to demonstrate
the patriotic loyalty of their tenants and populations respectively.

There is some evidence, moreover, that loyal papers were continuing to
attract a keen readership. Some time in 1797, Alexander Brown, an Aberdeen
bookseller, brother of William, wrote of the *Herald and Chronicle*, established,
as we saw above, with official support, as a merger of the *Edinburgh Herald* and
Patriot's Weekly Chronicle in 1796: 'The Herald is gaining ground much in this
& other counties ... William writes me that he has taken 200 subscribs from
the Mercury & Courant [presumably the *Caledonian Mercury* and *Edinburgh
Evening Courant*] since he began with it ....'[148] In Glasgow, two anodyne newspapers came to an end in 1795–6 – the *Glasgow Journal* and the *Glasgow Mercury*
– but the *Glasgow Courier* appears to have continued to flourish.

In March 1796, however, a new paper emerged which was to prove a tenacious critic of the Pittite war system and a powerful advocate for peace and
reform throughout the later 1790s. This was the *Scots Chronicle*, and the timing
of its foundation is, in some ways, surprising in that it coincided with the influence of the opposition Whigs in Scotland being at, or just reaching, its nadir. At

the general election in 1796, Dundas won an overwhelming victory, securing all but two of the forty-five Scottish seats. Nevertheless, as Emma Vincent Macleod has recently suggested, the opposition Whigs north of the border showed commendable persistence in very adverse circumstances in this period.[149] The impetus behind its formation came, in any case, not primarily from Scotland but from a group of Scottish opposition Whigs resident in London. Led by the Earl of Lauderdale, whose opposition to Pitt and the war had been consistent and very visible throughout the 1790s, and including Norman Macleod, who had played a prominent role in *British* reform politics in the early 1790s, it was this collection of individuals who financed the paper's establishment and selected the first conductor of the paper.[150] In Scotland, the main figure behind it was John Morthland, a young advocate who had been a member of the Scottish Friends of the People until the spring of 1793.

The *Scots Chronicle* quickly became the voice of the Whig opposition in Scotland and of Scottish opposition to the war.[151] This prominence also reflected its considerable qualities as a newspaper. Between May and August 1796, it printed John Millar's 'Letters of Crito', which sought to demonstrate that Pitt's war system was designed solely to perpetuate corruption in British politics and prevent reform. In early 1797, it lent its weight to calls for peace petitions to coincide with a national petitioning campaign led by the Foxite Whigs, also reprinting extracts from Thomas Erskine's influential *View of the Causes and Consequences of the Present War with France*.[152] On the issue of defensive patriotism in 1797–8, it spoke in contradictory voices, but in general chose largely to ignore it.[153]

Shortly after its establishment Morthland declared, in a letter to the paper's first manager, John Lauder:

> ... my friends in the west are indefatigable. There is already a train of agents fixed from Aberdeen, Dundee, and Perth through Stirling, Glasgow, Paisley, Greenock all along the west as far as Stranraer. Subscriptions are flowing in, many at something more than the minimum price at £2.2 for year for a single paper. The people are clamouring that we don't publish thrice a week.[154]

Some of these agents seem to have been the same individuals who had circulated radical and reform propaganda in the earlier 1790s, and the *Scots Chronicle* may well have established a readership which included many former members of radical societies who had remained disorganized following the suppression of the British Convention at the end of 1793. In 1797, a number of weavers in Cupar, Fife, suspected of being members of the Society of United Scotsmen, were clubbing together to purchase copies of the paper.[155] During the anti-militia disturbances, several contemporaries alleged that the paper was to blame for stirring up popular opposition to the measure. Sir William Murray described it as 'that damn'd Democratic paper', decrying its influence throughout the lowlands, and calling for steps to circumscribe its circulation; while William Brown, who, to be fair, had a professional interest in talking up its impact, declared the 'paper appears to me as much calculated as any other to set the country in a flame'.[156]

The paper's success was achieved, moreover, in spite of sustained official and unofficial harassment. Distribution through the Post Office of early issues seems to have been deliberately disrupted, and there are hints that a list of subscribers was collected through the same agency.[157] Morthland was denied credit to run the paper by the Bank of Scotland, despite guarantees for the sum from Lauderdale and one other individual. Steps were taken to discourage people from advertising in its pages. More ominously, in 1797 John Cadell of Cockenzie launched a claim for damages against the printer of the paper, John Johnston, and Morthland in the Court of Session. The case arose out of a letter printed in the paper on 1 September 1797 which described the notorious anti-militia riot at Tranent in East Lothian, at which twelve people were killed by a troop of English cavalry called on to protect local magistrates seeking to implement the Militia Act. The author of this letter, which was highly critical of the actions of the magistrates, and in which Cadell was named, was a relative of one of those killed. The principal motivation for bringing the case was almost certainly political. As Morthland later wrote: 'This account, tho' an extremely mitigated one, excited much party clamour and Animosity Against the Newspaper ...'.[158] Morthland had instigated an indictment for murder against the soldiers who had taken part in the policing of the disturbance. In September 1797, in response to this, Charles Hope proposed a motion to expel him from the Faculty of Advocates.[159] The prosecution in the Court of Session was only decided upon following a series of meetings of the county elite in East Lothian. In asserting the gravity of the slander, Cadell's counsel urged the significance of the political context – the upsurge of popular opposition to the Militia Act, evidence of disaffection in Scotland (a reference to the rise of the United Scotsmen) and Britain, and the war against France.[160] Morthland claimed in the course of the case that the *Scots Chronicle* was not making a profit, which suggests that it may have only been continued support from opposition Whig notables which kept it in existence.[161]

The record, therefore, of the *Scots Chronicle* indicates not only the continuation of a generally repressive political climate in Scotland in the 1790s, but also its limitations. As was emphasized at the beginning of this chapter, English radical papers continued to find readers in Scotland in this period, although, owing to repression south of the border, and disenchantment with the conduct of French armies in Europe, these generally pursued a more moderate, politically cautious line than their counterparts from earlier in the decade. In 1796–7, as we will see in a later chapter, radical pamphlets were again circulating around much of lowland Scotland, although the main source of these, the bookseller Alexander Leslie, was arrested in November 1797 and, like so many before him, opted to flee rather than face trial before the reactionary Scottish bench. Whether this prosecution was sufficient to staunch the flow of such material is currently impossible to say.

To a significant extent, the history of the Scottish press in the 1790s follows closely that of the rest of Britain. As Professor Dickinson has emphasized, loyalists and loyalist opinion tended to dominate the press in England as well as Scotland.[162] It was from Liverpool that William Roscoe wrote to Lord Landsdowne in late 1792:

> In the course of this fortnight the only newspaper that would admit an article on the cause of Reform has been obliged by the violence and threats of some intolerable individuals, to disavow its principles, and profess a thorough devotion to the prevailing frenzy; and though there are four weekly newspapers published, there is not one that will admit a contradiction to the grossest calumnies that can be devised against the friends of Reform, who have not now a public organ by which they can address the town of Liverpool.[163]

Radical newspapers were only a small minority of papers throughout Britain. One recent estimate suggests that, of around fourteen daily papers published in London in the first half of the 1790s, the maximum number of radical dailies was just four (between September and December 1792). Similarly, of between fifty and seventy-two provincial papers published between 1790 and 1795, the highest number of radical papers was eight, between May 1792 and February 1793.[164] The main English radical societies, the London Corresponding Society and the Society for Constitutional Information, quickly discovered that they were denied opportunities to promote their views in much of the press, hence their heavy reliance on handbills as a means of political communication. The radical press south of the border was fairly quickly crushed or weakened and worn down by repeated prosecutions. Those radical papers which did survive, moreover, were or became notably moderate in their politics. The Scottish radical press was, from the outset, moderate and cautious in nature, but did not thereby escape official and unofficial hostility. That said Scottish radical printers and publishers were not mobbed like some of their English counterparts,[165] although violent clashes between radicals and loyalists in Scotland were generally rare, partly because, as we will see in Chapter 4, Scottish loyalism in the early 1790s remained very much an elite phenomenon. While the final blow was delivered to the *Edinburgh Gazetteer* by concerted legal harassment of its conductor, Alexander Scott, and his staff following the suppression of the British convention, it seems, in fact, that it was already in a state of near-terminal decline, a decline which mirrored very closely the problems which came to afflict the Scottish radical movement in 1793 as its social base narrowed and as it came to rest on the support of artisans, lesser tradesmen and shopkeepers with strictly limited financial resources.

Dissentient voices were not, however, as John Cookson argued some years ago, completely eliminated from the British press in the later 1790s.[166] In an English context, it is nevertheless striking that these were most strongly represented not in the newspaper press but in more high-minded, serious periodicals. The latter were the mouthpieces of an affluent, well-entrenched dissenting intelligentsia present in many provincial towns – Norwich and Liverpool, for example – as well as in the capital.[167] There was no real equivalent to these groups in Scotland, and certainly no institutional base for them similar to that provided by the Unitarian chapels. Scottish dissenting intellectuals contributed little to the press in this period, although, we have seen, Millar was a notable contributor to the *Scots Chronicle*. The Earl of Buchan, armed with an overweening sense of his importance and political acuity, chose a posture of dignified retirement from the political fray, or so he presented it, following publication of his *Essays on the Lives and Writings of Fletcher of Saltoun, and the Poet Thomson* (1792), and following Charles Grey's careless disregard of his advice about the correct political tactics to employ in the crisis of political reaction of 1792–3.[168] Several other Scottish political dissenters only found their true political voices in print in England.[169]

Viewed in the round, the Scottish press suggests that the remarkable hegemony of the Dundas interest in Scotland in the 1790s, which reached its apogee in 1796, had its foundations, as David Brown has recently argued, not just in the construction of skilful political alliances with territorial political interests, but in strong, but short-term, currents of opinion.[170] As emphasized in the introduction to this chapter, and as will become clear in later chapters, the press did not reflect the totality of opinion on public affairs and the war. Indeed it seems likely that for some periods especially, for example 1795–6, certain views were very largely and deliberately excluded from the Scottish press. Not that they were thereby completely unavailable to Scots, who could, it is worth stressing again, gain access to them through English papers and pamphlets, which continued to circulate in Scotland throughout the 1790s. Nevertheless, papers like the *Aberdeen Weekly Journal* and the *Dumfries Weekly Journal* or the *Glasgow Courier* provided unwavering support to Dundas and his fellow ministers and their conduct of the war.

Lastly, the evidence of the press underlines the formidable difficulties confronting Scottish radicals in the early and indeed later 1790s. From the end of 1792, most Scottish newspapers constructed narratives, more or less deliberately, and largely through repetition of a few stock themes and images, which can only have been highly damaging to the cause of liberty and reform. This was especially true during 1793–4, at the height of the Jacobin Terror, which, influenced undoubtedly by the rise of sentimentalism and sentimental conventions of representation, was depicted in often very emotionally-charged language in the pages of the newspapers, and nowhere more obviously so than in the letters purporting to offer eyewitness accounts of conditions, say, in Paris which frequently appeared in a number of papers, for example the *Edinburgh Evening Courant*. Conveying political messages was, it should be stressed, not the primary purpose of newspapers, although it almost became so in the fraught political conditions of 1793–4; rather this was to provide timely and comprehensive news of national and international events. Nor did the press have anything like a monopoly of information on the French Revolution. Indeed, a vast penumbra of others sorts of publication poured from the presses to exploit the obvious demand for such information. In May 1794, the notable Perth publishers Robert Morison and Son wrote to the Edinburgh bookselling partnership of Bell and Bradfute for copies of a publication entitled *History of the Massacres at Paris in a Series of Letters*. As Morison observed, 'this pamphlet sells well', even bothering to underline his comment.[171] Eyewitness accounts of the Revolution appear to have been in considerable demand from the subscription libraries, which were being founded in increasing numbers in Scotland in this period.[172] It was, however, only newspapers that enabled the Revolution, and the associated war and developments in Britain, to be followed closely and continuously. As James Wodrow noted in 1792, this may have lent newspapers a peculiar importance in shaping popular political sentiments in a Scotland where political propaganda was less widely circulated and read than south of the border:

> I think within these two years the sentiments of our common people are growing much more liberal both in religion & Politicks than they formerly were not so much owing to any publications for very few of these are spread in this country, but chiefly to the French revolution which had awakened more attention than you coud [*sic*] easily imagine among them, set them a reading the news papers thinking & talking about this and other matters connected with it ....[173]

The reporting in the newspapers had unparalleled immediacy, while their pages contained a range of information that other forms of print, and private communications, could not hope to match. Newspapers had, in sum, a very distinctive role to play in the ideological and political battles of the 1790s, one which derived from much more than simply the breadth of their readership.

3 'THE TRUE SPIRIT OF LIBERTY': SCOTTISH RADICALS, 1792-4

This chapter examines the rise and fall of Scottish reform politics and radicalism as an open force between 1792 and 1794. To even talk of Scottish radicalism, however, in an unqualified sense may be a misnomer, other than from the very obvious perspective that Scottish radicals and radicalism were organized on a national (meaning Scottish) basis, more so than English radicalism, and Scottish distinctiveness – in religion, for example – inevitably impressed itself on radical views and outlooks. On the other hand, the salient question may be why the distinctively Scottish component was so negligible; or so British, for seemingly the overwhelming majority of Scottish reformers and radicals saw themselves as partners in a cause that was both British and more than British. The 'cause of liberty' was the 'cause of mankind'; universalist languages intertwined with national ones in radical circles with no sense of contradiction.[1] Thomas Muir, the radical martyr, may have talked of ancient Scottish liberty being fuller than its English equivalent, and some radicals called on the Claim of Right (1689) – the Scottish more-than equivalent to the English Bill of Rights[2] – to vindicate their right to petition in defence of reform, but in doing so they were not challenging the notion that liberty was to be created through a reformed Westminster Parliament, or that by the term 'people' was meant people throughout Britain. As we will see further below, from the inception of a parliamentary reform movement in Scotland, alignment and connection with English or English-based reformist and radical organizations were crucial, and this dimension only increased over time, partly in response to political repression throughout the British Isles.

A crucial thread in what follows, therefore, is interaction and interconnection between Scottish and English and, to a rather lesser extent, Irish popular politics in this period. In exploring the Scottish radical movement of these years, the chapter also seeks to do justice, however, to the experiences of reformers and radicals as they sought to develop and define their views and strategies against a very rapidly shifting domestic and international political background. This is something which, as emphasized in the introduction to this book, is not easily done since so many radicals and radical societies remain shadowy historical presences. Overwhelmingly, moreover, the record which survives to shed light on the history of radicalism in this period is of events in Edinburgh, especially at the three general radical conventions, the third of which was recalled on 14 November 1793 to quickly be transformed (on 23 November) into the grandiloquently titled 'British Convention of the Delegates of the People, associated to obtain Universal Suffrage and Annual Parliaments'. Even then, accounts of the discussions at these conventions are not very full, comprising official minutes, which were themselves subject to a measure of self-censorship, and the reports of a single spy.[3] Both Scottish radical newspapers of the period were Edinburgh-based, and, as we saw in Chapter 2, from late 1792 almost no other Scottish newspaper was prepared to open its pages to the Friends of the People. Fortunes and perspectives beyond the Scottish capital can, therefore, only be reconstructed with great difficulty. This is particularly true for the west, for such centres of radical strength as Paisley and other manufacturing communities in Renfrewshire, Lanarkshire and Dumbartonshire. It is doubtful that there are new sources waiting to be discovered which might fill in these gaps; and they should be borne in mind in what follows.

The chapter is organized thematically into three main sections. The first of these looks at the very sudden rise in support for organized radicalism in the second half of 1792 and its subsequent falling away during 1793 as the campaign for parliamentary reform sought to sustain its momentum and, increasingly, simply to survive in the face of official repression and loyalist counter-reaction. The focus of the second section is on the character and content of radical views and sentiment. An important thread here is the shifting relations between the Scottish reform societies and their counterparts elsewhere in the British Isles, which can tell us much about the changing nature and outlook of the former. The final section examines radical organization and the development of a radical platform. Several historians have emphasized the lack of a 'practical political imagination' on the part of the radicals of this period, which, in turn, was symptomatic of a deeper-rooted naivety about the prospects for political change at the end of the eighteenth century.[4] The case cannot easily be dismissed, although the obstacles which stood in the way of the construction of a radical political platform were, as we will see, massive. Radicals were trying to develop a new kind of politics in a climate of intense suspicion towards and open denunciation of their aims and indeed existence. By way of conclusion, the chapter returns to the theme which runs throughout this book – Scottish distinctiveness within British reform and radical politics of the 1790s.

The Rise and Decline of Radical Support

The Scottish reform alliance as it emerged in the second half of 1792 was comprised of heterogeneous parts. This owed much to the rapidly changing circumstances and political conditions in which the alliance was formed, and its relationship to longer-standing campaigns for burgh and county reform, both of which fizzled out in 1793, but which were ongoing in 1792. The first Scottish reform societies were formed in Edinburgh, Perth and Glasgow in the summer of 1792, and were the initiative of groups of propertied burgh reformers.[5] They were a response to what was widely seen as a decisive parliamentary setback to the campaign to secure reform of Scottish burgh government at Westminster, when on 18 April 1792 the Commons rejected Richard Brinsley Sheridan's motion in favour of reform, and on 30 April even voted to reject a petition from the 'burgesses associated for reform' praying to be heard at the bar of the house. A belated, and in the event abortive, proposal from the Lord Advocate, Robert Dundas, for a bill to ensure regular and transparent accounting in burgh government was viewed as a blind – 'a delusive and inefficient reform', as a meeting of the burgh reformers in Edinburgh put it.[6] Faced with this rebuff, while some, led by the leading opposition Whig and Dean of the Faculty of Advocates, Henry Erskine, argued for persisting with the campaign, but steering clear of the taint of innovation and association with the French Revolution, which any broadening of their objectives might cause, others among the burgh reformers began to view parliamentary reform as the only way to pursue their objective; an unreformed Parliament was never going to concede burgh reform.[7] From the middle of 1792, the influence on these individuals of the French Revolution was essentially a negative one, causing them to redouble their efforts to assert the conservative nature of the reform they sought and, increasingly, the independence of their cause from the political upheavals taking place across the Channel.

During the final months of 1792 this emergent reform movement was transformed in scale and nature, at a pace and to an extent which astonished contemporaries. Before September, the Scottish reform societies numbered just two or three; by the end of the year, the total had climbed to somewhere between eighty and a hundred, similar in number, in other words, to that of English societies by the mid 1790s, but drawn from a considerably smaller population.[8] Scotland, it briefly seemed, was becoming the most dynamic area of growth within British radicalism, and Scottish reformers might even overtake their English counterparts in importance. At the end of November, one contemporary declared: 'The spirit of Association and Remonstrance is stronger in SCOTLAND, as vegetation is most powerful in soil fresh and newly reduced from the forest'.[9] Around the same time, William Pulteney wrote:

It appears to me, that if mischief is to be set to work, it is likely to begin in Scotland or Ireland, or in both, & that great vigor to extinguish the first flame is of very great moment, for which purpose, preparatory measures cannot be too soon taken. The period of Christmas, when the work people are idle, is a likely time for beginning a riot.[10]

Pulteney's alarm reflected the fact that the rank and file membership of the new societies comprised artisans, especially weavers, and lesser tradesmen and shop-keepers. In late September 1792, Robert Watt, the Edinburgh wine merchant and informer, reported, 'all the weavers in and near Perth are disaffected'.[11]

Unlike the advanced Whigs and burgh reformers of the summer, those who joined reform societies during September, October and November 1792 were directly inspired by the French Revolution. They watched, intently and with mounting excitement, the tense drama of the declaration of the republic in August, its apparently imminent extinction by Austrian and Prussian forces; and its subsequent rescue by the French revolutionary armies led by General Dumouriez in October and November. Events across the Channel were eagerly followed in the pages of newspapers, circulation of which seems to have risen steeply in 1792, and in a string of publications providing first-hand descriptions of key episodes. Newspapers furnished their own such reports, usually in the form of private letters from Paris.[12] The French victories at Valmy and Jemap-pes, and Dumouriez's subsequent occupation of Brussels, were signals for rowdy popular celebrations. On 9 November, twelve or thirteen people styling them-selves the Revolution Club met at a bonfire at Langholm Cross to celebrate the success of the French at Jemappes. Three public toasts were drunk, which were reported as 'success to the French Revolution', 'George the third and last king', and 'liberty and equality to all the world'. Each was followed by a discharge of guns. That evening, candles were lit in the windows of club members' houses and a mob of boys went through the streets 'to oblige all the inhabitants to illuminate their windows'.[13] The explicit borrowing of the official script of civic celebra-tion of British military victories was a feature also of more serious disturbances in Perth and Dundee.[14] The erection of trees of liberty, in Dundee and several other places – Aberdeen, Forfar, Strathmiglo and Auchtermuty – was itself a further manifestation of the capacity of events in France to evoke powerful, posi-tive popular responses in the final months of 1792; from 1790, the tree of liberty had become the pre-eminent symbol of the French Revolution.[15]

The successes of the French revolutionaries and of their armies in late 1792 also sparked a sudden upsurge of confidence that Britain's 'old regime' was finished and that the progress of reform in Britain was unstoppable. There was, in short, an abrupt, and unprecedented, expansion in the sense of the politically possible. The excitement was palpable, and popular political expression in late 1792 frequently burst free of the trammels of Whig constitutionalism. Republican sentiments appear to have been widely voiced, which helps further to explain the rising alarm felt by ministerial supporters, as well as the tendency among many moderate, propertied reformers to disengage from reform politics from as early as the final months of 1792. On 15 December, it was, for example, reported from Perth: 'The Lower Class of People talk of nothing but Liberty and Equality – "No Dundas, No Bishops – and no King nothing but a republic for us" Such is the Spirit of the Times.' A month earlier, the Sheriff of Perth observed, 'it is not uncommon to hear the boys crying "Liberty, Equality and no King"'.[16] Handbills, often the closest the historian can come to genuinely demotic political expression in this period, encapsulated a message of inevitable emancipation – for Europe as well as for Britain. In the west, there was a brief flurry of these purporting to contain the apocalyptic prophecies of the thirteenth-century Thomas the Rhymer. This individual had supposedly foretold that after terrible convulsions in church and state, despots of all kinds – civil, military and religious – would be forced to flee, and in their place would come an era of peace where trade would flourish and 'true religion and an universal love to mankind shall be established unto the end of the world'.[17] Even the *Edinburgh Gazetteer*, normally a voice of studious caution and moderation within the Scottish reform movement, caught the heady, expectant mood in its early issues, calling, for example, on 21 November the French victory at Jemappes one 'for the whole family of the Human Race'.

Reinforcing and further stimulating popular political hopes and perceptions, Thomas Paine's *Rights of Man*, with its romantic, cosmopolitan vision of the French Revolution, and in Part 2 its explicitly 'redistributive' form of radicalism, was also circulating very widely throughout lowland Scotland during this period. Unlike in England and Ireland, Paine's influence in Scotland prior to the second half of 1792 seems to have been strictly limited.[18] His and other radical works – for example, Charles Pigott's the *Jockey Club* – were being sold, but at a cost which precluded a popular readership.[19] Before the second half of the year, the *Rights of Man* was also distributed by several booksellers who would just a few months later become staunch supporters of the anti-radical campaign, such as Peter Hill, William Creech's former clerk.[20] Even Creech himself, the arch loyalist who would in December become secretary to the Edinburgh loyalist association, was in March selling copies of the *Rights of Man* and in June of Mary Wollstonecraft's *Vindication of the Rights of Women*.[21] At the end of November 1792, Norman Macleod was to attribute the remarkable surge of interest in the *Rights of Man* to the impact of the May proclamation against seditious writings.[22] Partly in response to the proclamation, but also to requests from radicals in different parts of England, Paine arranged for the publication in May of cheap (6*d.*) editions of both parts of the *Rights of Man*.[23] In July Walter Miller, a cabinetmaker from Perth, wrote to John Horne Tooke of the Society for Constitutional Information (SCI) about the impact of the work around the town, informing him that copies which he had given to friends 'have already gone through about a dozen hands'.[24] In the same month John Thomson, an Edinburgh bookseller, was advertising the sale of an abridgement at just 1½*d*.[25] From August, a small coterie of his fellow booksellers in the capital – John Elder, Alexander Guthrie, James Robertson, Walter Berry and Cornelius Elliot – were advertising the 6*d*. editions, along with other notable radical works.[26] These were no doubt the 'unknown persons' in Edinburgh who James Wodrow credited with making 'very successful' efforts to circulate the *Rights of Man* in early October.[27] In November, Elder, who was almost certainly a member of the Friends of the People, and a key figure in the dissemination of Paine's writings in Scotland in these months, was advertising copies of the *Rights of Man* for sale at 30*s*. per hundred copies.[28] From the south-west, Sir William Maxwell of Springkell reported in the same month that 'Paine's pamphlet, or the cream and substance of it, is now in the hands of every countryman'.[29] Several radical periodical publications were also founded in Edinburgh between the summer and autumn. These included the two Scottish radical newspapers discussed in the previous chapter, the *Edinburgh Gazetteer* and the *Caledonian Chronicle*. A monthly magazine entitled the *Historical Register, or Edinburgh Monthly Intelligencer*, which had been founded in July 1791, also seems to have developed a new radical version at around the same time. According to Meikle – who saw copies in the Signet Library which I have been unable to locate – the contents of this version included outspoken assaults on the brutality of British imperialism in India, the slave trade, extravagance and immorality at court, and the greed of landlords which was causing mass emigration from the highlands.[30] In a direct echo of Paine, a national convention was portrayed as the principal vehicle for reform. Volume 13 (for July 1792) also included a portrait of Paine, almost certainly a copy of William Sharp's engraving of the Romney portrait.[31] With a complex publication history involving several radical booksellers – Elliot, Thomson, Robertson and Berry – the compiler of the *Historical Register* was, for some issues at least, the balloonist and printer-publisher James Tytler.[32] Tytler was forced to flee to Belfast in early 1793 under threat of prosecution for the publication of a handbill. Entitled 'To the People and their Friends', it contained a fiery attack on the 'despotism' of the Scottish landowning classes and dismissed the capacity of a parliament dominated by landowners to reform itself.[33]

The radical movement, therefore, grew very suddenly and in a febrile mood of great political excitement and optimism. The rapidity of its growth was both symptom and part of this, although popular emotions were not contained within organized radicalism, spreading more widely as reflected in the political disturbances of October and November. The circumstances of its expansion also help to explain why decline set in fairly quickly during 1793; the mood of heightened expectation at the end of 1792 turned quite quickly and easily to

one of demoralization and frustration when the radicals confronted not rapid
progress towards their political goals from the turn of the year but systematic
opposition and, in their eyes, crude misrepresentation of their aims.

Estimates of numbers of radicals by the end of 1792 are necessarily very
rough and contain large gaps. The few contemporary figures which exist are difficult to accept at face value, being susceptible to exaggeration on the part of
spies and authorities or deliberate underestimation by exculpatory witnesses at
the trials of radicals. As radical societies proliferated in late 1792, it was easy and
at times expedient to suppose they might continue to grow at a similar rate; fear
often did the rest. One report from late 1792 stated of Glasgow: 'The Reformers
are computed at 1200 they probably amount to a far greater number, as it is said
the number of Reformers in the west amount to between 40 & 50 thousand'.[34]
The origin of the 50,000 figure seems to have been a claim made by an advanced
Whig in Glasgow about likely *future* support in the context of urging the need
for immediate, moderate reform to forestall revolution; it may well, therefore,
have been an expedient exaggeration. The main urban centres of Scottish radical strength were, nevertheless, clear enough – Edinburgh, Glasgow and Perth.
In each, numbers joining radical societies probably reached between 1,000 and
1,500, although potential or unorganized radical support may well have been
rather greater than that, as was the case elsewhere.[35] Numbers were lower, somewhere between around 500 and 800, in Paisley and Stirling, and Kilmarnock,
judging by the number of societies formed and delegates sent to the general conventions.[36] In Dundee membership of radical societies was probably no more
than a few hundred by early 1793.[37] Elsewhere societies seem to have been small,
although extant figures are rare. A society in Saltcoats in Ayrshire comprised
60 members in early December, although it had only just been formed.[38] Some
parts of lowland Scotland also proved resistant to the radical message. There
were, for example, few radical societies in the borders or the north-east in Aberdeenshire and Banffshire. Neither were there any in Caithness and Invernesshire,
not surprisingly perhaps given the overwhelming dominance of agriculture in
their economies, and low levels of urbanization, although at least one individual
cautioned against complacency regarding the political views of the lower orders
in Invernesshire; such people were hardly likely to reveal their true views to
landowners.[39] The highlands remained immune to radicalism, although a Gaelic
edition of the *Rights of Man* was apparently produced.[40]

In manufacturing regions, however – Renfrewshire, Lanarkshire, Dumbartonshire and Ayrshire in the west, and Fife, Angus and Perthshire in the east
– radicalism spread very widely. In Angus, to focus on just one of these counties,
all but one of the main burghs – Dundee, Forfar, Arbroath, Montrose, Coupar
Angus and Kirriemuir – seem to have had radical societies or had hosted meetings of radicals by the end of 1792.[41] (The exception was Brechin.) From Forfar,

the county town, an Andrew Dundas, who for several years had been soliciting for a place in the excise service, so may have been embroidering his current plight, wrote to his namesake, Henry, in May 1793: 'for speaking in favour of our present Blessed Constitution and excellent Government, and on my name being Dundas, I have frequently been of late treated, by the factious party of this place, in a most scandalous manner, by having an Effigy burnt and hang'd at my door.[42] John Fyffe, employed as a government agent in Dundee from November 1792, reported in the immediate aftermath of the so-called tree of liberty disturbances there:

> As far as I can learn the Root from which all this has sprung has been Forfar & Ker-
> riemuir [sic] who seem to be the most inflammatory set of scoundrels I ever heard of
> and it is astonishing the notions that have instilled into the minds of the common
> people, such as the meaning of the word Liberty & Equality is nothing else than an
> equal distribution of property, a relief from Taxes, & such other stuff, which has been
> greedily swallowed by the multitude – in a society that has been formed at Forfar all
> descriptions of People are admitted to vote ...[43]

In these same regions, manufacturing villages, which were multiplying in the later eighteenth century, rarely seem to have lacked a radical presence. In Blair-gowrie, a manufacturing village in Perthshire, the local stamp master found himself the subject of investigation for alleged radical tendencies because a copy of the *Edinburgh Gazetteer* was being sent to his house, from where it was circulating around local weavers.[44] Several years later, William Murray of Ochtertyre observed: 'There are people in Crieff and a few in Comrie that have been on my suspicious list since the ninety-two'.[45] It was amongst weavers and other artisans in these sorts of communities that opposition to the Militia Act was often strongest in 1797 and the clandestine United Scotsmen found its recruits.[46] Even several parishes on the Carse of Gowrie, a rich agricultural region bounded on one side by the Tay and on the other by the Sidlaw Hills, in which spinning and weaving of linen had established themselves from the later seventeenth century as by-employments, were home to small numbers of radicals.[47]

Explaining the map of Scottish radicalism in the early 1790s in detail is difficult since much must have depended on local circumstances, conditions and personalities which are largely lost from view at this distance of time. Of general relevance, however, were, first, the presence of leadership from members of the middle or upper ranks; and, second, the paternalism, politics and attitudes of local employers and landowners. As in many places in England, the initial rise of popular radicalism often seems to have depended on the leadership and patronage of individuals from the propertied classes.[48] In 1792, Thomas Muir was meeting with groups of radicals in weaving villages in Dumbartonshire, advising them, amongst other things, on what they should read.[49] In Perth, the early leaders of radicalism were wealthy burgh reformers.[50] Prominent among them was

George Meliss, a cotton manufacturer and merchant. Meliss, who lived for most of the 1790s in Rosemount House, a villa-style property across the River Tay, was a prominent abolitionist, as well as burgh reformer.[51] It was Meliss, supported by a large number of weavers and other tradesmen and artisans, who successfully proposed a pro-reform amendment to a series of loyalist resolutions put to a public meeting in the town on 18 December 1792.[52] In 1798, George Paterson of Castle Huntly, a small estate to the south-west of Dundee, was to note, with not a little satisfaction, one suspects: 'Meliss of Perth the Great Democrate has stopped pay[men]t & the Cromwell Perth Comp[an]y all failed. This discharges a nest of 400 Democrates.'[53] In Dundee, the 1780s had seen the development of a strong opposition Whig group. In June 1790, the local Whig Club, which included among its membership a number of leading merchants, as well as several professionals and ministers, sent a congratulatory address to the French national convention. A list of subscribers or recipients of the *Edinburgh Gazetteer* in the town drawn up in 1792 comprised seventeen individuals, including several wealthy merchants and manufacturers.[54] The first of the two Dundee reform societies to be formed in the early 1790s, the Friends of the Constitution, invited the neighbouring landowner, George Dempster of Dunnichen, who had also been the MP for Perth burghs, which included Dundee, up until 1790 and who had been president of the Whig Club in 1790, to become their first president. They were firmly rebuffed by him. 'Honest George' may have been a notable independent in politics, but he was no friend to parliamentary reform or lower-class radicalism. By late 1792, he was advising friends of government on measures to combat the influence of Paine's writings.[55] They also approached Lord Kinnaird, whose Rossie estate was on the Carse of Gowrie, but received a similar response.[56] Other local propertied opposition Whigs with reputations for being friends of reform – men such as the Revd Robert Small, wealthy surgeon Dr Robert Stewart and Dr John Willison, another well-heeled medical man, a physician – do not appear to have joined either of the local radical societies.[57]

This pattern was to be repeated elsewhere. From Glasgow, Robert Dundas was informed in early October that a 'Mr Pattison', presumably a local opposition Whig, 'will keep clear of them' (i.e. the parliamentary reform societies).[58] Similarly in Aberdeen, where the burgh reform movement had been strong in the 1780s, and in 1790 had, like the Dundee Whig Club, issued an address to the French national convention, rather than turn to parliamentary reform in 1792, the energies of the reformers were consumed with arguments about proposed police reform in the city. While there was a radical society in Aberdeen, it was short-lived and seems to have been very poorly supported.[59]

Edinburgh was also, on the face of it, an unlikely place of radical strength. Its large legal establishment and interlocking governing institutions – Burgh Council, Board of Trustees for the Improvement of Manufactures and Fisheries, the

Royal Bank and Bank of Scotland – had been since the early 1780s firmly dominated by the Dundas interest.[60] The city's clergymen were from the Moderate
wing of the Church of Scotland, men whose strong commitment to cultural and
economic liberalization was matched by an equally firm commitment to political conservatism and rule by an enlightened, landed elite.[61] Men of similar views
prevailed in the university, as was emphasized in Chapter 1, not surprisingly
given the source of patronage for academic posts – the Town Council. By the
later eighteenth century, the capital's economy also included a large and expanding luxury sector, reflecting its growing role as a place of winter resort to the
landed classes.[62] Many of its tradesmen were heavily dependent on elite custom
as a result, and very susceptible to economic pressures to disavow their support
for the radical cause. It was the Edinburgh goldsmith David Downie who proposed the following resolution at the British convention in late 1793:

> Seeing that the enemies of the Constitution & of the People have ungenerously
> combined together to withdraw their employment and assistance from the friends
> of Reform, knowing that self preservation is the first law of nature, we the Friends of
> the People do think it a duty incumbent on us to assist one another in our different
> employments and in whatever concerns procuring assistance for support of ourselves
> and familys and also that every one in particular who is or may be persecuted for their
> laudable principles in the cause of reform shall be supported by the whole mass of the
> People conjoined for the Purpose of Parliamentary Reform.[63]

A similar, abortive proposal had been made at the first general convention twelve
months previously. In supporting it, one delegate informed the convention that
the Duchess of Buccleuch had discharged her haberdasher for being a member
of the Friends of the People.[64] The same difficulties were present in other towns,
especially county towns which attracted the patronage of neighbouring gentry
and in the many smaller burghs of Scotland in this period. In Haddington, for
example, the premises of radicals were allegedly being pointed out by the local
magistrate for avoidance by the 'wealthy part of the Towns men'.[65] From Dunfermline, a teacher of a private school asked rather desperately that his name be
omitted from a letter he had written to Fyshe Palmer for inclusion in the *Edinburgh Gazetteer* since to include it would 'highly injure' his 'private interest'.[66]
Probably nowhere, however, were such pressures felt as intensely as the capital, and by the later 1790s Edinburgh seems to have proved a notably unfertile
environment for radicals for precisely this reason. In 1797, one radical declared
in relation to the capital: 'The reason for the timidity of the friends of liberty
may easily be traced to its source. They are in general poor – and dependent
almost solely for their daily support upon the Aristocracy, in whose hands all the
business of the town either mediately or immediately lies.'[67] In 1792, a radical
leadership was forthcoming, however, from the ranks of the capital's advanced
Whigs and former burgh reformers, and under this leadership reform societies

spread and grew, to between ten and fifteen in 1793, and spreading to several of its suburbs, including the New Town and Portsburgh.[68] Moreover, the very strength of the dependencies created by the luxury economy, together with the increasingly visible social divisions manifest in the city's changing form and lay-out with the development of George Square on the south side and the first New Town, probably created their own deep resentments. Normally hidden or sup-pressed, these may well have found temporary expression in membership of a radical movement which held out, however fleetingly, the promise of bringing into being a society marked by equality of opportunity and of social and political regard for all of its citizens.

If, therefore, leadership from higher social ranks was frequently important in facilitating the emergence of popular support for reform, also influential in sev-eral places was religious dissent and the presence of dissenting ministers actively supportive of reform. Several dissenting ministers were active in Perth radical circles, and hack writer Robert Heron emphasized the contribution or 'religious zeal and pride' to political divisions in Perth in the early 1790s.[69] With regard to Dundee, the Unitarian Fyshe Palmer is only the best known of the local radical dissenting ministers owing to his trial in 1793 and subsequent transportation. Others included James McEwan, an anti-burgher minister who was the town's delegate to the second general convention; James Donaldson, Berean minister, former shoemaker and delegate to the second and third general conventions; and Neil Douglas, a minister of the Relief Church, and a delegate at the third and British conventions of radicals. In early 1795, a Methodist minister in Dundee attracted suspicion on account of the supposed political content of his sermons.[70] In Montrose and St Cyrus, the Christie family, who were Unitarians, were the leading figures in radicalism locally, while the Montrose delegate to the second convention was Frederick MacFarlane, an anti-burgher minister.[71]

In their degree of influence, the role of the dissenting ministry in radical-ism on Tayside was in a Scottish context unusual, although several dissenting ministers from elsewhere in Scotland supported the radicals. Why this should have been so is hard to say. Tayside provided a fertile environment for dissenters in the eighteenth century, as evidenced, for example, by the foundation of the Glassite church first in Dundee and then in Perth. For much of the eighteenth century, influential Dundee ministers came from the popular, evangelical wing of the Church of Scotland and much of the population seems to have of a rigidly orthodox Presbyterian cast. Dundee's most famous minister of the first half of the eighteenth century was Dr John Willison, the Church of Scotland's foremost early opponent of Moderatism, and a proponent of rehabilitation of the Seced-ers. In the 1760s, Dundee attempted, unsuccessfully, to call John Witherspoon to one of its charges from Paisley.[72] In 1784, it was reported that opposition to an overture against patronage in the Presbytery of Dundee would have been 'dangerous ... as the inhabitants of that place are madly orthodox'.[73] Yet this is at best a partial explanation since, in the first place, we can find similar conditions present in, for example, Paisley and other towns and villages in the west and central lowlands. Some dissent – Unitarianism – was also of a rational kind, and radicalism, nationally and locally, often seems to have involved alliances between rational and Calvinist forms of dissent. In 1804, an early historian of Dundee wrote: 'Although divided into different sects, and unavoidably connected with party opinion – the greatest liberality of sentiment prevails, while a scrupulous strictness of morals is observable in all ranks'.[74] This mood may help explain the emergence of Dr Robert Small, who was referred to briefly above, as a leading figure amongst the local ministry. Small, whom we met in Chapter 1, was seemingly a popular figure locally and certainly no defender of rigid orthodoxy, being very much on the Moderate wing of the Church and a man of broad intellectual interests.[75] The relationship between religious dissent and political radicalism was, moreover, as emphasized in Chapter 1, far from a straightforward one, and not all or probably most dissenting ministers and congregations were supporters of the radical cause. David Sangster, minister of the Relief Church in Perth, was in 1794 denounced by a member of his congregation for preaching in favour of the French Revolution and against the war.[76] Unitarian influence in Scotland was very confined geographically in the 1790s and very recently implanted.[77]

Dissent may have been important in less direct ways. In manufacturing villages it was a factor potentially weakening landlord control.[78] More broadly, as again alluded to in Chapter 1, it nurtured a critical attitude honed on theological and religious dispute, as well as a profound respect for the printed word, although such characteristics were also strongly entrenched in the popular wing of the Church of Scotland, which was very strong in the west around Glasgow and Paisley. As Robert Heron observed of the weavers of Kilbarchan, in Renfrewshire, 'whatever appears in a printed book or paper, derives the highest consequence in their eyes, from the circumstance of its being printed'.[79] The rise of radicalism in Stirling and its environs in the early 1790s may well have been linked to the local strength of the dissenting tradition, although local burgh and electoral politics were also unusually contentious from 1774 onwards.[80] There may have been apocalyptic religious traditions buried in dissenting communities which resurfaced under the impact of events in France. We have already noted the circulation of millenarian prophecies in handbills in the west in late 1792. The early eighteenth-century Presbyterian minister Robert Fleming's millenarian tract *A Discourse on the Rise and Fall of the Papacy* was republished in Edinburgh in 1792 and in Edinburgh and Falkirk in 1793. Unlike in some Ulster Presbyterian communities in this period, there is very little evidence, however, of the influence of these tracts or the traditions they recalled.[81]

The simple fact of isolation could also influence whether a society was formed, or how and whether radicalism spread to an area. Weavers were a very mobile section of the population, and, as a result of a series of moves, could easily have personal and family connections to nearby villages and towns. This was one reason why the United Scotsmen was able to develop almost entirely beyond the gaze of the authorities from 1796. Communications between towns within economic regions were multiplying in this period. Thus, towns like Forfar and Kirriemuir, as well as many linen-weaving villages throughout Perthshire, Angus and Fife, formed the natural economic hinterland of Dundee. Towns and their hinterlands were strongly connected in other ways, through the marketing of agricultural produce, for example. Radicals in communities, meanwhile, which were located in areas generally hostile to radicalism did not form such connections, and, as a result, could be and were deterred from forming reform societies. From Newburgh, Fife, James Blyth reported, in disgust, on 18 November 1793: 'We sit in the midst of a blind intoxicated and prejudiced people, the majority of whom are possess'd with a spirit synonimous [sic] to the herds of the stall'. A radical from Selkirk talked explicitly a few months earlier about isolation as adding to local radical demoralization.[82] Individuals in such places and areas were also more likely to be influenced by pressure from landlords and employers to keep clear of radical societies. Radicals in East Linton failed to form themselves into a society probably because of this vulnerability.[83] In July 1792, considerable pressure had been exerted by landlords to prevent tenants from attending a dinner in East Linton to celebrate the anniversary of the fall of the Bastille. As a Mrs Hamilton wrote on 16 July to a correspondent in Edinburgh: 'There was a printed Ad: on Thursday inviting all Farmers and others who lov'd Freedom &c to dine at Linton the 14 to Celebrate the French Revolution. I hear about 20 went. None of mine & Lord Weems sent a Message to his not to go, otherwise to expect no New Lease.'[84] No doubt such pressures only intensified from the final months of 1792 into 1793. Few farmers joined the radical cause; vulnerability to landlord pressure was one important reason for this.[85]

The final factor which helped determine the spread of radicalism was, as already implied at several points above, the presence of an independent, or relatively independent, skilled labouring class. The wages of most skilled workers in Scotland were rising, up at least until 1793 and the effects on manufacturing of the credit squeeze caused by British entry into the war against revolutionary France (in February). The 1780s had seen a 'massive increase' in demand for handloom weavers, pushing wages upwards and creating greater opportunities for upward mobility in the labour market.[86] During 1792, there is evidence of continued shortages of labour and higher wages pushing prices up in several areas of the urban economy.[87] Support for the 'cause of liberty' amongst this stratum of society was therefore, in contrast to the post-Napoleonic war period, a consequence more of aspiration than desperation. With regard to the weavers of Perth, Heron talked of a 'spirit of turbulent independence produced by weekly freedom and opulence'.[88] Political developments of the early 1790s reopened older debates about the desirability of high wages amongst the labouring classes as part of wider discussion about how far manufacturing progress brought benefits to society or instead produced consequences which undermined its stability and cohesion. In fact, the independence of weavers was beginning at the end of the eighteenth century to come under challenge from merchants seeking higher profits from enhanced control of labour, but there were other, more immediate means of pursuing economic disputes than seeking political reform. In what was still a tight labour market, especially close to large manufacturing centres, striking could prove effective; while there remained before 1812 the option of appeal to Justices of the Peace, and, failing that, the Court of Session.[89] Weavers especially were a highly literate and cultured group who sought political recognition commensurate with their sense of independence and worth. They were, at the same time, seemingly quite receptive to the message of cheap government which underpinned the radicals' appeal. If Paine had a central importance to radical politics in the early 1790s in Scotland it was probably in terms of the popularization of this message. This may well have reflected, in turn, an acute awareness at this level of society, fuelled by personal experience and folk memory, of the often sharp fluctuations in living standards in eighteenth-century Scotland.[90] Equally, however, short-term economic hardship was not necessarily a strong recruiting tool for the radicals, as we will see below.

Support for radicalism in Scotland reached its height in the 1790s in late 1792. Thereafter, although new societies continued to appear in a few areas into the early months of 1793 – for example, in the borders, Ayrshire and in Renfrewshire, Paisley especially – support seems to have fallen away quite quickly in the face of government and legal repression, but also political setbacks, notably the failure of Charles Grey's reform motion of May 1793, which was strongly supported in Scotland by petitions from radical societies. From Edinburgh, the authorities were being informed early in 1793 about demoralization in radical ranks. On 5 February, it was reported that attendance at meetings in the capital was declining, either from 'despondence' or the fact that there was no 'immediate object in view'. The informant's report concluded, 'possibly the people may get tired of them [the meetings]'.[91] The first general convention of Scottish radicals, which convened in the capital, in early December, was attended by around 170 delegates, around 50 per cent of whom came from societies elsewhere in Scotland. Attendance at the second general convention, which assembled in Edinburgh on 30 April, was significantly lower at 117; a higher proportion of delegates were also from the capital.[92] Of quite a few of the Scottish societies, we hear nothing further from early 1793.

The decline quickened during the second half of 1793. By early July, 'most societies' in Renfrewshire were postponing meetings for between one and three months, while the delegate meeting was monthly.[93] The sentences passed on Thomas Muir and Thomas Fyshe Palmer, in July and September 1793 respectively, which shocked radicals and many others with their severity, seem to have arrested the slide in the capital at least.[94] This was, however, not true of everywhere. Beyond Edinburgh, the call by William Skirving, as secretary of the general committee of the Edinburgh Friends of the People, for a third general convention of Scottish radicals to assemble at Edinburgh at the end of October met with a very mixed response. Glasgow elected nine delegates, but four of these declined to attend. John Dunlop was able to inform Henry Dundas in December that since his last letter, on 27 October, the Glasgow Friends of the People had attempted to hold several general meetings, but unsuccessfully.[95] Paisley, where local radicals were reported on 18 October as being 'much cast down', elected only one delegate to the convention.[96] From Montrose, William Christie reported the 'happy effect' of the trials in 'fanning the flame of patriotism', but also the 'present languid frame' of the radicals.[97] Similarly equivocal was the message from Dunfermline, Fife, from where it was reported that while the 'two memorable tryals' had been the cause of new members joining the local society, the society was 'not so very numerous as we once was ...'.[98] Perth radical societies had sent nine delegates to the first convention, and seven to the second one. Only one representative may have been present at the third, although three were elected to attend.[99] The Dundee Friends of the Constitution initially decided to send just one delegate to the third convention; the appointment of a second only occurred after receipt of a letter from Skirving urging them to do this.[100] On 19 November, it was reported from Dundee that a meeting of radicals had been called but was poorly attended and adjourned for a few days. Apparently hardly anyone attended the reconvened meeting. The same informant observed: 'The People here much soured particularly as money is wanted – There are no persons of any respectability that now attend their meetings.'[101] From near Dunbar, a Thomas Watt talked of an area cowed by 'clerical & Aristocratical influence' and of the lukewarm reaction to Skirving's initiative from his fellow radicals.[102] The small number of delegates at the third convention (around a hundred), and the absence of individuals of high social rank, led one official to declare 'there is nothing to be fear'd from the operations of these people at present'.[103]

How do we explain this falling off in support? Apart from the effects of government repression and loyalist hostility, which are examined in the next chapter, a strong source of demoralization in radical circles was the failure to develop a convincing political strategy once the petitioning campaign of the spring of 1793 had failed, or even before this. Before the meeting of the second convention, advanced or Foxite Whigs were advocating a strategy of passivity while waiting for the outcome of the petitions to be known; one such individual – Richard Fowler, a medical student – even called on the Friends of the People to recognize the futility of their cause and disband in the face of general public hostility. These same individuals had opposed the calling of the first general convention.[104] There was no agreement either about how best to voice their opposition to the war, whether through petitioning or publishing resolutions. At the second general convention, there was a further motion to disband after the petitions for parliamentary reform had been forwarded to Parliament, although this was also defeated.[105] Before the meeting of the third convention at the end of October, there was no specific plan of reform; the failure of the petitions had not produced any accession of support to the radical societies, as some had anticipated. One reason why union with English societies was so eagerly embraced in late 1793 was the vacuum which existed in the direction of the movement at this point.[106]

Second, economic depression in 1793 took a heavy toll. This was especially true in the west, in and around Glasgow and Paisley, where manufacturing was hardest hit.[107] Both the local and national authorities were very concerned that radicals would exploit discontent arising from the resulting unemployment, and the press contained much comment about unemployment, with supporters of the ministers either denying its seriousness or attributing it to the actions of radicals supposedly undermining business confidence.[108] And while petitions against the war were drawn up in Glasgow and Paisley in July, and gained significant support,[109] the salient question is why economic hardship did not produce more of a boost to radicalism, and if anything seems to have contributed to its further decline. Part of the answer lies in the actions of the authorities and local employers. Dundas, with his very close links to the Glasgow mercantile elites and authorities, ensured that government support was quickly forthcoming to stabilize credit conditions in and around Glasgow as part of a wider programme of support for finance and business in Britain.[110] On 3 May, four days after the Commons had endorsed the ministry's proposals, Gilbert Hamilton wrote to Dundas about the measures to be adopted by the authorities, remarking that had no such scheme been forthcoming the consequences would have been 'dreadful'. 'I do not suppose', he declared, 'that less than 100,000 persons, men, women, & children would have been deprived of the means of subsistence'. As it was, he estimated that 'many thousands' had already been dismissed.[111] According to Richard Saville, thanks to Treasury support, by the summer most companies were able to resume 'normal working', also aided by an increased flow of government funds for war materials.[112] Either in late July or the beginning of August a subscription was opened in Glasgow for the 'relief of the distressed poor' owing to the 'stagnation of trade', probably in emulation of similar subscription established in Manchester in the spring.[113] In the autumn, when an unofficial public meeting was called in the city to examine the causes of unemployment, the Lord Provost and magistrates were quick to attend and ensure that it could not be used to focus potential anger against the war and its economic effects.[114] In Paisley, the 'principal inhabitants' met and agreed to open a subscription for relieving the unemployed in November.[115] In the following month, recognizing that kirk session funds and other charities had been drained by recent events, a further subscription was launched in Glasgow to create a fund to provide relief to the poor during the 'severity of winter'. This fund was to be divided among the city parishes, and administered by the sessions together with subscribers; the sessions provided detailed lists of the poor to guide the distribution of relief.[116] Some employers, meanwhile, may have attempted to shield workers from the worst effects of the downturn.[117] Radicalism was, moreover, only one possible response to hardship. Many seem to have opted for emigration or recruitment into the armed services. One estimate put the number of those who had entered the ranks of the armed forces from Glasgow in 1793 at 5,000.[118] On 7 October 1793, James Wodrow commented on two ships which had sailed from the Clyde 'full of emigrants consisting of Manufacturers Bleachers & two persons have been sent from America on purpose to entice them'.[119] Those who remained were probably forced to work harder to sustain a reasonable income, while still others may have returned to rural areas, notably the highlands, from whence they had come. One contemporary argued that radicalism had been a symptom of relative economic prosperity; under the conditions prevailing in 1793 there was less time or inclination to attend radical meetings.[120] Whether this was so or not, lack of funds had become a pressing problem for the radicals by the final third of 1793, and this, in some places, was directly attributable to economic depression.

Scottish radicalism was already faltering, therefore, well before the suppression of the British convention in early December 1793, the political trials of early 1794 arising from this convention, and the discovery of the so-called Watt or Pike Plot and a further round of arrests of radicals in the early summer of that year. The composition of the movement also changed over the course of 1793 as the reform alliance narrowed significantly in social terms. Propertied reformers, especially advanced Whigs, who had provided the initial leadership to the parliamentary reform campaign, abandoned the cause from the spring, and quite a few them well before then. Robert Graham of Gartmore, a prominent burgh reformer, told Robert Dundas in November 1792 that all those of 'respectability' who had joined the Friends of the People 'on account of the Burrogh Reform' had 'withdrawn with the strongest expression of their dislike to the doctrines now broaching'.[121] From the spring of 1793, new radical leaders, locally and nationally, began to come forward who were significantly lower in social status than their predecessors. These new leaders included men such as George Mealmaker, the Dundee weaver who was the author of the handbill against the war which formed a major element of the bill of indictment for sedition against Fyshe Palmer. Mealmaker went on to play an important role in the United Scotsmen in the later 1790s, a role which was, in many ways, a natural extension of the one he was already playing in 1793, travelling widely, visiting radicals throughout Angus and probably Fife.[122] Robert Sands from Perth was another of these individuals. A weaver like Mealmaker, he first appears in the historical record in late 1792 attending a public meeting called to agree to a set of loyalist resolutions, the purpose of which was subverted by a large radical presence; by the spring of 1793 he was secretary to a local radical society and a delegate to the second general convention. It was Sands who proposed a motion at this convention to persevere with the reform campaign, even in the event of petitions failing to achieve any result in Parliament.[123] In Paisley, men such as Archibald Hastie, a baker, and William and James Mitchell, both weavers, came to the fore. When the loyalist press published a list of delegates to the British convention, showing their occupations as well as their names, this was designed to show how insignificant and socially marginal a group they were. More importantly in the present context it served to confirm how far Scottish radicalism had become by late 1793 a movement of the skilled labouring classes, lesser tradesmen and shopkeepers. Journeyman weaver was the most common occupation among the delegates.[124] As we will see later, the most important formative influence on the politics and political outlook of these individuals may well have been their experiences of and responses to repression and loyalist hostility since late 1792.

Moderates or Radicals

Recent writing on Scottish radicals in the 1790s has tended to emphasize their moderation and caution.[125] This characterization is undoubtedly substantially correct, although several important qualifications are required. First, even in the early phases, the Scottish radical societies contained divergent political tendencies. These were, however, largely held in check or balance up until the early summer of 1793. Thereafter, different faces of radicalism came to the fore the movement changed in response to the pressure of events and repression, as well as to shifting connections with radical bodies and radicals south of the border and in Ireland. As Mark Philp has argued, radicalism could be and often was a transformative experience, and this was no less true of Scotland than other places in Britain, although it is a facet of popular politicization in this period only occasionally directly glimpsed in the sources.[126]

The clearest sign that the political path on which the Scottish reform societies set out was one of prudent constitutionalism were the connections which were quickly established with the Whig Association of the Friends of the People. The formation of this body in London on 17 April 1792 may have been influential in the initial decision to establish the Edinburgh Friends of the People, although, as referred to earlier, this also represented a response to the recent parliamentary setback to the burgh reform campaign.[127] The establishment and publicization of the London group were, nevertheless, extremely timely in the latter context, acting as an inspiration to burgh reformers looking for a new way forward following their disappointment in April. Led by Charles Grey, Sheridan and the Earl of Lauderdale, and also possessing a considerable Scottish membership in addition to Lauderdale, the Whig Association of the Friends of the People explicitly disavowed any connection to events in France, arguing instead that reform was the best way to avoid revolution.[128] An important intermediary between the Edinburgh Friends of the People and the association was Norman Macleod, a former officer in the 42nd Highlanders who had served in India, and until 1796 MP for Invernesshire. Macleod, who joined the Glasgow Associated Friends of the Constitution and of the People, was a member of another body with links to opposition Whigs and reformers in London, the Friends of the Liberty of the Press. He was present in Edinburgh in late October–November 1792 and again in January 1793, when he attended meetings of several radical societies. When he was in London he seems to have corresponded quite frequently with the Edinburgh Friends of the People. Two of his letters to this society were subsequently published in pamphlet form and widely circulated in radical circles, north and south of the border.[129] His commitment to the Scottish Friends of the People continued after the spring of 1793, when many advanced Whigs dropped away from the cause of reform, and he showed solidarity with the Scottish radicals into the autumn. On 11 May, that is after the second general convention had sat, he wrote to Skirving from London: 'I shall soon be in Edinb[urgh] & there shall converse with you & our other Friends on the best plans to be followed in future'.[130] On 29 October, a four-man delegation from the third convention was sent to visit Macleod to 'see if he stood to his principles', to which he gave

> assurances ... of his steady adherence to the cause, but expresses his opinion at the same time That the People were not ripe at present for Universal Suffrage & Annual Elections, which more than in his opinion wou'd be granted; though the principles thought they were justly intitled to it; and would support them as far as possible so far as the people went on in a Constitutional Way.[131]

The SCI initially hoped that he would act as their delegate to the British convention, but he declined, and appears not to have been present at it. Events there were almost certainly too extreme for him, and he was not offering his support at that stage.[132] Another important intermediary was Lord Daer, eldest son of the Earl of Selkirk, of whom little is known, apart from the fact that, like Macleod, he was closely involved in the burgh and county reform movements, and he seems to have been part of the Earl of Shelburne's Bowood circle in the 1770s and '80s.

Through his suffering from consumption, from which he was to die in 1794, he shared an interest in pneumatic chemistry with men such as Joseph Priestley and Thomas Beddoes.[133] In the 1790 general election he stood as a reform candidate in two English constituencies. As we will see below, his radical connections in London were not confined to the Whig Friends of the People. Daer, who was present at the first general convention of Scottish radicals in Edinburgh in early December 1792, as well as the third and British conventions, was a keen advocate of cooperation with reform societies in London and 'the supporters of freedom at a distance'.[134] In January 1793, it was reported that without the influence of Daer and Macleod 'the Friends of the People could not go on'.[135]

Other Scottish societies, in addition to the Edinburgh Friends of the People, were strongly influenced by the Whig reformers. The Glasgow Associated Friends of the Constitution and of the People, the society of which Muir was a prominent member, strongly advocated cooperation with the London body. On 17 October 1792, several weeks after its establishment, this society voted its thanks to Charles Grey, while on 7 November the chairman and secretary wrote to the London association informing them of their existence, and declaring that they had been 'associated for the purpose of cooperating with the Friends of the People in London'.[136] Members had to sign resolutions to the effect that the society would cooperate with the London association in all proper measures to achieve an equal representation of the people in parliament and shorter parliaments. In late November, the Dundee Friends of the Constitution wrote to the Earl of Buchan about their existence and purpose. Buchan was a high-profile Scottish member of the Whig Association, albeit in an honorary capacity, and this is almost certainly the reason they wrote to him.[137]

What was distinctive, however, about the Scottish reformers' stance in late 1792 was less its constitutionalism – this, after all, was the predominant position of most British reformers and radicals before the mid 1790s, including members of the popular reform societies[138] – but the strength of their urge to appear moderate and peaceable. This could lead to some strange situations, and in retrospect seems doomed to failure, although the turn which events took in France and Europe – the establishment of Jacobin dictatorship, the Terror and British entry into the war against revolutionary France – which were to play such a major role in undermining the cause of reform, were not widely foreseen at the time. (As Philp has pointed out, radicals did know their historical destiny was to fail – indeed they thought otherwise; neither did their opponents know this.[139]) Yet their stance needs to be understood, first, in terms of a wish to maintain as inclusive a reform alliance as possible; there remained the possibility, or so they thought, of creating a broader alliance with the burgh and county reformers. Second, it was constructed against the background of a sharply polarizing political environment. In this context, the series of popular protests which broke out in Scotland in the late summer and autumn of 1792, some of which were referred to above, posed a further problem. Radicals' efforts to dissociate themselves from the protests, which included issuing resolutions in support of magistrates's efforts to maintain public order, almost certainly did nothing to allay the rising alarm and suspicions.[140]

The consequent pressures were only too apparent in the deliberations and actions of the first general convention of Scottish radicals, which met in Edinburgh in late 1792. The delegates set themselves the task of rebuffing unfair attacks on the movement from loyalists, as they saw them, and also trying to sustain the momentum which had built by late 1792. In order to continue the goal of being as inclusive as possible, calls for reform were kept deliberately general, although this was also a further step designed to align the movement with Whig reformers south of the border. To the same end, it was agreed to petition Parliament in conjunction with the Friends of the People in London.[141]

The unity which was achieved amongst Scottish reformers in late 1792 was limited and deceptive in several important ways; and tensions surfaced during the debates at the first general convention on a range of questions. In this context, considerable attention has been devoted in recent years to the response to an address from the Dublin United Irishmen. Written by William Drennan in, for him, typically emotionally-charged, vivid language, and appealing directly to nationalist aspirations to liberty, it was deemed by a majority of delegates, albeit a small one, to contain sedition and inappropriate nationalist overtures, but was strongly supported by Thomas Muir.[142] As significant, however, as the debates surrounding this address, and how to respond to it, are the hints of divided views about petitioning, with some country delegates wishing to see immediate action to maintain the momentum behind the reform campaign.[143] Fyshe Palmer was a proponent of immediate steps to draw up petitions for the same reason.[144] Behind these divisions were almost certainly currents of opinion not fully reflected in the decisions of the leadership of the Scottish radical campaign in late 1792, opinion which was less cautious and less willing to subordinate the Scottish movement to the needs and views of the London-based Whig Friends of the People.

There are other hints of the existence of these strands, although their significance is difficult to evaluate. Although a degree of rhetorical posturing was commonplace among radicals in this period, as referred to earlier, republican sentiments appear, nevertheless, to have been widely voiced in late 1792. William Peddie, a member of the Canongate Society of the Friends of the People, declared in late November that 'the Era of British Liberty' was approaching, even arguing that the outcome would be a republic, and that, in the event of civil war, British democrats could expect help from their French brothers.[145] Those responsible for voicing republican principles may not always have been members of radical societies, but, like Peddie, not all members of the societies were anx-

ious to follow a very cautious approach in late 1792. A proposal at a meeting of
Perth radicals to correspond with the French National Assembly in this period
was only narrowly defeated. As one informer reported: 'had it not been for one
or two of their more moderate members, who saw & represented the impropri-
ety of the measure a Resolution to that purpose would have been adopted'.[146]
From Glasgow, a year later, the Lord Provost warned Robert Dundas that the
views of the leadership of the radicals were not necessarily shared by the rank
and file, writing that he did not 'think the people here, have confidence in the
leaders of the party, although *I believe the general principles of it, have taken very
deep root, and are making daily progress*' (my emphasis).[147]

In this context, a number of ambiguities which ran through the reform
movement have added significance. These ambiguities were not necessarily self-
conscious, but they give Scottish radicalism in this period a protean character
which is not always recognized, but which again makes it more similar to radicalism south of the border than is sometimes acknowledged. Alongside the at times
near-comical defensiveness of those who met at the first general convention was
the attempt to put the principles of liberty into action. This was radicalism as the
actualization of liberty. Some of the commissions of delegates were addressed
to the 'Citizen president'.[148] The convention's chair was elected daily in order to
ensure that the deliberations were as open as possible. During the final session of
the convention, Thomas Muir

> Congratulated the Convention on the propriety of their conduct and the happy
> result of their deliberations. He particularly complimented them upon the free spirit
> of inquiry and jealous attention which had pervaded all their debates. They had paid
> no respect to the authority of leaders. They had not assented to a single clause in their
> various resolutions in compliance to great names. They had entered into the minutae
> of everything, and scrutinized every syllable before they gave it their consent, instead
> of tamely yielding their judgements to those of others. This was the true spirit of lib-
> erty which, now that it was fairly begun to be understood amongst his countrymen,
> he hoped would never cease till it became universal, and till every object they wished
> for was accomplished.[149]

Sometimes, any clear division between moderate reformers and radicals disap-
pears. It was Richard Fowler who moved that the convention should take the
French oath 'To live free or die'.[150] (This oath was prudently omitted from the
published minutes.) Fowler was one of the advanced Whigs who disappeared
from the radical cause in the spring of 1793, but his intervention is a further
reminder of the different voices in which reformers could talk on different occasions and in different contexts. When several delegates argued that petitioning
Parliament should be supported because its inevitable failure would open the
eyes of the people and thus further the cause of reform, they were loudly cheered;
this was a line of argument widely heard in radical circles south of the border.[151]

Muir's politics are more elusive than they first appear. While he seems to have been in touch from the summer or autumn of 1792 with the Dublin United Irishmen whose radicalism, even then, moved beyond the conservative reformism of the Whigs, he was a strong advocate of the alliance with the Whig Friends of the People.[152] At the same time, however, he was telling weaver radicals how reform would bring cheap government and lower taxes, and thus greater prosperity, precisely one of Paine's main messages. His ultimate ambitions for reform were also focused firmly on annual parliaments and universal suffrage.[153]

Contacts with English reform societies were not confined before the summer of 1793 to those with the Whig Association of the Friends of the People. The extent of these connections, which have been overlooked by most historians, is almost certainly not fully revealed in the extant sources, depending as they often did on personal initiative and contacts; nor is the origin of the relationship often revealed. The Glasgow reformers had links to the SCI. It was to this society, it will be recalled, that Walter Miller wrote from Perth in the summer of 1792 regarding the circulation in and around the city of the *Rights of Man*.[154] Scottish members of the SCI included Lord Daer, proposed by the veteran reformer Major Cartwright and seconded by Paine; Thomas Christie, son of William, the St Cyrus radical leader; and Dr William Maxwell, friend of Burns. The main point of contact seems, however, have been to Glasgow, a link facilitated by membership of the society by Lord Sempill. Sempill, a frequent attender of SCI meetings, proposed another of the leading propertied Glasgow reformers, Colonel William Dalrymple, as a member.[155] Sempill and Dalrymple were, along with Macleod, cashiered by the King on 3 December because of their connections to the Friends of the People and the reform movement in Scotland. It was through Sempill that various SCI resolutions and SCI-sponsored publications were distributed in and around Glasgow, including 400 copies of Paine's *Letter to Mr Secretary Dundas*.[156] On 21 December, the society agreed that its resolutions in response to the 'calumnies' of the loyalists, together with similar resolutions from the Manchester Constitutional Society, should be published in the Scottish newspapers, and to this end these were sent to Captain William Johnston, the leading Edinburgh reformer and proprietor of the *Edinburgh Gazetteer*, of whom more below.[157] Johnston was probably the source of a letter the society received from 'a most respectable correspondent' in Edinburgh regarding the trial of three journeymen there for allegedly seeking to suborn the loyalties of soldiers at the Castle. In response, it promised to 'take into serious consideration the state and circumstances of the judicial proceedings in Scotland'.[158] Links with the London Corresponding Society (LCS), meanwhile, were facilitated by Daer, who was a member of that body, as well as the SCI. It was to Daer that Thomas Hardy, Scottish-born secretary of the LCS, wrote in July 1792 asking for information about the spread of liberty north of the border.[159] Scottish influence in the LCS appears, initially at least, to have been considerable, reflecting the substantial Scottish artisan presence in London.[160] In the autumn of 1792 Walter Berry, the radical bookseller jointly responsible for publication of the *Caledonian Chronicle*, was introduced to a meeting of the LCS by Thomas Christie, another Scottish member. Hardy wrote, again in a letter to Daer, that the LCS had been 'highly pleased with the informations' that Berry had 'communicated' from Scotland. He went on:

> If you now judge it proper and have opportunity to promote a correspondence between any of the societies in Scotland and the London Corresponding Society it will tend to cement us together for by uniting we shall become stronger and a three-fold cord is not easily broken – It appears absolutely necessary by communicating with each other we shall know one another's mind and act with one heart in the same important cause.[161]

During the winter of 1792–3, letters to the LCS were forthcoming from Paisley, Edinburgh, Glasgow, Dundee and, more surprisingly perhaps, Banff.[162] There was also communication between the Sheffield Society for Constitutional Information and the Edinburgh radicals, although only fragments of this survive. The connection may well have been forged through the Sheffield radical periodical the *Patriot*, which was being sold in Edinburgh by Alexander Guthrie from April 1792.[163] In October 1792, the *Patriot*'s editor, Matthew Campbell Brown – whose name suggests Scottish origins or parentage – wrote to the LCS informing them of the recent upsurge in radical activity in Edinburgh. He also declared that the Sheffield radicals had been impressed by 'some most spirited communications' from Edinburgh, which led to the observation:

> We clearly foresee that Scotland will soon take the lead of this country, and conceive it will be necessary to take the greatest care that an universal communication should be constantly kept up between the several societies, however distant, and that all should determine to act upon the same principle, and move together, as near as may be, in regular and active unison.[164]

The correspondence continued during the spring and summer of 1793, when several further contacts were made between English and Scottish radical societies.[165]

These contacts are further evidence of the divergent tendencies within Scottish radicalism in its early phases, but also of the importance of connections between Scottish and English radicals well before the meeting of the British convention. It was Skirving, one of the main architects of the British convention, who at the first Scottish general convention proposed, although unsuccessfully, a series of far-reaching measures designed to achieve much closer and continuous cooperation and communication between the Scottish Friends of the People and their counterparts in London and England.[166]

Nationally, however, Scottish radicalism was, at least up until the summer of 1793, dominated by a leadership which was, whatever its divisions, and its capacity to speak in various voices, fundamentally cautious in its outlook, a stance in which it was confirmed by government repression and loyalist hostility. The Scottish radicals did not, for example, join in the congratulatory addresses to the French National Convention in late 1792 from the SCI and LCS, despite an invitation to do so from Hardy.[167] Representative of this cautious leadership was Captain William Johnston, a half-pay officer from the New Town who chaired the meeting at which the Edinburgh Friends of the People was founded on 26 July 1792, and who played a leading role in Edinburgh radical politics in the second half of 1792 and at the first general convention. Johnston was the proposer of two resolutions at a meeting of the Edinburgh general committee, which were adopted and widely published in Scottish and English newspapers, one of which declared that any person found guilty of involvement in rioting would be expelled from the Friends of the People.[168] As chairman of the convention, he led a delegation of the Friends of the People which attempted to sign, in the name of the convention, the Edinburgh loyalist resolutions.[169] He was also, as referred to above, the first proprietor of the *Edinburgh Gazetteer*. In this capacity, along with the paper's printer, he was prosecuted in early 1793 for a report in the *Gazetteer* of a High Court trial of three Edinburgh journeymen who were found guilty of attempting to suborn the political loyalties of soldiers at Edinburgh Castle. Found guilty of contempt, he was sentenced to three months' imprisonment and, on his release, had to find £500 surety for good behaviour for three years.[170] By the spring of 1793, he was anxious to divest himself of the paper and its attendant responsibilities, and on 2 April Alexander Scott assumed control of it. He appears to have been considering emigration to the United States, a route followed by several Scottish radicals and reformers in this period.[171] He made brief appearances at the third general and British conventions, but his role in radical politics by this stage was a minor one.[172] And while by 1793 he was a supporter of annual parliaments and universal suffrage, in a letter to Skirving he memorably described his political stance as one of 'intrepid moderation'.[173]

The loss in the spring and summer of 1793 of men such as Johnston, and also advanced Whigs such as Robert Fowler and John Morthland, as well as other propertied reformers, inevitably acted to change the character of the Scottish radical movement. The changes in trajectory and nature in the second half of 1793 also need to be seen, however, in the context of, first, the experience of and reactions to repression, and, second, the strong influence on Scottish radical politics of a small number of English and Irish radicals present in Edinburgh in the final months of 1793.

The heavy sentences handed down to Muir and Fyshe Palmer were, as referred to above, received with anger and shock by the radicals. The two men remained in Scotland until late 1793, the former in Edinburgh and the latter in Perth, where he had been tried before the circuit court, and their continued presence acted as a strong focus for radical discontent. Reports of reviving radical fortunes as a consequence, and rumours that an attempt was to be made to free him, led Robert Dundas at the end of the October to call for Muir to be transported to England sooner rather than later.[174] As early as the beginning of September, calls for his 'speedy removal' had been made by the capital's magistrates and members of the local loyalist association.[175] During the third and British conventions, deputations of delegates were dining daily with Muir. The third convention also sent congratulatory letters to both men, and opened a subscription to collect funds for their benefit.[176] Fyshe Palmer received regular visits in the Perth toll-booth from radicals on Tayside.[177] Just as importantly, the trials and sentencing of Muir and Fyshe Palmer were seen as part of a wider programme of repression and indeed suppression of radicalism which spanned the different parts of the British Isles in 1793. News of the Irish Convention Act, passed in the Irish Parliament in April, and which prohibited such assemblies, was widely seen in Scottish and British radical circles as a signal of similar measures to follow in Britain. The mood was increasingly one of crisis, of imminent confrontation between government and the radicals. The third and eventually British convention met against this background, and was conceived in part as a response to it.[178] The presence of the United Irishmen Simon Butler and Archibald Hamilton Rowan, as well as several English radicals, in Edinburgh in early November also served to increase awareness of the common interests and shared fate of radicals throughout the British Isles. Butler, who had just spent six months in prison in Ireland, spoke at length at the British convention about political conditions in his country, declaring that 'when a law like that [the Irish Convention Act] shou'd take place here – he was afraid freedom w.d vanish'.[179]

On the face of it, the actions of the British convention, before its suppression on 5–6 December, provide strong evidence of the hardening of radical views in response to the experience of repression and fears about imminent suppression. Steps were taken for convening a future emergency convention of British radicals should the government take measures which threatened the existence of liberty and therefore radicalism, possibly through the adoption of a convention bill in Britain. The adoption and publicization of French forms of address and organization based on those of the new French National Convention – through most obviously the creation of divisions, the singing of French revolutionary anthems, the addressing of one another as 'citizen', and the dating of its proceedings from 'the first year of the British Convention' – indicate an altogether less cautious stance than the one adopted a year earlier. As John Barrell has recently written: 'It invited the charge not only that it wished to introduce French and therefore republican principles of government but that it was thereby representing itself as a legislative, not a petitioning body'.[180]

It has been argued that the Scots were led into this new extremism by the English delegates – Maurice Margarot and Joseph Gerrald from the LCS, Charles Sinclair from the SCI and Matthew Brown from the Sheffield Society for Constitutional Information.[181] The arrival of Margarot, Gerrald and Sinclair in the Scottish capital in the first week of November galvanized the Scottish radicals, causing, in the first place, Skirving and the Edinburgh general committee to re-call the third convention for 19 November. Margarot and his English colleagues played crucial roles in guiding this reconvened convention to adopt several controversial measures and initiatives, notably the idea of the emergency convention, but also the organization of business into French-style divisions.[182] The reports they gave of levels of English support for radicalism were also much exaggerated, thereby giving the Scots a false notion of potential *British* radical strength. Margarot claimed that 'the societies in London were very numerous – tho sometimes fluctuating', continuing

> In some parts of England whole towns are reformers – Sheffield & environs there 50,000. In Norwich there are 30 societies in one. If we could get a Convention of England & Scotland called we might represent 6 or 7 hundred thousands males which is a majority of all the adults in the Kingdom & ministry w.d not dare to refuse us our Rights –[183]

The key question, however, in the present context is how far Margarot and the other English delegates were working with rather than against the grain of Scottish radicalism at this stage.

There is no simple answer to this question since the views of radicals remained quite diverse. Some were alienated by the trajectory of radical politics in late 1793, the turning away from the moderate stance which had characterized Scottish radical politics to that point. They included the Dundee Friends of the Constitution, for example, the more moderate and socially mixed of the two Dundee radical societies.[184] The need to continue to avoid confrontationalist tactics and 'violent measures' was urged on Skirving by several individuals prior to the meeting of the third convention.[185] On the other hand, even before the arrival of the English delegates, the Scottish radicals had finally declared unambiguously that the political reform sought was universal suffrage and annual parliaments. The vote on this at the third convention was unanimous, with several delegates arguing that this move would be strongly supported by their constituents.[186] The political views of those who made this decision had been confirmed, perhaps even transformed, by their experiences of radical politics, but also loyalist and government hostility. Their sense of injustice was more profound, their language more uncompromising. At the British convention, Mealmaker, referred to above, proposed an address to their fellow citizens expressing their grievances. For Mealmaker, reform was both an act of political purification, and a reinstatement of the people in their natural rights; it was the means to rescue people from the poverty and oppression which a corrupt and corrupted political system imposed upon them. Mealmaker was an elder in the Relief Church, and his politics seems to have been a peculiar mix of the moral and secular, universalist and national. Like several other radicals in late 1793, he looked too to the liberation of the highlands and highlanders from oppressive lairds and chiefs. His address was also evidence of how radicalism subsumed long-standing national grievances – the law of patronage, burgh misgovernment – within a more explosive ideological politics.[187] Another list of radical grievances from this time, drawn up by one of the divisions of the convention, ran to thirty-four items, and included the lack of proper provision for the education of the poor, which may well reflect the influence of Paine.[188]

Government repression, and fears about future repression, pushed radicals on to ever more ambiguous constitutional territory, as it did south of the border. While in some ways it is the continued adherence to prudent constitutionalism which stands out in the autumn of 1793 in the Scottish context – through, for example, the urging of radical supporters to avoid any disturbance in response to the news that Muir and Fyshe Palmer were to be removed to London, continued support for petitions to parliament in support of reform, and the preoccupation with demonstrating the constitutionality of their aims through insistence that they sought the recovery of ancient rights and the recommendation that the Bill of Rights be transcribed into every society's minute book – the duty to defend constitutional liberties in the face of despotic government and arbitrary courts was powerfully expressed.[189]

Union with their English counterparts, the other key aspect of the British convention, was also enthusiastically supported by Scottish radicals in late 1793. Plans for closer cooperation between radicals in different parts of Britain appear to have been widely discussed in the autumn of 1793. In mid-October, a meeting of the Fife radical societies advocated the establishment of committees of correspondence in different parts of Britain.[190] Around a month earlier, one radical wrote from Cromarty of the advantages which union promised to the cause. 'This union betwixt the two nations', he enthused, 'shall not, like the former [i.e. the Union of 1707] be effected by the distribution of sordid gold; but result from the genuine impulses of Patriotism, uniformly tending to one centre'.[191] When the proposal for union was made at the re-called third convention, it received unanimous support. One of the divisions, or 'sections', in which the delegates met in the mornings, drew up a document entitled 'Hints on the Question of Union'. The first of these hints read:

That the people of Great Britain (disclaiming every distinction of Scots & English) from this Period, & forever, doe unite themselves into one Mass, & in an Indissoluble Union, Bold appeal to this Island & to the Universe; that they demand the restoration of the Rights, from which demand they shall never depart.

In order to achieve this end, the division recommended that delegates from national conventions in England and Scotland meet twice yearly on the banks of the River Tweed. This would be a symbolic meeting place 'where the Ashes of their Ancestors now Lye', ancestors who had been condemned to die because of the 'caprice of the few in the Paltry Feuds of Court Etiquette'. It was also suggested that a weekly communication be opened up between 'South' and 'North' either by letter or in person so that 'Occurrences maybe known from one end of the Kingdom to the other' in order to 'strengthen & instruct every individual of this great but one indivisible Mass'.[192]

The suppression by the authorities of the British convention and subsequent trials for sedition of Margarot, Sinclair, Gerrald and Skirving marked the end of the open phase of radicalism in Scotland in the 1790s. It also drove some Scottish radicals to contemplate insurrection as the only means to rescue or continue to pursue the radical cause. This is not the place to review in exhaustive detail the murky events and plotting which lay behind the so-called Pike Plot of 1794, in which former spy Robert Watt played a key role.[193] What is worth emphasizing is the level of alienation and resentment which was current amongst radicals at this time, however much it was, ultimately, also a response to political impotency. In January 1794, a handbill appeared in Perth, which declared, in the light of the suppression of the British convention, 'Behold the era of an important revolution is at last come ... shall we be free or shall we be slaves'.[194] In April, radical graffiti appeared on the bridge at Perth, including the words 'Britain must be a republic, liberty and equality'.[195] From Montrose, the spring and early summer brought reports of alienation and provocative language, at least in private, from radicals.[196] From Ayrshire, James Wodrow was similarly convinced of the 'sullen discontent' of the 'tradesmen and manufacturers', even regarding the current 'spirit of disaffection' as considerably more dangerous that the 'open petulance about reform' which had given rise to the initial alarm in the autumn of 1792. As he went on:

> ... the meer Mob have certainly imbibed levelling principles to a higher degree than ever. I know before and by any thing I can learn their attachment to the French still continues & what is surprising in those who had a considerable sense of religion & the French cruelty & open impiety makes little empression to their prejudice chiefly for this reason their friends are resolved not to believe this or anything at all to their disadvantage.[197]

A few months later, Wodrow was remarking that the 'spirit of discontent' had 'almost universally seized the great bodies of our sectaries & not a few of the lower manufacturers in the establishment'. A French invasion, he urged, could precipitate an 'explosion'.[198]

Among the authorities, there was particular concern about Paisley and the surrounding area, the economy of which had been hard hit by the economic downturn in 1793, and where opposition to the war seems to have imparted a strong socio-economic dimension to radical views.[199] In early December 1793, the Sheriff of Renfrewshire committed three weavers and a grocer to Paisley prison for drinking toasts in a tavern club, which were reported to be 'Confusion to H M arms by sea and land'; 'Confusion to the *Duke* of York [commander of British forces on the continent at this point]'; 'Confusion "all aristocrats"'; and 'Success to the French and British in all lawful undertakings'.[200] In January 1794, Margarot visited the town, sparking an upsurge of further concern in ruling circles. What was happening in the town at this stage is almost entirely hidden from view, and the only source we have is an account of his expenses drawn up by the Sheriff Depute of Renfrewshire later that year for the Sheriff Clerk.[201] From this source, it appears that Margarot's visit either coincided with or led to an open-air meeting of a 'great body' of people. In response, warrants were issued for the arrest of three individuals – Archibald Hastie, whom we met earlier, William Mitchell and James Smith – who had been most active in the meeting. In May, the authorities received information about the presence of 'daggers, bayonets and other lethal weapons', and of 'considerable numbers' of people assembling in military array. This led to a proclamation being drawn up and pasted around Paisley and other local towns prohibiting such assemblies. A warrant was issued for the arrest of James Colms, a weaver from Kilbarchan, said to have played an 'active part' in this affair. A search was made in the manufacturing village of Neilston for concealed arms. Mention is also made of military arrays in Neilston and one other manufacturing village, Barhead. Meanwhile, several weavers from Paisley were arrested for drinking seditious toasts and for seeking to suborn soldiers from their duty. John Finlayson was alleged to have 'declared that he would for a penny cut off His Majesty's head'. Their arrest led, in turn, to a meeting in the High Church, Paisley, where resolutions were taken to liberate those arrested. The authorities responded by stationing the military the keep the peace in the town. Robert Reid, an ironmonger, was said to have concerted measures for the liberation of two of the arrested radicals at the home of another radical. James Kennedy, a Paisley radical who had been assistant secretary to the British convention, fled Edinburgh following the discovery of the Pike Plot, turning up in London, where, through the radical bookseller Daniel Isaac Eaton, he published a volume of poems which bear the unmistakable and heavy imprint of Paineite ideology.[202] (Eaton's bookshop seems to have acted as a magnet to quite a few Scottish radicals who sought refuge in the British capital in this period.[203]) Kennedy had close links to several of the individuals involved in the meetings of the spring of 1794, notably William Mitchell, and Kennedy may well be the unnamed Scottish radical who, visiting a meeting of the LCS in June 1794, was described in a spy report as a 'violent democrat'. This individual talked, apparently, of 'the Scotch to be in great force, and resolved in obtaining a reform and redress of their grievances, that would long ago have proceeded to violent measures, but had been induced to wait from favourable reports they had heard of the London Corresponding Society ....'[204]

Talk of arming may have been quite widespread in these months, and not just in Paisley. From Dundee, following the British convention, an informant described Mealmaker as a 'daring, dangerous fellow'. Mealmaker and fellow radicals in the town were apparently openly boasting about plans to 'try their strength'.[205] In February, Dundee radicals were reported to be 'commissioning pistols from Sheffield, with daggers and bayonets concealed in them, which upon touching a spring started out.'[206] From Perth, Walter Miller was accused of commissioning 'Guns and Bayonets from Birmingham'.[207] In East Lothian, there were widespread rumours of a rising to coincide with the King's birthday (4 June) in 1794.[208] Just how much of this activity was coordinated, or connected to the plans emerging from Edinburgh, in which Robert Watt was a central figure, is elusive, although we do know that Watt sent emissaries to Paisley and Dundee in early 1794, amongst other places, and that several radicals in Perth were implicated in the so-called Pike Plot.[209] At the same time, certainly not all radical activity was focused on such plans, and radicals in several places, as our unnamed 'violent democrat' referred to, looked to the LCS for leadership and direction, responding positively to calls from the London body to elect delegates to a new emergency convention in the spring of 1794.[210] Equally, it is clear that talk was not the same thing as capability. The same informant who warned of Mealmaker's 'daring' words noted that, currently, Mealmaker and his allies had 'no arms'.[211] The authorities executed various searches for arms in the spring of 1794, but none were found apart from those which were accidentally discovered as a result of the bankruptcy of Robert Orrock, an Edinburgh blacksmith. A search of Walter Miller's premises in Perth, for example, revealed only five 'fowling pieces'.[212] In Edinburgh, there were occasional confrontations between the authorities and radicals in the first half of 1794 – for example, at the theatre in April, and during the trials arising from the British convention – but these were relatively minor.[213] The radical societies, meanwhile, in the capital and elsewhere, seem to have largely collapsed between the end of 1793 and the early months of 1794, although small numbers of radicals were still meeting privately or in 'sections' to avoid detection.[214]

Building a Radical Platform

The failure of the radicals in Scotland and indeed elsewhere in Britain to achieve their political goals can seem inevitable, and historians have not been slow to identify weaknesses in the radical campaign.[215] Yet the challenges which the radicals came up against in their efforts to build a new sort of politics and a political organization which might sustain their campaign and realize their ambitions were formidable. This would have been so, moreover, if they had not faced the intense official hostility and repression and the onslaught from organized and spontaneous loyalism which they did.

At first glance, however, through the conventions, Scottish radicals seem to have achieved a degree of unity and coordination which was unmatched south of the border, and perhaps in Ireland before the mid to later 1790s, although first the SCI and then the LCS did exercise some strategic direction over many English radical societies from 1792. This achievement may well have been as much apparent as real, however. In so far as there was central direction, it was a function mainly of the dominance of Edinburgh within Scottish radicalism, and the fact that, as the country's natural political centre, the capital hosted the conventions of the Friends of the People. Edinburgh's influence on the radical movement only increased during 1793–4 as demoralization and lack of money took its toll on radical societies elsewhere in the country. To some extent this dominance was also reflected in organizational form. Presiding over Edinburgh radicalism was a general committee, formed prior to the first general convention, and comprised of the secretary of the Edinburgh Friends of the People and the presidents and secretaries of the various societies in and around the capital. When the conventions were not sitting, the general committee, together with the Edinburgh finance committee, seems to have been given or assumed responsibility for the movement as a whole.[216] In October 1793, prior to the third general convention, the Edinburgh general committee established a committee of correspondence to communicate with other societies.[217] It was also this committee which was deputed by the third convention to collect the views of other societies and, from these, draw up an address to the public.[218] William Skirving's influential role in Scottish radical politics in 1793 reflected his role as chairman of the general committee.

The model for this kind of central organization or coordination was almost certainly the burgh and county reform campaigns, and beyond that the annual meeting of the Convention of the Royal Burghs. Conventions of delegates from the burghs or counties tended to meet in Edinburgh twice yearly, precisely the arrangement followed by the radicals. Thomas Hardy was to use, as part of his defence in his treason trial in 1794, the fact that Robert Dundas had been present at a convention of county reformers in Edinburgh in December 1792 in rebuttal of the idea that a convention was necessarily an instrument of revolution.

Centralization only went so far, however. The first general convention explicitly recognized the right of 'individual societies to regulate their own internal order'.[219] Resistance to too much centralization was evident also in the rejection of a proposal at this same convention for a central publications committee.[220] And while the Edinburgh finance committee was given responsibility for control of national finances, 'districts' were expected to establish their own finance committees which would communicate with the central one.[221] In 1793, as the radicals looked to renew their campaigning in preparation for the third general convention, there appears to have been considerable discussion about organizational renewal, although the motivation behind this was mainly financial. The Friends of the People were in debt, and few funds were coming in from outside the capital, partly because of the effects of the economic depression referred to in an earlier section of this chapter.[222] Several suggestions were forthcoming to increase the flow of monies to the centre, including one which was adopted, that members of societies should make half-yearly payments which would be collected by delegates and brought to the conventions.[223] At the same time, there was recognition of the need to achieve greater unity, if only as a means of survival in the face of government and loyalist repression. On 1 November, it was resolved to recommend that societies 'in the country to hold frequent intercourse with each other and to meet at stated periods for that purpose'. A proposal at the British convention was to divide the country into sections or 'departments' and to appoint provincial conventions.[224]

Such proposals almost certainly reflected a reality of sporadic and uneven coordination between societies beyond the capital. In several places – Perth, Paisley, Glasgow and Stirling – societies were confederated as they were in Edinburgh. In Glasgow, as numbers increased new branches were set up which sent monthly reports to the central society and delegates to a convention of local associations. How regularly the convention met is not known. The central society had a Committee of Direction which initially met weekly.[225] The Edinburgh general committee performed the same function as the convention of local associations in Glasgow. This federal or confederal structure may have been copied from English societies, notably the Sheffield Society for Constitutional Information, which Scottish radicals would have read about in print. County conventions met in Fife and Renfrewshire, while the Edinburgh radicals also met in conventions.[226] In Dundee, however, the two radical societies remained quite separate. It is also probable that, in Perth and Stirling, the federated structures collapsed fairly quickly, probably some time in the spring of 1793.

As important, however, as organizational arrangements in achieving a sense of unity between radical societies was face-to-face communication between radicals from different places, but this is what has left least record. As referred to earlier, George Mealmaker appears to have travelled quite widely in this period, meeting with radicals in different part of Angus, Fife and the north-east. Muir did likewise in and around Glasgow before his arrest. Dundee and Perth radicals appear to have cooperated in various ways in the early 1790s, while Dundee radical ministers appear to have had an influence well beyond the town.[227]

Print constituted another important bridge or link between the radical societies across Scotland and indeed Britain. This helps to explain the importance which the radicals placed on maintaining the *Edinburgh Gazetteer* in existence in late 1793, a subject which was discussed at length at the third and British conventions.[228] The first general convention published 15,000 copies of its minutes for circulation to the societies, as well as throughout Scotland.[229] The minutes of the second convention were printed in the *Caledonian Chronicle,* and those of the British convention in the *Edinburgh Gazetteer*.[230] When Mealmaker, Fyshe Palmer and the Dundee Friends of Liberty issued their anti-war handbill in July 1793, the design was very specifically to circulate it to every radical society in Scotland. As Fyshe Palmer wrote to Skirving on 9 July 1793: 'We want a copy to be sent to all the societies of the friends of the people'.[231] In the autumn of 1793, Skirving was proposing publication of a monthly periodical as part of the proposals to renew the unity and organization of the radical movement.[232]

In their efforts to exploit print's potential as a medium of communication and instruction, the radicals again came up against the problem of lack of money. As we saw in the previous chapter, the financial condition of the *Edinburgh Gazetteer* was precarious and the third and British conventions could do nothing to tackle this, apart from urging fellow radicals to pay up their subscriptions.[233] Several pamphlets were distributed through the radical societies. In the case of an account of the parliamentary speeches on Grey's motion of 6 May, which ran to a hundred pages in octavo format, societies were offered one pamphlet free for every six that they purchased.[234] The relatively high cost of a pamphlet account of the trial of Fyshe Palmer acted as a major deterrent to its purchase by societies. As James Brown wrote from Glasgow: 'It is but few people that are disposed could they afford it, to pay so high for such publications ...'.[235] This issue of expense lay behind a proposal, emanating from Glasgow, that the radicals look to publish cheap pamphlets on coarse paper to disseminate their message.[236] Several collections were made at the third convention to help defray the costs of publishing 'tracts on the subject of reform'.[237] There were also calls for measures to be adopted for 'instructing the people at large' in proper political principles.[238] Such calls probably reflected a perception that much needed to be done, and that little had yet been done. In 1795 George Mealmaker was to write about the cost of propaganda as a significant obstacle to the circulation of the radical message in a letter to the LCS.[239] The fact that most Scottish newspapers were, from late 1792, hostile to the radicals only magnified the difficulties they faced in this context. Cheapness also helps to explain, together with relative immunity from suppression owing to the ease and secrecy of their production, the importance of handbills, written as well as printed, as a form of communication and publicity on the part of Scottish radicals in this period.[240]

Radical politics exploded spectacularly into life in Scotland in late 1792. Having erupted so dramatically, however, and extended its reach into many different communities, especially in manufacturing regions, it was relatively quickly suppressed or driven underground. Historians have explained this collapse in terms of several factors – social and economic, as well as political. Crucial was the timing of the emergence of the societies, and the circumstances in which they were founded. In late 1792, faced with what seemed to be a very threatening conjunction of domestic and international political conditions, the propertied classes began, in quick order, to close ranks in defence of the existing political and social order, or to dissociate themselves from the kind of politics represented by the new radical societies. This meant, amongst other things, that the radicals were denuded of potential leadership almost as soon as the societies came into existence. This process of political polarization occurred elsewhere in the British Isles, but probably nowhere as rapidly or as starkly as in Scotland. While France was sliding into violent mob rule – 'mobocracy' as Horace Walpole described it – so Scotland appeared to many to have its own 'Jacobin' mob in late 1792. The emotions on which the radical movement was launched were also inherently unstable. Political talk in late 1792 spread not just well beyond the traditional political nation, but was infused with a license to re-imagine in their entirety political and social life. The ruling elites sensed this mood, and were genuinely very frightened by the frenzy of political speculation which they often only dimly apprehended around them. Yet the hopes unfettered in late 1792 made the task of leadership of Scottish radicalism all the more difficult, and it was in respect of leadership that it was weakest.

Poor leadership derived from inexperience – reform politics of the kind which emerged in 1792 were new to Scotland – but also divisions, divisions which again are traceable to the circumstances and timing of the movement's emergence. The advanced Whigs and burgh reformers who largely directed the early phases of the reform campaign were cautious, conservative reformers, looking to modest reform as the best means to prevent revolution or deflect popular demands for more fundamental reforms. What many of them also sought was a movement firmly subordinate to the needs of Grey and the Whig reformers in Parliament. There was no coordinated attempt to exploit the downturn and hardships created by British entry into the war against revolutionary France because the advanced Whigs saw or feared this as a diversion from their central goal. When Fyshe Palmer proposed issuing resolutions opposing the war at a meeting of the Edinburgh general committee, he was rebuffed, hence perhaps his enthusiasm for circulating the anti-war handbill approved by the Dundee

Friends of Liberty to radical societies across Scotland.[241] Such tensions and divisions added to a creeping demoralization which rapidly overtook the radicals from the beginning of 1793. It was also why the role of men such as Macleod and Daer was so critical in providing advice and direction, as well as connections to leading reform and radical societies south of the border.

Were Scottish radicals weaker, more cautious and more moderate than their counterparts elsewhere in the British Isles? In terms of numerical strength, at least in late 1792 the radicals probably commanded a support more or less similar to that which obtained south of the border, and from a significant smaller population. Where England was different in this context was in the resilience of London radicals and, to a slightly lesser extent, those of Sheffield and Norwich. English radicals also seem to have gained strength and numbers in 1794–5 from adverse economic conditions in a way that Scottish radicals did not in 1793–4. Explaining this difference is hard, although weak leadership and recent experience of sharp wage rises must provide part of the explanation. Demoralization and declining support in 1793 was not solely a Scottish phenomenon. A similar trend was evident in the Dublin United Irishmen, as well as smaller English provincial societies vulnerable to repression, particularly at the leadership level, and to loyalist hostility and pressures from 'above' to disavow radical politics. Constitutionalism and commitment to peaceful means to achieve reform were also key features of radicalism throughout the British Isles before 1794–5, with the probable exception of Ireland, although the militancy of the United Irishmen before 1795 is the subject of vigorous debate amongst Irish historians.[242] It was the SCI which resolved in December 1792, in the face of loyalist propaganda to the contrary: 'That this Society disclaims the idea of wishing to effect a change in the present system of things by violence and public commotion ...'.[243] Nevertheless, most Scottish radicals seem to have been less sceptical than many of their English and certainly Irish counterparts about the intentions and trustworthiness of parliamentary reformers, and less alienated from current structures of government, although warning notes were sounded. This was one reason why Scotland featured so heavily in the petitioning campaign in support of Grey's reform motion of 6 May 1793. Even in late 1793, when repression was forcing them to contemplate the right and duty of armed resistance in defence of their liberties, there remained a commitment to petitioning Parliament as the only constitutional means of achieving their goals, at least in the short term; and there was continued hope that petitions could be drawn up in such a way as to prevent their summary rejection, as had happened to some of them in the spring of 1793. Not that everyone was convinced, however, as disclosed by support at the third convention for an address to the King as the better means of realizing their goals.[244] Around this same time, Thomas Noble quoted Lord Kames in support of a view of Parliament as a legislature of landowners which sought to keep

down the burden of land tax while burdening the 'common people'.[245] In the
longer term, radical aims would be realized by a revolution in public understanding and knowledge. Constitutionalism was not abandoned by the Scots, at least
before the suppression of the British convention. After this event, many appear
to have given up the cause, if they had not already done so, while among those
who remained committed and active stances became more ambiguous, and certainly some – probably a small minority – were prepared to talk about, and, in a
few cases, plan for, insurrection.

Like their counterparts elsewhere in the British Isles, the Scottish radicals
were also a diverse group, and this cautions against over-generalization. Indeed,
the Scottish reform movement as it emerged in late 1792 has been described as
an 'uneasy alliance' of advanced Whigs, burgh reformers, dissenting ministers,
shopkeepers, tradesmen and the skilled labouring classes.[246] About the views of
some of these groups we know very little, even assuming they were uniform or
broadly similar, which they may well not have been. The precise contribution
of religion to radicalism is elusive, as we began to see in Chapter 1. Opposition
to patronage was frequently voiced, although this was as much a political as a
religious concern.[247] Some dissenting ministers may well have been prominent
in the movement by virtue of their education and the authority which came
from ministering to a congregation; they also had the resources to attend conventions in a way many artisans did not. A somewhat patronizing view of the
abilities and judgement of many of these artisans may lie behind the Revd James
Donaldson's proposal at the third convention that the secretary 'recom.d to the
various societies to send up those gent.n as Delegates who are most able for that
station.'[248] Ironically, Donaldson was a former shoemaker. For some, religious
theology did, in Jim Smyth's phrase, 'transmute into political ideology', although
direct evidence on this is slight.[249] Mealmaker was an elder in the Relief Church,
and one of several proponents at the third convention of calling a day of fasting
to solicit God's favour for their cause, but the historical record of his opinions
tells us little about the relationship between religion and his politics. Apart from
this, there are hints of religious influence and inspiration among the records
of speeches of radical delegates. The informer 'J.B.' reported William Skirving
as arguing, in a debate in the Edinburgh general committee on who should be
given the vote, that all government was 'derived from God' as a 'Law of Faith and
Love'.[250] Millenarian views were occasionally expressed, but only occasionally.
James Tytler, who fled Scotland in 1793, seems to have written a millenarian
tract which he published in exile in the United States.[251] Radicals could easily
equate political with moral and spiritual reform; political reform, in this view,
was an integral aspect of wider moral reform. The concept of elect nationhood
was deeply rooted in the Presbyterian tradition, and it is unsurprising to see it
drawn upon in support of a vision of liberty restored and a reformed polity and

society. Nor was this without precedent, as the writings of James Burgh, a British and Scottish radical from an earlier era, can illustrate. Significantly, the Dundee relief minister Neil Douglas republished Burgh's earliest political tract, a call to reform from the crisis of 1745–6, in 1792 as an appendix to a poem urging for a new campaign of moral reform to rescue the nation from its current dangers, as Douglas perceived them. For Douglas, political reform was instrumental, not an end in itself, and it is perhaps not so surprising that in the later 1790s his vision of a nation uncorrupt was being sought, not through political reform, but by membership of the newly formed missionary societies. Douglas is the only minister who was a member of a radical society who has left a significant body of writing from which to reconstruct his views, however.

Conservatives regularly associated dissent with support for radicalism, as did, on occasion individuals of independent views, such as James Wodrow.[252] Nevertheless, it seems likely that this was often as much symptomatic of the stark polarization of opinion after late 1792 as a reflection of any accurate appraisal of opinion among the various strands of dissent. As we saw in Chapter 1, officially the dissenting churches sought to keep out of the 'political muddle', as one dissenter put it in 1792.[253] In September 1794, the Glasgow burghers held a day of fasting and humiliation in which people were enjoined to 'fear God, honour the King, and lead quiet and peaceable lives in godliness and honesty'.[254] In the political conditions of the 1790s, and with the new and intense demands to demonstrate publicly their loyalty, such a stance inevitably drew suspicion upon them. Passivity was often construed as alienation, if not disaffection.

If the extent, therefore, of religion's influence on Scottish radical views remains uncertain, conclusions about the attitudes of those amongst the labouring classes who were drawn into radical politics in the early 1790s must also be tentative owing to gaps in the evidence. Views current among this group were, nevertheless, almost certainly more populist and often Paineite than some historians suppose, although direct confirmation of this is slight. Artisans may well not have read Paine primarily as a republican, but rather as an advocate of cheap government and lower taxes. Those who remained within the ranks of the radicals during 1793 and beyond had their view sharpened by the experience of involvement in radical politics and the hostility they encountered from loyalists. It was from such individuals that the United Scotsmen recruited from 1796–7, and their views and political goals may well have changed very little between the two periods.

Most Scottish radicals, finally, were British or even Anglo-British radicals who happened to be Scots, and to this extent their history is one which is best viewed in a British context. They were, and saw themselves, as members of a cause that transcended nation, but which looked to nations (in this case Britain) as the vehicles of political, moral and social regeneration. Being British radicals meant, for most, more than eschewing a nationalistic outlook, it meant looking to union as the means of achieving reform. Union was at the core of Scottish radical strategy from the inception of the movement, as the establishment of the link to the Whig Association of the Friends of the People showed. This was partly a reflection of the need for strategic direction; partly it was also a consequence of the conviction that unity of sentiment amongst the 'people' was the only real means of delivering the hoped-for reform; and by 'people' was naturally meant the people of Britain of whom the Scots were a part. For some, perhaps, the early 1790s presented an opportunity to eclipse the Union of 1707, to produce a genuine union bred of shared goals and attitudes; a people's union, in short, and not a corrupt bargain between elites. The British convention was the high point of this tendency to look for cooperation and unity with radicals in England, but it was a culmination and continuation of something, not an isolated episode, as we have seen. Being British or Anglo-British in outlook also reflected just how steeped Scottish radicals were in English radical ideology. To this extent, the languages in which they constructed their politics were borrowed ones, but they were also ones which it was natural for them to adopt as 'North Britons'. Indeed, being British came more naturally to them than to many English radicals. It was, after all, James Burgh who first advocated the idea of a convention of the people as the crucial means to achieve parliamentary reform. It was also two Scots, one in Edinburgh and one in London – William Skirving and Thomas Hardy – who were the principal architects of the British convention of 1793.

4 CHECKING THE RADICAL SPIRIT

Prior to the autumn of 1792, there was limited concern amongst the Scottish ruling classes and propertied society about the domestic impact of the French Revolution and, from the summer of that year, the rise of a domestic parliamentary reform movement. The King's birthday riots in Edinburgh between 4 and 6 June were met by a thorough investigation of their possible causes, but no clear link to the Revolution or reformers was found.[1] When the 'Friends of the French Revolution' met in Edinburgh on 14 July, there was no special alarm, although the Sheriff noted that the authorities would not 'fail ... to be on our Guard'.[2] Even the formation of the first Scottish parliamentary reform societies in July and August – in Edinburgh, Glasgow and Perth – appears not to have caused any marked change in attitudes or mood. The Royal Proclamation of 1 May against seditious writings did not produce an overwhelming response in the form of loyal addresses from Scots.[3] Between October and November, however, as we have seen in previous chapters, a dramatic and sudden change took place in political life in Scotland and in attitudes and emotions. Against the background of the creation of a republic in France, the marked intensification of political violence in that country, which reached a ghastly climacteric with the notorious September massacres in Paris and the outbreak of war on the continent, and the widespread circulation of cheap editions of Paine's *Rights of Man*, new radical societies sprang up in large numbers across lowland Scotland, particularly in the fast-growing manufacturing regions.[4] If this were not sufficient cause for concern, in the summer and autumn a succession of popular disturbances broke out.

The prevailing mood among the elites in the final months of 1792 was jittery and alarmist. In Edinburgh, the Lord Advocate, Robert Dundas, was inundated with letters from different parts of the country conveying the profound concern of the elites and, on occasion, their near panic about the activities of supposed 'emissaries of sedition' in their neighbourhoods.[5] Rumour and hearsay, and often a paucity of solid information, fuelled the sense of alarm. From Glasgow, Allan Maconockie informed the Lord Advocate: 'their [the reformers] secretary told a Gentleman this morning that in a month they w[oul]d have 50,000 subscriptions – and that if the Ministry did not agree to their Resolutions they might <u>stand</u>

for the consequences'.[6] George Home of Wedderburn was convinced that 'many People' were determined to bring about a revolution similar to that in France in Scotland, dramatically describing Edinburgh as having become 'the Paris of Scotland'.[7] The events of the autumn were also witnessed by Henry Dundas, from the summer of that year Home Secretary and as such responsible for domestic order and security throughout Britain, who was then on a visit to his native country. In October, he aborted a trip to a meeting of the Perth Hunt in anticipation of popular demonstrations against him. In the event, the protests went ahead anyway, and he was burnt in effigy in the town, as well as in several places nearby (Scone and Crieff).[8] According to one historian, the Home Secretary returned to London convinced of the reality of a 'Scottish insurrection',[9] a notion which formed a central plank in the defence of the government's repressive policies in the Commons in the winter of 1792–3, although such a portrayal of events in late 1792 was ridiculed by several opposition Whigs, including Norman Macleod.[10]

It was also while he was in Scotland that Henry Dundas formulated, or helped to formulate, the authorities' response to the emergent radical threat north of the border. This response was described in a letter from Dundas to William Pitt, the Prime Minister, written from Arniston House, home of his nephew, Robert, on 12 November.[11] Identifying Edinburgh, Glasgow, Paisley, Perth, Dundee, Montrose and Aberdeen as the 'great scenes of attempts to do mischief in this country',[12] Dundas explained that he was concerting measures in the Scottish capital with the Sheriff, Provost and crown lawyers. He was also talking to leading magistrates in Glasgow. As yet, he had not spoken to anyone from beyond the two main cities, but he was planning to talk to others, including sheriffs, in the coming days. Dundas was clear that an effective response would involve measures to watch and guard against the radicals, through spies (although they were not specifically referred to), but also attempts to win back the loyalties of the lower orders. Key to the peace of the country were the clergy. This reflected, in Dundas's view, the importance of popular adherence to religion. Newspapers should be won over. Meanwhile, while the present 'fermentation of the people's minds' continued, the military establishment should be strengthened, while tax reductions on necessities should, if necessary, be sought. This emphasis on military force as the final guarantor of order was reiterated a week or so later, when Dundas called for five regiments to be posted at Perth, Dundee and Montrose, the 'seats of sedition'.[13]

Dundas was a British politician, and the campaign to extinguish the Scottish radical threat was a dimension of a British-wide strategy of political repression. The royal proclamations against seditious writings of May and December 1792 covered Britain. The establishment of barracks in manufacturing and other strategically-positioned towns, which was first discussed in the autumn of 1792 and which began to be implemented in 1794, was a natural extension of a policy introduced in England in June 1792.[14] The courts throughout Britain and Ireland were used to decapitate the radical movement and intimidate the radical press. As John Barrell has shown in his authoritative investigation of shifting conceptions of treason in the 1790s, *Imagining the King's Death*, definitions of treason, and strategies of repression, were worked out in courts throughout Britain.[15] Not for the last time, Scotland was in effect a laboratory for measures and arguments which would later be applied, or sought to be applied, to England. Radicals were, with reason, utterly convinced that repression in the different parts of Britain and Ireland were elements of a single political strategy. Muir and Fyshe Palmer were, although this is not how they are usually remembered, British (not Scottish) radical martyrs.[16] The suppression of the British convention in early December 1793 was a move against radicals in England as well as Scotland, and events in Scotland featured strongly in the 'discovery' of the well-laid international plot to turn Britain into a republic, laid bare in the widely-circulated and much-quoted first and second Commons secret committee reports on treasonable activity of 1794.[17] The suspension of habeas corpus in the spring of that year was matched by the suspension of the 'act anent wrongous imprisonment' (1701) for Scotland. New repressive statutes – notably the Seditious Meetings Act and Treasonable Practices Act of 1795, but also changes to stamp duty on newspapers (1789, 1794 and 1797), and later legislation against unlawful oaths (1797) and the registration of printers and publishers (1799) – were British in conception and application, although the Gagging Acts were primarily aimed against the London Corresponding Society. It was a Scot, John Bruce, who appears to have compiled the precedents for the changes to the treason laws.[18] There was coordination in other ways, in terms, for example, of watching the activities of radicals. In June 1794, following information received from Robert Dundas, the London magistrate Richard Ford was having George Ross, who had fled south following his indictment for treason, watched; he was also confident that another Scottish radical who had fled to the capital, James Kennedy, would be apprehended in a few days.[19] As was the case south of the border, the effectiveness of the authorities' efforts relied on the cooperation of local authorities and, as importantly, the mobilization of a supportive, intimidatory loyalist opinion. Repression and persuasion were not so much different tactics as complementary strands of a single political intent.

This chapter will not describe in great detail the unfolding campaign of repression, although it will sketch its principal elements. Much has been written, for example, about the famous radical trials of 1793–4, and controversy continues, without any sign of resolution, on the issue of whether the legal system was abused to crush the radicals.[20] Rather, in keeping with the central themes of this book, the main focus will be on two aspects. The first is the similarities and differences, as well as interactions, between loyalism and repression in Scotland and their counterparts in England and Wales. Second, the emergence and creation of loyal opinion amongst the wider Scottish population will be closely examined.

To date, little has been written about this, although it has not prevented some strong claims for the breadth and depth of loyalism north of the border.[21] The chapter concentrates on the period between 1792 and 1794 when radicalism existed as an open, mainly constitutional force.

Repression

Dundas's letter of 12 November spoke of the need to maintain a close watch on radical meetings; once the true nature of their activities had been established, proper measures could be taken to counteract them. The authorities, as elsewhere in Britain, relied very heavily on local officials to keep them informed about radical meetings and activities. How widely spies and informers were used is unclear. Paid spies appear to have been few, although extant secret service accounts for Scotland in this period are frustratingly opaque.[22] The most important informer used by Robert Dundas in Edinburgh was 'J.B.', whose identity to this day remains a mystery. He provided very detailed reports on the discussions which took place in radical meetings in and around Edinburgh, including the three general conventions of Scottish radicals. Between late 1792 and early 1793, Dundas also took into pay Robert Watt, an Edinburgh wine merchant. Watt had contacted Dundas in the late summer of 1792, but already by the spring of 1793 his services were dispensed with, seemingly because he was beginning to make unreasonable and suspect demands for payments, but also probably because he was no longer providing valuable information.[23] Outside the capital, Robert Graham of Fintry, Scottish Commissioner of Excise, was employing informers in and around Dundee in late 1792, presumably in response to the tree of liberty riots of November of that year. Within the town, the key figure in this network was John Fyffe, son of wealthy returnee from Jamaica, David Fyffe of Drumgeith. Fyffe's efforts were to be repaid by finding him a lieutenancy in the Royal Navy. In 1797, he appears to have acted as a government informer during the naval mutinies at Nore and Spithead.[24] James Mitchell, a local excise officer, also had an informer at work in late 1793. This individual was spying, through a wooden partition, on radicals, including George Mealmaker, meeting privately in a room in the upper part of a house in the Overgate. Mitchell reported, however, that his informer was likely to be discovered soon.[25] Another informer used by Graham of Fintry was Montrose innkeeper Susan Bean. Bean sent her reports by private carrier to Arbroath to escape detection, although by 1794 it appears that her political sympathies were public knowledge and thus radicals were avoiding her tavern.[26] I have come across no direct evidence of paid spies being employed in the west, for example in Glasgow and Paisley, although it is certain that magistrates in these and several other places used informers.

In the later 1790s, the authorities had few sources of information about the clandestine United Scotsmen, although one Jamieson, an LCS agent, was tracked, detained and turned in 1797.[27] This absence of informers partly reflected the extent of organized radicalism's defeat in Scotland in 1793–4. The radical threat had apparently been extinguished, so, while ordinary vigilance was maintained, there was no presumed need to take extraordinary measures.

In addition to employing spies and informers, from late September 1792 the letters of several leading radicals (Capt. William Johnston, William Skirving and Thomas Muir) were intercepted by the Post Office.[28] Copies of the two Scottish radical newspapers – the *Edinburgh Gazetteer* and *Caledonian Mercury* – were also being sent by Robert Dundas to his uncle in London.[29] This last measure was an extension of a press policing operation which had been established for England and Wales, and represented a revival of arrangements which had existed in England in the early eighteenth century.[30]

There was also a clear intention to use the first opportunity which arose to prosecute radicals. In the third week of September, the Lord Advocate and Solicitor General were meeting to consider 'seditious publications' which were appearing in the capital.[31] Shortly thereafter (probably at Blair Castle, home of the Duke of Atholl) the decision was taken to investigate the publication of a radical declaration from Partick in the *Glasgow Advertiser*, an investigation which led to the prosecution in early 1793 of James Smith and John Mennons, the paper's printer and editor respectively.[32] Between 1793 and 1794, the Scottish courts became a formidable tool of repression, beginning with the trials of several publishers and printers in the spring of 1793, among whom were Smith and Mennons, followed later in that year by the trials of Thomas Muir and Thomas Fyshe Palmer, and, in early 1794, several English as well as Scottish radicals following the suppression of the British convention. Unlike in England, no cases against radicals in Scotland in the 1790s failed; cases were not dismissed because of technical or other inaccuracies in drawing up indictments; and swingeing sentences were handed down for leading Scottish and English radicals in 1793–4. A good number of the radicals – James Tytler and James Thomson Callender in 1793, George Ross, Alexander Callander, James Kennedy and Alexander Scott in the following year – fled rather than face the justice of Braxfield and the High Court. In justifying his flight, Alexander Scott, conductor of the *Edinburgh Gazetteer* from the spring of 1793 until its collapse in early 1794, asserted:

... if my cause be good and if I am conscious of my innocence, why did I not stand trial? MEN OF SCOTLAND, hear my answer – The goodness of my cause has itself been my offence; for, to knaves and hirelings, what is so offensive as Virtue and Truth? And that innocence is not a shield is evidence, since men, supported by integrity and enabled by talents to defend those principles which they spoke, and which I only printed, have fallen victims to a brutal and ignorant Bench, and a corrupt, trembling, and packed Jury.[33]

The escape while on bail four years later of the United Scotsman Angus Cameron led to calls for this system to be amended to prevent such occurrences. Robert Dundas was convinced of the necessity of doing this, but there was a division of opinion on how best to achieve the desired reform. Under the current system, the judge had no discretion about the sum of bail to be fixed, a sum which was, in Dundas's description, 'ridiculously small'.[34] In the event, no change was made, probably because few similar cases arose in the next few years.

As referred to earlier, a considerable amount of discussion has taken place about whether, and how far, the judges abused their authority in the radical trials of 1793–4.[35] The cards were heavily stacked against the radicals, although several hardly helped themselves through decisions made and actions taken. Muir, for example, refused the services of a defence counsel because of his determination to use the court as a stage on which to defend the cause of 'liberty' and, as importantly perhaps, his role in it; no doubt, in choosing martyrdom – if this is what he did – he did not anticipate the severity of his sentence (fourteen years' transportation).[36] (Radicals' insistence on exploiting the court room as a political platform, while wholly understandable given the possibilities it offered for broadcasting a political message and vindication in the form of newspaper reports and pamphlets, was in the narrow context of the trials themselves counterproductive, serving simply to alienate bench and jury.[37]) Most importantly, and in contrast to the English system, there was no scope under Scottish law for challenging the composition of the jury other than on the grounds of 'insanity, outlawry, deafness and dumbness'. Judges also exerted close control over the selection of jurors, and there is evidence that special attention was paid to ensuring the political soundness of jurors in the sedition trials of these years.[38] Even more influential was the fact that Scotland's judges accepted the government's view of events, and were overtly and intensely hostile to reform. Indeed, the attitudes of the judges coincided entirely with those of ministers to the extent that the former could seemingly make no distinction in their minds between seeking reform and seeking to overthrow the government. In January 1793, when the Lord Provost and magistrates of Edinburgh visited the Court of Session, they were told by Ilay Campbell, the Lord President:

> Those who associate in meetings to devise impracticable and unnecessary plans of reformations, sometimes from good design, and oftener from bad, affect to disdain the pernicious tenets which have been imported to use from another country [i.e. France]. They tell us, they have no view to disturb the peace of society, or to encourage licentiousness. Many of them, it is believed, speak sincerely when they use this language; but perhaps they are not aware that their actions have precisely that effect, whatever their intentions may be; for they have brought men together for the purpose of instilling prejudice into their minds, and making them believe that they feel grievances which do not exist. The consequence of this is obvious. They have not duly

considered how dangerous it is to tamper with the minds and passions of uninformed men; and how impossible to say to a mob; 'this far you go, and no farther.'[39]

It was naked class prejudice and widely shared, although rarely so starkly articulated as it was by members of the Scottish bench in the sedition trials of this period. It was also thoroughly typical of the sort of constructive reasoning which put radicalism beyond the constitutional pale by construing intention from action or rather the possible consequences of action. In the context of Muir's trial, the phrase used by one contemporary was 'links of proof'.[40] Objections to the composition of juries as comprising members of a loyalist society were beside the point given such ways of reasoning. Lord Eskgrove announced during the trial of William Skirving in 1794: 'This gentleman's objection is, that his jury ought to consist of the convention of the Friends of the People; that every person wishing to support government is incapable of passing upon his assize. And by making this objection, this panel is avowing, that it was their purpose to overturn the government.'[41] At Joseph Gerrald's trial, objections to William Creech being a member of the jury, on the grounds that he had said in private that he would condemn any member of the British convention, were simply brushed aside. A report stated: 'One of their lordships observed that, if jurymen were to be disqualified for saying that the members of the convention deserved to be published, he believed that there was not a gentleman in court qualified to be a juryman, that should not be said aside'.[42] Lord Swinton told Muir at his trial that torture was the only punishment appropriate to his crime. That Swinton was a liberal, if we can talk in such anachronistic terms – he was a strong advocate of reform to the Court of Session, including the introduction of juries to civil cases – is only indicative of the fiercely reactionary temper which swept over the bench in 1793–4.[43]

The conduct of Scotland's judges, particularly the jeering, abrasive Braxfield, led to embarrassment and political difficulty for Dundas and the authorities in London. The legality of the sentences handed down to Muir and Fyshe Palmer were the subject of four debates in Parliament during the session of 1793–4, initiated in the Commons by Sheridan and William Adam, MP for Rosshire and opposition Whig political fixer, and in the Lords by the earls of Stanhope and Lauderdale. This culminated in March in a motion, proposed by Adam, for the postponement of Muir's and Fyshe Palmer's sentences until an enquiry had been held into the trials and the issue of whether the crime of sedition existed under Scottish law.[44] In public, ministers defended, even praised, Braxfield and the Scottish courts; in private, there was irritation about his conduct.[45] While it may have been soundly defeated, Adam's motion received great attention in the Scottish and indeed English press, as well as a report of the debate appearing in a pamphlet published by the Scottish radical printer-publisher close to the Friends of the People, James Robertson.[46] Muir had made contact with the opposition Whigs on his trip to London as self-styled martyr of liberty in the spring of 1793.[47] Fyshe Palmer was quick to do likewise. On 29 October, while still in Perth tollbooth, he wrote to Charles Grey requesting:

> If you should think proper to endeavour to get a bill passed to put a stop to this despotism, to restore to the Scots a trial by jury and the privileges of British subjects, I hope that from the illegality of the proceedings and from the enormous dispropor- tion of the punishment to the offence (if any) that you will see it just to have my sentence reversed by a clause in the bill and restoring me to the rights and privileges I before enjoyed.[48]

He also enclosed a pamphlet account of his trial, which was widely circulated amongst radicals north and south of the border.[49] On 11 December, Grey, Lauderdale and Sheridan had an interview with Henry Dundas in which they questioned the legality of the sentences, also handing in a memorial on the sub- ject.[50] On the hulks in London awaiting transportation, Muir and Fyshe Palmer were visited by leading opposition Whigs.[51] Fyshe Palmer wrote several letters to the opposition Whig paper, the *Morning Chronicle*, which had already taken up the cause of the 'Scottish martyrs'. It was probably to avoid such difficulties that the authorities chose to have Robert Watt and David Downie tried for treason by a commission of oyer and terminer under the terms of the 1709 Treason Act, passed in the aftermath of another, much earlier threat to peace and security in Scotland and Britain (the 1708 Franco-Jacobite invasion attempt). This way a court could be convened which was not presided over by Braxfield, although he did sit as an ordinary judge.[52] Moreover, the very severity of the justice in the Scottish courts for the radicals had a double-edged effect. In Edinburgh, if not elsewhere, the sentences passed down on Muir and Fyshe Palmer served, as we saw in the previous chapter, to galvanize a demoralized radical movement, imparting a new energy to their activities which they took into the third general and then British radical conventions.[53] Muir's continued presence in the capital following his trial acted as a further provocation to radicals, hence the anxiety to see him removed as quickly as possible to London.[54]

Viewed overall, however, the very repressive character of the Scottish legal system was a major contributory factor in the collapse of an organized, open radical movement north of the border and in intimidating political dissent more broadly. As we saw in an earlier chapter, the demise of the two Scottish radical newspapers was at least in part owing to legal intimidation and prosecution. In Dundee in 1793–4, attempts to raise a subscription to help pay off the debts of the profligate opposition Whig leader Charles James Fox failed because of the sense of 'terrour' felt locally amongst opposition Whigs, a feeling directly linked to the outcome of the recent treason trials.[55] The 'stormy days of Muir and Palmer'[56] cowed moderate political dissent, at least for a few years, and drove radicals to ever more desperate gestures. From Perth, merchant John Richardson, a burgh reformer and opponent of the war against revolutionary France, wrote to his brother, Robert, in March 1794: 'I forbear entering upon Politics which indeed is not safe to speak upon in this part of the Country with any prudence as the most innocent and meritorious sentiments may be construed sedition and I have no inclination for a voyage to Botany Bay'.[57] More broadly, the actions of the courts gave further sanction to a view of radicals as, despite what they said in public, committed to a republican political order and, quite possibly, the despoliation of property in pursuit of equality. The British convention and, a few months later, the discovery of the so-called Pike Plot only served to confirm this view, and further to alienate moderate opinion from the radicals.[58] Watt's declaration, in which he appeared to confess to the reality of a British-wide radical plot to overthrow the government, was circulated extensively in the form of a cheap pamphlet, as well as being widely published in newspapers.[59] His execution in the Scottish capital in October 1794 was carefully staged by the authorities as a further lesson in the realities of the radical threat. Watt's death, by beheading, seems to have been genuinely shocking to the modest-sized crowd which gathered at the site of execution.[60] Watt was the only radical to be executed for treason in Britain in the 1790s.

If the courts were very willing participants in the assault on radicalism, the ultimate guarantor of order and peace in society was the military, as Dundas had asserted on 12 November and again on the 20th. Following the disturbances of the autumn of 1792, Dundas had called for a strengthening of the military establishment in Scotland, and its deployment in barracks in notable 'seats of sedition'. By 1793, troops were permanently stationed at Edinburgh, Stirling, Perth, Montrose, Dundee, Aberdeen, Banff, Forts Augustus, William and George in the highlands, and at Dumfries, Annan, Kirkudbright in the south-west and Kilmarnock and Hamilton in Lanarkshire.[61] How far the burgh authorities wished see any increase of military force is a moot point. As elsewhere in Britain, local magistrates knew that recourse to use of the military during protests could undermine their authority and standing, and there was evident reluctance to do so. What was prudent tact in the eyes of these magistrates could easily be seen as weakness by others. A Captain Maclean complained from Perth in December 1792, in the context of the disturbances there involving the erection of a tree of liberty: 'All this was very distressing to me, and many others, but we could not help ourselves – The Chief Magistrate is a good, easy man, and will not call for troops because it is disagreeable to the pretended friends of the people'.[62] Soldiers, meanwhile, were not necessarily a welcome presence in towns, and tensions arose on a range of issues, including recruitment, the predatory sexual habits of soldiers, and public order. Even more burdensome was billeting, the subject of several cases brought by burgh authorities in the Court of Session in the 1790s.[63] The construction of barracks had the advantage, as far as the burgh authorities were concerned, of alleviating the burden of billeting, hence the eagerness of many in authority for such establishments to be located in their towns. In the summer of 1792, James McDowall, the Provost of Glasgow, wrote separately to Robert Dundas and the Duke of Richmond, Master General of the Ordnance, calling for the establishment of barracks in his city, a message to be repeated eighteen months later by John Dunlop. At the end of October 1793, it was the turn of William Anderson to make a similar call with respect to Stir-ling.[64] From 1794, barracks were established in several places, including Perth and Aberdeen. Even then, given the scale of the military mobilizations of this period, the burden of furnishing accommodation to soldiers remained a very heavy one on certain communities.

In early 1793, to supplement the regular forces, Dundas raised again the issue of forming a Scottish militia. The English militia had been revived by Parliament as long ago as 1757, and this inequality rankled with some Scots, helping to spark agitations for revival of an equivalent force in Scotland at the end of the Seven Years War and again during the War of American Independence. At the beginning of 1793, Dundas solicited views about how practical and helpful such a revival now might prove. Most opinion was opposed because of scepticism about the political loyalties of the lower orders and the advisability, therefore, of arming them.[65] The scheme was dropped at this point. Dundas did, however, proceed with the establishment in 1794 of a system of lords lieutenant, envisaged as the lynchpin of a new, strengthened means of maintaining order and domestic security in the face of related external (meaning France) and internal (meaning radical) threats. This was made clear in the scheme for maintaining order which was unveiled in May 1794.[66] This plan envisaged the major reinforcement of the system of constables at parish and country level, as well as the creation of an additional supplementary force for maintenance of peace. It was also under this plan that volunteer forces were to be raised. The implementation of this plan is examined below. Meanwhile, it was the lords lieutenant, and their deputies, on whom government in London and Edin-burgh relied for executing their wishes in maintaining order and responding to the French invasion threat for the rest of the 1790s. To that end, the lords lieutenant were drawn from among the highest rank of Scotland's landed elite, for example, the Duke of Atholl in Perthshire, or the Duke of Buccleuch in Midlothian. These new officials were expected to provide the lead in their counties in support of ini-tiatives to support government and the political status quo, starting with the plans for internal defence in the summer of 1794. The system of lords lieutenant had long been established south of the border.

Persuasion

Repression and persuasion were, as argued above, in reality inseparable. Propaganda was designed to shape opinion, but also to mobilize loyalists to intimidate radicals. Loyalists who sponsored and supported the circulation of propaganda also engaged in acts of harassment of radicals or attempts to deter potential supporters of radicalism. Volunteer companies were valuable as much for very public demonstrations of support for loyalism as for any military contribution they might make. Other public demonstrations of loyalist support – whether through celebrating the King's birthday or subscribing to a loyalist fund – were also designed to pressurize waverers and dissenters, as much as to confirm the existence of a loyal constituency. Nevertheless, there is merit in distinguishing between repression and persuasion, if only because the latter was even more dependent than the former on the willing and enthusiastic cooperation of a large group of people in society.

Support for the political status quo was demonstrated in several ways in Scotland in the early 1790s. In broad terms, these were the same as south of the border: resolutions, loyalist associations and subscriptions, public demonstrations of loyalism, and the production and circulation of anti-radical propaganda. Nevertheless, there were several important differences. There were very few loyalist associations formed north of the border – three, possibly four, at current count, compared to 'hundreds' or maybe even as high as two thousand in England.[67] There were almost no Tom Paine burnings in the winter of 1792–3, perhaps just two, one at the village of Ruthwell in the south-west and one in Newburgh in Fife.[68] In England, these were numerous and widespread, symptoms of a noisy, vocal plebeian loyalism, although many were organized and orchestrated from 'above'.[69] John Brims has suggested that loyalism in Scotland was more dominated by the clergy than south of the border.[70] How to explain these differences is an issue we will need to turn to later.

Another important difference, albeit one of degree, was the role which the authorities seem to have played in providing the impetus behind the initial mobilization of loyalist opinion. In early November, Henry Dundas was concerting measures with officials in the Scottish capital. One part of the plan seems to have been to organize a public resolution which would, it was hoped, be copied elsewhere, a reasonable assumption given Edinburgh's traditional political dominance in Scotland, and also given the tendency of landed Scots to visit the capital in the winter.[71] In line with Dundas's concern about the distribution of popular pamphlets, he was arranging for the funding and circulation of such items before he left Scotland. It was, for example, Dundas who was responsible for having George Hill's sermon *The Present Happiness of Great Britain* printed in 'many thousands of copies at a Price not higher than a penny'. What were described as 'many thousands' were also to be 'circulated for nothing'.[72] At about the same time, a number of loyal pamphlets were sent to Robert Dundas through the agency of Charles Long, a joint undersecretary to the Treasury. Others were sent from England direct to several manufacturing towns through the Post Office.[73] This represented an extension of existing efforts to disseminate such propaganda south of the border.[74] The full range, meanwhile, of measures taken to secure newspapers for the anti-radical cause is currently unclear, as we saw in Chapter 2, although before 1794 most support was focused on the *Edinburgh Herald*. These efforts began, moreover, well before late 1792, probably in the spring of 1791, when, through novelist Henry Mackenzie, discussions appear to have taken place with James Sibbald, the editor of the *Herald*.[75]

Dundas was also present in Edinburgh at the time when the Edinburgh loyal association, more often known as the Goldsmiths' Hall Association from its meeting place, was established. The role of ministers in the formation of the much more famous Association for the Preservation of Liberty and Property (APLP) in London has been the subject of protracted debate, with Michael Duffy recently arguing that while the initial meeting took place without the knowledge of ministers, it did subsequently receive their support and approval.[76] The establishment of the APLP almost certainly was responsible for commencing discussion in Edinburgh about establishing a similar body, and Pitt may have sent Dundas the initial declaration of the society.[77] Once the Edinburgh body was established, contact between the societies was quickly made. Two members of the Edinburgh association, the Revd Thomas Hardy and the advocate George Ferguson visited the APLP in London. One member of the association declared that its committee 'wish for ye sake of that common good cause in which both Associations are engaged, to keep up a constant correspondence & communication with the London Association to interchange ideas on the subject & the publications which either end of ye Island produces'.[78] Dundas refused, however, to give official backing to an Edinburgh counterpart, although he was privately encouraging. Ironically in view of later events, one source of concern may have been the difficulty of members serving as jurors in political cases, although it was also because of the 'delicacy' of being seen to encourage one sort of association and not others (i.e. reform associations), a prudent stance in view of the defences offered by radicals in their trials in the early 1790s.[79] The relationship between the society and the authorities was very close, nevertheless, perhaps unsurprisingly given the close-knit, intimate character of Edinburgh politics and society. Thomas Hardy was a Dundas protégé. The secretary, John Wauchope, a writer to the signet, held a minor government office, and may well have agreed to perform this role at the behest of individuals close to the Dundases, if not directly through their influence.[80] On 9 December, Robert Dundas informed his uncle: 'A copy of every Pamphlet you wish circulated should be sent to him

[John Wauchope, 'secretary of our General Association']. You may let Mr Long know this.' A few days later, he was again reporting to his uncle, in terms which also seem to indicate a high degree of official involvement: '*Our Association* proceeds with vigour – Pulteney is one of the committee & a most active member of it ... John Wauchope's conduct is really most meritorious. Without him, *I would not have succeeded to any purpose or effect*' (my emphasis).[81] Pulteney, MP for Shrewsbury in England – a true Anglo-Scot with property interests in Bath and an important role in the British Fisheries Society – was a political ally of both Dundases.[82] Another influential member of the association was Archibald Campbell of Clathick. Sheriff of Perthshire, Campbell was a staunch, even violent anti-radical, and important ally of Robert Dundas.[83]

However, even more suggestive is the role of Henry Mackenzie. Best known as a sentimental novelist and writer and editor of polite periodicals, Mackenzie has probably the strongest claim to being the guiding figure behind the Scottish authorities' anti-radical propaganda campaign of the 1790s.[84] As well as acting as the Dundases' agent in negotiations with the press in the early 1790s, he had links to Pitt, for whom he wrote several political pamphlets, but also to other important individuals involved in the production and circulation of anti-radical polemic in London, notably Charles Long and George Chalmers.[85] Together with Campbell of Clathick and Wauchope, he appears to have been an important figure on the publications committee of the Edinburgh association. The radical newspaper the *Edinburgh Gazetteer* claimed that he was in receipt of a £300 annual pension from the government.[86] I have found no corroboration of this, but he did contribute widely to newspapers in the anti-radical cause. As already mentioned, under the pen-name 'Brutus', he wrote the major political articles which appeared in the vehemently loyalist *Herald*, and he could not help boasting in letters of several other contributions, including a call, published in the press, for people not to employ tradesmen who were members of the Friends of the People.[87] In the later 1790s, it was Mackenzie who was author of 'The Address to the Inhabitants of Scotland from the Committee for Conducting the Contribution for the Defence of the Country', which was very widely reprinted in the press.[88] Other writers who contributed to the Edinburgh association were the prolific hack Robert Heron, who received £50 from secret service funds in 1793, and William Brown, whose role in the loyalist press was discussed in Chapter 2.[89]

The hand of the authorities is, therefore, not hard to detect in the loyalist campaign launched in late 1792. Its success (or not) was determined, however, by other factors, not least its ability to draw on the collaboration of people across Scotland – ministers, urban magistrates and merchants, county elites – and to engage the enthusiasm or at least acquiescence of a broad cross-section of society. Here the evidence, such as it exists, is more ambiguous and at times contradictory.

As we saw above, a key plank in the loyalist campaign as it unfolded in late 1792 was the drawing up of loyal resolutions. Prior to the end of the year, such loyal resolutions as had been forthcoming from Scotland had tended to be issued by local authorities and official bodies.[90] The new resolutions were different, subscribed to by as wide a body of people as possible, for example, at a public meeting, and publicized widely in Scottish and English newspapers. To this extent, they were more similar to petitions to Parliament, such as those promoted by the abolitionists in the first half of 1792, than traditional loyal addresses. On the face of it, this element of the campaign was a striking success. From late 1792, addresses poured in from different parts of the country and from a wide range of groups, including presbyteries, incorporations and associations of different professions, farmers, landholders, freemasons, on occasion labourers, but most commonly 'the inhabitants' of counties, burghs, towns and villages. At Ayr, on 26 December, there was what was claimed to be 'the fullest meeting of the community of the burgh and parish as ever appeared on any former occasion, to agree a set of loyal resolutions.'[91] In Cromarty, on the north east coast, 280 out of 300 heads of families signed the loyal resolutions, and had time been extended a few more days, it was declared that all but three would have done so.[92] So numerous were the loyal addresses and resolutions that the *Edinburgh Advertiser*, a thrice-weekly publication, was forced to announce in its issue of 21–5 December that, while they would continue to be published in the paper in the order in which they were received, it would be impossible to print them on the days specified by those who sent them in. Yet behind the addresses were some fierce battles and embarrassments for loyalists. Many of them reveal too the degree to which sections of the Scottish population continued to support political reform, albeit of a more moderate kind than that now being promoted by the parliamentary reformers. Any loyal consensus was, in short, uneven, diverse and loosely defined in the winter of 1792–3.

A major problem for those who sought to instigate loyal resolutions at public meetings was that, particularly in large manufacturing towns – Dundas's 'seats of sedition' – these were vulnerable to being taken over by radicals. This occurred in Perth on 18 December, in Dundee a few weeks later (8 January), in Montrose, and may well have happened in Forfar. It also occurred in several other places across the country, including, for example, Dalmeny in Fife, and Strathhaven, Hamilton and Kilmarnock in the west. In Perth and Dundee, backed by weight of numbers, local radical leaders managed to force meetings to include pro-reform clauses in the resolutions. The Perth resolutions, following an amendment put forward by George Meliss, included specific reference to the desirability of reintroducing triennial elections, as well as to the need for 'more general, as well as more true representation'.[93] The response, in both Perth and Dundee, was to issue new sets of resolutions, but subscribed by individuals; the holding of public meetings to gather loyalist support was abandoned. In Dundee, two sets of new resolutions were drawn up – by the Dundee Club, a body which spanned the urban and local landed elites – and by a group comprising leading merchants and a few professionals.[94] The small numbers subscribing to these resolutions (61 and 56 respectively) suggest that support was hardly overwhelming, and was limited to the wealthy, although it did cut across normal political boundaries.[95] The second set of Perth resolutions, agreed on 31 December, was signed by a slightly higher number, 132, but this was in a town with a population of around 19,000. As in Dundee, the signatories, led by Provost John Caw, comprised members of the merchant elite, professionals, public servants, and just a few artisans and tradesmen.[96]

In Glasgow, the authorities encountered fewer difficulties in having resolutions as initially proposed agreed. The first main set of Glasgow resolutions was put forward at a joint meeting of the Town Council and Trades House on 10 December, a few days after Edinburgh's resolutions had been agreed. As John Dunlop noted in a letter to Henry Dundas, written on 11 December, complete unanimity had not been achieved, but the overwhelming feeling of the meeting had been against the reformers:

> Two patriots which were the only dissenting voices insisted that we should say 'we were not enemies to constitutional reform at a proper time' – These Gentlemen were told that we considered the word Reform in the present times, as tantamount to Rebellion & that it could not be admitted into our resolutions.[97]

When the merchants, manufacturers and other inhabitants met, however, at the Merchants' Hall on 14 December, debate was more protracted, the meeting dividing between those who wished to see specific mention of reform and those who sought resolutions which were 'unequivocal, not clogged with reform'. In the event, a compromise amendment was agreed, which read, 'the more especially as we are convinced, that if any abuses have crept into the Constitution in itself has the means of rectifying them.'[98]

Glasgow's merchants and manufacturers had very strong lines of communication to Dundas and the ministry, in part through the agency of the MP for Glasgow Burghs, William McDowall, which may to some extent account for the ready and staunch loyalism of many of them.[99] While the opposition Whigs did have supporters in the town, most merchants and manufacturers seem to have been strong supporters of the Pitt ministry, not least because of these points of contact, but also because of Pitt's support, actual and perceived, for commerce and manufacturing.[100] In 1793, Glasgow and the west received the bulk of Exchequer support for credit in Scotland, although this was because they were most adversely affected by the credit squeeze which followed Britain's entry into the war in February. It is perhaps worth noting in this context that Patrick Colquhoun, a London magistrate and enemy of the London Corresponding Society, was a former Lord Provost of Glasgow and had been the first president of the Glasgow Chamber of Commerce.[101] Colquhoun is representative of a strand of opinion – politically conservative, but economically progressive – which was powerfully entrenched north of the border, but particularly in the west.

Gathering support for county resolutions could involve similar problems to those met in larger towns. At the Lanark county meeting to draw up loyal resolutions, William Dalrymple of Cleland and Fordell proposed a motion in support of reform. While this was defeated, Dalrymple did manage to gain the support of eighteen other attendees. Dalrymple's motion, significantly, was omitted by those who prepared an account of the meeting and resolutions for publication.[102] From Perthshire it was reported that 'L[or]d Kinnoul proposes some Resolutions in the country but can get nobody to sign them but his gardener'.[103] Perth radicals had a handbill printed in Dundee for circulation in rural parishes 'to counteract the Resolution of the Gentlemen of the County'.[104] In Angus it was decided to send copies of the resolutions to ministers to encourage as broad-based support as possible.[105] It may have been radicals who were behind a notion which seems to have taken root in some places in the county that those who signed the resolutions would be obliged to enlist as soldiers. To counteract this, Sir James Murray of Ochtertyre apparently stuck up a handbill that if an 'apprehending act' were passed, 'those who did not sign would be looked upon as suspicious persons and made soldiers'.[106] The pressures which were brought to bear on groups and individuals to sign such resolutions or otherwise testify to their 'sound' principles are occasionally glimpsed elsewhere. David Johnson of Lathrisk visited towns and villages in Fife where he owned a 'good deal of property'. There he 'spoke and reasoned with the principal people as well as with my tennents'.[107] What might seem to be paternalistic responsibility from the perspective of men such as Johnson no doubt appeared in a different light to many tenants and labourers, particularly those with radical or reformist sympathies. In April 1793, James Smithson wrote to William Skirving, Secretary of the Edinburgh Friends of the People, from Selkirk about the dependency of the townspeople on the elites. He also talked of the 'country farmers' being under the influence of the nobility and gentry and 'in a manner compelled to sign [a] loyal address last winter'.[108]

The resolutions were also far from a simple endorsement of the political status quo. A good number specifically declared, to a greater or lesser degree, more or less unambiguously, the need for reform. The 'Proprietors of the County of Linlithgow' urged that the reform of abuses was the best way of 'quieting' discontent, precisely the argument of opposition Whig reformers.[109] One anonymous individual close to the authorities described the resolutions passed at Dalmeny and Queensferry on 14 December as 'weak'; these resolutions were among those which acknowledged the need for reform.[110] The terms of the resolutions were also typically very broad and capable of being interpreted in a variety of ways, although this was not true of all. This was their potential strength as a means of demonstrating consensus, but their weakness for the historian as a guide to opinion. A good example would be the resolutions agreed by the 'heritors and inhabitants' of Culross in Fife on 23 December. These contained explicit condemnation of the 'Levellers and Republican incendiaries' who were seeking to produce a revolution similar to the one across the Channel in Scotland and Britain. Yet they also contained the following clause:

> We earnestly recommend to such of our countrymen as are advocates for a reform, or more properly speaking an alteration in our Parliamentary Representation, and who are not infected with the principles of Republicanism or Equality, that they would join with us, and other good subjects, in securing to ourselves, with God's assistance, the measure of blessings we at present enjoy, and postpone reform, except the necessary reformation of our lives and conduct, until it had pleased God to remove the dark cloud which now hangeth over the nation. *We then pledge to give it the degree of consideration and support it deserves* [my emphasis].[111]

Several opposition Whigs in Dundee were happy to sign loyal resolutions in early 1793.[112] In a well-known incident, representatives from the first general convention of Scottish radicals, led by Captain William Johnston, attempted to add their signatures to the loyal resolutions drawn up by the Goldsmiths' Hall Association on 7 December.[113] This might be seen as political mischief, but it was more. The Scottish radicals thought of themselves as patriots and as committed to a balanced constitution of King, Lords and Commons; in their eyes, they were seeking to restore this constitution to its original state. The superiority of the British constitution, and the need to defend this and the peace of society against internal and external enemies, were accepted by many radicals. At the Glasgow meeting on 14 December, one reform-minded gentleman asserted that he was: 'Opposed to means used to conduct reform; reform not been refused by Parliament. With regard to the present resolutions, he was determined to sign them as they stood; he saw nothing in them unfriendly to reform; nor any thing which should prevent a man who signed them to day from going to a constitutional meeting for reform tomorrow.'[114] In a comment which demonstrates how influential English example could be in this period, he also declared that he was an admirer of the 'London Resolutions' which stated that the principles of the constitution contained within them 'sufficient means for correcting any abuses which may have crept into it'; similar formulations appeared in many of the Scottish resolutions.

The resolutions of the winter of 1792–3 can, therefore, easily mislead about the depth and nature of support for loyalism, at least at this point. Described by Robert Dundas as a 'steady friend of government', George Paterson of Castle Huntly was prepared to acknowledge this fact. His words of warning, recorded in a letter to Dundas, are worth quoting at length:

> Constitutional Associations have been formed, and Resolutions published in con-
> sequence, signed by many respectable names, strongly expressive of loyalty and
> attachment to the constitution and declaring themselves ready to sacrifice their lives
> and fortunes in support of Government. But in general these have been Men of Rank
> and fortune, or of such a superior class of men whether in Town or Country from
> which the militia cannot be drawn.

He added: 'In many places several have signed these or similar resolutions, who
are indeed not of the highest ranks in life: but many such will be found to have
done so from an influence, or from interested motives, and not from principle'.[115]
As already referred to, just three loyalist associations are known definitely to
have been established across Scotland in the early 1790s – the Edinburgh Goldsmiths' Hall Association, the Glasgow Constitutional Association, and a similar
body in Dumfries in the south-west – the Dumfries Association for Preserving
Peace, Liberty and Property, and for Supporting the Laws and Constitution of
the Country. The sole surviving membership list of the Edinburgh association
fully supports Paterson's contention, with the overwhelming preponderance of
members being drawn from the legal, professional and mercantile elites.[116] The
role of 'influence' is not always or often discernable in the sources many historians use to examine loyalism, but was pervasive, as alluded to above and as will be
seen further in this and a subsequent chapter when examining other, later loyalist and patriotic initiatives.

Alongside the drawing up and publicizing resolutions, loyalist propaganda
was produced and circulated in very large quantities. How much of this was the
product of the loyalist associations, as opposed to private, uncoordinated efforts,
and simple commercial opportunism on the part of printers and publishers is
unknowable, as are the sorts of quantities of pamphlets and handbills involved.
Several of Edinburgh's booksellers were notable loyalists, most famously William Creech, Burns's canny publisher, and secretary to the Goldsmiths' Hall
Association. Others included Creech's erstwhile clerk Peter Hill, John Bell and
John Bradfute, who were responsible for one of the earliest loyal publications
produced in Scotland – *The Constitutional Letters*, published from July 1792
– and James Dickson.[117] All were signatories to the Goldsmiths' Hall Association
declaration, while Hill and Bell joined Creech as jurors at the trial in 1794 of the
English radical Joseph Gerrald. These booksellers also had long-standing links
to publishers in London, some of them Scots, acting, on occasion, as the latter's
agents north of the border. This ensured that notable English loyal propaganda
was readily available in Scotland, although there were other sources, as we will
see below. These booksellers also had counterparts in other towns across Scotland, for example Alexander Brown in Aberdeen, brother of William Brown,
the Dundee bookseller and writer who had become a loyal newspaper editor.
The Edinburgh and Glasgow associations were certainly very active, and their

influence extended beyond these two cities. In some cases, this entailed circulating or encouraging the circulation of loyalist items from London, although the
exchange was not only one way.[118] Subscriptions were established to raise funds
to defray the costs of producing loyal pamphlets and facilitating their distribution in large numbers amongst the artisan and labouring classes. Publication of
William Brown's *Look Before Ye Loup: or, A Healin' Sa; for the Crackit Crowns
of country politicians, by Tam Thrum, an Auld Weaver* (1793) was, for example,
subsidized by the Edinburgh loyal association. Both associations recommended
various pamphlets for dissemination, including, in the case of the Glasgow Constitutional Association, a cheap edition of John Young's *Essays on Government*
and, in both cases, Thomas Hardy's *The Patriot*.[119] The Edinburgh association
was also offering pamphlets to other associations at 'low prices' on application
to Creech, the scretary.[120] The publications committee of the Edinburgh association was responsible too for seeing into print several loyal pamphlets, including
several adaptations for a Scottish readership of notable English loyal pamphlets
and a statement about the relative insignificance of the burden of taxes which
fell on the common man in contemporary Scotland and Britain, a direct riposte
to Paine, and the perception that the economic case for radical reform was the
most likely to sway weavers and fellow artisans.[121] George Chalmers's hostile
Life of Paine, published under the pseudonym 'Francis Oldys', was distributed
by the committee of the Edinburgh association.[122] The associations may also
have supplied a considerable number of articles to the press. Robert Heron, the
hack writer referred to earlier as in receipt of pay from the government for his
efforts on behalf of the Edinburgh association, contributed some of these. Henry
Mackenzie noted that the Edinburgh publications committee, impressed with
Arthur Young's *The Example of France; a Warning to Britain* (1793), 'means to
extract & publish in the Newspapers, a channel which in the local circumstances
of this country ... we find by much the most efficacious for general Distribution
of either writings or sentiments'.[123] It may well have been the same committee
which was behind the appearance in the *Herald* in December 1793 of the names
and occupations of the 'motley group', in John Wauchope's phrase, who made up
the delegates to the British convention.[124] Similarly, it seems quite likely that a
series of letters published in the *Edinburgh Advertiser* and *Edinburgh Herald* in
1793 purporting to be between members of the Friends of the People, and which
exposed their revolutionary ambitions, had a similar source.[125] The *Glasgow Courier* printed a series of loyal items in later 1792 aimed explicitly at the working
man, including a series of spoof radical advertisements and 'The Paisley Weaver's
Letter to his Neighbours and Fellow Tradesmen'.[126] Again no evidence survives
regarding origin or authorship, but it seems likely that they were the product of
official encouragement or intervention. On 15 December 1792, Gilbert Hamilton reported from Glasgow: 'A considerable number of pamphlets and little

Essays have been published & circulated lately, a number of others are in forwardness which I hope will help to open people's eyes to their own true interest ...'.[127] In 1793, the committee of the Glasgow Constitutional Association took considerable pains to refute a series of paragraphs which appeared in Scottish and English newspapers regarding the alleged strength of support in the city for a peace petition organized by a group including radicals in the spring of that year.[128]

Beyond the two main cities, loyal propaganda was circulated by private individuals and local officials. In Dundee, the Dundee Club, referred to earlier, raised a subscription to fund the dissemination of such material; a similar fund was set up in Paisley.[129] Ministers were used to distribute loyal pamphlets, as were stamp masters, and excise and customs officers.[130] From Cupar, Fife, Sheriff Claud Boswell reported in January 1793 that 2,000 loyal pamphlets had been distributed.[131] The use of stamp masters was at the initiative of Graham of Fintry, although John Wauchope wondered whether the 'disaffected' would pay any notice to 'any thing that may be distributed by your officers'.[132] In Blairgowrie, a manufacturing village in Perthshire, allegations, strongly denied, that the stamp master had failed to circulate some loyal material to local weavers were carefully investigated.[133] The Royal Burghs received loyal material from the Edinburgh Goldsmiths' Hall Association, for which they were thanked by the General Convention in 1794.[134] In some places, there were efforts to produce loyal propaganda tailored to local conditions. In Angus, a statement was drawn up regarding the contribution of the bounty on exports of coarse linen, introduced first in 1742, to local prosperity.[135] This was aimed squarely at weavers, who dominated the labouring populations of the towns and many villages throughout Angus and also in Perthshire and Fife. Below these efforts were those of individuals acting on their own initiative, or in some cases perhaps taking the advice of the Goldsmiths' Hall Association to circulate loyal publications 'amongst the journeymen and apprentices of tradesmen and manufacturers and the working people of Scotland'.[136] Known examples include the Dundee linen merchant Archibald Neilson and the Fife landowner David Johnson of Lathrisk.[137] Neilson was one of those 'endeavouring to turn the attention of the weavers to the great object of the linen bountys'.[138] In December 1792 James Boswell (of Auchinleck) sent several loyal pamphlets to his overseer, including two which were to be pasted up in the 'smithy's and lent about'. The overseer was also instructed to paste up a further copy of one of them in the estate office for Boswell's tenants to see.[139] No doubt many other landowners did similar things. John Fyffe, who as we saw earlier was employed to make enquiries in and around Dundee following the political riots in the town in November 1792, was another distributing loyal pamphlets in the winter of 1792–3.[140]

Contemporary views on the impact of this propaganda differed. Some, including Mackenzie, but also George Dempster of Dunnichen, were strongly convinced of its efficacy.[141] More cautious assessments were offered, however, reflecting in part the recent memory, deeply etched, of the excitement with which Paine's *Rights of Man* had been read by labouring people in late 1792.[142] There was also the question of which groups in society were influenced. It is doubtful radicals were swayed by reading loyal pamphlets; indeed, they may simply have served to confirm them in their political convictions. The Perth radicals were apparently recommending that radicals read some of these pamphlets to reinforce their sentiments.[143] In the parish of Peterculter in Aberdeenshire, authors of loyal pamphlets were branded 'ministerial tools, court sycophants, the slaves of despots &c'.[144] Secession congregations could prove notably resistant to the loyalist message, although this was not universally the case. John Young, antiburgher minister of Hawick, faced a formal complaint because of his defence of the British constitution in his influential *Essays on Government*; his efforts also apparently led to 'an almost total Desertion of his Auditory'.[145]

Printed propaganda was not the only form of persuasion used to deflate and destroy the radical cause, although print was crucial to the wider effects of several others – resolutions, which have already been examined, loyal subscriptions, bounties to encourage enlistment in the armed services, as well as various public demonstrations of loyal fervour and support. Loyal subscriptions – including ones to support wives and families of soldier and sailors who fell in war and to provide flannel waistcoats and other warm clothing to British soldiers on the continent in the winter of 1793–4 – proliferated from 1793, receiving very detailed coverage in the press. Some were local initiatives, others national, and some British-wide. When London instituted a ladies' subscription to support the provision of flannel waistcoats to Britain's soldiers in Europe in the winter of 1793–4, Edinburgh quickly followed suit.[146] Organizers of subscriptions were careful to ensure that notices appeared in newspapers showing not only amounts collected, but details of individual donors and their designations.[147] Linking all of these manifestations of loyal sentiment was the aim of creating an impression of a firmly and enthusiastically loyal Scotland, an impression conveyed and created through the cumulative impact of reports in newspapers. By publicizing them, additional pressure was also created for communities and individuals to demonstrate their loyalty. The power of emulation as a motivating force underpinning much loyalist behaviour in this period should not be underestimated.

Being seen to be loyal was not only important, however, in terms of civic and individual reputations at the national and indeed British level; it was also an aspect of demoralizing and defeating radicalism at the local level. To this end, from early 1793 burgh authorities in Scotland's 'seats of sedition' also sought to wrest back control of public spaces from the influence of the radicals and regain control over the construction of political meaning in those spaces. This was not so much a deliberate, coordinated policy, but a habit of action engaged in by most burgh magistrates and their supporters, especially in 1793–4. Military victories were ostentatiously celebrated, while the King's birthday became again the principal occasion for demonstrations of political loyalty north of the border, as it had been earlier in the century.[148]

Any assessment of the success of these efforts again needs to be a carefully balanced one. From the final third of the eighteenth century, there was a shift in the nature of urban celebrations on the King's birthday, with a gradual withdrawal in some places of the elites from the public elements of the day and growing intolerance of the licence which could be displayed by elements of the crowd.[149] These divisions and tensions continued in the 1790s, not least of course during the famous King's birthday riots in Edinburgh in 1792; calls for economy in public expenditure could work in the same direction.[150] The centrepiece of most celebrations in this period was a dinner involving burgh magistrates and council members and invited local notables; in other words, an exclusive occasion which took place away from public view. In later years, there was also great care to ensure that disorder did not mar the celebrations. In 1794, special constables were enrolled in Edinburgh and Perth in advance of the day. These were designed, as we will see below, for a wider role than simply policing this occasion, but they were mobilized on the day, and the timing of their enrolment seems to be explained by the importance of the anniversary as a moment of potential disorder.[151] In Edinburgh, marines from Leith were used to reinforce the forces of order, as they were at other moments in this period. Significantly, in Perth arrangements were made to exclude the regular soldiers from the celebrations in 1794 because of a fear this might lead to disorder. In order to avoid 'turbulent meetings', Col. Moncrieff was requested not to assemble his soldiers on the day for either a dinner or drink 'on the Inch or any where else', as had been customary in former years.[152] In the capital, the same concern and attention was shown during the treason trials of 1794. This was partly because of demonstrations which accompanied the trial of Maurice Margarot. Similar attempts to create a mob to accompany Alexander Scott to the court were frustrated by the vigilance of the authorities.[153] From 1795, the embodiment of volunteer companies added a new element to loyalist celebration, including elaborate volunteer reviews; there also seems to have been less concern about the likelihood of any subversion of such occasions or disorder, although this did occur in relatively minor ways in Dundee and Edinburgh in 1795 and 1796, respectively.[154]

In many ways, however, the greatest test of the depth and character of loyalist feeling in the first half of the decade came in the spring and summer of 1794 when Dundas unveiled, as referred to earlier, plans to strengthen the forces of domestic security. The plan, passed by Parliament on 14 March 1794, and sent to local officials for implementation in May, was British-wide in implementation, and had several strands, including, first, the formation of volunteer cavalry companies partly funded by voluntary subscriptions but also by various allowances from government and, second, the appointment of extraordinary officers of peace in the counties.[155]

Again at first glance the Scottish response to this plan provides powerful evidence for the strength of loyalist feeling north of the border, especially when compared to events in England. Led by Edinburgh, Glasgow and other places in the central lowlands, but rapidly followed by towns up and down the east coast, volunteering spread rapidly in Scotland. By 1796, according to John Cookson, one in three infantry volunteers belonged to Scottish corps.[156] Volunteer companies appear to have rapidly filled. In Dunbar, two companies were quickly embodied, only one which was being paid for the days it exercised; the Provost was 'at all the Expence & trouble' with respect to the other. In Kelso, it took only a 'few hours' to enrol a company of infantry comprising sixty privates, two drummers and nine officers.[157] In Stirling, two companies of infantry were quickly followed by a third. Perth's citizens agreed to raise three infantry companies, comprising sixty privates each, and these were filled without delay or difficulty.[158] In Keith in the northeast, the full complement of a company of infantry was made up in 'a few hours ... such is the loyalty of the inhabitants'.[159] Burgh authorities offered bounties and other incentives to volunteers, while farmers in several places also funded bounties to encourage early volunteers to create light cavalry companies.[160] The farmers of Fife offered to raise an additional troop of cavalry at their own expense, an offer which was refused.[161] In Angus, plans to embody volunteer cavalry appear to have proceeded less smoothly, although this may simply have been because of confusion about the terms under which they were to be raised. Whatever the source of confusion, the plans were dropped or at least significant revised. In place of volunteer cavalry, two companies of infantry were raised, partly funded by subscription. An association was also formed committing members to form themselves into a body of cavalry under the command of the lord lieutenant, but only to be called out in cases of emergency. These men were to serve without pay, supplying their own clothes and horses; government was simply to provide arms and accoutrements.[162] In Stirlingshire, there appear to have been more deep-seated frictions in that several present at the meeting of the county called to consider internal defence favoured raising a militia rather than volunteer forces.[163] The overall impression, nevertheless, is of a series of communities across different parts of Scotland enthusiastically responding to Dundas's plan.[164]

Little is known about the social composition of these early volunteers since no muster lists of companies survive for the period before 1798. Many of the companies were probably formed mainly from the ranks of the urban elites and middling sorts, partly reflecting the costs incurred by volunteers, who often were required to pay for their own uniforms, a sum which may well have come to around £6.[165] The Royal Aberdeen Volunteers served without pay and were 'under a very considerable Expence in Dress ...'.[166] The Provost of Perth reported that it would be difficult to raise more than between 100 and 120 men in his town because of the expenses entailed by volunteering.[167] Around half of Edinburgh's 700 or so royal volunteers were connected to the law courts.[168] Not all were drawn from these and similar groups, however. In the case of the Kelso infantry company, referred to above, one individual later wrote, regarding the origins of the company: 'A Journeyman Tailor or Shoemaker was as good for our purpose as the biggest little man in our village'. Uniforms were funded by the county, while the times of the exercise were carefully chosen to fall outside the working day, between 6 and 8 in the summer; in the winter, the volunteers were paid 6*d.* a day for exercising, but were only called out once every two months.[169] In Stirling, the expenses of craftsmen joining the volunteer companies were defrayed by wealthier volunteers giving up their allowances and raising a subscription.[170] In the case of Montrose, there is even better evidence because the Town Council agreed that volunteers should be admitted as burgesses and members of the guildry without payment of normal dues. In late 1795, the Town Clerk duly recorded the names and occupations of fifty-six volunteers who were entered on the burgess role. Of this number, twenty-four were weavers, nine were shoemakers, and five were flax-dressers; the others were also artisans and tradesmen.[171] Even before 1797–8, therefore, when the social depth of companies extended markedly, volunteering was not confined solely to the upper and prosperous middling ranks.

There is also the issue of what the volunteers actually stood for. In an English context, several historians have tended to downplay the links between loyalist associations of 1792–3 and the volunteers, and to portray the latter as an expression less of loyalism than defensive patriotism.[172] We possess limited evidence for the motivations of Scottish volunteers; nevertheless what does exist tends to point to loyalism, understood as opposition to the perceived radical threat, as a significant factor. The Stirling volunteers subscribed to the following declaration: 'We the subscribers inhabitants of the Town and Parish of Stirling do hereby agree to inroll ourselves as a volunteer corps for the defence of the present happy constitution under which we and our forefathers have so long lived in peace and security ...'. They swore 'to bear faith and true allegiance to his said Present Majesty King George the Third so help us God'. They also declared their intention to protect their town from 'all ill disposed and disloyal persons who might attempt to make an insurrection or disturb the peace'.[173] One Perth volunteer, a Robert Scott, described his reasons for seeking membership as follows: 'As a loyal citizen, I make offer of myself to serve in the corps of the Perth Royal Volunteers for the Purpose of crushing & subduing the Enemies of our King's Constitution at all times & on all occasion when necessity requires'.[174] The Perth volunteers were, ironically given Scott's forthright motivation, subject to criticism because they did not subscribe to an overtly anti-radical oath or declaration.[175] The explicit contrast being made here was with the Edinburgh volunteers. As Meikle has noted, nothing was said in the articles of the Edinburgh volunteers regarding a foreign enemy. Rather the members formally disavowed the doctrine of universal suffrage and Jacobin political principles, disapproved explicitly of the Friends of the People and the British convention, and undertook to prevent such societies being formed or such meetings being held in the future.[176] The spectre, raised so clearly by the British convention and the revelations related to the so-called Pike Plot, remained that of 'domestic treachery'.

If the Scottish contribution to volunteering in the mid 1790s was a noteworthy one, the record in respect of the second plank of the plan for domestic defence is rather more mixed, and begins to suggest again some of the limitations surrounding the reach of loyalism in the first half of the 1790s. The rationale, detail, but also the anticipated sensitivity surrounding this second strand is fully revealed in two sets of private instructions, one regarding extraordinary and other ordinary constables, drawn up by the Duke of Atholl for Perthshire.[177] Prospective extraordinary constables were to be contacted individually by deputy lieutenants or heritors, not at a public meeting. They were to be reassured that their service, which would be on an annual basis, would be limited to preserving peace within the county, not serving against a foreign enemy. They were only to be called out by a civil magistrate or the lord lieutenant. The extraordinary constables were to comprise peace officers, to number between ten and twenty, each with five or six assistants. The peace officers were to be drawn from the ranks of farmers and substantial householders, and their assistants from farmers, householders or creditable inhabitants. The political loyalties of both peace officers and their assistants were to be certain, and deputy lieutenants were told to be on their guard for seditious individuals offering their support: 'The seditious will often be most disposed to offer their pretended services'. Pressure was to be applied to those who were reluctant to sign: 'It may perhaps be proper to inform such as ought to but have not signed, that they cannot expect the same assistance in protecting them and their property, as they who declare their willingness to aid the civil magistrate may Expect but this should be done in a Gentle but not in a threatening manner'. The main aim with respect to ordinary constables was, in addition to ensuring their political soundness, to renew and reinforce a system that was currently failing to produce candidates of sufficient social standing and number, at least in Perthshire. As Atholl declared:

> Too little attention has been hitherto paid to their appointment and care should now be taken by the deputy lieutenants to inform the proper persons to serve ... In England persons of the better class act as constables and conceive themselves bound to perform that part of their public duty which they accordingly discharge willingly and faithfully – It is proper that the Farmers and householders both in Country Parishes

and in villages should in Perthshire be taught that it is their duty which in their turn they must perform.

In Perth, it was noted, that there were currently fifty constables, but that this number might be increased if it were thought expedient. That these arrangements were political, in the narrow sense of being aimed against a perceived domestic threat from radicalism, is disclosed by one further instruction in relation to the extraordinary peace officers. Deputy lieutenants were told to ensure that a sufficient number of these should attend all fairs and markets to 'prevent attempts to circulate seditious and inflammatory papers, and to apprehend the vendors or distributors of such'.[178]

In the event, Atholl's concerns about likely reaction to these plans, implicit in several parts of the instructions, were fully justified since the scheme quickly ran into difficulties in some parts of the county. George Drummond of Blair Drummond, after discussing the proposals with his neighbours, returned his commission as a deputy lieutenant, urging that Scottish farmers, in contrast to their English counterparts, were too poor and busy for military duties.[179] George Haldane of Gleneagles had duly called farmers and heritors to a series of meetings at the local kirks, but they only brought a series of objections; and only a small minority had signed.[180] While the response in Blairgowrie was quite positive, in nearby Rattray there were many refusals, and a number of the local population (around 48) had signed a petition for parliamentary reform drawn up one Andrew Thom, a land surveyor.[181] There were similar reports of reluctance to sign declarations from parishes on the Carse of Gowrie.[182] Perthshire landowners had to work extremely hard to elicit any level of cooperation, however qualified, from their tenantry in 1794.

Similar problems arose in East and West Lothian. In late May, it was reported from East Lothian:

> A great many of the Tenants have proposed to subscribe to raise money for the purpose of giving an additional bounty to the East Lothian Fencible cavalry, and one Gentleman to whom the tenants communicated this plan, askd if they would rise and join their landlords to preserve the peace of the county, the answer was not a man it was believed would rise.

Proposals for peace officers to act in any part of the county in the event of an emergency had to be dropped.[183] From West Lothian, a deputy lieutenant reported: 'I find the people in the district containing the parishes of Kirknewton East Calder Mid Calder & West Calder in general much averse to the idea of Enroleing'.[184]

Why was there so much opposition to these schemes? In East Lothian, political factors seem to have been influential. Rumours were current in May of a planned rising on the King's birthday and, linked to this, there was profound concern about the political disposition of the 'lowest class of people' and also tenant farmers. The latter, who had 'crept into wealth, by the long continued high price of corn', had supposedly begun to aspire to greater influence in society, including performing 'the Duties of representatives in Parl[iamen]t, of justices of the peace & the like offices'. They had also 'formed plans for having the right of election extended to them', as well for several other things, including capping rents and converting temporary leases into feus. Armed with these plans and desires, they were looking, or so it was reported, 'with sullen complacency upon the rising storm', while in public they were complaining about the 'enormous expence of Government, of the war, and the consequent heavy Burdens of the accumulated rate of tastes upon the Poor'.[185] In West Lothian, there were fears that those who signed declarations would be enlisted into the army. There was evident distrust about the political sympathies of farm servants who would be left behind in the event of the farmers being mobilized. Another source of opposition was economic, the feeling that farmers could not afford the time and potential loss of income involved in serving away from their farms.

Similar factors were at work in Perthshire, including the fear that subscribing to the scheme would prove a preliminary to enlistment in regular forces, and the relative poverty and lack of time of tenant farmers. George Drummond of Blair Drummond, referred to above, reported in early December that the original plan would never succeed and that 'there was no reasoning with ignorant country people'. He also noted that tenant farmers in his locality were 'but a very few degrees above the level of day labourers'.[186] The proposals also appear to have provoked some class tensions, with some maintaining that it was a scheme simply to arm the 'higher orders' against the 'lower', which, in a way, it was.[187] John Ramsay of Ochtertyre spoke of his tenants, all of whom refused to be enrolled as peace officers, as 'totally devoid of zeal', although not disaffected.[188] In parishes bordering or close to towns, especially Dundee and Perth, 'fear of the mob' seems to have acted a major deterrent. As Sir John Wedderburn explained, their 'timidity seemed to proceed from the fear of the town of Dundee'.[189] Another important factor in Perthshire may have been religion. Seceders in several parishes were refusing to sign declarations or enrol as peace officers. Sir William Ramsay reported on the case of one William White, a blacksmith, who had refused to sign the declaration, claiming that it would do more harm than good. White was a Seceder and member of the 'Reforming Societies'. Archibald Stirling of Garden, Leadhills, observed that all Seceders in his district had refused to sign the declaration.[190] While White may have been a reformer, such resistance was not necessarily or perhaps in many cases motivated by support for radicalism. Rather it reflected self-conscious distancing amongst Seceders from a state which had failed to respect a strict separation of Church and State, or in the case of some denominations to subscribe to the Solemn League and Covenant.[191] The

Glassites, for example, while committed to peace and order in society, and not wishing to meddle 'in no shape with them that are given to change', considered it incompatible with their religious views to sign declarations committing them to support the civil power in the event of disturbances.[192]

Opposition to establishing new peace officers was not uniform across the country, however, or indeed across Perthshire. Stewart of Ardvorlich persuaded over 200 farmers and householders in his district to sign the declaration and take up arms if called upon. David Campbell, of Glenlyon House, forwarded lists of 126 loyal men from Kenmore, Dull and Weem. All were, according to Campbell, loyal and had signed of their own accord.[193] Despite some talk of signing declarations entailing military enlistment, from Midlothian the Duke of Buccleuch was able to report in December that 580 extraordinary constables had been nominated 'besides a vast number who had offered to act when called upon as assistant constables'.[194] As we have already seen, in Edinburgh and several other towns, large numbers of citizens were happy to offer their services as extraordinary constables from the spring of 1794. The Perth citizens enrolled as peace officers in 1794 included merchants, weavers, shoemakers, fleshers and glovers, as well as a significant number of other sorts of tradesmen and artisans.[195] Urban authorities may, paradoxically perhaps given concerns about popular disorder and the contagion of disaffection, have found it easier to mobilize loyal opinion than rural magistrates and landowners.

Those active in the Scottish loyalist campaign of the early 1790s maintained that their efforts had been instrumental in helping to extinguish a radical threat which in the winter of 1792–3 especially had caused huge alarm amongst the authorities and many amongst the landed and urban elites. John Wauchope, Secretary to the Goldsmiths' Hall Association in Edinburgh, asserted in January 1793:

> The Times were critical and did not admit of much Deliberation. Something required to be done. And trusting to support I agreed to do my best. Fortunately the tide turned almost instantly and in the course of a very short time those stiling themselves the Friends of the People were Resolved Declared and wrote Down.[196]

There is no doubt that the overwhelming majority of the propertied classes quickly closed ranks in defence of order and peace in society from early 1793. As we saw in an earlier chapter, moderate political dissent amongst the propertied retreated fast in 1793–4, and became embattled and sporadic thereafter. Actions to suppress radicalism and disorder were greeted with strong support, such as the Edinburgh magistrates' suppression of the British convention in December 1793. Loyalism also greatly amplified the pressures on radicals and reformers, actual and potential, to either disavow or mask their true political principles. Partly stimulated by a call from Henry Mackenzie in the press, 'disloyal' tradesmen found they quickly lost custom. This was a particular pressure in Edinburgh with its large luxury economy, but was not confined to the capital. Radicals became conscious in many places of operating as a small minority in a hostile environment and this could, as happened south of the border, act to deter and demoralize them. More generally, demonstrations of loyalism reinforced the sense of persecution imparted by the actions of the courts in 1793–4. Radicals were watched closely, their words subject to hostile scrutiny and, very often, in their eyes, gross misrepresentation.

What is less clear is how far the loyalist campaign was able to win back the loyalties of the bulk of the population, or at least immunize them against the radical message. The resolutions, loyal associations and volunteering were before the later 1790s primarily manifestations of the loyalty of the propertied classes. The same was largely true of loyal subscriptions and bounties, which drew on the same groups in society as the other demonstrations of loyalty. The more astute recognized that the upper ranks could easily delude themselves about the political views of those below them on the social scale, or who were vulnerable to pressure from above. Telling your landlord you were loyal did not make you so.[197] On the other hand, as suggested above, one of the achievements of the loyalist campaign was precisely the pressure it did contrive to create, not least through publicity in an expanding press, on groups and individuals to demonstrate that they were loyal. This did not prevent groups from resisting such pressures, if loyalist schemes were not, or were felt not to be, compatible with economic circumstances or to involve too great a burden, as illustrated by the events of the summer of 1794 when counties sought to create a strengthened force for internal order, in addition to the volunteer companies. The stuttering implementation of these schemes begins to expose some of the tensions and suspicions – political, religious and economic – which could readily fracture any loyalist consensus. One of the main appeals of volunteering was that it represented a revocable contract, the terms of which were decided by the volunteers; it was compatible with civilian status and imperatives. The urban companies were also run as subscriber democracies with elections and management committees, something which could readily compromise discipline and undermine their utility as a military force.[198] Their function in 1794–5, however, was to maintain internal order, not to help defend Britain against an invasion, although this changed in the later 1790s.

Loyalism in Scotland in this period relied heavily on the initiative, commitment and leadership of local officials, as well as direction from Edinburgh. At one level, this was a reflection of a much smaller, more cohesive political community, or series of communities than south of the border. This was one reason perhaps why so few loyalist associations were formed; the Edinburgh Goldsmiths' Hall Association had a reach into other parts of lowland Scotland which the Reeves Society in London could never have had in England, at least not in the same way. It was also a function of a society in which the average size of towns was much smaller. Moreover, in quite a few parts of the country there was confidence that radicalism had failed to gain a significant foothold. What has to be explained is why places like Perth, Dundee and Paisley did not see the formation of loyalist associations, nor did Crail or Kinghorn.

Ministers of the Church also loomed larger in loyalism than clergymen south of the border, again suggesting a movement led strongly from above. Their loyalism was vocal and very visible. As William Duncan, a Dundee versifier of little talent but keen loyalty, wrote in 1796: 'it is a comfortable reflection, that clergymen of all denominations, with only a few exceptions, have stood forth in defence of religion, law and government, with distinguished ardour'.[199] Presbyteries and synods issued loyal resolutions and 'warnings and admonitions' to their congregations, as they had done in earlier crises, for example, the '15 and '45.[200] Roman Catholic and Episcopalian congregations made very public avowals of their loyalty.[201] Fast days provided good opportunities for loyal sermonizing.[202] Ministers from different branches of the Kirk, but also various Secession churches, featured very heavily as authors of loyal propaganda, although this also reflected how few professional writers there were in Scotland, apart from ministers and academics. Aspirant Scottish journalists and writers – for example, James Perry of the *Morning Chronicle*, by birth an Aberdonian – who were not in possession of such posts went south to London in search of their fortunes. Clerical commitment was also reflected in a myriad of other actions, most of which probably remain hidden from view. As we saw earlier, the Revd Thomas Hardy, author of the highly regarded loyal pamphlet *The Patriot*, was a member of the Goldsmiths' Association publications committee. In Dundee, the Revd James Blinshall was chair of the Revolution Club, which organized loyal celebrations on key calendrical occasions.[203] Both were rewarded for their roles with appointments as King's chaplains. At an individual level, their prominence partly reflected ideological conviction, especially amongst most Moderates. In 1793–4, the anti-religious tendencies of the French Revolution, and Robespierre's elevation of the cult of reason, made defeating radicalism a religious as well as political imperative, in so far as these were ever separable. It is no accident that it was in 1794 that the Kirk launched a further drive to re-establish strict Sabbath observance.[204] The prominence of ministers also, however, reflected the continued influence of the Kirk, especially in rural parishes, where there had been no significant diminution in its authority by the 1790s, unlike in larger towns and cities.[205] Differences in the structure of local government north of the border offer a further explanation. There was no real equivalent to the parish government of south of the border. Justices of the peace were much weaker figures. The system of constables, as we have seen from the example of Perthshire, appears in normal times not to have attracted men of any social standing. The institution of the system of lords lieutenant and deputy lieutenants in 1794 was designed to fill this vacuum.

How, finally, can we explain the absence of Paine burnings, which were such a prominent feature of the loyalist reaction south of the border in the winter of 1792–3? The burning of effigies as part of a political demonstration was not unknown in Scotland prior to the 1790s, although it was nowhere near as common as south of the border, which may provide part of the explanation. Scotland largely lacked, or had done since the 1710s or thereabouts, a robust, lively political culture which embraced popular demonstrations and participation.[206] This was another factor which helped make the political demonstrations of the summer and late 1792 so alarming to the elites. From the later eighteenth century, there was also a growing fear of the mob, a fear crystallized by the renewed waves of food rioting in the 1770s and early '80s, but even more pointedly by violent anti-Catholic riots in the Scottish capital in 1779. It was the widening gap between elite and popular cultures which partly deterred the elites in larger towns where radicals were present in significant numbers from seeking to encourage crowds to gather in the winter of 1792–3, but also the recognition that they would not be able to control such events. In the winter of 1792–3, the fear and some cases reality was that it was radicals who appeared to be able to subvert public meetings for their own purposes; 'turbulent meetings' were to be avoided. It was only once the radicals had been crushed, and greater confidence had returned amongst magistrates and local elites in these towns, that major public demonstrations of loyalism were staged. Even then these were carefully policed by constables, peace officers, regular soldiers and, from 1795, the volunteers.

5 VOLUNTEERS, THE MILITIA AND THE
UNITED SCOTSMEN, 1797–8

The years 1797–8 present the historian with sharply contrasting, at times seem-ingly downright contradictory, images of the state of Scottish public opinion and political and social stability. Britain appeared in this period to stumble from crisis to crisis. In December 1796, a French fleet evaded Britain's navy to rendez-vous off Bantry Bay on the Cork coast, thereby reviving, and in a very dramatic manner, the prospect of a French invasion of the British Isles. In February 1797, against the background of the alarm created by this threat, the Bank of Eng-land was forced to suspend payments in specie; Scottish banks were compelled immediately to follow suit. This was quickly followed by mutinies in the navy at the Nore and Spithead. The north of Ireland was placed under military rule, as Dublin Castle struggled to contain the spread of disaffection in Ulster. The war against France saw further military failure and diplomatic isolation, with Spain allying with France in October 1796 and the withdrawal of Austria from the conflict in the subsequent year. Naval victories at St Vincent and Camperdown in 1797 and at the battle of the Nile in 1798 were rare bright points. Peace over-tures on the part of the Pitt ministry were rebuffed by the French in 1796 and 1797. In early 1798 a massive invasion force took shape in the French Channel ports, while in August Ireland erupted in bloody rebellion.

In Scotland, 1797 began with a new campaign of defensive military mobi-lization, which proceeded in fits and starts during 1797–8 and continued until the end of the war (1801). The initial emphasis was on a further expansion of volunteering, but this was quickly joined by other ways of preparing to repel the French. As in 1794–5, the newly-introduced system of lords lieutenant played a key strategic role in leading and organizing the defensive patriotic reaction in the counties, in response to direction from Whitehall. Lords lieutenant had similarly crucial roles to play when, in the autumn of 1797, the focus on national defence planning switched to implementation of the Scottish Militia Act, a process which led to intense and, in a Scottish context, largely unprecedented popular opposition to government and parliamentary statute north of the border. For several weeks, authority seemed to be on the point of collapse in much of central lowland Scotland and parts of the highlands. Only the application of military force enabled the protests to be subdued. Notoriously, on 29 August 1797, twelve people were killed by English cavalry troops during an anti-militia protest in and around the village of Tranent, East Lothian. Whether the troops had overreacted, or whether the cause of the deaths was the degree of resistance and violence with which they had to contend, was vigorously argued about at the time.[1] Whichever was the case, the ruling elites were shocked by their inability to control the 'mob' without the help of military force, although, aided by an influx of 3,000 troops from the south, they managed fairly quickly to recover their collective nerve. Those lords lieutenant who momentarily lost their sense of resolve – for example, the Duke of Hamilton in Lanarkshire and the Duke of Atholl – had this stiffened by the Home Secretary, the Duke of Portland, directly or through the Lord Advocate, Robert Dundas, the former of whom was determined that no concessions should be made in the face of the crowd's defiance of statute law.[2] The year 1797 also saw the reactivation of radical politics, the most notable manifestation of which was the growth of the Society of United Scotsmen, a covert body modelled on the Irish insurrectionary radical society the United Irishmen. Alongside this revival, however, a more moderate opposition and reformist politics also reasserted itself, or sought to do so, in the form of a campaign for peace in the spring of 1797. One of the major challenges facing the historian in respect of this period is disentangling these overlapping and interlinking strands of oppositional political activity and trying to assess their relative importance.

Historians have tended to examine the expansion of volunteering and defensive patriotism of this period, the anti-militia riots and rise of the United Scotsmen largely in isolation from each other. It is partly for this reason that they have reached divergent conclusions about their significance for our understanding of Scottish politics and society in the 1790s. This chapter examines them alongside one another in an effort to understand better their interrelationships and the fluctuations and contours of public opinion in this period.

The chapter is divided into sections which are organized partly on thematic and partly chronological lines. The first section explores the patriotic reaction of early 1797 in response to the scare created by the arrival of a French fleet off Bantry Bay. The focus of the second section is the reactivation of radical and opposition politics in this period, including the spread of the United Scotsmen. The third examines the anti-militia disturbances and in particular the motivations of the protestors. A final section again takes up the story of patriotic mobilization from 1798.

Reactions to Bantry Bay

The invasion scare at the end of 1796 provoked an immediate and wide-ranging patriotic reaction in many parts of Scottish society. The first symptoms of this were offers from several of the largest volunteer forces, led by the Royal Edinburgh Volunteers and Royal Glasgow Volunteers, to serve in towns in place of regular forces called elsewhere to repel an invasion.[3] Quickly, however, these offers were overtaken by new initiatives, most notably proposals to establish further volunteer companies and offers of free use of horses and carts to move troops and military supplies in the event of an invasion.[4]

The inspiration behind the latter came from publication in the press in early January 1797 of an 'Address to the Farmers' by Sir John Sinclair, Caithness landowner, improver and first president of the Board of Agriculture.[5] The response was rapid. On the Carse of Gowrie, in Perthshire, Sir John Wedderburn, who years earlier as a young man had been out at Culloden, but who had rescued his family's fortunes through plantation ownership in the West Indies, had, on seeing Sinclair's proposal in the press, got together with his neighbouring landowner, George Paterson of Castle Huntly, and circulated a paper for subscription among the leading farmers of the district.[6] Already by the end of January, 'A Briton', writing in the *Edinburgh Advertiser*, felt able to advocate arming the farmers following the success of Sinclair's appeal.[7] Even before the dissemination of Sinclair's address, however, similar offers by the farmers of Midlothian and Dalkeith had been widely publicized in the press.[8]

Proposals for additional volunteer companies seem to have emerged largely spontaneously. A small number of new companies had continued to be established in 1795–6. The first company of what, after 1797, became the first battalion of the Royal Glasgow Volunteers had been raised in June 1794; a second company had been established in April of the following year; while a third was formed in early February 1797.[9] In the third week of January, it was reported in the press that the inhabitants of Irvine on the Ayrshire coast had, on hearing news of the arrival of the French fleet off the Irish coast, immediately formed themselves into a volunteer company.[10] Around the same time, in Peterhead, on the north-east coast, an additional company of volunteers was raised.[11] In Edinburgh, various meetings seem to have taken place towards the end of January regarding proposals to add to the city's volunteer establishment.[12]

In so far, however, as any sort of lead was forthcoming, this came from the Duke of Buccleuch and the Midlothian landowners, who met on 17 February to consider their response to the invasion scare. Robert Dundas, the Lord Advocate, was present at and spoke to this meeting, which agreed a set of resolutions strongly supportive of a major expansion of volunteering.[13] The meeting also voted thanks to the inhabitants of several towns and parishes, a glass manufacturer and a firm of ship's carpenters from Leith for their recent offers of service, emphasizing again that the meeting was, to a significant extent, lending its weight to a set of initiatives already in train rather than initiating something. This widely-publicized meeting was the first of a number which took place at county level during the following eight weeks or so, many of which agreed resolutions almost identical to those endorsed by the Midlothian landowners, although several – notably those from Perthshire, Fife and Roxburghshire – also included clauses calling for the establishment of a militia as the most effective means of national defence.[14]

To the extent, therefore, that the patriotic reaction to the invasion scare was directed from above this was, in the first place, through the actions of lords lieutenant and their deputies. In many places, ministers of the church played a prominent role in encouraging support for patriotic initiatives. In several counties – for example, the County of Wigton – the resolutions agreed at county meetings were sent to ministers for reading out to their congregations.[15] The press, which was, as we saw in an earlier chapter, overwhelmingly loyal by this stage, also had an important role to play, both in terms of publicizing proposals and initiatives – for example, the resolutions of county meetings – and also, as a consequence, in creating pressure for emulation. There is plenty of evidence too of landed and burgh elites playing a prominent role in encouraging and supporting the patriotic reaction. In Cupar, Fife, the initiative behind the formation of a new volunteer company came from the magistrates, and the commander was the Provost, John Cheap of Rossie.[16] Tenants of leading landowners, such as Sir William Maxwell of Springkell in Dumfriesshire, were, no doubt, strongly encouraged by these individuals or their factors to demonstrate very publicly their patriotism.[17] In some cases, this seems to have involved hints about the renewal of tenancies being dependent on farmers coming forward as volunteers.[18]

Nevertheless, if the influence of important landowners and members of the urban elite is readily discernable in the patriotic reaction of early 1797, the response their efforts evoked was enthusiastic, or certainly appears to have been such. The contrast with 1794, in this context, is stark; and there is scant evidence of the earlier reluctance to support internal defence. This was especially so amongst the farmers, who had, in many areas, stubbornly resisted pressures in 1794 to join loyalist forces.

One county where we have better evidence than most for the marked change in sentiment and behaviour is Perthshire. From early February, the Duke of Atholl, as Lord Lieutenant, was writing letters to London urging ministers to provide arms for volunteers and impressing upon them the upsurge of loyal spirit across the county. On 2 February, he declared that, although there were still 'mischievous persons' in Scotland, the 'phrensay among the manufacturers' which had been apparent in 1792–3 had died down. He also claimed that loyalty was now at a 'very high pitch' in the county.[19] A few weeks later, he was reiterating the same message, asserting that if the government would provide 600 stands of arms, he could readily enrol between 4 and 5,000 men as volunteers.[20] In writing in such terms, Atholl was no more than responding to communications from his deputy lieutenants expressing their determination to support the patriotic effort and the readiness of those within their districts to volunteer. To cite just one example, on 28 February Mungo Murray of Lintrose reported on a recent district meeting which he had convened as a deputy lieutenant. Encouraged by local ministers, in just two hours 110 individuals had enrolled as volunteers. According to Murray, the sooner arms were available the better, since the men were enthusiastic.[21]

What makes this activity all the more striking is that any central direction was quite weak in Perthshire. It was only at the end of March that a county meeting was held, although Perthshire landowners had met at Moulinearn on 21 February under the chairmanship of James Robertson of Lude to discuss measures to be taken in response to the threat of invasion.[22] There was also a meeting of Perthshire gentry on 22 February at Edinburgh, a meeting called by Sheriff Archibald Campbell of Clathick.[23] Nor were all of the deputy lieutenants convinced that volunteering represented the best answer to the threat. George Paterson of Castle Huntly, for one, was an advocate of a militia, a view that was quite widely shared at this time, and which was made more relevant by the fact that the possibility of such a measure being introduced was being discussed by ministers and others at this time.[24] From the end of February, ministers discouraged new offers of volunteer companies as they sought to agree on a new plan of internal defence. On 17 April, Atholl received a circular letter from the Duke of Portland informing him that he should exercise discretion in submitting further offers since the government were proposing to submit plans to Parliament for raising a further military establishment. In future, infantry volunteers were to be limited to the principal towns on the coast, although yeomanry cavalry would continue to be supported elsewhere. The King, however, had been pleased to accept a proposal for four additional volunteer infantry companies in Perth, one at Coupar, two at Dunblane and one at Culross. Earlier, a proposal for a company at Dunkeld had been accepted.[25]

There is abundant evidence that the attitudes and behaviour in Perthshire were not untypical of the patriotic reaction witnessed elsewhere in Scotland in the early months of 1797. As we have already seen, farmers from across the country were quick to sign agreements to provide horses and carts in the event of an invasion. From Dalmeny, Fife, it was reported that 'almost every individual, possessed of horses and carts' had signed a subscription paper to provide them in the event of an invasion, and that 'several who had none undertook the expense of hiring them'.[26] In just one issue of the *Herald and Chronicle*, similar offers were reported from Blairgowrie, Rattray, Kinloch and part of the parish of Bendochie in Perthshire; Crail and Kingsbarns in Fife; Luss and Row in Dumbarton; Lesmahagow in Dumfriesshire; the farmers club in Kilmarnock; and from 'every parish' in Renfrewshire.[27] The keepers of post-chaises in Perth agreed, in event of an invasion, to convey troops one or two stages in any direction free of charge; they also agreed to lend the soldiers the use of their carts 'within the usual limits from Perth'.[28]

The story with respect to volunteering was similar, leading the *Edinburgh Advertiser* to boast of a revival of the 'old martial spirit' of the Scots. The papers printed numerous reports about the alacrity with which new volunteer companies were filled and new offers of companies were made. In Cupar, the county town of Fife, over 100 enrolled in a new volunteer corps of infantry in a day. Throughout Fife, 22 new companies were formed in the burghs, including two in Cupar. Other companies were also formed in several of the more populous villages, such as Aberdour, and in the parish of Cults, where David Wilkie's father was the minister. A press report on all this activity concluded: 'In short, it is highly pleasing to observe the truly patriotic zeal that animates every rank of citizens in the county; there seems to be but one mind, one heart, and one hand united in the protection of every thing sacred to free, independent, and happy people'.[29] It was a similar picture in the Stewartry of Kirkudbright, where a total of 1,509 individuals came forward as prospective volunteers from 28 parishes. In the burgh of Whithorn, in Wigtonshire, over 100 subscribed as volunteers in around two hours.[30] In many ports and coastal communities in Fife and elsewhere, fishermen came forward with offers to man boats during an invasion scare.[31] At Port Glasgow, shipowners offered their services for the defence of the coast.[32]

Although press reports of loyal activity and demonstrations tended to give very optimistic readings of manifestations of loyal spirit, contemporary correspondence suggests that in this instance the papers were not exaggerating unduly the scope and energy of the patriotic reaction. James Stedman reported on 7 March that the people of Kinross were 'so much in one mind & spirit in becoming volunteers for the Defence of the shire'. New subscriptions were coming forward 'every hour'. He continued: 'I had almost forgot to say that none of the people in Milnathort have as yet subscribed the report of the day is they mean to have a company by themselves & I have no doubt that they will get that number'.[33] From Aberdeen, February brought reports of the 'laudable spirit which now pervades all ranks'.[34] The Lord President, Ilay Campbell, returning from a visit to Glasgow and its environs about a month earlier, remarked:

> I was happy to observe that the Alarms of an Invasion had no effect there but to increase the spirit of loyalty & to add considerably to be Number of volunteers every day coming forward to offer their services. In short the People of Glasgow & in that quarter, so far from entertaining any apprehensions, are in the highest spirits, & seem to be possessed of only one sentiment upon the occasion.[35]

From Ayr, the Earl of Eglinton, the Lord Lieutenant, remarked to Henry Dundas that the county meeting called to consider a response to the invasion threat had been 'very fully attended' and 'unanimous that every exertion should be made to put it in a proper state of defence'. Farmers were proving ready and supportive of measures being adopted. Eglinton also reported that he had sent to Portland offers to form volunteer companies from Kilmarnock, Irvine, Saltcoats and Newtown of Ayr.[36]

Conversely, there are few signs of resistance or foot-dragging. In Ayrshire, while all farmers in most parishes had signed a subscription to supply horses and carts in the event of invasion, two had been 'a little backward' – Stewarton and Fenwick. In Fenwick, only two had signed.[37] In early January of the following year, the Earl of Eglinton was again noting the disloyalty of Fenwick's inhabitants, amongst whom there were 'a number of seceders ... sour saints, and bad subjects'.[38] In Edinburgh, while recruitment to the 2nd battalion of the 2nd regiment of the Royal Edinburgh Volunteers was eventually successful, attempts were made initially to 'thwart' the initiative, presumably by disaffected individuals. These seem to have involved spreading rumours that enrolment in the volunteers was a preliminary to enlistment in the regular forces.[39] A notice denying this, issued on the authority of the Duke of Buccleuch, the Lord Lieutenant of West Lothian, had to be published in the form of a handbill and in the press.[40] In Musselburgh, a handbill appeared seeking to persuade people against enrolling in a new volunteer company, which was countered by a notice similar to that issued in respect of the Edinburgh volunteers.[41] Even in 'loyal' Perthshire, patriotic feeling was certainly stronger in some areas than others. In early April, Paterson of Castle Huntly reported to Atholl about a meeting of thirty farmers who had agreed to serve in a volunteer cavalry troop in Perthshire, but who were not enthusiastic.[42] James Stobie drew a sharp contrast between the loyal tenantry of Strathord, Huntingtower, Glen Almond and Tullibardine, and the tenantry on the Logiealmond estate which, he remarked, is 'full of seceder Democrats'.[43] The *Scots Chronicle*, mouthpiece of the opposition Whigs and lone dissenting voice amongst Scottish newspapers by this period, printed a letter in late February arguing that volunteering was a 'snare' designed to perpetuate the power of ministers and to distract attention from real issues at stake – namely, the need for their removal and the negotiation of peace. Nevertheless, in the same issue of the paper, another letter urged opposition Whigs to join in the defensive initiatives as properly consistent with the 'cause of freedom'.[44] In a subsequent issue, a letter from Glasgow alleged that volunteers were only coming forward very slowly in that city, and then only either 'through necessity, or overbearing influence'. The author repeated the same warning contained in the earlier letter about shoring up ministers in power through support for volunteering. At the same time, however, they acknowledged that opposition was fragmented.[45]

Some argued that peace was the only proper solution to the invasion threat, but it seems that many opposition Whigs were coming to see defensive patriotism as fully consistent with their political stance, a viewpoint even more clearly articulated by some in 1798.[46] Members of the Royal Edinburgh Artillery Company, formed in the spring of 1797, included the reform-inclined Edinburgh Professor of Moral Philosophy and tutor to a new generation of early nineteenth-century Whigs Dugald Stewart and the opposition Whig lawyer Robert Cranstoun.[47] This trend towards a broadening patriotic consensus was a British-wide one.

Many of the volunteer companies formed in 1797, especially those established in larger burghs, were composed of men from significantly lower down the social scale than those of 1794.[48] To some extent, this must be inferred from numbers enrolled in volunteer companies, since extant muster rolls are relatively rare from this period. The new Edinburgh and Glasgow volunteers mainly comprised lesser tradesmen and apprentices.[49] One private in the first regiment, which had been formed in 1794–5, noted that the new companies being established were 'composed chiefly of journeymen and tradesmen'. In an interesting comment on the concerns about social rank which pervaded every aspect of volunteering, he also wrote of 'writers clerks, apprentices & shop keeper clerks & apprentices' who could not afford to join the first regiment of Royal Edinburgh Volunteers but who were averse to joining the new companies, the implication being that this was because of the low social standing of the rank and file.[50] In the case of the Royal Highland Edinburgh Volunteers, formed in the spring and early summer of 1797, we possess a muster roll from 1799. This shows, not unexpectedly, that the most common occupational group represented was chairman. Other well represented groups included bookbinder, change keeper, clerk, grocer, painter, porter, printer, servant, shoemaker, tailor, waiter and writer.[51] The Nairnshire volunteers were described in early 1798 as predominantly 'tradesmen and small farmers'.[52] A 'loyal subject' wrote to Henry Dundas in February 1798 describing the second battalion of the Dundee Volunteers, formed in 1797, as 'made up of the common or work people'.[53]

The expansion of volunteering in 1797 brought new challenges and threats, including those of control and the possibility of the disaffected gaining arms. From one perspective, however, what stands out is how little concern was expressed about the latter when the new companies were forming. No doubt, this was partly because people were, like Atholl, more impressed by the contemporary effusion of patriotic fervour. Several people did express anxiety, nevertheless, and in quite pointed terms. Archibald Campbell of Clathick, Sheriff of Perthshire and a staunch anti-radical, wanted officers of volunteer companies to be appointed rather than elected. To admit the latter would be, he wrote, 'most dangerous & is recognizing a hurtful French Principle'. Officers should be drawn from the ranks of county gentlemen, respectable manufacturers or master tradesmen. On being posted to particular corps, men should, he also urged, be asked to produce certificates of their loyalty, take the oath of allegiance, and sign a declaration of loyalty.[54] There was evident concern about the political principles of new Glasgow volunteers, concern shared by the Duke of Hamilton. This led James McDowall, the Lord Provost, to reassure Hamilton in the following terms: 'Such precautions would have been taken as to prevent any improper person enrolled and we flatter ourselves that it would not have been a difficult matter to procure 1500 able men of sound principles out of more than 60,000 inhabitants'.[55] The Duke of Buccleuch warned: 'To render them [the volunteers] useful against the attacks of a foreign enemy, and harmless with regard to ourselves requires great attention and superintendence'.[56] Buccleuch's scepticism about the military utility of the volunteers was very widely shared, a reflection of their often intense localism, rigidly contractualist attitude to military service, and prickly sense of self-regard, although, in default of a militia already being in existence, the volunteers were grudgingly viewed as the best possible solution to the current invasion threat.

Some infiltration of volunteer companies by the disaffected did take place, albeit probably on a limited scale. In Irvine on the Ayrshire coast in early 1798, twenty volunteers were disbanded for this reason, although the rest were said to be loyal. One volunteer, the suspected ringleader of this group, had allegedly told his officer that 'It was in his own heart what he would do, even if the French were to land'.[57] An annotated list of Dalkeith volunteers from March 1797 includes several individuals who were identified as possessing either 'questionable' or 'suspected' principles.[58] On the other hand, a number of volunteer companies played a significant, if secondary, role in policing anti-militia disturbances in the second half of 1797, and with no indication of unreliability.[59]

The evident popularity of volunteering in early 1797 requires explanation. Part of the reason was undoubtedly that, unlike in 1794, the invasion threat was immediate and incontrovertible. In 1794, as we saw in an earlier chapter, mobilization for internal defence had been as much against a domestic as an internal threat. A major appeal of volunteering was that it was a form of military service which was compatible with civilian status. Time and again, the terms of service under which offers were made emphasized this fact. Volunteers, as noted above, took a keenly contractualist view of their service, and were notably sensitive to officers failing to consult or ignoring the management committee of the company. Most officers were elected, and as such seen as accountable to the company for their command. Discipline relied less on a culture of command and obedience than a sense of common purpose, which could readily be frayed by an officer assuming too dictatorial a posture.[60] Volunteers could resign at any time, a point frequently emphasized in the founding resolutions.[61] There was, in short, no great enthusiasm for military service except under very specific conditions.

To this extent, those who had chosen to listen carefully in early 1797 would have heard clear hints that militia service would prove altogether less acceptable, or of fears about military service that would resurface much more intensely with the implementation of the Militia Act. Fears than volunteering might lead to conscription into the regular armed forces were frequently heard, and had to be allayed before companies were filled, as was referred to above in relation to the 2nd battalion of the 2nd regiment of the Royal Edinburgh Volunteers.[62]

This raises one further possibility: namely, that volunteering was embraced so readily because it would secure exemption from militia service. It is hard to know how widely this motivation was held. The prospect of a militia act for Scotland had been raised and dropped in early 1793, raised and dropped again in late 1796, and was under discussion again in early 1797.[63] Several county meetings called, as we saw earlier, for the introduction of a militia in March. In one case, however, we have direct evidence of a link between the appeal of volunteering and hostility to a militia. In early May, William Stewart of Ardvorlich wrote to the Duke of Atholl about volunteering in his district. In four days 140 men had come forward, and had paraded at Balquidder in highland dress and armed with oak cudgels. The plan was for them to wear bonnets and the tartan of the 42nd. Stewart emphasized that the district was much opposed to the militia bill and ready to submit to any hardships as volunteers to avoid this. Part of their opposition was that in that area there were no substitutes available since all 'the loose people' had already been recruited as fencibles or to other corps.[64]

In one other way, the defensive patriotism of the first half of 1797 was to have a strong bearing on reactions to the implementation of the Militia Act. Only a minority of offers to form volunteer companies were ever accepted, especially in inland areas. In the third week of February, the Duke of Montrose complained, in the context of ministers' refusal to accept an additional company of volunteers in Stirling: 'It is unpleasant to engage men in exertions, & afterwards to tell them they are not wanted'.[65] In Kirkudbright, the government's refusal of offers from inland areas provoked a meeting which described this refusal as 'injurious and insulting'. Ministers had accepted an offer of three companies of 60 men each from the burgh, but rejected offers of a further 2,000 volunteers drawn from inland districts. There may have been a class dimension to this reaction in that those who voted for the resolutions at the meeting were mainly tradesmen and artisans, in other words, individuals who would be liable to service in the militia and who were least able to afford the purchase of a substitute.[66] Not all reacted in this way. The Loyal Dalgety Volunteers, who numbered between 80 and 100, had, following a meeting on 7 March, begun to learn their military exercise from several military veterans, and even chosen their officers (on 14 April). When they made their offer of service to the Lord Lieutenant of Fife, the Earl of Crawford, he declined it on the grounds that a plan of defence was to be put before Parliament. The volunteers simply declared their readiness to come forward again should their services be required.[67] Some of the places which had their offers of service as volunteers rejected were, nevertheless, precisely those which were to be sites of violent opposition to the Militia Act later in the year. This was true, for example, of the planned village of Blairgowrie, in Perthshire, and of several weaving communities in Fife. In early April, Atholl was seeking to impress on Portland and ministers the potential dangers of dampening the 'present zeal' for volunteering by passing a militia act. The root of his concern was partly that it would take too long to pass and implement such a measure – a view Henry Dundas had shared in the previous November – but also the clash between any militia scheme and the offers already made to enlist in volunteer corps.[68] Atholl's warning was prescient. In the eyes of many, compulsory military service was poor return for the ready patriotism which they had shown in the spring.

Radical Revival

The radical revival of 1796–7 has left only a sketchy, broken and often opaque documentary trail. The authorities in Edinburgh were relatively slow to recognize the renewed threat from radicalism, probably because it had been so comprehensively crushed in 1793–4. And when they did begin to do so, partly under the impact of information from Dublin, delivered via London, their efforts at gathering information showed limited results, hence a heavy reliance on 'discoveries' which officials hoped would follow waves of arrests.[69] In March 1797, the Earl of Eglinton, Lord Lieutenant of Ayrshire, wrote to Robert Dundas about the threat posed by the influx of Irish fleeing the north of Ireland, and evidently took steps to have them watched.[70] There was a strong suspicion that communication was taking place between disaffected individuals in Ireland and the west of Scotland. Two months later, Eglinton received an anonymous letter, probably from or about Girvan, about the establishment of a secret society. One of his deputy lieutenants had taken steps to 'get to the bottom of the matter', but had only limited success. Nevertheless, from the information he had collected, he had been convinced that an oath-bound society was coming into being, and that members communicated with one another using secret signs. He also reported that it was believed that the society maintained communication with the disaffected in Ireland. Concluding, Eglinton reassured Dundas: 'Every precaution is taken, and trusty people employed to procure information of their meetings and what is going on at them'.[71] Between December 1796 and January 1797, at the request of Portland, who was himself acting on information supplied from Dublin, Robert Dundas had had Portpatrick carefully watched for Irish incomers, but this watch had lapsed at the end of January partly because of the cost of maintaining it. In May, Dundas reported to London that he was convinced that something was 'afoot' in the west, but without further help from ministers, and especially from Ireland, he was unable to discover more.[72] One reason that officials in Edinburgh were prepared to use the London Corresponding Society (LCS) agent Archibald Jamieson as an informant in 1797–8, despite scepticism about the value of the information he provided, was because they had few other potential sources of information, and that arrests of suspected radicals were not producing any real discoveries.[73] In late July 1797, the Procurator Fiscal William Scott received a letter from Perth concerning the activities of radicals there. It is unclear at whose behest this was collected, although the source of the information was evidently someone who had the confidence of the radicals.[74] Only the chance discovery of a handwritten copy of the constitution of the United Scotsmen on the street in the town in late 1797 confirmed their presence in this part of Scotland.[75] Arrests in 1798 of suspected members of the Fife United Scotsmen only took place because of 'the apprehension of some of the concerned'.[76] The real strength of the United Scotsmen lay in small weaving communities largely impervious to elite scrutiny; and the organization spread through personal contact amongst a mobile population of textile workers. Meetings typically took place in private houses, and communication was often eased by the existence of family networks linking towns and villages in a particular area. Just what its precise aims were, how it was seen by its members as joined to insurrectionary plans elsewhere in the British Isles, indeed how well organized and coherent a body it was, are questions which are not susceptible to definitive answers. Nevertheless, if much about the United Scotsmen remains elusive, there is enough information to reconstruct the main elements in the radical revival of this period.

As was described in an earlier chapter, Scottish radicalism was left in a broken, fragmented and demoralized state following the authorities' and loyalists' campaigns of repression and counter-propaganda in 1793–4. What slight evidence exists suggests little change in this condition in the following year or so, with knots of radicals continuing to meet sporadically at the local level.[77] That the revival, when it did come, occurred at a time when many Scots were demonstrating their patriotism was in large measure simple coincidence since much of the impetus behind the former came from external sources. In so far as volunteering had any significance in this context it was probably as a means of masking disaffection, or as an opportunity to infiltrate a military body. As we saw above, officials were certainly aware that this might be taking place, and in several places steps were taken to ensure that only those who were loyal to the constitution were admitted to the expanded ranks of the volunteers. Throughout the British Isles, attempts either to suborn the loyalties of the military or to infiltrate armed bodies were a key tactic of radical groups committed to insurrection as the means to achieve their political goals in the later 1790s.[78]

One of the main catalysts of radical revival, and the one which has in recent years received most attention, was events in Ireland. Elaine McFarland has recently explored the role in the formation of the United Scotsmen of an Irish politics of insurrection seeded by the repression in Ireland of open radical politics and the defeat of hopes for Catholic emancipation in 1793–5.[79] As McFarland sensibly remarks, the relative importance of this Irish influence is hard to assess, and may well be exaggerated in the extant sources; suspected United Scotsmen under detention might well have had an interest in portraying the society as the product of incomers.[80] Nevertheless, Irish influence was important and substantial, particularly in Ayrshire and the west and west-central regions. The organization of the United Scotsmen – an ascending pyramid of committees culminating, at the apex, in a national committee – was explicitly borrowed from the United Irishmen. Designed to facilitate expansion, it also aimed at maintaining maximum secrecy within the society.[81] As the authorities were well aware, and as alluded to above, large numbers of Irish were arriving from Ulster in the Ayrshire port of Portpatrick in 1797, from where they were dispersing to weaving villages in particular in the west and west-central areas. Here they came into contact with former members of the Friends of the People. Union with radical bodies in other parts of the British Isles was an element of strategy of the United Irishmen. In 1796 two agents were sent to Scotland from Belfast; and further agents arrived from Ireland in 1797–8.[82] Several leading figures in the United Scotsmen were Irishmen, and in some places it was Irishmen who were mainly responsible for swearing in new members. In Perth, two of the main radicals active in this period were James Craigdallie and Thomas Winluck, both Irishmen, although the former had been resident in Scotland for some time. By the summer of 1797, Craigdallie was 'united', although not, it seems, Winluck. It was reported that among the radicals, the system of uniting was termed 'planting Irish potatoes'.[83] Robert Sands was in 1798 to blame the spread of the United Scotsmen on the activities of 'incendiaries from the west'.[84] Under examination in April 1798, James Jarvie, a cotton spinner from Thornliebank, Renfrewshire, claimed that at the meetings of delegates from the United Scotsmen held at Pollokshaws, he 'never saw any but of the lower order, and mostly Irishmen'.[85] David Black, a Dunfermline weaver, declared that 'persons from Ireland ... were the original founders of the Society of United Scotsmen'.[86] William Murray of Ochtertyre took up two Irishmen in the summer of 1797, who had visited Crieff, Auchterarder and Dunning, the last of which was described by Murray as a 'democratick nest'. Murray had 'no doubt' that there were United Scotsmen in both Auchterarder and Dunning.[87] Meanwhile, in May 1798, the magistrates of Maybole in Ayrshire took up five Irishmen who were suspected of holding seditious meetings. According to their informer, who was one of the five, the swearing in of Irish weavers there into the secret society had been going on for twelve months. The Deputy Lieutenant of the district which contained Maybole reported that there was no appearance of sedition amongst the inhabitants, apart from the Irish.[88] During the summer of 1798, as rebellion broke out in Ireland, official concern about the influx of Irish, especially disaffected Irishmen, through western ports peaked. Sheriffs and magistrates were ordered to seize all Irishmen in their districts not possessed of passports, and volunteer corps in several places were called out on permanent duty to take up the Irish, a duty which included searching houses on the coast to prevent their concealment.[89]

The Irish connection was, as McFarland acknowledges, far from the full story behind the radical revival, however.[90] In Fife and Angus, the leading figure in the United Scotsmen was George Mealmaker, and his involvement highlights, as emphasized in an earlier chapter, the continuities in radical politics between the earlier and later 1790s. In so far as we can tell, Mealmaker's political goals had not changed since 1793, remaining focused on universal suffrage and annual parliaments, although his political message, contained in his *The Moral and Political Catechism of Man* (1797), which was being circulated on Tayside and in Fife, was a strange mixture of menace and moderation, Paineite republicanism and conditional constitutionalism. Other United Scotsmen missionaries who were Scots included Archibald Grey, who was active in the west and west-central regions, and probably Angus Cameron, a native of Lochaber and key figure in the Perthshire anti-militia disturbances.[91] Unlike in the case of Perth, there is almost no evidence regarding the activities of the United Scotsmen in Dundee, apart from the exiguous details which emerged from Mealmaker's trial for treason in 1798. There is similarly little information regarding Fife, although of twenty-six United Scotsmen societies mentioned in official sources, eight were in Fife, which, along with Angus and Perthshire, formed an east coast linen-producing region focused on Dundee.[92] A list of suspected United Scotsmen members from Fife in 1797 seems to indicate that their strength lay amongst weavers from weaving villages such as Ceres.[93] There is no direct evidence of Irish influence in such places in this period. Interestingly, Fife was to see some of the most disciplined, well-organized opposition to the Militia Act in the autumn of 1797, involving meetings of delegates from towns and villages in the county at Falkland (21 August) and later at Freuchie (8 September) to petition against the Act.[94] It also, as we will see below, saw considerable support for the opposition Whig-led peace campaign in the spring.

If developments in Ireland and exiled Irish provided part of the impetus behind revived radical activity in this period, another was provided by the renewal of connections to the LCS. Following the suppression of the British convention and resulting trials of radicals, the connections appear to have largely lapsed. Thus, an attempt to re-establish a link in 1794 by the LCS came to nothing. In late 1795, however, new attempts were made to reforge links.

The initiative again came from the LCS, at this stage looking to rebuild radical politics in the aftermath of the passage of the Gagging Acts. Two individuals who were contacted were Mealmaker and the Perth radical Robert Sands. Sands's response in particular shows how far, following the British convention, Scottish radicals looked to the London body for a strategic and political lead.[95] The contact between the LCS and both men had been an individual visiting Scotland from London, and there may well have been other personal contacts which have not left a historical record. In 1797, the LCS sent an agent to Scotland, Archibald Jamieson, referred to above. Closely watched by the authorities, on arrival in Glasgow Jamieson was arrested and only released on agreeing, it appears, to act as an informer.[96]

A further important link between the LCS and Scotland was provided by Edinburgh bookseller Alexander Leslie, whose activities shed valuable light on radical communication in this period. Leslie arrived in the capital from Jedburgh in the borders as an apprentice shoemaker some time in the early 1790s, before setting up in the bookselling business on the south side of Nicholson Street in the Scottish capital in March 1796.[97] His bookshop was described in 1797 by an Edinburgh radical printer as a 'haunt' of 'democrats'.[98] He quickly contacted the LCS offering to act as agent for its publications in Scotland, an offer which was duly accepted.[99] Leslie, like Mealmaker, was arrested in late 1797, but, unlike Mealmaker, he fled on bail rather than face a trial for treason in the spring of 1798.[100] At his arrest, various papers were seized by the authorities, including a day book, correspondence and a catalogue of his stock.[101] These show that, through his bookshop, radicals in Scotland had been gaining access in 1796–7 to a wide range of radical pamphlets, songbooks and poems. They included Jacobin classics, such as Joel Barlow's *Advice to the Privileged Orders in the Several States of Europe*; Paine's major publications, including the *Rights of Man* and the *Age of Reason*; translations of the major works of the European Enlightenment; as well as an array of more populist metropolitan radical literature, much of which was published by Daniel Isaac Eaton. In March 1796, Leslie advertised Eaton's *The Catechism of Man. Pointing out from Sound Principles, and Acknowledged Facts, the Rights and Duties of Every Rational Being* (1794) at 3*d*. or 2*s*. per hundred copies.[102] Important contacts of Leslie's in the capital included, in addition to Eaton, John Smith, J. S. Jordan, John Bone and Thomas Evans, all members of the LCS, and land reformer Thomas Spence. He also did business with more established booksellers in the capital, for example, the dissenting publisher Joseph Johnson. Leslie saw himself as part of a radical publishing network or community which naturally looked to London for support and publications. In addition to selling and distributing radical works printed and published in London, he was joint publisher of several pamphlets with the metropolitan radical printing fraternity.[103] He also published several works on his own account, including Edinburgh editions of Paine's *Agrarian Justice*, a translation of Helvetius's *Catechism*, and a radical songbook which appeared in parts, entitled *Patriot Songs; or Patriot's Musical Companion*.

At least as significant, however, as the works which Leslie was responsible for distributing, is to whom and where he was distributing them; and in the record of his day book and bits of correspondence we can glimpse circuits of radical communication being rebuilt or reactivated. He did business with booksellers and printers from Edinburgh, Leith, Glasgow, Paisley, Hamilton, Muirkirk, Alloa, Kelso, Hawick, Jedburgh and Dunbar, and Newcastle south of the border. A significant number of these individuals had been active in the first phase of radical politics in the early 1790s, men such as John Elder in Edinburgh, who we will recall was responsible for distributing cheap editions of Paine's *Rights of Man* in the second half of 1792. Leslie sent substantial orders of publications to both Edward Leslie and James Martin, booksellers in Dundee. Edward Leslie had been active in Dundee radical circles in the earlier 1790s. In Glasgow, Alexander dealt heavily with Alexander Cameron and John Murdoch, but also with the well-known firm of Brash and Reid, and with a Mrs Galloway, almost certainly the widow of a Glasgow radical bookseller of the early 1790s.[104] In Paisley, he dealt with two individuals, sending one of them substantial orders of Paine's *Agrarian Justice*, while in Kelso he sent books and pamphlets, including copies of the *Rights of Man*, to James Palmer, printer and publisher of the *Kelso Chronicle*. Among those of his customers who were not booksellers were a shoemaker from Tranent; James Craigdallie, Robert Sands and Alexander Aitchison from Perth; James Wilson from Strathaven, who was to become one of the radical martyrs following the radical rising of 1820; William Moffat, solicitor and former Friend of the People, who had fled Edinburgh following the suppression of the British convention; and James Kennedy, assistant secretary to the British convention who also fled to London from Edinburgh, but after the exposure of the so-called Watt or Pike Plot. Sands ordered thirty copies of *Patriot Songs*, clearly intended for circulation in and around Perth, while Andrew Scott, a print-cutter from a printfield near Perth, wrote in October 1797, at Sands's recommendation, 'wishing to procure a few patriotic books to disseminate in this part of the country'.[105] One further name to appear in the day book was that of Thomas McCleish, almost certainly the same man who organized the printing and circulation of George Mealmaker's *The Moral and Political Catechism of Man* and the *Resolutions and Constitution of the Society of United Scotsmen*. McCleish, like Leslie, appears to have had dealings with booksellers in other parts of lowland Scotland, many of which, again like Leslie, were the result of personal contact.[106]

That Leslie was a republican and deist is evident from his correspondence. In one letter to a fellow radical, a weaver from Kilsyth, he referred to 'these cursed Brigands or Ruffians, for they are a race of Monsters that ought to be exterminate the Earth, Kings & Priests have in all ages been a Curse to Mankind in Making Ruinous & Bloody War'.[107] It also seems likely that he was a supporter, if not himself a member, of the United Scotsmen. Among the papers seized on his arrest was a handwritten document entitled 'Caution to the Friends of Liberty & Peace' which described an oath-bound secret society dedicated to the 'sacred cause of Liberty and Universal Peace'.[108] From Dunfermline one of Leslie's correspondents wrote in November 1797: 'Fife seems to yield a pretty good crop of Pattatoes this season but not good in this corner as might been expected. The soil of this corner seems to produce the Royal Blood kind best, the new kind you know fore kings from what I hear this sort of crop has not been very luxuriant around Edinburgh.'[109] In the previous August, another fellow radical wrote to him from Linlithgow: 'I think the Soceity [sic] in London is doing well. I hope they give Arastockrats a Sweet very Soone ....'[110] Quite what metropolitan society was being referring to is open to question, but it may refer to the LCS, which continued to exist at this date, or perhaps to the British Union Society, a breakaway group of impatient extremists from the LCS formed in August 1797. This sense of connection to, and dependence on, events in London and south of the border was a major feature of insurrectionary radical politics in this period, reflecting in part lines of communication between them, but also the belief that such connections existed; indeed at times they may have existed as much if not more in the imagination than in reality.[111] Leslie, meanwhile, was a frequent visitor to Glasgow, where he married Janet Gow, daughter of a Glasgow weaver, in 1797, visiting radical groups in various places en route to the city. Among the pamphlets seized from his ship were two in the name of the British Union Society, referred to above.

There is one further main piece in the jigsaw that is the radical revival in this period, one which connects at several points to the worlds we have been discussing above. This was the reanimation of opposition Whig politics in 1796–7. Scottish opposition Whigs had removed themselves from the radical campaign at the latest by the spring of 1793 and remained a cowed, embattled force for much of the two years which followed. In 1795, however, in line with opposition Whigs in London and south of the border, they led opposition in several places to the Gagging Acts and in support of peace. In the general election of 1796, they lost further ground to Dundas and his allies. March 1796, however, had seen the establishment of the *Scots Chronicle* on the initiative of a group of Scottish opposition Whigs based in London led by the Earl of Lauderdale. This paper is discussed in detail in another chapter in this work, but what requires emphasizing here is the extent to which its success in Scotland appears to have depended on the involvement of individuals who had been prominent in earlier radical politics. Agents for its sale included the Edinburgh booksellers John Elder, Walter Berry and James Robertson, and Edward Leslie in Dundee. Elder, Berry and Robertson were also distributing in this period anti-war pamphlets, most notably Thomas Erskine's *View of the Causes and Consequences of the Present War with France*, along with other reformist works.[112] Extracts from Erskine's pamphlet were printed in the *Scots Chronicle*, while cheap pirate editions appeared in Edinburgh.[113] We know the *Scots Chronicle* was being read by groups of weavers in Fife in 1797, and it seems likely that it very widely circulated amongst radicals across lowland Scotland.[114] At least one supporter of the government blamed it for the outpouring of opposition to the Militia Act in the autumn of 1797,[115] an opposition in which weavers and other artisans and lesser tradesmen were very prominent. Other reformist papers published in England continued to circulate north of border, including the press vehicle of the Foxite Whigs, the *Morning Chronicle*, two copies of which were being taken in 1798 in the Paisley coffee house.[116]

It was in large part through the *Scots Chronicle* that the opposition Whigs sought to extend the campaign for peace in the first half of 1797 to Scotland. In this, they were only partially successful, in that support was hardly overwhelming, as was reflected in the pessimistic tone which on occasion intruded into the contents of the *Chronicle*.[117] But it was not insignificant, as Emma Vincent Macleod has recently emphasized.[118] From Edinburgh, Glasgow, Paisley, Perth, Haddington in East Lothian, and Cupar and Dunfermline in Fife, and one or two other places, well-supported petitions were forthcoming, and this despite concerted efforts to disrupt them by ministerial supporters and loyalists.[119] The bulk of support for these petitions seems to have come from artisans and tradesmen rather than members of the middling sort, and almost certainly included radical supporters. Thus, one opposition Whig supporter reported from Scotland in relation to the petitioning drive, 'of us, as you say there is little to be expected', continuing, 'Tho' Glasgow, Dundee, Perth & Edin[r] are all Petitioning here there will be a great number of subscriptions but very few people of name ...'.[120] The reason given was partly fear among the middling sort, but also the staunchly pro-administration sentiments of the upper ranks in Scotland.

The precise relationships between these different strands of political activity are hidden from view, although there was substantial overlap between them. The United Scotsmen appear to have spread quite widely, especially in areas of former radical strength. However, not every former member of the Friends of the People joined the society; in Perth there was considerable resistance to 'uniting'.[121] What becoming a member of the United Scotsmen meant to individuals is unclear, in particular whether it meant in many cases much more than a recommitment to the political goals of radical parliamentary reform. The goals expressed in the resolutions of the society did not go beyond this, or indeed beyond the popular radical political platform as it had developed by 1793, although one source of Robert Sands's suspicions regarding the society was that, by being secret, 'more might be meant than was actually expressed'.[122]

Other witnesses at Mealmaker's trial gave divergent testimony about this, although most insisted, unsurprisingly, that the society was committed to pursuing its aims by peaceful means.[123] At the same time, the opposition Whigs spoke of the removal of ministers and peace as the only means of national salvation, and a letter to the *Scots Chronicle* emphasized the pro-reform credentials of Fox and Lauderdale.[124] On the other hand, the Glasgow reformer Lord Sempill, who would become an object of official suspicion in the late autumn,[125] refused to attend a meeting called in Edinburgh in January 1797 to celebrate Fox's birthday because he objected to its private nature. Sempill's message was a bleak one: only a 'thorough reform' of the current political system could rescue Britain, but there was no hope of this given the current 'abject state of the public mind'. Given this, the only solution was exile to the United States, a path taken by other reformers earlier in the decade.[126] 'A Perth Weaver' contributed a poem to the latter paper which included the verse:

> My sov'reign – if I might advise –
> Our just petitions don't despise,
> If John and Sandy e'er arise,
> Pitt fair will rue that mornin'.[127]

Weavers from Fife arrested in 1797 as suspected members of the United Scotsmen were happy to admit to involvement in petitioning for peace in the previous year.[128] What the evidence suggests is that the opposition Whig-radical alliance was, at least temporarily, being re-knit in the early months of 1797.

Some may also have sought ways to achieve independence and a sense of self worth other than political ones. The mid 1790s saw a proliferation of reading rooms and societies amongst the labouring classes in Scotland. Described in a series of letters in the *Scots Chronicle*, they were formed in the image of the more famous subscription libraries which emerged in urban Scotland from this period.[129] A key difference, however, was their membership was smaller and their charges lower. Between eleven and twelve such societies existed in Paisley, for example, with thirty to forty members each drawn from the ranks of the 'working people'. The societies met monthly, members contributing between 6 and 9*d*. The societies lasted for a fixed duration, after which the books were auctioned off to the members, and the proceeds divided equally between them.[130] It is possible that some of these societies were linked to, or even a cover for, radical political activity. Archibald Jamieson was offering officials in Edinburgh a scheme to close down the reading societies at this time, presumably because of their radical connections.[131] Following a visit by Mealmaker to Coupar Angus, a news room was established.[132] The librarian of the Dundee Public Library, whose members, according to a letter in the *Chronicle*, comprised 'mostly tradesmen and labourers', was James Martin, one of the Dundee booksellers who had business connections with Alexander Leslie.[133] At Muirkirk, in Lanarkshire, a small group of artisans and tradesmen set up a society which called itself a 'reading society' in public but a 'society for political information' in private. We only know about this because its members were believed to be behind local opposition to the Militia Act.[134] One commentator portrayed these popular reading societies as part of the European phenomenon of the lower orders rising to a proper sense of their importance.[135] It may be that the link is that both – politics and reading rooms – were symptoms of a radical version of the Enlightenment that took hold amongst elements of the artisans and lesser tradesmen in burghs and manufacturing villages at the end of the eighteenth century.

Anti-Militia Protests

If the authorities knew relatively little about the United Scotsmen before the end of 1797, this was also because their attention was, in the main, focused elsewhere. As summer turned to autumn in 1797, a wave of intense popular protests took place against implementation of the Militia Act. Initially dropped by Henry Dundas in February following proposals for its revival in late 1796 at the time when a supplementary militia was being enacted for England, the Scottish Militia Act was passed in haste by Parliament on 19 July 1797.[136] Quite why Dundas went ahead, in the face of advice to the contrary from leading figures in Scotland, who anticipated popular opposition,[137] is not entirely clear; but it almost certainly reflected his conviction that 'military feeling' in Scotland needed to be spread further to defend against external threats, and a more widely-shared acceptance of the limitations of volunteers as a military force. In several letters, he spoke of the desirability of introducing a general military training for 'every man' of between nineteen and twenty years old in order to create a defensive force that was economical but also sufficiently extensive.[138] As several historians have pointed out, the successful introduction of the system of lords lieutenant in 1794 prepared the way for the creation of a militia.[139] Dundas viewed this system with great pride, and saw it as the lynchpin of order and security. In early August 1797, he declared to Colonel Alexander Dirom, with whom he had an extensive correspondence about internal defence: 'I trust it has been in my Power in the course of my Political Life to be of service to my native Country in more particulars than one, but I value upon none more, than the introduction in Scotland of that respectable and usefull office of lieutenancy under the Crown'.[140] Whatever Dundas's precise reasoning, those who had foreseen popular opposition were to be proved frighteningly correct as implementation of the Act got underway in the late summer. Although they began as early as the end of July, protests properly began in Berwickshire, Stirlingshire and Abernethy and several other parishes in Perthshire in mid-August.[141] Few counties or areas in the lowlands were completely unaffected, although in several counties unrest was particularly serious – East Lothian, Ayrshire, Dumbartonshire, Fife and the south-western counties of Dumfriesshire and Galloway. At the end of August, parts of highland Perthshire rose in opposition to the Act in what the Duke of Atholl described at the time as a 'kind of phenzy',[142] while upper Deeside in Aberdeenshire was the scene of the final spasm of unrest in mid-September.

If anti-militia protests were widespread throughout lowland Scotland, the detailed pattern was, nevertheless, quite a complicated one. Several counties saw little or no unrest. They included Midlothian, which included Edinburgh, and perhaps more surprisingly the manufacturing counties of Renfrewshire and Angus.[143] Kinkardine, Nairnshire, Banff, Elgin, Caithness and Ross in the north-east, and Argyll and Invernesshire in the highlands were completely free of disturbances.[144] Even within those counties badly affected by protest, far from every parish saw resistance to implementation of the Act. In Fife the burghs of Newburgh and Kirkaldy remained quiet, despite very widespread disturbances elsewhere in the county, while much of lowland Perthshire remained relatively quiet.[145]

Resistance to the Act also took several forms, and was far from always violent or straightforwardly intimidatory. The most notorious episode of violence, referred to in the introduction to this chapter, took place at Tranent in East Lothian on 29 August, an incident which has been very well described elsewhere by Logue.[146] Most agreed that the soldiers had come under severe provocation and assault, in the form of stone throwing and attacks with heavy bludgeons from crowds partly formed from colliers and salters from the surrounding area; where there was disagreement was about whether the military's response, which led to twelve deaths, was proportionate.[147] In various places – Crieff, for example, Denny in Stirlingshire, or Shotts, New and Old Monkland in Lanarkshire – opposition took the form of petitioning campaigns calling on the King to suspend the Act.[148] These campaigns were often highly coordinated, involving meetings of delegates to discuss measures against the Act. Indeed, meetings drawing people together from across a parish or number of parishes to discuss the Act seem to have been commonplace, and were, on occasion, the prelude to direct action.[149] The organization evident behind the protests was one of their aspects which most alarmed the authorities.

Where direct action was taken, moreover – for example, seizing lists of men eligible for the militia ballot from schoolmasters or compelling deputy lieutenants to sign bonds committing them to take no further role in implementing the measure – the level and nature of violence employed by, and the temper of, the crowds varied considerably. In some places, crowds were, according to reports, calm and good humoured; in others, they bristled with anger and violent intent.[150]

Explaining these differences is very hard. As we will see below, many were convinced that political disaffection lay at the root of the disturbances, but if so not all places with a radical presence or recent radical history saw unrest. In Dundee and Perth in the east and Paisley in the west, for example, there were no anti-militia disturbances, yet each had a considerable and determined radical presence.[151] And while Renfrewshire as a whole, with its many manufacturing villages, remained quiet, the borders, which had seen few radical societies formed in the earlier 1790s, and from where there is no evidence of the United Scotsmen being active, saw considerable unrest. Much seems to have depended on the actions and responses of those in authority to popular concern and alarm about the Act. The composition of crowds and their relationship to local landowners and officials also had a bearing on the role of violence in protests; where deputy lieutenants were known to crowds, and vice versa, there was generally less violence; bonds of deference and respect were strained almost to breaking point, but not quite. Credit for Renfrewshire's quiescence has been given to its Lord Lieutenant, William McDowall, who took much personal responsibility for implementation of the Act, deliberately staggering district meetings of deputy lieutenants to collect lists of men eligible for the militia ballot in order that he could be present at every one.[152] McDowall also took very deliberate steps to explain the Act before seeking to implement it; in many other places, efforts at explanation were slower to emerge or followed protests.[153] Similarly in Midlothian, the close attention and determination of the authorities, including the Lord Advocate, helped to prevent overt opposition to the measure.[154] Also critical was whether troops were present or available to back up authority. Although volunteers were frequently used to police district meetings and deter protests, no great reliance was placed on them.[155] Civilian peace officers – ordinary and extraordinary or special constables – seem to have largely disappeared in the face of the intensity of popular opposition to the Act.[156] Only regular forces, and especially dragoons, were effective as deterrents or in suppressing disorder. As the Duke of Roxburghe reported from the Borders: 'The Populace yet hold them [volunteer yeomanry] in contempt as soldiers, But they dread the appearance of the Dragoons'.[157] Recognition of this fact explains why Lord Adam Gordon, the Commander of Forces in Scotland, and the Edinburgh authorities were so quick to call on London to supply additional troops to put down the protests, a request which was readily acceded to, with 3,000 troops being sent north to aid the civil authorities.[158] Even with this accession of military strength, the number and scale of protests made it impossible to respond immediately to all outbreaks of disorder. This was one reason why the Perthshire disturbances were only brought under control relatively slowly; it took time to withdraw troops from elsewhere – notably Fife and Stirling – to move into the affected areas; at the same time, it was deemed inadvisable to leave Perth denuded of any significant military force.[159] Similarly in Fife, lack of quickly available military force allowed protests to spread unchecked there in the first week of September.[160]

If, therefore, patterns of resistance and opposition to the Militia Act were more complicated than they are sometimes represented, what most struck the ruling elites was, notwithstanding this, the intensity of popular anger which it aroused; the signal defiance by the lower orders of elite rule and authority; and, as emphasized above, the apparent degree of organization behind the protests.[161] Poorly-paid parish schoolmasters, upon whom was placed responsibility for compilation of lists of men eligible for the ballot, were similar in social standing to many of those protesting; and their vulnerability to intimidation is unsurprising. The schoolmaster in the parish of Falkirk was evidently determined not to compile any list, repeatedly refusing directives to do so, even on one occasion leaving his home, and having those left there inform the local deputy lieutenant that they did not know when he would return.[162] The house of the schoolmaster in Carstairs in Lanarkshire was set on fire, and a mob refused to let the fire be extinguished until all the parish registers had been produced and burnt.[163] Similar incidents were widespread in many counties, and many schoolmasters, like the one in Falkirk parish, refused to act.[164] (One flaw in the Militia Act was that it made no provision for compelling schoolmasters to draw up the lists of men eligible for the ballot.) In Stirlingshire, it was the deputy lieutenants who had, in many parishes, to draw up the lists themselves. According to the Lord Lieutenant for the county, the Duke of Montrose, in doing so they had met no resistance.[165] In many other places, however, deputy lieutenants found themselves treated with novel disrespect and open intimidation when they attempted to collect lists at district meetings. A significant number were forced to sign undertakings to discontinue their efforts to implement the measure.[166] What must have struck those in authority were the scale of opposition, the determined defiance of entreaties to desist from opposition to the Act, and the intensity of feeling which underlay this opposition. One deputy lieutenant responsible for the district which contained Strathaven, scene of an anti-militia riot at the beginning of September, wrote to the Duke of Hamilton in alarm in early September urging delays in taking any precognitions from witnesses concerning this disturbance since such action was only likely to lead to further assaults and violence on those in authority. As he declared: 'The tendency of this bill ... has been to detach from us the country part of the parish and united them with the people of the town, [so] that we have none now to depend on'.[167]

Historians agree that much of the explanation for this anger and resistance is to found in the specific terms of the Act, rather than any underlying political disaffection or discontent with the continuance of the war.[168] Ironically, one aspect which aroused opposition was the restriction of eligibility for the ballot to those men aged between eighteen and twenty-three years – ironic because this narrow range was probably chosen to lighten the burden of service on communities.[169] By restricting the range to this extent, however, those eligible were much more likely to find themselves balloted for service. People of this age were also quite often the support of the elderly. There appears to have been widespread suspicion that service in the militia would be a preliminary to forcible enlistment in the regular army.[170] The fear that the terms of service would be violated was especially strong in highland Perthshire. These suspicions may have reflected the recent experience of seeing fencible regiments raised for service in Scotland deployed in England and overseas. The highland communities in the county also seem to have viewed the militia as an alien force not in keeping with local traditions. Inhabitants of several highland parishes openly stated their willingness to defend 'internal peace and tranquillity' when called upon to do so by justices of the peace. They also declared their willingness to raise funds to pay for volunteers to serve under the Militia Act, but these men were not to be drafted into the regular army and were to be commanded by a 'gentleman of the Country'.[171] If they were going to serve in defence of the country (a term which usually meant simply parish or immediate locality), they wished to do so on a voluntary basis and under local leadership.[172]

In some lowland areas, there was a class element in the opposition to the Act. The *Scots Chronicle* reported the following conversation between Charles Hunter of Burnside and a widow on the links of Barry near Arbroath:

> Mr HUNTER told a widow woman who had some of her sons inrolled, that all his sons were in the Army or Navy; but the widow replied, 'That this was greatly to his advantage, and his sons too; and that these would domineer and lord it over her's, and other poor people like them.'[173]

The Stirlingshire militia proclamation, issued on 29 August 1797, explicitly stated that the Act fell equally on all sections of the population: 'No Gentleman, or the Son of a Gentleman (as has been supposed by some) is exempt from Militia Duty'.[174] How widely such concerns were articulated, however, is hard to say, and there would seem to be a contrast here with the anti-militia disturbances in England in 1757, which had a very marked class dimension.[175]

Those in authority quickly became convinced that behind the disturbances was misrepresentation of the terms of the Act. In quite a few places, rumours or fears about the effect of the Act – for example, that those forced into service in the militia would be sent to the East or West Indies[176] – took hold. To counteract these and other misperceptions, lords lieutenant issued handbills and notices in newspapers seeking to correct misunderstandings and instruct the population as to the correct terms of the Act and militia service. Such efforts appear in many counties to have arisen spontaneously, often at the initiative of individual deputy lieutenants,[177] although by the end of August, officials in Edinburgh were circulating copies of printed addresses to lords lieutenant and sheriffs, while at the beginning of September Portland was recommending use of printed notices on parish churches and 'conspicuous situations' as part of wider range of strategies designed to deal with resistance to the Militia Act and enable its continued implementation.[178]

At bottom, however, popular protest and anger reflected sheer dislike of compulsory military service, however this was dressed up. A Fife petition against the measure talked of the 'utter and irreparable aversion' to the 'profession' of soldiering, and of 'strongest and most unconquerable abhorrence' of the 'military life'.[179] One of the ways in which resistance to the Militia Act was defused was to make clear that substitutes could serve in place of those balloted, and the launching of subscriptions at parish level to pay for these substitutes. Atle Wold has recently suggested that the first such subscription to be launched was at Rutherglen in late August and, based on contemporary newspaper reports, Wold estimates that around thirty subscriptions were instituted.[180] These subscriptions appear in many cases to have been supported and promoted by members of the landed classes, but not in all cases. In one parish in Stirlingshire, the young men seem to have got together and asked a local notable to draw up a subscription paper to establish such a fund. In a letter to William Forbes of Callendar, the leading local landowner, the individual concerned noted that 'none of them have any desire to serve in person'. He also reported that they were relying heavily on Forbes's support, concluding: 'they have in this business behaved with great moderation – and are of course I think intitled to all the assistance possible'.[181] However the subscriptions emerged, the connection between them and the damping down of disturbances was explicitly made by contemporaries. From Muirkirk, it was reported that, while all young men of the parish were on the list of those eligible for service, each had subscribed 10*s.*, while other inhabitants had also added sums. The result was that 'this will prevent completely, any inconveniency to any individual in the parish, consequently all future cause of complaint'.[182] In some cases, moreover, a subscription seems to have been established as the *only* way to dampen down unrest, even at considerable financial cost to landowners. Thus, one East Lothian deputy lieutenant wrote feelingly in 1800 to the Duke of Hamilton:

> You know the trouble I was at formerly when the mobs were prevailing in the country & had then Old Bertram's parishes & my own to manage no fewer than 9 in number and I was put to Expence of above £230 in finding substitutes for the militia lads that were Balloted to serve for those parishes in order to get the mobs dispelled & the People kept quiet ...[183]

In highland parts of Perthshire, the institution of subscriptions for substitutes seems to have been closely linked to the quieting of the region after the unrest, although the initial cause of this had been the concerted deployment of military force.[184] In Edinburgh, a militia insurance scheme was launched by Robert Allan, the loyalist newspaper printer and publisher of the *Caledonian Mercury*, which had the same effect. This initiative seems to have had the support of Robert Dundas.[185] When the militia was first embodied in 1798, at just half strength – 3,000 – so as not to arouse further protests, what probably made it palatable to the labouring classes was the role of substitutes.[186]

Compulsion seemed poor recompense too for the enthusiasm for volunteering displayed earlier in the year. Time and again, this issue was raised by those opposed to the Militia Act. From Sanquhar, it was reported that people were complaining that they had volunteered, but were now being 'pressed into service', and would be 'made soldiers of whether they will not'.[187] Robert Grierson wrote from Dumfriesshire that people in the parishes round about him would 'cheerfully come forward as volunteers under the direction of men possessed of their confidence', but were strongly opposed to the Militia Act.[188] Patrick Murray reported that his and Ardvorlich's volunteers, the latter of whom we met in an earlier part of this chapter, were 'very much irritated' that after putting themselves to considerable expense as volunteers they were now faced with the potential burden of militia service.[189]

Opposition to the Militia Act could be and was portrayed, therefore, as emerging from 'loyal' sections of the population. Yet at the same time, quite a few contemporaries detected the hand of the 'disaffected' behind the protests.[190] At times, this seems to have been based on little more than supposition. If rumours were circulating which misrepresented the terms of the Militia Act, then it naturally followed that the source of these rumours were malcontents seeking to stir up popular anger. The geography of protest also seemed to point to a similar conclusion, in that it was in industrial villages and communities where radicalism had taken root in the early 1790s that resistance was often strongest, although this was not universally so, as we have seen. The Duke of Montrose, for example, spoke, in the context of opposition to the Act, of the role of the 'old districts' – Falkirk, Kilsyth, Bucklivie, Kippen, Gartmore and Balfron – in other words, former areas of radical strength.[191] Kirkintilloch, Cumbernauld and Strathaven were other centres of opposition to the Act in the west which had a recent radical history.[192]

If suspicion of radical involvement was, then, often no more than that, in several cases there was more substance to these assertions. Threatening letters to magistrates on occasion hinted at deeper-lying grievances and political opposition to current power structures. William Cunninghame of Lainshaw, Ayrshire, was told: 'As we have been under your tyrannical power so long and been so much kept under by your old headstrong, unjust ways of dealing with us about this town [Stewarton], we therefore have taken it into consideration that neither you nor your Lord Lieutenant, as you call him, but we can call you and him no other thing but two old damned tyrants ...'.[193] In Dalry and Beith, also in Ayrshire, trees of liberty appeared as part of the protests.[194] In two other parishes in the same county, Kilmaurs and Fenwick, which had, like Stewarton, stood outside the patriotic consensus of early 1797, there were reports of associations forming to oppose implementation of the Act, meetings, a subscription and, more alarmingly, efforts to procure arms. Eglinton, the Lord Lieutenant, wrote of these parishes: 'I look on this as the very worst part of the whole county – other parts may be led away by bad advice, and folly, but there they are, and have been for long, a sett of obstinate and determined democrats'.[195] In East Lothian, a servant of a 'democratical tenant' supposedly told a 'respectable' inhabitant of Haddington that the Militia Act was against both the Union and the Confession of Faith.[196] It was reports like this which lay behind the idea that the disaffected were deliberately stirring anger against the measure through the power of malicious rumour. Radicals were suspected to be behind the protests in several parishes in Lanarkshire, notably Muirkirk and Strathaven, while in Fife at least one radical was influential in the anti-militia campaign there.[197] Key figures, meanwhile, in the unrest on Strathtay were Angus Cameron and John Menzies, both suspected members of the United Scotsmen, and both of whom certainly had close links to radicals in and around Perth.[198] Lord Fife claimed that the militia had been a 'pretence' in the highlands, and alluded to political causes behind the protests. Copies of abridgements of the Act of Union were, he reported, dispersed widely, in which it was claimed that the Union was 'broke' and that there was no government. He hinted too at a heady element of socio-economic radicalism, with talk of taking property back from landlords, regulating rents and removing controls on taking timber and fish.[199] Another source talked of having 'heard murmurs about reducing the Lairds Rents and the ministers stipends and about making the king reside at Edinburgh',[200] which perhaps indicates the strange blending of traditional and radical voices stirred up by Cameron and the agitation in Strathtay. A schoolmaster who was examined after the disturbances alleged that one individual, now a tollkeeper on the Dunkeld Road at Perth, had held a 'Democratical Club and instilled French Principles into the Tenants of Edradour', for which he had been turned away by the local landowner.[201] Much was made of oath-taking as an element of these protests, but most witnesses testified that the oath had nothing to do with the United Scotsmen.

Logue's conclusion, therefore, that the main wellspring of opposition to the Militia Act was to be found elsewhere than in the actions of knots of disaffected radicals must in general be correct, although their role was probably significant in several areas.[202] It is also far from clear that the disturbances aided the radicals in terms of attracting further support to them. In one obvious sense, they were counter-productive in that they helped to steel the authorities to act against the United Scotsmen, with the first big wave of arrests commencing in November

1797. There was also a determination to ensure that the radical leadership, in so far as it was known, should be prosecuted and subject to harsh punishment. Mealmaker was sentenced to fourteen years' transportation in early 1798, and his trial was closely and widely followed in the press.[203] Cameron, who, along with Menzies, was hunted down by the military in mid-September, fled Edinburgh on bail, probably ending up in London.[204] And while the United Scotsmen survived this first series of blows, further arrests followed in February and April 1798, the latter series concentrated in and around Glasgow and Renfrewshire weaving villages. These actions seem to have successfully cowed the United Scotsmen before the outbreak of rebellion in Ireland, and they almost entirely disappear from the historical record until a brief reappearance in 1801.[205]

Patriotism Continued, 1798

In retrospect, one of the most striking features of the anti-militia disturbances is how quickly they were sparked off and equally how relatively quickly they died down. By mid-October, Lord Adam Gordon was unconcerned about the return of two troops of dragoons to England.[206] Part of the explanation for their rapid subsidence was the concerted use of military force to suppress disorder and official determination and activism, both at the centre and locally through the actions of the lords lieutenant and their deputies, which included arresting ringleaders and seeking to ensure that their trials followed quickly.[207] From Perth, Archibald Campbell wrote at the beginning of October of the 'spirit of the refractory' being 'compleatly subdued by terror', although he also acknowledged that a 'democratical spirit' continued.[208] Events at Tranent and the evident determination of the authorities to defend the actions of the military, which included publication of a 'narrative' of the riots to counter 'false and unfounded reports' regarding the role of the soldiers,[209] and to punish some of the supposed ringleaders, may have caused some to step back from direct action.[210] There is evidence too that explanations of the terms of the Act helped to reconcile popular opinion, and there was to be no recrudescence of the violence and protests when the militia was initially embodied in 1798.[211] Rather, this seems to have gone ahead peaceably and without significant tension, although continued persecution of schoolmasters in some places may indicate a deeper undercurrent of hostility and alienation.[212]

From early 1798, the continued threat of French invasion, as Napoleon's *armée d'angleterre* mobilized in the French Channel ports, also called forth further displays of defensive patriotism. The degree of central direction was greater than in the previous year, however, in that the main initiatives were driven from London. Additional volunteer companies were encouraged, but in the context of new legislation and plans for national defence circulated to the counties in

April 1798.[213] 1798 also saw the experiment of Pitt's voluntary contribution to help fund the continuing war effort.

These initiatives were on the face of things successful north of the border, and they certainly helped to create an image of a Scotland which was solidly united around defence of British liberties and the British constitution and in opposition to France under the Directory. The reality, however, may well have been more mixed and ambiguous. Volunteering remained popular, and new volunteer companies continued to be formed. Although first planned in September 1797, June 1798 saw, for example, the formation of the 120-strong Glasgow Armed Association, a strictly local force of volunteers which was not eligible for government financial support. In the following month, 62 of the 'loyal inhabitants' of Hamilton offered their services as a 'Volunteer Corps in Defence of our King and Constitution' in the military district which included Lanarkshire.[214] Other offers were forthcoming from the same county in what one group described as 'a season of danger, of alarm, & national exertion'.[215] From the Carse of Gowrie, George Paterson reported in June 1798 that 'our volunteering goes on very rapidly'. Within his district, it was designed to raise four companies of infantry and a troop of yeomanry. His tenants had given in 100 names, from which Paterson intended to select 60 'good men'. In a demonstration of the fact that enthusiasm was not always matched by military utility or potential, Paterson also reported: 'All the rusty guns in the country were mustered on the Kings birthday & 30 of them fired with great exactness, at my village of Longforgan'.[216] Brechin in Angus raised its first volunteer company in 1799.[217] Opposition Whigs could be found establishing or supporting companies, a widening of a trend first evident in 1797. The Duke of Montrose noted, for example, following a county meeting in Stirlingshire called to agree measures for local defence: 'Those who were in opposition to the Administration seem to make a point of coming forward & offering their services for the defence of the country against an invading Enemy ...'.[218] One of Paterson's collaborators in raising volunteers on the Carse of Gowrie in 1798 was Lord Kinnaird, a supporter of the opposition Whigs, although Kinnaird's claims for a volunteer or militia command for himself and his son were opposed by Paterson and others who had shown staunch loyalty throughout the 1790s.[219] Yet even by 1801, the numbers involved in volunteering are easily exaggerated. It is also noteworthy that volunteer numbers were greatest in highland counties, where economic motives for volunteering were almost certainly strongest.[220] Moreover, the importance of economic factors in facilitating, if not encouraging, participation in volunteering across Scotland was very clearly revealed in January 1798 when ministers sought to reduce the allowance for training from two days to one a week.[221] The reaction north of the border was vehemently hostile, and Portland and Dundas were inundated with letters complaining about the likely adverse impact of volunteer morale and pointing out the contribution of volunteers to checking seditious principles in Scotland.[222] Patrick Crichton, the lieutenant colonel of the 1st battalion of the 2nd regiment of the Royal Edinburgh Volunteers, warned of the 'no small hazard of the entire dissolution of the corps themselves'.[223] Several people also emphasized the handle which such a decision would give to the disaffected to attack the ministry, a reminder that while radicals were cowed they had not disappeared.[224] Faced with the barrage of criticism, ministers rescinded the decision.[225]

Membership of the volunteers also brought immunity from militia service,[226] while people clearly expected, as they had in previous years, the terms of service to recognize the imperatives of civilian life. The Earl of Morton was told in July 1798 that plans to create new companies were likely to prove successful, although this depended on the terms of service being 'agreeable'. What this meant in practice was the place of rendezvous for drilling being fairly close to homes, the men not being called out very often, and a 'total suspension from drill during harvest'.[227]

The response to the national defence plans in 1798, which involved an unprecedented effort to collect and collate information about local preparedness and willingness to contribute in different capacities in the event of invasion, was also not one of unreserved support. In Renfrewshire, while William McDowall was satisfied with the patriotic spirit present in the county, he instructed those who filled in the schedules of those willing to serve also to make out lists of those not prepared to participate. He explained the reason for taking this course of action in a letter to Henry Dundas in early June:

> I am sorry to say that they met with insolence & even some abusive language in some instances not only among the lowest classes of the people, but among farmers & others, whose principles I considered as favourable to Government – Have taken [...? word indecipherable in MS] arundo of French liberty & equality, which may be bent but cannot easily be broken – with this list, I shall however be enabled to crush it more effectually than I would otherwise have done –[228]

In Stirlingshire, the completion of schedules ran into difficulties because of suspicions about why the information was being collected. Some farmers and others appear to have believed that it might be used to help raise rents or in the collection of taxes, and considerable effort was needed to allay these concerns.[229]

The record of the voluntary contribution was also more mixed than reports in the press might suggest. From the capital, Thomas Elder reported on 2 March 1798: 'We are here all quietness and voluntary contributions going on tolerably'.[230] The capital's elites rallied round, however, and set a strong example for others to follow. The Duke of Buccleuch committed £6,000 a year for the duration of the war, Robert Dundas £2,000, and the Faculty of Advocates and Town Council both gave £2,000.[231] Burgh authorities and other corporate bodies evidently felt pressure to contribute, or to be seen to contribute, reasonable sums. The initial contribution for the Forfar Town Council was £50, but this was doubled just over a week later. The reason is explained in the town council minutes:

> The Magistrates & Council, taking into their further consideration, the necessity of giving as much aid as possible to government in the present critical State of affairs by the threatned [*sic*] invasion of the French and the Provost having represented that other Burghs of less ability and extent had contributed to a much greater amount than the sum agreed to be given from the funds of the Town; The Council unanimously agree to give the sum of Fifty pounds Sterling in addition to the like sum resolved to be given by minute of the 12th current ...[232]

From Bath, George Paterson was able to report to Robert Dundas at the beginning of March that 'By my letters from Dundee this day, I find the Contribution there is going on with spirit ...'[233] Towards the end of March, James Stobie, the Duke of Atholl's factor, informed his employer that the country people were 'subscribing fast for the assistance of Government', and that the parish of Tippermuir looked set to subscribe £300 exclusive of taxes.[234] The second Earl of Cassilis reported from his part of Ayrshire that, while the overall sum might not be huge, the numbers of subscribers were 'beyond idea' and that even the 'poorest cottars' had made contributions.[235] The miners of Wanlockhead gave contributions of between 1s. and £10.10s. each.[236] The lists of contributors which filled many pages of the press had the effect of emphasizing the social depth and extent of support, including many very modest donations.

Like many earlier loyal and patriotic initiatives, the success of the voluntary contribution depended to a significant extent on the support from and example shown by the landed and urban elites and from other leaders of communities, notably ministers of the church. Lords lieutenant and their agents seem to have deliberated long and hard about how much to pledge, acutely conscious of the interpretation which might be placed on a less than generous donation.[237] Owing to indebtedness, Lord Tweeddale initially omitted to make a donation, but eventually put his name down for £1,000 since, as Lord Lieutenant, not do so 'would be a reason to prevent the lower class of people from subscribing'.[238] In Stirlingshire, committees, comprising deputy lieutenants, justices of the peace, and clergymen 'of all denominations', were formed at parish level to encourage contributions for 'all ranks of inhabitants'. The clergy were also directed to recommend support from their pulpits.[239] In Lanarkshire, the Earl of Hyndford reported to the Duke of Hamilton, the Lord Lieutenant, that a meeting in Hamilton to commence a voluntary subscription had been 'poorly attended'. As a result, it was decided not to open a subscription immediately, but rather to establish one in each parish 'under the patronage', as it was described, of the clergymen and deputy lieutenants.[240] Almost a month later, one clergyman reported to Hamilton that he was taking steps to support the contribution, but was predicting that their success would be limited.[241] Clergymen seem to have played an important role in other places. From Blairgowrie, one such individual wrote on 18 April: 'Some influence will be necessary to ensure degree of success – The people seem very averse to the measure'. In his view, only the influence of the proprietors on tenants would produce the required results; his entreaties from the pulpit had been unavailing.[242]

If the patriotic consensus was, therefore, far from universal and on occasion manufactured with difficulty, it was, nevertheless, a broadening one in the later 1790s. We have already seen how it included opposition Whigs, who might condemn the conduct of the war, but who could not ignore the patriotic call in defence of their country and constitution against the French. Other groups who had hitherto remained outside this consensus took steps to enter it. In the spring of 1798, a loyal address to government was forthcoming from the burgher Seceders.[243] We lack information on some of the other dissenting churches, although it is striking that the Stirlingshire authorities felt able to call, as referred to above, on the services of clergymen from 'all denominations' in support of the voluntary contribution. From Dalkeith, it was also reported in March 1798 that a recent fast day was observed 'even by the seceders & other sectaries here'. The same writer declared: 'the tide begins to turn, the eyes of the vulgar are open'd; they dread the French invasion & I am perswaded now that the bulk of the "Friends of the People" see their error with contrition'.[244]

What wider lessons can be drawn from this attempt to map the broad contours of shifting popular and indeed elite opinion in Scotland in 1797–8? In some ways, what stands out is, first, the mutability of popular opinion. Parishes which saw violent anti-militia protests might, by the spring of 1798, show exemplary willingness to volunteer or make financial contributions towards national defence. In this context, there were frequent calls in the spring of 1798 for leniency to be shown towards those who had been found guilty of rioting against the Militia Act.[245] Second, this period demonstrates very clearly the limits of popular quiescence under elite rule. Patriotic mobilization might have paradoxical effects in this context, as Linda Colley and others have emphasized.[246] It is likely, for example, that tenant farmers, normally passed over quickly in discussions of popular politicization in this period, became more independent and restive in the 1790s. This was partly a reflection of their achieving a greater sense of collective identity through the formation primarily of farmers' clubs and societies, although these very often had a landowner patron. However, it was also because of the concerted efforts to enlist them in patriotic initiatives. One contemporary commented in March 1797, in the context of the formation of yeomanry cavalry companies of volunteers in West Lothian, comprising farmers and gentry: 'By this our farmers have obtained a sort of political consequence they before had not'.[247] During the later 1790s, there are signs of farmers as a group becoming more vocal on a range of issues, but especially taxation and the commutations of road service and creation of turnpike trusts.[248]

Volunteering was also one of the ways in which burgh elites reinforced their standing within their local communities, and at the same time brought them into closer cooperation with members of the landed elites. Like subscription charities, which were proliferating in this period, volunteering can be seen as part of wider process in which notions of civic identity were being reshaped to reflect the collective strength, concerns and outlook of the prospering urban middling ranks. And while many rural volunteer companies formed from the summer of 1798 were a projection of landowner power and influence – the captain of the company formed on Lord Kinnaird's estate on the Carse of Gowrie, for example, was his factor[249] – many urban volunteer companies were altogether less tractable bodies. Disputes flared up about leadership, disputes which reflected the sense that command of the volunteers should be accountable and decision-making transparent.[250] The resolution of divisions within the Stirling volunteers, which appears to have taken on a class dimension, required the corps to be disbanded and two new companies formed.[251] In Perth, disputes arose over commanding officers altering order books without consulting the management committee of a corps, attempts to make changes in the running of the corps without proper notice being given before general meetings, and on ensuring properly transparent accounting.[252] In Scotland, where urban electoral politics was so narrowly based, such disputes were more novel and may have had a greater impact than south of the border, although in some ways they were a continuation of struggles over burgh reform from the 1780s.

Nevertheless, with the benefit of hindsight, the main story of these years is one of continuing loyalty north of the border, especially among the elites. The opposition Whigs made limited headway with their peace campaign in the spring of 1797, and there are very few signs of anything other than unity amongst the propertied and ruling classes in the face of domestic and international threats to the status quo. A division in 1797 amongst the Angus gentry caused by opposition to the quota acts stood out because it was so unusual, and seems to have reflected broader political divisions, usually muted or hidden, within the county.[253] Edinburgh became, even more so than in the early 1790s, the loyal capital of north Britain, in contrast to the political divisions which ran through the London populace and political institutions. Perhaps this is no surprise, given how susceptible Edinburgh politics was, as we have seen in earlier chapters, to management and manipulation by the governing and ruling elite, and the growing dominance of the luxury sector in the capital's economy; nevertheless, given how far much of the rest of Scotland, urban and landed, looked to Edinburgh for a political lead it was, nonetheless, significant. The patriotic mobilization in response to the abortive French invasion of Ireland at the end of 1796 was impressive and involved a broad cross-section of society. The rage of volunteering was striking and never more than very partially exploited by ministers, whose principal concern was with national defence, not shoring up patriotic morale. Volunteering became genuinely popular in this period, hence one conservatively-inclined clergyman's complaints about a shift from 'an armed aristocracy' to 'a promiscuous armed Democracy',[254] although motives for participation were undoubtedly mixed, as elsewhere in Britain. Whether many volunteers maintained their zeal for training and parading during subsequent years may also be doubted, although this is hardly surprising. In June 1799, evidently quite a few volunteers in Paisley were absenting themselves from parade; and while privates had been discharged, commissioned officers had proved more difficult to deal with. According to one contemporary, the latter had the 'impunity to laugh at what they term the folly of the rest in giving themselves so much unnecessary trouble'.[255] More importantly, some were concerned about the potential dangers surrounding the social expansion of volunteering. Yet as noteworthy is the confidence of others that any risk involved in arming the populace was a minor one, if indeed it existed at all.[256] The political utility of the volunteers, as a means of undermining and demoralizing radicals, was widely recognized, seemingly by radicals and those supportive of the status quo alike.[257]

Meanwhile, attempts to reconstruct the history of radicalism in this period will always be very frustrating ones. Certainly initially, the authorities showed few, if any, signs of alarm or panic about the spread of the United Scotsmen, although then again they knew very little about what was going on; and even when they were more concerned, their ability to gather intelligence was extremely limited. The numbers involved in the society were probably very small. (The only figures we possess, which suggest a membership of several thousand, come from the United Scotsmen themselves, or agents of the United Irishmen reporting on the strength of the United Scotsmen.[258]) The bulk of membership came from a layer of 'Jacobin' radicalism which had been deposited in 1793–4. Profoundly influenced by Paineite ideology, these individuals, mostly weavers and other artisans and lesser tradesmen, eagerly consumed radical propaganda emanating from London's radical printing fraternity, when it was available. Mealmaker was untypical only in his prominence and in his willingness to put his political views into print. Another radical from the early 1790s who seems to have been active in this period was James Kennedy. A Paisley weaver by origin, Kennedy had been arrested in the aftermath of the exposure of the so-called Pike Plot in 1794. His political views, which reflected very directly the influence of Paine, were contained in a volume of radical poems published in London in 1795 by Eaton. When he was arrested at the end of 1797, a small number of these volumes in his possession were seized.[259] More generally, what the spread of the United Scotsmen indicates is how deep rooted were the political beliefs and traditions given rise to by the politics of the earlier 1790s, and how relatively easily relationships and circuits of political communication were revived under the stimulus of external events and influences. This is what contemporaries meant when they referred to a 'democratical spirit' being cowed but not extinguished. Even as late as 1801, a visitor to Perth spoke about the weavers' 'talk of liberty'.[260] Whether the United Scotsmen was ever very well organized, or even had a coherent sense of purpose, is open to question. What membership did offer were reaffirmation of the political faith and a sense of connection to a radical alliance throughout the British Isles. With the recent memory of harsh repression, its secrecy and oath-taking contrary to law seems to have been too much for quite a few Scottish radicals. However, these individuals continued to read radical propaganda, follow events in France very closely, and support peace as an essential preliminary to a wider political transformation.

The convulsion of opposition to the Militia Act has, finally, been interpreted in very different ways. McFarland has emphasized the contrast between the relatively restrained anti-militia disturbances in Scotland and the much more destructive anti-militia protests in Ireland in 1793 which led to over a hundred deaths.[261] Recently, Christopher Whatley has used evidence of popular resistance and protest against the initial implementation of the Act to support a portrayal of Scottish society in the 1790s as much less quiescent and passive than is sometimes suggested.[262] The latter issue is taken up more fully in the next chapter. There is no doubt that some officials and landowners in the counties were shocked by the ferocity of the popular response, although, as was emphasized earlier, responses to the Act varied greatly and were far from always violent. Robert Dundas in Edinburgh was mostly sanguine, confident that opposition could be readily defeated or defused.[263] Local elites also recovered their sense of resolve quite quickly. There was no complete collapse in authority similar to that which took place, for example, in the West Riding of Yorkshire during anti-militia disturbances in England in 1757.[264] By 1798, most Scots seem to have learnt how to live with and manage the burden of the militia, principally by avoiding it.

The real significance of the anti-militia disturbances is elusive, therefore. On the one hand, it provides plenty of evidence that the Scottish people were far from docile and perfectly capable of resisting their landlords and rulers if pushed too far, or they thought this was so. With rule and stability ultimately reliant on opinion, and with little coercive force to regulate society, it was, as several contemporaries were not slow to point out, extremely inept that no attempt had been made to explain the Act prior to its being implemented.[265] More interestingly, newspapers were seen as a natural medium through which to do this, a demonstration of their growing presence in society in the later eighteenth century. Indeed, from this perspective, the episode reinforces the growing power of print as a medium of communication in Scottish society, a power which had been steadily growing in the later eighteenth century. Pressure was placed, for example, on newspaper print-ers to exclude descriptions of anti-militia protests from their papers so as not to encourage copycat actions, while several lords lieutenant ensured that abstracts of the Act, as well as the Act against unlawful oaths, appeared in the most influential local paper.[266] In the south, there was concern about the inclusion of a 'misrepre-sentation' of the Act in James Palmer's *Kelso Chronicle*. Palmer, who may well have had reformist sympathies, was described as having circulated 'poison amongst the minds of the people of the south of Scotland for many years ...'.[267] At the request of the Provost of Dumfries, the printer of the *Dumfries Weekly Journal* was insert-ing everything 'favourable to the business in the different parts of Scotland, and nothing of an adverse nature'.[268] Resistance to the Act took peaceful as well as violent forms, but the demonstration of purpose was manifest either way. On the other hand, during the disturbances the system of lords lieutenant and deputy lieutenants introduced in 1794 showed its effectiveness, albeit military support was needed in many places to bring crowds under control.

Perhaps the more significant lesson, however, not just of the anti-militia pro-tests, but of the events of these years, was that there were deeper-lying forces at work making Scottish society and public opinion less tractable, and that while dissenting opinion might be crushed temporarily it could not be eliminated. This truth can be glimpsed in some responses to the protests, for example, the observation of the Lord President, Ilay Campbell, that only coercion could con-trol the printfield workers in and around Dumbarton or the discontented in the weaving parish of Kirkintilloch.[269] Sir John Menzies complained to his father-in-law, the Duke of Atholl, from Castle Menzies at the head of Loch Tay during the anti-militia unrest on Strathtay, that only the 'better sort of tenants' could be relied on, and that the 'cottars, servants and manufacturers' were 'tinged strongly with principles very unreliable to good government and that subor-dination necessary for society'.[270] It was in the fast-developing manufacturing communities in rural and semi-rural areas, not in the towns, that existing struc-tures of authority were weakest and most readily subject to challenge. There were other perceived threats to established structures of authority at around this time. The rise of lay preaching associated with the Haldanite missionary movement was another source of concern in this context. While not directly 'meddling' in politics, these preachers often attacked the authority of parish ministers. They also disseminated pamphlets which were, in the words of one establishment figure, 'calculated to produce discontent, to foster an aversion to the present order of things and to increase the portentous fermentation in the minds of the people'.[271] That these concerns may have been built on more than just general-ized alarm at anything which challenged the status quo is suggested by the fact that one supporter of the missionary cause was the Dundee relief minister Neil

Douglas, who had been a delegate of the Dundee Friends of the Constitution to the third general convention of Scottish radicals in 1793.[272] Meanwhile, the perception that popular opinion could not be taken for granted was not entirely lost sight of despite the relative quiescence of most of the population during the next three years in face of the strains of rapid, unexampled rises in food prices and economic depression.

6 BREAD, DEARTH AND POLITICS, 1795–1801

From the later 1770s up to 1793, Scotland saw rapid, unexampled economic growth, especially within the textile sector. The picture for the remainder of the 1790s was more mixed. In 1793 and 1797 tight credit conditions precipitated temporary depressions in manufacturing.[1] In the first case, the cause was British entry into the war against revolutionary France and in the second the suspension of cash payments by the banks caused by fears of a French invasion. In 1793, fine linen manufacturing in Glasgow and Paisley and cotton spinning and weaving in and around Glasgow and Paisley and in the south-west were particularly badly hit. In October 1793, a petition from the cotton manufacturers of Glasgow and Paisley claimed that the number employed in the industry had fallen by half since 1792.[2] Visiting Cupar, Fife, in April of that year, an Edinburgh burgess noted in his journal: 'Money is unusually scarce owing to the late numerous Failures'. Higher than normal prices for provisions were, he also reported, adding to difficulties.[3] In and around Perth, trade seems to have been dull in the early summer. On 3 June, the town's carters petitioned the magistrates for an increase in the rates they were able to charge, arguing that 'times are so very hard in this and in all other places and so little trade to be had or any employment whatsoever...'.[4] In early August, it was reported from Perth: 'The manufactures are still very idle especially the Cotton – The Linen are not quite so bad ...'.[5] For many sectors and firms, recovery was, nevertheless, fairly rapid, both in 1793 and 1797. Even cotton manufacturing, which had been very adversely affected in 1793, was booming by 1798. Suppliers of war materials flourished. In the summer of 1795, an enquiry about whether a recruiting party should be sent to Dundee elicited the response that the take-up was likely to be poor because manufactures there were buoyant owing to wartime demand for sail cloth and brown linen.[6] As we will see further below, 1800–1 saw renewed problems in several areas and sectors of the economy because of a combination of a collapse in domestic demand and the closure of important European markets under the impact of changing conditions of diplomacy and war.

As several contemporary authors of agricultural reports for the newly-formed Board of Agriculture noted, in manufacturing towns and agricultural regions close to them, demand for labour remained strong for much of this period, which pushed wages upwards.[7] Recruitment into the armed forces seems to have added to labour shortages in some places. It was only in the 1800s that conditions in the labour market shifted decisively against many workers, especially in unskilled and semi-skilled jobs. At the same time, rising prices began to erode the impact of earlier wage gains.[8]

Harvests were relatively abundant in most years and, in a society in which food purchases accounted for up to two-thirds of the budget of a labouring household,[9] this was extremely important for social and political stability. There were some fears articulated in the autumn of 1792 about the state of the harvest, owing to wet weather in the late summer and autumn, and during disturbances in Dundee in November, the so-called tree of liberty riots, not only was it alleged that recent changes to the Corn Laws were a source of popular anger, calls were made to have grain on a ship in the port unloaded.[10] Such facts have misled one or two historians about possible food shortages in late 1792 as a major contributory factor to popular protest and unrest in that period. Enquiries initiated by the Lord Advocate, Robert Dundas, revealed no serious shortfalls, and prices show no unusual rise in late 1792.[11] Where there was difficulty was in respect of access to coal, owing to the unusually wet weather in the autumn adversely affecting supplies of peat. The consequent surge in demand caused prices of coal to rise steeply in the winter of 1792–3. In Perth, prices doubled in this period. A similar rise occurred in Edinburgh, from where it was reported towards the end of December 1792: 'Coals are amazingly scarce'.[12] This was the background to Henry Dundas's decision in 1793 to have Parliament remove duties on coal moving coastwise north of the Red Head near Arbroath, a tax imposed in 1707 to protect the interests of the Scottish coal industry, which, in effect, meant Midlothian landowners.[13] In 1793 and 1794, fortuitously for the authorities given broader economic and political conditions, the harvests were good. In at least two periods, however, economic conditions led to serious distress for the lower orders. The first and less serious was 1795–6, when an unusually harsh and protracted winter in 1794–5 was followed by sporadic food shortages and protests on the east coast between August 1795 and the following March. Much graver were conditions in the period 1799–1801. A very poor harvest in 1799 was followed by a below-average one in 1800, again especially on the eastern side of the country, which caused food prices to rocket, reaching unprecedented and dramatic peaks in the spring and autumn of 1800. In 1800–1, these very high prices were combined, in some sectors of the economy, with depressed economic conditions.

In England, it has been argued by Roger Wells that the crisis of 1799–1801 was of profound importance as part of the longer-term process by which the lower orders became alienated from the state and political system – Thompson's 'making of the *English* working class'.[14] The challenge of popular protest was far-reaching, and in 1800–1 was overlaid with a further political challenge of revived radical feeling as a close connection was forged between dearth and war and a corrupt, narrow political order, although the extent of the politicization of these events is the subject of debate amongst historians.[15] If the ruling elite survived this crisis, it did so not because of its unity and efficiency, but precisely because of its disunity; if it was cohesion it showed in adversity it was 'disordered cohesion'. John Dinwiddy has argued that the later 1790s witnessed a 'subterranean shift' in the political loyalties of the population, from support for the status quo to a stance he describes as 'passive disaffection' by the end of the decade.[16] In contrast to the first half of the 1790s, no longer could Pitt and his fellow ministers take the anti-Jacobinism of the bulk of the population for granted.

Of the crisis in Scotland, much less is known since it has largely been neglected by historians. This probably reflects the perception that the strains were much weaker north of the border, and any political disaffection far more muted. Logue's work on riot and disorder, published in 1979, revealed dramatically fewer food protests in this period than in England. Logue found evidence of just fourteen such disturbances across Scotland in 1795–6, and twenty-two in 1799–1801.[17] Even allowing for the fact that the sources on which such enumerations are based are likely not to be comprehensive, the contrast with England is stark, where the number of disturbances ran into the hundreds.[18] Nor were the Scottish disturbances as threatening or long-lasting, as we will see later. Once again, the conjuncture seems to provide strong evidence for the relative stability of Scottish society and its seeming immunity from the popular anger and political currents which were fraying the political and social order south of the border. If we wish to explain this Scottish orderliness, then we need look to the greater role of paternalism in Scotland, bonds of deference and hierarchy, and the unusual cohesion of urban society, or so it has been forcefully argued.[19]

This chapter re-examines the periods 1795–6 and 1799–1801 in order to provide, in the first place, a fuller, more detailed picture of economic and social conditions in Scotland. It also explores the ways in which local and national authorities and elites responded to the evidence of food shortages and strains in order to assess the quality and nature of Scottish paternalistic responses to hardship in this period. How, if at all, different were they to the measures taken south of the border to alleviate suffering and reduce social tensions? It may well be that it is similarities across the national border in this context which are most striking, although this should perhaps not surprise us. Local authorities throughout Britain were responding in ways shaped by national debates about appropriate measures and in response to directions and initiatives from London and Westminster. The establishment of the system of lords lieutenant in 1794 aided matters in this respect, as it was partly through this system that relief efforts were coordinated at the county level. It was not just government that encouraged similar responses, but also voluntary agencies. Count Rumford was fêted south of the border in this period for his advocacy of soup kitchens financed by public subscriptions, so it is perhaps no surprise that this happened when he came north of the border in 1800 to visit Edinburgh.[20] Separate legal systems did not mean, moreover, that well-publicized decisions taken in English courts were without influence on attitudes and opinion north of the border. That said, there were important contrasts between the actions of the English High Court and the Scottish Court of Session. If the English judges, led by the Lord Chief Justice, Lord Kenyon, were very visible and vocal supporters of 'moral economy' in this period,[21] views among the Scottish judges seem to have been more equivocal, even contradictory in the face of a growing conflict in this period between the imperatives of 'moral economy' and 'free trade'. In 1795–6, the Scottish judges helped to lead the defence of the case for magisterial intervention in the bread market; in 1801, in a judgement which may have prefigured the rapid victory of 'laissez faire' ideology in the next ten years or so, the bench handed down an important decision which cast doubt on the legality of a key power in this context – the power of magistrates to force farmers and dealers to bring grain for sale in public markets in times of shortage.

Markets and Magistrates

By the 1790s, the market, and the corn dealers, merchants, millers, bakers and retailers who constructed that market, were vital to ensuring that supplies of grain and meal reached Scotland's expanding wage-earning population, located in rapidly expanding towns and a growing number of semi-urban villages. Some time in the middle of the century, rather earlier than England, Scotland became a net importer of grain.[22] In every year from 1760, Scottish ports were open at some point to allow imports of grain. In the ten years preceding 1793, grain had been imported into the port of Ayr in every year bar three (1786, 1790 and 1793) and Irvine in every year bar one (1793).[23] Imports from Ireland, 'the granary of the west of Scotland',[24] were of growing importance in the later eighteenth century, and not just to the highlands and islands where they had been significant from at least the early eighteenth century. By the 1790s, it has been estimated that as many as 40,000 Scots were dependent on Irish imports of grain or meal.[25] In 1795–6, a contributory cause of problems of supply within Scotland, particularly the west, was the closure by the Irish executive of the Irish market to exports, and in 1799–1801, the failure of the Irish harvests leading to a simple lack of grain there for export. Within Scotland, supply in west and west-central manufacturing regions depended on flows of oats and oatmeal from high producing areas – Galloway, Dumfriesshire and, to a lesser extent, Ayrshire and eastern counties from Berwickshire northwards – to high price markets.

Much about the extension of the market in grain in Scotland in the eighteenth century remains currently hidden from view. We know little, for example, about the dealers, merchants and millers who were critical to its operation, although some corn merchants were evidently operating on a very considerable scale in what was not merely a national but an international marketplace. In 1795–6, and even more so in 1799–1801, critical to maintaining supplies in local markets was access to imports from north German (Hamburg) and Baltic ports (Danzig) and North America, sometimes sourced directly by merchants in Scotland and sometimes through London contacts. In the summer of 1795, a contributor to the *Caledonian Mercury* declared that imports were the only 'effectual relief from scarcity of wheat', advocating, in this context, a 'croisade' against the 'modern female Atila of the North' (i.e. Catherine the Great) to establish a reasonable constitution and government in Poland which would give sufficient security to the peasantry to renew cultivation of grain there.[26] How far and widely the rise of tenant farmers paying their rent in cash rather than kind after 1760 transformed the sale of grain on many farms by the end of the century is again unclear from existing research. In an English context, Thompson made much of the reduced importance of the public market in the eighteenth century, and the rise of sale by sample behind closed doors.[27] In Scotland, during periods of shortage, alarm was periodically expressed about dealers buying up grain while it was still in the field, in other words, before it had been harvested, a type of purchase which was defined under Scottish law as 'regrating'.[28] In 1795, one commentator from Dumfries pointed out the advantages to farmers of selling in large quantities to merchants rather than at public markets:

> The Farmers of this Country are very much more disposed to sell their Grain by the lump for shipping, than in small quantities for the consumpt of certain classes of People at home; because though the price may be the same, they thereby avoid the trouble attending the sale of small quantities in the public market, when, on the other hand, they sell and deliver in large quantities, and receive their payment in one sum.[29]

During the shortages of 1795–6 and 1799–1801, stocks of grain held by farmers, once their own subsistence and need for seed grain was provided for, formed a key element in relief efforts, alongside meal or oats, or other types of grain, sourced from beyond the locality, either in Scotland or Britain or overseas. Some farmers seem to have committed themselves publicly in these crisis years to selling in the public market, which may reflect the enduring ideological force of this model, but not necessarily its operation in years of normal or low prices.[30] In larger towns by this period, the bulk of the labouring population depended not on buying meal weekly at the meal market, but smaller purchases from retailers of meal or of bread from bakers. Edinburgh, for example, had no wheat market, relying on the major grain market at Haddington. Key to the supply of wheat bread in the capital were a number of flour-mills located at places just outside the city – Water of Leith, Stockbridge, Canonmills, Bell's Mills – and operated by bakers.[31]

From wherever, or in whatever form, meal and indeed other foodstuffs – potatoes and other vegetables or fish – were purchased, from the point of view of the labouring classes, the rising importance of the market, and the growing proportion of the population dependent on purchasing their food, meant increased vulnerability to dislocations in the system, whether through natural causes (poor weather rendering roads impassable or during the growing season and harvest) or artificial ones (monopoly or speculation).[32] This, and its potential impact on wage and labour costs, is why the issue of the Corn Laws was, as we saw in Chapter 1, such an extremely sensitive one in urban Scotland during the second half of the eighteenth century. In 1741, during an earlier period of shortage and popular protest, the Westminster Parliament gave the Lords of Session the responsibility for opening ports for the importation of victual from Ireland or elsewhere, under terms laid down by a Scottish act of parliament of 1703. (Prior to its abolition in 1709, this responsibility resided with the Scottish Privy Council.) In 1773, however, Scotland was absorbed within the English (now British) system of Corn Laws. From this point, proposed and actual changes in these laws generated intense debates, pitting the 'landed interest' against an urban-manufacturing interest or series of interests. Mirroring to some degree those which took place in England, the debates focused on how, and in whose interest, price levels determining the opening of ports for imports of grain should be ascertained – the 'landed interest', which comprised landowners and farmers, or the manufacturing interest, which comprised manufacturers and workers.[33]

Second, attitudes towards the supply of foodstuffs did not change in accordance with or at the speed of the changed realities of supply; or perhaps more accurately, the assumption that there was a responsibility to protect the poor from shortages and very high prices proved extremely tenacious. Across social ranks, from the labouring poor to the landed elites, it was believed that meal should be available to the labouring poor at a price they could reasonably afford. In so far as there was dispute about this, it was about how this should be done, and, increasingly towards the end of the eighteenth century, whether a free market in grain and the 'public good' were compatible, especially in times of shortage.[34]

Just how powerful the notion of 'paternalistic duty' was in relation to magistrates' conduct during food shortages is revealed by two cases involving the defence of personal reputations from the mid-eighteenth century. In 1753 Alexander Livingstone, sometime Provost of Aberdeen and merchant, launched an action at the High Court against those who had accused him of recently doubling the price of meal in Aberdeen. The effect of these slanders was, or so it was asserted in support of his case, that neither Livingstone nor his wife could walk through the streets of Aberdeen in safety for fear of 'that many headed monster a Mobb' which had been stirred up against him.[35] In the same year, James Coutts, former Lord Provost of Edinburgh and grain merchant, petitioned the current magistrates of the city against the inclusion of a paragraph in William Maitland's history of the city which claimed that, under suspicion that he was responsible for a 'devouring famine', he had fled the city during the shortages of 1740 in fear of his life. Coutts's petition against what he claimed was a flagrant misrepresentation of his role in the crisis, was indignant in tone. 'Any one who reads this account', the petition read:

> would be led to believe that Mr Coutts had entered into a Concert with other Corn Dealers to keep up the Grain they had in their possession, Nay even to let it spoil rather than sell it under the price agreed on; and that to avoid the Resentment of the People for such a Conduct he had been obliged to leave the City otherwise He would have been torn to pieces by the enraged Multitude. Nothing can be more false than these Allegations. It is well known That the defunct never kept up Victuall from the Mercates when he had it in his possession; That at the period in question he was so far from keeping it up That after his own Granaries were exhausted he bestowed his whole time and labour in purchasing and importing immense Quantities of Victuall wherever it could be had and gave it all into the Committee who had the provision of the City under their Care without the smallest Return of Profite. That instead of leaving the City, He was constantly present at every meeting whether of the Committee or Town Council which were then so frequently held for no other purpose but to provide means for the Relief of the Inhabitants, to which by his extensive Correspondence & Knowledge in these matter he Contributed in a very remarkable Degree.[36]

Maitland, who had been granted 'every assistance' by the Edinburgh authorities in researching and writing his account, had, Coutts argued, failed in his duty as a 'faithfull and Impartial Historian'. He called on the magistrates to grant him such relief as they judged most appropriate. The outcome was that Maitland, who was called before the magistrates, was compelled or persuaded to compose a new paragraph which replaced the old one in the second edition of the history. The new one stressed the extent and vigour of Coutts's and his fellow magistrates' endeavours to remedy the problems of shortage in 1740.

If images of responsible authority involved looking after the well-being of vulnerable sections of the population in periods of shortage, this reflected a practice of intervention, which may in some burghs date back to 1720 but which spread more widely in 1740–1, to ensure markets were kept stocked with reasonably-priced grain in Scottish burghs during periods of high prices and shortage.[37] In responding to the problems of 1795–6 and crisis of 1799–1801, magistrates drew, therefore, on a very well-established repertoire of measures. Common initiatives undertaken during earlier periods of hardship and shortage (1720, 1740–1, 1756–7, 1773, 1778, 1782–3) included raising funds or subscriptions to purchase grain to sell at or below market price. Losses resulting from sale of the grain at below current market price were met by the town councils, other urban bodies or subscribers. In Dundee in 1771, the Town Council, the trades incorporations and kirk session disputed liability for payment of such losses, although the initial agreement seems to have been that each should be responsible for one-third.[38] Farmers were encouraged to bring their grain to local markets, usually through direct approaches from burgh magistrates or landowners.[39] To the same end, security and indemnity was offered to those farmers and dealers who sold their grain in the local market against any losses resulting from crowd action. In 1740, the Edinburgh Town Council not only bound themselves to 'secure the importers of grain and victual of all kinds into the Port of Leith' and against any 'violent and masterful Attempts, that may be made by any mobs, or riotous Assemblies of the Populous', they also declared that they would recompense dealers for any grain seized by rioters at market prices.[40] Market dues might be removed from essential foodstuffs, while bounties were paid to farmers and dealers who brought significant quantities to market. In 1782, the Society for the Relief of the Poor in the town and suburbs of Paisley offered a bounty for one month of 6*d.* per boll to any individual who brought above nine bolls of meal and sold it in the Paisley market in one week.[41] Trades incorporations bought grain and coal to sell at below market price to the poor, or, as alluded to above, joined with burgh councils in arranging for the purchase of supply.[42] In rural areas, landowners and the Kirk took measures in periods of shortage to relieve the hardship of the labouring poor, often, like the burgh magistrates, providing meal at below market price.[43] Most recently, in 1782–3, when a late and poor harvest created serious dearth in the north-east, highlands and islands, and difficult conditions in the south, national and local government had combined to take measures of relief.[44]

As in other parts of Britain, Westminster and national government had a crucial role to play in periods of shortage and social tension. This could create problems, as well as helping to solve them; action which was too hasty, or based on inaccurate information, could precipitate panic and thus add to alarm and difficulties. To a degree this is what occurred in Scotland in the summer of 1795, as we will see below, although the problem was really the ministry's and Parliament's focus on England and disinterest in Scottish difference. On the other hand, if central government waited too long, local authorities could be faced with widespread disorder and protest. Central government action included impositions of prohibitions on exports of foodstuffs, the provision of bounties on imports, and bans on distilling. All of these would be used during the crisis of 1799–1801, while in 1795–6 a ban was imposed on distilling in Scotland. The Privy Council also purchased grain for distribution to markets. This was mainly targeted on the strategically and politically crucial London market, but it was circulated more widely, as, for example, in the highlands and islands in 1783–4.[45] The actions of national government, and of Parliament in convening committees to investigate the causes of scarcity in 1795 and again in 1800, strongly reinforced the expectation that relief would be forthcoming; that this was indeed the responsibility of those in authority.

Statute law and decisions of the Court of Session provided, meanwhile, legal authority for interventions by magistrates in the food market. Parliament abolished the statutory offence in English law of forestalling and regrating in 1772, although they were still offences under common law.[46] Under Scottish law they were covered by an act of 1592, which clarified several pieces of earlier legislation, and which in addition provided magistrates with the power of ensuring that grain and meal was carried to local markets before it was circulated to more distant ones.[47] On this last point, there seems to have been some uncertainty about the legal position, although in 1757 the Court of Session passed an act of sederunt supporting the actions of the Justices of Midlothian in seeking to ensure that the capital's markets were supplied by tenants and farmers during a period of shortage. The crucial part of the act stated:

> And the said Lords are of opinion, that, in case the farmers of this county shall prove refractory, and shall not comply with the reasonable demands of their respective heritors, that it is the duty of the Justices of the peace, and they are sufficiently authorized by law, to compel those within their county, possessed of oats, to contribute their proportion for relieving the inhabitants of Edinburgh from their present distress, and thereby to prevent the dangers that may justly be apprehended by the want of oatmeal, which is the principal means of subsistence of many of the inhabitants.[48]

In 1795, reference was made to this decision in support of magisterial activism in intervening in the market place.[49] During the crisis of 1800, at a point when Eskdalemuir was 'almost entirely out of meal', the Baron-Baillie of Langholm issued a warrant to seize meal, suspected to be for dealers rather than to supply local needs, from a barn belonging to a Mr Burnet. The warrant seems to have been issued partly as a preventive measure to stop an 'exasperated people' destroying not only the grain but Burnet's house. It seems that Burnet had been in the habit of allowing his barns to be used by purchasers of grain from Annandale for sale in Selkirkshire. In defending their actions, the individuals who had applied for the warrant declared:

> But the theory of the wealth of nations, and the demonstrated expediency of invariably leaving grain, like other things, to find its own level, was not thoroughly understood in the heights of Eskdalemuir, where the clamorous wants of their children made fathers and mothers look with an evil eye on professed dealers, who hoarded grain up for the purpose of raising the markets. *The general belief was, that the Magistrate had the power to compel such persons to supply the pressing demands of the day, by selling part of their stores at a reasonable profit, and that this was a necessary and proper exercise of his powers* [my emphasis].[50]

It also followed that magistrates had the power, or were believed to do so, to force the sale of grain in transit. As we will see below, in 1799–1801, as in England, the pressure from popular expectations, the growing power of free-trade ideology and the force of pragmatism and tradition led to even greater incoherence in attitudes towards markets and securing food supplies; and in the contradictions space was created for beliefs to flourish about unscrupulous dealers and profiteering as the cause of famine.

Food markets were also subject, at least in theory, to paternalistic regulation or superintendence by magistrates on a daily basis; and this provides a final context for understanding popular and official attitudes towards intervention in the marketplace for food at the end of the eighteenth century. The law against forestalling and regrating has already been referred to. Prices charged by bakers in urban markets were set by the bread assize in an effort to prevent their taking advantage of any monopoly. In 1800 the Edinburgh magistrates were advised to suspend the bread assize, which they did, presumably in the belief that unfettered competition would bring prices down.[51] Markets or dealers were subject to inspection for possible adulteration of grain or use of false or light weights and measures. The salient question, however, is not whether such powers existed, but how regularly and widely they were used. Dean of Guild records, where they survive, contain few examples of actions taken against individuals for use of false weights and measures.[52] A preliminary search of burgh court records for Perth in the eighteenth century has revealed relatively few cases of forestalling; and it may well be that magisterial activism in this context was largely confined to periods of dearth and social tension, or that their posture was basically reactive, intervening if and when called upon to do so. Certainly, in the period 1799–1801, magisterial rigour in, for example, taking action against forestalling and false weights and measures was one aspect of a wider strategy of attempting to deal with the dearth and potential social unrest.[53] On the other hand, there is evidence of more regular inspection and action at least in the case of Edinburgh, although this highlights the contradictory pressures that magistrates and officials could face in seeking to ensure that supplies continued in a system dependent on circulation of meal; over-zealous regulation and policing could impede supply. The evidence comes from a series of memoranda made by a police superintendant, John Hutton, covering the years 1792–6. One entry, for 25 June 1793, reads:

> Went along with Mr Laing, Deacon Smith & Murray, Bakers to the Meal Market on considering the present scarcity of oats of home growth & the bad quality of foreign grain, put off the inspection of the market, fearing it might create a scarcity of that necessary article.[54]

Elsewhere, Hutton records summonses issued to forestallers of various articles, fines issued for use of false weights, and inspections of measures used in shops.

In May 1794, one Anne McKenzie was found to have used a measure for potatoes which was 'greatly deficient', and was sentenced to be drummed through the town with the measure hung at her neck. She was saved this fate, however, when she was able to show that she had bought the measure in its present state.[55] In December 1794, another woman was summoned to appear before the magistrates for concealing several barrels of haddock and thereby 'creating a scarcity, in order to keep up the price'.[56] In the summer of 1795, anonymous letters about bakers using false weights led to five of them being fined, the highest fine being £29.[57] The impression created is of fairly responsible and responsive regulation of the marketplace in the capital. Whether beyond Edinburgh similar practice was followed is currently unclear, although in the case of Perth a full record survives of the operation of the bread assize. This indicates that there at least this aspect of regulation was assiduously and regularly carried out in a manner which sought to balance the interests of the bakers against those of the town's population, especially in periods of heightened social tension created by shortage and high prices.[58]

Shortage 1: 1795–6

In an English context, it is reasonable to talk of two periods of acute distress in the 1790s, 1795–6 and 1799–1801. Scotland was somewhat different, in so far as conditions in 1795–6 were less threatening and serious north of the border. Indeed, to a significant degree, climbing prices in the summer of 1795 were the consequence of shortages south of the border. It is, nevertheless, probably significant that the problems of 1795 followed a very severe and protracted winter. In Edinburgh, snow led to a shortage of coal for domestic fuel. A combination of labourers and soldiers were used in January to clear the roads to nearby collieries. In early February, it was reported from the capital: 'It is very cold and snow is lying deeper than known since 1740'.[59] As late as the middle of March, Parliament Square had to be cleared of snow in preparation for the meeting of the courts.[60] Work in some areas for labourers was more than usually scarce in such conditions.

It may well be that, as in England, the 1790s saw an extension of the support customarily given in winter to the poor.[61] Certainly, the sorts of schemes established in the winter of 1794–5 were very similar to those which emerged in 1795–6 and 1799–1801, often involving the raising of funds by subscription, and the donation or sale of meal and coal to households based on close enquiry into their needs. Ministers and kirk sessions would play a key role in assessing need, along with committees formed from subscribers. In Dumfries, a subscription was opened at the beginning of February, and similar schemes were established in surrounding parishes.[62] Aberdeen seems to have established a permanent 'coal fund' at this time, to provide subsidized coal to its poor.[63] In Dundee, the Council agreed at around the same time to distribute 60 bolls of meal among the poor.[64] In January, around 700 individuals or families were being relieved in Edinburgh with supplies of meal, coal and doles of money. This number did not include around 400 people who could not be 'entered on account of the advanced period of the day' but 'who had mostly waited two days almost perishing with cold' and who were given either 6*d.* or 1*s.* depending on the size of their family.[65] By the beginning of March, 2,986 families, comprising around 11,000 people, were being supported by the 'Committee for Relieving the Necessitous Poor' in the capital.[66]

The English harvest in 1794 had been a poor one. This was followed by a late and poor harvest in 1795, although it was yields of wheat which were significantly down on normal, not of barley or oats. Wheat was the main grain used in making bread in England, unlike Scotland where it was oats. Rapid price inflation occurred in the spring of 1795 in anticipation of shortages increasing in the summer. When these duly occurred, prices surged in midsummer.[67] The Scottish harvest in 1795, meanwhile, also appears to have been deficient, at least in some areas, although not to the same extent as the English one. The Perth magistrates claimed that in their part of the country, in November the harvest had been thought to be down by about a third on normal, although on subsequent threshing out of grain on some farms yields had been found to be only around half of normal.[68] In February 1796, Archibald Campbell of Clathick, Sheriff of Perthshire, wrote that he *thought* that crops had not been deficient in Fife, Perth, Stirling and Angus, although yields had been down on normal. He also noted that farmers had been bringing less to market than usual during the winter in anticipation of higher prices, and that poor weather had made its impossible to thresh out as much grain as usual.[69] The Duke of Atholl prepared, as Lord Lieutenant of the county, an account of the harvest in Perthshire for the Duke of Portland, the Home Secretary, probably some time towards the end of 1795. This declared that, in lowland areas, the oat crop, while down on 1794, was equal to a normal year, although the quality was less good. In highland areas, the oat crop had been 'full', but again poorer in quality than usual and between a quarter and a fifth had been lost owing to 'rain and wind'.[70] In Berwickshire, it was reported in December that, while yields of oats were lower, the quantity of the crop was greater than usual; it was only the wheat crop which was seriously deficient.[71]

If crops in Scotland were poorer, in quantity and quality in 1795 than in normal years, therefore, it was not by a very significant amount, and oats, the Scottish staple, were in reasonably good supply. The principal cause of the rising prices was, then, initially at least, not the state of the harvest, but the fact that, from July, agents from English towns and localities engaged in 'frantic competition' to buy up available stocks of wheat and other grain. From the late summer and into the autumn, this competition extended to Scotland, as northern ports especially sent agents north of the border to secure supplies. Towards the end of July, for example, it was reported in the Edinburgh press from Liverpool that in the past week no less than eleven ships had arrived from Scotland laden with wheat, oats, oatmeal and barley.[72] Around a month later, the Provost of Perth was assured: 'We have been pretty well supplied hitherto with meal here [i.e. Perth], tho the Price high, & a good quantity of Barley & pease ship'd to the English market, which we could spare'.[73] English agents were buying up grain even before it had left the 'farmers corn yard' which seems to have caused prices to climb very sharply, largely by inducing localized panics about future supply.[74] Further contributing to the pressure on prices, and growing alarm, was the actions of magistrates, who, in turn, were responding to directions from national government. On 6 July, in the face of the outbreak of disturbances over grain in England, the Privy Council entered into an engagement to eat only standard wheaten bread, news of which was circulated to lords lieutenant throughout Britain a few days later by the Duke of Portland.[75] Meanwhile, Parliament passed an act prohibiting use of grain for distilling in Scotland until the following February. This was followed by further resolutions from the Privy Council later in July calling on people to discontinue the use of fine flour, in support of free circulation of grain, and urging magistrates and local authorities to call meetings of inhabitants to take this measure under consideration, and also to adopt measures best calculated to ensure supplies of 'bread to the people'.[76] In response to these resolutions, magistrates in Scotland duly called meetings to consider supplies of grain. These meetings, which tended to take place in early August, largely as a preventive or pre-emptive measure, while rejecting the applicability of the adoption of standard wheaten bread to Scottish conditions, called for other measures of economy, and agreed that steps should be taken to secure stocks of grain in case of future shortages. On 3 August, a meeting of the deputy lieutenants of the County of Dumfries resolved that heritors and farmers should ensure that they 'reserve as much Grain and Oatmeal in their different possessions, as will be necessary not only for the consumption of their own families, but also for that of the other inhabitants, till the new crops are got in'.[77] A number of major urban authorities were even more anxious to ensure that the possibility of future scarcity be guarded against. On 5 August, the Dundee Council resolved

> ... considering the great demand there has been of late in this quarter for oats and meal from different parts of the county and holding to be their duty to take every prudent measure to provide for and prevent any scarcity when there is the least appearance of it, they do hereby authorise the present Magistrates ... to purchase on account of the town any quantity of oats or meal not exceeding one thousand bolls.

This grain was to be stored in granaries and used to supply the market 'from time to time as circumstances may appear to them [the magistrates] to make it advisable ...'.[78] Several weeks later, the amount which the magistrates were authorized to purchase was increased by 50 per cent, while their efforts were supplemented by a private subscription to fund any losses on further purchases of grain by the managers of the subscription.[79] Edinburgh's magistrates had been purchasing meal from the end of June, while on 5 August the Lord Provost was authorized to obtain up to £18,000 credit to make payments for this when they became due.[80] A number of other burghs – Montrose, for example – took similar steps at this time.[81]

The consequence of these actions was that English agents and agents of Scottish towns, often merchants specially deputed for the purpose, were from the summer of 1795 competing with one another to buy up available stocks of grain, especially, it seems, in northern counties of Scotland, notably Banffshire and Aberdeenshire, but also in border counties – Dumfriesshire and Berwickshire. The result was climbing prices, particularly but not solely for wheat, and unusual speculation in the grain market. We have already seen that farmers in some places may have been holding back grain in anticipation of prices rising higher, something which may have been quite widespread. In the following May, it was reported from Dunfermline that, following the arrival of a considerable quantity of imported corn from abroad, local farmers, 'even those who were borrowing meal for their own use', had begun 'eagerly' disposing of it at local markets at the 'very reduced' prices now obtaining.[82] The inference must be that they had been hoarding in hope of further price rises before the new harvest. In Edinburgh, it appears that bakers were, 'tempted by high prices', disposing of stock to agents which would normally have provided the daily consumption of the population of the capital. The bakers were examined on this before the Sheriff, following which an order was issued for seizing the flour and disposing of it locally.[83] Sharp practice, exploiting the unusual pattern of demand, seems to have further pushed prices upwards. David Stewart, a former Lord Provost of Edinburgh, seems to have offered to sell the city a quantity of oats and oatmeal but only 'at the same rates such articles might be worth at London, Hull or Newcastle'. The meeting of subscribers of the fund to purchase grain for Edinburgh inhabitants rejected this offer since these were places 'where grain was dearest'.[84] Stewart, it appears, had on first hearing of the looming crisis from London secretly organized to purchase grain in the north of Scotland through an agent. He was now unwilling to forego any potential profit on his speculation.

The spectacle of grain being exported, while prices were rising and fears of shortage were current, led to a wave of disturbances, beginning in Dundee in August 1795 when a ship in the port was disabled and grain removed and sold in the marketplace. The removal of troops to bring order to Dundee seems to have provided the trigger for disturbances in Perth, although these were quickly brought under control by the Perth volunteers and troops from the Ayrshire light dragoons, then stationed at Perth.[85] In 1795, there was a further disturbance at Annan, while February–March 1796 saw protests at Dumfries, Dingwall, Stonehaven, Montrose, Aberdeen, Peterhead, Inverness, Portsoy, Nairn and Oban.[86] In each case, the targets of the mob were exporters of meal, or dealers and farmers believed to be ignoring local needs at moments of actual or imminent shortages. In Dumfries, for example, where the catalyst appears to have been a decision, against the background of falling stocks of grain, to lessen the allowances of public meal sold to the poor, the disturbances began with the seizure of meal from carts transporting it to ships in the port. The crowd then seized potatoes from carts throughout the town, before proceeding to the town's mills to take further quantities of meal. On the two following days, various places surrounding the town were visited to secure more grain. All the grain and potatoes were sold in the public market.[87]

The number of protests was, as referred to earlier in this chapter, small compared to south of the border, and they were relatively easily contained, albeit that this usually required the intervention of regular troops supported by volunteers and patrols of peace officers, and, often, concessions to the crowds' demands. The protests were also very largely confined to the north-east and south-west; the west and west-central regions appear to have been unaffected.[88] No one was killed or seriously injured during them, and they appear to have been less serious than the protests which swept through Tayside, for example, in 1773 and 1778.[89] A contemporary diarist wrote in relation to the disturbances in Dumfries: 'I think a mob never took place that did less real mischief. They seemed to have no other object in view except bringing in meal which there was an absolute necessity for as the farmers seemed to be determined to starve the town as they would bring it in nor sell it at any price.'[90] The courts showed, by and large, a lenient face towards the rioters, imposing harsh sentences on only three individuals, two from Inverness and one from Aberdeen; in the case of the Aberdonian he would undoubtedly have received a lesser sentence had he confessed his guilt. The cases of fifteen individuals were postponed indefinitely.[91] Robert Dundas took the view that the disturbances in Dingwall did not warrant any prosecution of the ringleaders at all, while in Dumfries deterrent action was limited to the arrest and interrogation without trial of twelve of the rioters.[92]

If the protests were relatively modest affairs, however, shortages and relatively high prices endured for nearly a year, and to this extent we should be careful about not underestimating the problems which arose, and the consequent tensions. The early months of 1796 saw renewed fears of shortage, which in part explain the wave of protests in February–March, that and the continuing quantities of grain being shipped from ports, especially on the eastern side of the country. In early

February, the Dundee committee for purchasing meal reported that they had purchased further quantities of grain as a result of continuing reports of scarcity, but also because 'fears of want having excited great discontents, and threatening and dangerous meetings among the inhabitants of the town and neighbourhood'. The main sources of the purchases, apart from several local landlords, notably Lord Kinnaird and George Paterson of Castle Huntly, were merchants at Peterhead and Banff disposing of north-country meal. In 1797, it was reported that the losses sustained on buying grain for Dundee in 1795–6 had amounted to over £2,500.[93] As in the previous summer, the efforts of towns to secure further supplies from late 1795 and into the early months of 1796 may well have been a major source of tension in ports on the north-east coast. At the end of January, the Provost of Perth reported that magistrates there had secured 3,000 bolls of oatmeal and were hoping to buy enough to ensure a normal consumption of 100 bolls weekly until the end of September.[94] On 4 February, the Provost was informed that several gentlemen in the county had meal to spare on the terms offered by the town, 'but they uniformly answered that they were afraid of the vengeance of the populace', if they sold any of it in the meantime.[95] It was probably at about this time that the Perth magistrates decided to prevent vessels from departing with grain by purchasing the grain which was due to be loaded on to them at the shore.[96] In this case, the threat of disturbances was enough to compel drastic measures from the authorities. In March, the Edinburgh magistrates were selling oatmeal at 1s. per peck, when its current market price was 1s. 8d., a price, in Logue's words, 'unprecedentedly high in living memory'.[97] At around the same time, merchants in the west were applying for leave to import meal from Ireland.[98] In one East Lothian parish, the local heritors and farmers agreed in March to provide oatmeal at reduced prices to labouring people in the parish who did not receive wages in corn. Similar schemes were still being established elsewhere in the country in the following month.[99] At the end of April, a mob in Glasgow gathered in the butter and egg market, destroying produce until the disturbance was brought to an end by magistrates and the military. High prices seem to have been the cause, and one newspaper recommended a consumer boycott rather than mob action as the best response, a strategy which was pursued in several places in 1800.[100] In early May, a committee of East Lothian gentry and the Edinburgh magistrates was recommended by a meeting of the East Lothian quarter sessions to investigate the present state of the corn market and to look for the most likely means to 'procure a more plentiful and cheap supply'.[101] In the same month, the Provost of Montrose saw fit to purchase between 140 and 150 bolls of meal which had been lying in the town's market and which the proprietor, who was from Berwick, had been proposing to remove elsewhere. No doubt, the Provost was unwilling to see grain taken away from the market, which might trigger further disturbances there.[102] From April, however, prices began to fall, albeit interrupted by several further rises – itself a source of considerable tension and suspicion about speculative activities – before prospects of a good harvest drove prices further downwards in the summer.[103]

Evidence that the disturbances took on a political dimension, or that radicals were seeking very actively to exploit them to strengthen anti-war sentiment, is also limited, but not totally insignificant. On the King's birthday (4 June) in Edinburgh, which traditionally brought crowds into the streets and which in 1792 had been the occasion or cause of major riots, a crowd, comprising, according to one witness, several hundred tradesmen and trades lads, gathered outside Robert Dundas's house in George Square crying 'No bribery here – Peace and cheap meal'. Stones were thrown at the windows of the house. Twenty individuals were apprehended after the intervention of several gentlemen and the military caused the mob to disperse. Only one prosecution stemmed from the disturbance, however, which does not seem to have troubled the authorities unduly, and certainly not anything like to the same extent that those of 1792 did.[104] Logue discovered no overt connection between the disturbances on 4 June and the food riots in the north-east earlier in the year.[105] Late April–early May in the capital did see, however, an upsurge of social tension caused by suspicions regarding speculative and fraudulent activity in the grain market. On 26 April, the magistrates were forced to issue a proclamation denouncing rumours and stories circulating to the effect that the managers of the committee for purchasing meal for the poor had been mixing the meal with other meal which was of inferior quality, and that they were employing individuals to buy up any grain which came to market in order to raise the price. Behind these stories were 'turbulent and seditious persons whose aim is obviously to produce discontent and uneasiness and to mislead the minds of those whom they are capable of seduceing [*sic*]'.[106]

That some disaffected individuals were seeking to stir up crowds in this period is also hinted at in several other cases. One of the Dundee rioters of August 1795, a John Rodger, had been a member of the Friends of the People. Rodger denied under examination having said to the crowd that 'we ought to have had a revolution long ago, [and] ... that if they wanted a revolution the present was the properest time to obtain one'.[107] Archibald Campbell of Clathick was convinced that 'seditious men' who had been circulating 'ill founded reports and false stories' lay behind the Perth disturbances which followed rapidly on from the Dundee ones.[108] Campbell was a staunch anti-radical, and his comments may simply have reflected the authorities' confusion about the causes of rioting in the summer of 1795 when supplies of grain were still readily available and urban authorities were taking steps to limit price rises and ensure continued availability of bread and grain. The state of the harvest was unclear in August, and prospects may well have looked less good in some places than they eventually turned out, which, together with the alarms south of the border, may explain the rumours which lay behind the disturbance. There are hints of a political aspect to tension at Montrose, with one participant in the disturbances in February describing the houses attacked as belonging to 'a parcel of royal rascals'.[109] Dundee, Montrose and Perth were sites of substantial radical activity in the early 1790s, as we saw in a previous chapter. In Perth, the role of the military in suppressing food disturbances in 1795 seems to have created, or added to, considerable tension between soldiers and civilians in the town, although there is no direct evidence that political grievances were part of the underlying causes. The tension also reflected the sheer number of soldiers stationed in Perth in the 1790s, and the tendency of redcoats in all periods to be a source of trouble in urban life, whether through sexual license, general rowdiness, or tensions over enlistment.[110] Perth burgh court records contain numerous cases from the 1790s relating to enlistment, usually involving alleged malpractice on the part of recruiting parties.[111] In November 1793, a fight took place between some bakers' lads and several dragoons, and there may have been an undercurrent of tension and resentment building in the town towards the redcoats even before their role in the suppression of rioting in August 1795.[112] In that month, an additional four troops of dragoons were stationed in the town following a request for reinforcement from the Provost and magistrates.[113] Following a series of clashes between townspeople and the new soldiers, horse patrols took to going through the town with swords drawn.[114] By October, the magistrates, concerned that their own authority was being undermined, and to remove the source of tension, were forced to request that the regiment be removed. 'If they remain longer here, there will soon be an End of all Authority', it was claimed in support of the call.[115]

The connection between dearth and war may well also have been quite widely made in 1795–6. William Duncan saw fit to seek to refute this link in the preface to a published volume of his poems, in which he acknowledged, however, that 'The Chief complaints at present are Bad State Ministers – The War – Dearth of Provisions'.[116] James Anderson, Lord Kinnaird's gardener, was reporting to Kinnaird in February 1795 about the strength of feeling in and around Dundee in favour of peace.[117] The same month saw a peace petition strongly supported in the town.[118] At the beginning of December 1795, 473 people signed a petition in Forfar against the repressive legislation and in favour of a speedy peace. Among the resolutions passed at the meeting which produced this petition was one declaring that 'the present disastrous war has been one of the principal causes of the high price & threatened scarcity of the necessaries of life'.[119] Much more significant was the meeting held in Edinburgh at the end of the previous month, at which Henry Erskine moved resolutions against the Gagging Acts and in favour of peace. The ensuing petition gathered around 8,000 signatures.[120] In Edinburgh, anti-war feeling in 1795–6 was evidently quite widespread, amongst the elites and middling ranks as well as tradesmen and the labouring classes.

Among the former groups, the main causes were probably not so much dearth, however, as the wider economic effects of war, and concern about the conduct of the war and its aims. One female resident of the capital wrote to her son in late 1795 about stagnation in public building in the capital because of shortages of money, and also the lower demand for houses caused by 'great number' of the Edinburgh elite serving overseas in the war. At the beginning of January 1796, she commented: 'Every body wishes for Peace and would God it were restored as trade and every thing languishes ...'.[121] From the west, James Wodrow reported in mid January 1795: 'The discontent of our lower people is considerably encreased since the opening of the present Parl.t Mr Pitt is considered by them as having no feeling for the expended blood & treasure of the Nation'. He also declared that he could not recall seeing the manufacturing workers 'in a more discontented & irritable state'. At the end of the year, his message was similar; the 'lower ranks of the people' were 'sullenly discontented & indignant'.[122] The year 1795 saw Holland over-run by the French, the removal of Prussia from the anti-French coalition, and the failure of the Royalist landing at Quiberon; the Jacobin dictatorship was also replaced by the Directory, which to many seemed to promise stability and order in French politics and thus the political foundation for a secure peace settlement. The war, in other words, had a very different face to the one it presented, to British eyes, in 1793–4. The strength of anti-war feeling in 1795–6 is a reminder of how volatile public opinion was in this period in the face of rapidly shifting domestic and international circumstances.

There are two further aspects of the shortages and protests of 1795–6 which are worth noting at this point. The first is the role of volunteers, embodied in 1794–5, in policing crowds and maintaining order in 1795–6. Roger Wells has argued, in an English context, that urban companies were much less reliable than rural ones in this capacity during the crises of 1795–6 and 1799–1801.[123] In Dingwall and in Peterhead in 1796 local volunteers were involved or implicated in disturbances. In the aftermath, the Dingwall Company of Volunteers appear, on the advice of the Lord Lieutenant, to have been totally disbanded.[124] These were, however, isolated cases, and in general Scottish urban volunteers appear to have proved a reliable police force during the tense months of 1795–6. They were used, for example, without incident in Perth in August 1795, alongside the dragoons.[125] In one sense, their dependability is no surprise, since before 1797 Scottish urban volunteer companies were recruited, in the main, from the upper and middling ranks of urban society. As one individual noted of the first company of Dundee volunteers, shortly after their establishment in 1795, 'a great part of them are Gentlemen'.[126] However much these men might sympathize with the plight of the poor during a period of high prices and shortage, they were steadfastly opposed to all symptoms of popular protest and rioting. Indeed, the rationale behind their establishment had been to support 'the civil magistrate for the preventing and suppressing of riots, tumults or disorder within the burgh'.[127]

Second, the disturbances and tensions of 1795–6 disclose just how far local authorities in Scotland continued to see intervention in the marketplace as the best means, often the only means, of preventing shortages and defusing social tensions in periods of unusually high prices and threatened scarcity. To a degree, the circumstances of the crisis of 1795–6 north of the border pushed them in this direction, in that 'speculation' or agents buying up grain were evidently a major contributory cause of rising prices and fears of scarcity. Nevertheless, Scottish magistrates sought or recommended new powers of intervention faced with this problem; free markets could not guarantee public order. The Provost of Dumfries described the crisis of 1795 as one of 'fictitious scarcity', proposing that magistrates be given the right of pre-emption to force farmers to supply local markets in preference to exporting grain.[128] In March, John Dunlop, writing from Glasgow, urged the creation of the right of magistrates at ports to direct sales from ships in the local market.[129] The Duke of Atholl was calling in late 1795 for temporary restrictions on the export of oats and oatmeal from Perthshire to prevent excessive price rises. In this, he was almost certainly influenced by communications from the Provost of Perth, an advocate of measures to curb 'speculators in grain'.[130] On 29 December 1795, the magistrates and Town Council of Perth petitioned the Privy Council to take measures to prevent speculators purchasing grain 'while it remains in the farmer's corn yards', which, they claimed, was responsible for the current alarm and rising prices.[131] Ministers were opposed to such measures, but Portland did forward a letter from Atholl of 7 February recommending bounties be granted on the import of oats and oatmeal to the Privy Council and the Commons select committee considering the high price of corn.[132] In his capacity as Lord Lieutenant, at about this time, Atholl directed his deputy lieutenants to make close enquiries about the quantity and quality of grain available in their districts before the next harvest in order that any real scarcity could be dealt with. The deputy lieutenants were asked to report on whether farmers had been holding grain back or whether their stocks had been purchased by forestallers to create a monopoly. Farmers were to be informed that it would be 'neighbourly and friendly' to ensure that their conduct did not lead to undue scarcity in their own neighbourhoods.[133] The strength of the consensus that farmers, together with landowners and urban magistrates, had a responsibility to secure local supplies in periods of hardship may have been more important than legal powers in shaping conduct in 1795–6 and during the next crisis. As referred to above, farmers in some areas joined schemes, apparently readily, to stockpile grain for sale to the labouring poor at or below a fixed price. The farmers of the parish of Newabbey agreed on 29 October to secure a stock of oatmeal for sale to labourers, tradesmen and the poor at a rate of 2*d.* per stone under

the lowest shipping price. Meal to be furnished by individual farmers was pro-
portioned according to rents. On the 4 November, the Dumfries and Galloway
Farming Society recommended the adoption of similar schemes at parish level
throughout the region.[134] In this case, the commercialization of farming did not
prevent recognition of the claims of the 'moral economy'.

The view that speculation was the root of the trouble in 1795–6, and that
magistrates had a duty to take action against this, was strongly supported too
from the bench. The charge of the English Lord Chief Justice, Lord Kenyon, to
the grand jury of Shropshire, in which he called on justices of the peace to be
'champions against this hydra-headed monster' – as he termed forestalling – was
widely publicized north of the border and may have strengthened Scottish magistrates' determination to prevent such abuses.[135] Among the Scottish judges,
meanwhile, Lord Swinton made a very public declaration of his belief that the
current scarcity was artificial in April 1796. Addressing magistrates, justices of
the peace and sheriffs at Stirling and Glasgow, he declared: 'that it was the duty
of all magistrates ... to make enquiry concerning these circumstances, and if they
were found to be true, to take proper measures to have these hoarded grains
brought to public market, and sold at market prices'.[136] Swinton's comments were
made at a time when prices, having fallen somewhat, subsequently rose again,
deepening suspicions that market manipulation was the root of current difficulties. The Midlothian corn committee, established at about this time, as referred
to earlier, made its own enquiries into the causes of the continuing high prices
in the spring of 1796, discovering no shortages to explain the trend. They also
took a series of precognitions (statements from witnesses) in an attempt to find
out if forestalling and regrating were actually taking place. The authorities were
'determined' that those who were guilty of such practices should 'not go unpun-
ished, but be held up as examples to deter others for such nefarious practices in
future'.[137] In the previous month, the Edinburgh Council had issued a new set
of regulations regarding the operation of the flesh, veal and fish markets in the
city designed to ensure the immediate supply of these markets and to prevent
forestalling or regrating.[138]

One final symptom of how widely shared the conviction that manipulation
of the markets was prevalent in 1795–6 is the support expressed during 1796
for a proposed bill to provide for sale of corn by weight and not measure in
England, which was designed to reduce opportunities for fraudulent selling, to
be extended to include Scotland.[139] In Scotland in 1795–6, there is, in brief, little
evidence of a clash or confrontation between advocates of 'free trade' and 'moral
economy', although one writer was to claim, retrospectively, in terms which were
to be heard more insistently during the next period of shortage, that had matters
been left to their 'ordinary course' – i.e. the market – prices of bread would have
been 20 per cent cheaper.[140]

Shortage 2: 1799–1801

If the shortages of 1795–6 were, to a significant extent, a consequence of the impact on Scotland of harvest and market conditions in England, the shortages of 1799–1801 were different in nature, being caused by successive poor harvests which affected Scotland and England equally, and much of the rest of Europe besides. In 1799, the harvest was late and of poor quality, owing to 'never ceasing rains in August, September and October'.[141] One individual wrote in March of the following year, in relation to the northern counties, of the 'failure of the crops in many places', while from Fife it was reported that the corn crop, not only in that county, but in 'most other Counties of the Kingdom' was 'not only scanty, but very inferior in Quality.'[142] The poor harvest in 1799 meant prospects for 1800 were already adversely affected, in that there were shortages of good quality seed grain. Seed oats may well have been damaged by frost in 1799. James Twaddle, a farmer from Spittal, launched a claim in the Court of Session in 1801 against another farmer for a refund of the cost of four bolls of seed oats which had failed to produce a crop in 1800. In support of his case, Twaddle remarked on the 'great quantity of frosted oats sold last year for seed, and which proved so prejudicial to the crop in many parts of Scotland'.[143] Reports, nevertheless, of a good harvest circulated widely in the summer of 1800. A minister from the Mearns, for example, reported in late August 1800: 'all around the brae country and west thro' Angus the appearance is very fine and harvest by this time commenced. Upon the whole I cannot help thinking that the Lord has in the months lately past over us only been shewing us famine at a distance telling us what he can inflict if we return not from the evil of our ways.'[144] In the middle of the same month, the opposition Whig *Scots Chronicle*, a fierce advocate of a free market in grain and food, declared: 'The harvest of oats in England is now completely ascertained; and in memory of man there has not been a harvest so abundant, or that promises to be so general in all varieties of human provision. We trust that this year will then have the effect of teaching innovators not to build schemes of permanent revolution upon temporary circumstances ....'[145] The reports seem to have been caused by undue optimism resulting from a very hot, dry summer, which led to an early harvest in parts of Scotland and England.[146] Whatever their origin, they were to be one important cause of tensions in the autumn as prices, having fallen somewhat in August, rose again and remained high in the autumn, partly because heavy rain in late summer again interrupted and damaged the harvest.[147] By October, it would be reported with regard to East Lothian, that the 'greatest part' of the oat crop was worse than in living memory, while the potato crop, although good in quality, had been about half the usual quantity.[148] There may have been a difference in conditions in 1800 between, broadly, east and west. The Lords committee on the scarcity of grain in 1800 reported that crops had been around two-thirds of a normal year on the eastern side of the country, while deficiencies were much less in the west.[149] By contrast, the 1801 harvest was early and 'prodigious', bringing to an end the 1799–1801 crisis.

How serious the shortages were in Scotland is not easily judged given current research, although the consensus among historians currently is that there was no famine in the lowlands, while conditions in the highlands contributed to a surge of voluntary emigration.[150] The rise in meal prices was, nevertheless, from the autumn of 1799 relentless and unexampled, although some of the increase may be attributable to inflationary pressures caused by government fiscal policy. In Edinburgh meal prices peaked in April 1800 at the previously unknown level of 3*s.* 7*d.* per peck, remaining at a very high level until July before dropping to 2*s.* – still an extremely high level – in September, rising again in the final months of 1800, before commencing their final decline in June 1801. Between January 1799 and the following year, the rise in prices had been a dizzying 358 per cent. In Fife, between 1798 and 1800, the price rise was over 180 per cent, in Roxburghshire over 200 per cent.[151] The evidence is that price rises in other places were of a similar magnitude, although local patterns could be distinctive. In late April 1800, when prices peaked in the capital, they climbed to between 3*s.* 3*d.* and 3*s.* 4*d.* in Dundee.[152] In the case of Aberdeen, which is unusually well documented thanks to price data published in the *Aberdeen Weekly Journal*, prices peaked in early January 1800, at between 3*s.* per peck and 3*s.* 2*d.*, dropping somewhat between February and June, before falling more sharply in August–September, on hopes of a good harvest, but rising once more in the autumn and remaining at high levels until September 1801. Behind this picture of climbing and sustained high prices was one, at the local level, of often sharp fluctuations of price, which had a further disorientating effect. One merchant pointed out in 1802, referring to the July of two years previously: 'Under these circumstances [of great scarcity], the price of a commodity becomes altogether arbitrary ... every person followed such loose conjectures as arose from the imagination than from judgement ... and the prices underwent the most unprecedented fluctuation ...'.[153] The effect, meanwhile, of sustained high prices on the labouring population was to exhaust any savings they may have had, perhaps by as early as the summer of 1800.

By early 1800, there were frequent expressions of alarm about shortages. February–March saw a brief flurry of disturbances in Elgin, Dalbeattie, Glasgow and Macduff.[154] From Glasgow, the Provost and magistrates appealed to the Treasury in February for assistance, holding out the prospect of 'most serious and fatal consequences' if nothing was done to 'quiet the minds of the people, and to afford them some prospect of relief from absolute famine which at present stares them in the face'.[155] In January 1800, some Ayrshire towns were faced with acute supply problems, part of the cause of which was harvest failure in Ireland and lack of usual imports from there. In the following year, in the Court of Session, it was argued by the magistrates of Ayr that 40 bolls of meal were needed every week to feed the town's population of 7,000. On 24 January 1800, only 3 bolls had been brought to the market, even though the current price was 2*s.* 6*d.* per peck. Between 24 and 31 January, magistrates were unable to find further meal to supply to market, and were, therefore, faced with 'the evil of absolute famine, with its attendant miseries'.[156] At the end of March, there was a disturbance in Perth, while one was only avoided at Dundee by having the military mount guard in the market to deter the collection of a mob.[157] At the end of following month, a rumour took hold in the latter town that poor-quality oatmeal was responsible for the death of a child in the manufacturing district of Chapelshade.[158] The popular mood was brittle and tense. Edinburgh and its environs were affected by disturbances, and threatened disturbances, at the beginning of May.[159] The targets of the Edinburgh crowd were mealsellers and granaries. On 29 April, soldiers and volunteers, struggling to control a crowd which appeared in several parts of the city and Leith, were unable to prevent the destruction of a house of a mealseller in Leith, which led to his claiming £255.15.7¾ in damages from the magistrates in 1803.[160] In Glasgow in July, the windows were smashed of several dealers who, it was believed, were sending meal to other places.[161] At the end of the following month, several carts were stopped in Portsburgh, an Edinburgh suburb, on their way to and from the capital's public market.[162] Meanwhile, trouble spread to the western manufacturing districts in the autumn of 1800, with disturbances and a period of heightened tension affecting Ayrshire, Glasgow, Paisley and Pollokshaws.[163] Further disturbances occurred in 1801, although these were not numerous and almost certainly reflected localized rather than general conditions of shortage, and the fact that in the autumn of 1801 prices remained high in quite a few markets when compared to Edinburgh, and in face of expectations of more rapid reductions owing to the good harvest. In Kirkudbright in January the shipping of potatoes led to protests.[164] On 23 June 1801, the attacks in the capital of the previous year on millers and bakers were renewed, while a mob also visited mills nearby in an attempt to seize meal.[165] In the final months of 1801, Errol, a weaving village on the Carse of Gowrie, Dundee and Arbroath were the sites of disturbances.[166] A further disturbance also occurred in the Cowgate, Edinburgh, in late October 1801, when a journeyman smith led a crowd which seized a cart loaded with oatmeal and distributed it for free, an action which again seems only to be explicable in terms of local market conditions since prices had fallen significantly since the summer.[167]

Conditions were made worse in 1800–1 by economic depression caused by the collapse of domestic demand, itself another consequence of the unrelenting high prices, and international developments. In early 1801, the prospect of conflict with the Baltic powers caused the price of Russian flax to surge. As a result, the manufacture of osnaburgs was almost at a stand in and around Dundee. The only sources of demand in the local economy were government orders for sail cloth and privateering.[168] In February, a correspondent wrote to the opposition Whig William Adam that 'scarcity and dearth' pervaded 'every parish' in Angus, the reason being given that brown linen was under 'a deadness in demand and depression of value'.[169] In May, a letter in the press spoke of continuing stagnation in 'almost every branch of trade'. An additional problem was the prohibition on trade between the West Indies and Spanish territories, which was further depressing demand for sail cloth and brown linen.[170] In April 1801, it was reported that the state of the muslin and cotton industry in and about Glasgow and Paisley was 'truly lamentable and distressing'. High prices of provisions, a lack of work and low wages were, it was said, leading to poverty, beggary and emigration. Two thousand looms, it was also reported, had been 'laid aside in the past few weeks'.[171] A year earlier, a similar report came from Glasgow, observing that since the previous November over 3,000 weavers had enlisted in the army. The only market where there was any demand for Glasgow textiles was Hamburg and Emden.[172]

The number of disturbances in Scotland in 1799–1801, so far as we can tell, was again, compared to south of the border, low, and again as in 1795–6 they tended not to be very serious or protracted, although they were symptoms of considerable social tension. Behind them were suspicions that specific individuals, whether farmers in the countryside, or mealsellers and dealers in towns, were exploiting conditions of hardship, or failing in their 'responsibility' to supply local markets before more distant ones. The notion of a 'pacte de famine' never caught hold in quite the same way as in England in the autumn of 1800, but there were strong echoes of it, and for similar reasons. As in England, the press played a significant role in that, as emphasized earlier, carrying frequent reports in the summer moving into the autumn of 1800 of a good harvest and prospects for falling prices. On 24 July, the *Glasgow Courier* reprinted a letter from a 'house of the first respectability in the Corn line, to a gentleman in Glasgow, dated Limerick, 12 July 1800', which reported on the 'fine state' of the crop in that part of Ireland and declared that there was 'every prospect of being able to send large supplies' to Scotland. The same issue also quoted an eminent corn merchant from Norwich stating that there was 'every reason to hope and expect' that the harvest 'will prove abundant and of fine quality'. Almost every issue between then and early September contained similar reports.[173] Prices failed to fall, however, causing people to look to artificial causes of current problems. The Glasgow Farmers Society, meeting in early November, noting that it had been 'industriously reported that [the] last crop was abundant', and that farmers were unwilling to bring stocks to market, called on the lords lieutenant of each county to order an inspection to be made to establish the quantity of grain being held in their counties, the purpose being to satisfy the 'public' about the 'real stock in the hands of farmers'.[174] In Dumfries, popular belief in the existence of a 'nefarious system of monopoly' was reinforced by evasion of restrictions on exports of grain to England by merchants moving the grain south from Dumfries 'at the extremity of Scotland', and then transporting it overland into England.[175] Tensions in Ayrshire were exacerbated by farmers transporting grain at night, despite being urged not to do so by magistrates.[176] In the neighbourhood of Peterhead, landowners and tenant farmers were, it appears, only selling their surplus grain at the public market in the town in order to undermine suspicions of meal being bought up for export before townspeople had any opportunity to purchase it.[177] Newspapers frequently contained paragraphs which alluded to speculative activity on the part of farmers and others at the expense of the public.[178]

There was much propaganda, originating from ministers and others in England as well as Scotland, denying that dealers and speculation were the causes of the shortages, and promoting free circulation of grain as the best solution to shortages.[179] The actions of many magistrates at the local level pointed, however, to a different conclusion; or perhaps more accurately, threats to public order required immediate, decisive measures to allay public anger and anxieties and to secure supplies for markets. In March 1800 a mob in Perth seized a load of bear from a vessel, and loaded it into carts for transport to the town mills. They were stopped by regular soldiers and the local volunteers, and the meal was carried back to a warehouse. The Perth magistrates, in face of widespread alarm, decided to conciliate rather than confront. The ship was sent from Perth the next day, but without its cargo, and a handbill was issued to allay public fears.[180] In Edinburgh in July 1801, a meeting of those who had suffered at the hands of the meal mobs in 1800 and 1801 expressed its lack of confidence in the promise of protection by the magistrates of those who bought or sold in the capital's meal and corn markets, declaring, 'some other authority ought to be pledged in security of life and property without which no regular supply at Market can be expected and this measure appears the more necessary, in as much as the Mob do avowedly proceed under the ideas that their depredations are tolerated by the magistrates'.[181] We have already seen that in Eskdalemuir a local magistrate issued a warrant for the seizure of meal being moved to distant markets. This also occurred in Ayr in 1800.[182] Prosecutions against forestallers and other market abuses were also common in this period, as magistrates sought to demonstrate their diligence and vigilance in seeking to defend the interests of the labouring population in the face of acute suffering. The Sheriff of East Lothian, for example, examined corn dealers from Tranent and several other places in the county in late October on suspicion of forestalling and regrating. All those examined were bailed to stand trial, while some were also fined for use of defective measures.[183] In Lanark, magistrates, finding meal short in the public market in early

November, discovered that meal dealers were being stopped on the road by 'pests buying and laying up' grain before it reached the market. One individual was duly fined as a forestaller and regrator, while a meal dealer was jailed for 'gross prevarication'.[184] Against this background, the strength of popular belief that supplying local needs was a duty of magistrates and indeed farmers and dealers, and given that some individuals clearly did seek to exploit strained conditions for personal gain, it is hardly surprising that suspicion that speculation was taking place led to direct action against this.

The conviction that high prices and shortages had causes other than a deficient harvest was also fuelled by English reactions to the contemporary dearth. In the spring of 1800, it was reported: 'Several Publications of alarm from England did great injury in Scotland, by encouraging the Forestaller, and intimidating the Fair Trader'.[185] Through reading English and Scottish newspapers, the Scots were only too aware that the English courts were prosecuting large numbers of individuals, under common law, for forestalling and regrating in this period. The high profile cases at the Old Bailey of the King versus Waddington, a hop dealer, and the King versus Ashby, a corn factor, which provided Kenyon with further opportunities to lambast the forestallers and speculators, were widely reported in the Scottish press.[186] In Edinburgh, it was reported that the English trials 'for forestalling and engrossing are talked of ... as a complete refutation of the speculations of theorists on the ... corn trade'.[187] The reports of the English trials directly contradicted the frequent assertions that free circulation of grain was the only effective solution to shortage and famine, and of magisterial confidence in dealers and retailers of grain.

What needs explaining, however, is not primarily that some disturbances took place in 1799–1801, but why they were so few in comparison with England and why those that did take place were relatively minor. An explanation strongly favoured by several historians is the strong sense of paternalistic responsibility among the Scottish ruling elites and wider propertied classes, and the extent of their efforts to alleviate suffering in the crisis months of 1799–1801.[188] This explanation has much to commend it in that there is abundant evidence for the assiduity and efforts of Scottish elites to respond to the surging prices and shortages. Responses included, as in 1795–6, purchase of meal and its sale at below market prices. In the spring of 1800, the principal heritors and farmers of Coldstream agreed to assess themselves an additional quarter's poor rates in order to purchase wheat and oats to sell as flour and meal to the 'necessitous'. In order to enable the purchases to be made immediately, three individuals pledged credit to the bank for the amount of the assessment.[189] In some places, a scale of prices was established at which meal would be sold linked to household need and income, a type of Speenhamland system of relief pioneered in this period in the southeast of England.[190] In an extension of a role which they appear to have played throughout the eighteenth century in periods of hardship, landowners provided donations of meal and coal to tenants and labourers, as well as to urban and semi-urban populations. In Perthshire, the Duke of Atholl supplied 100 bolls of meal for Blairgowrie, 70 for nearby Rattray, 12 for Kinloch, and 20 for Bendochy in the spring of 1800.[191] Burgh councils paid premiums to encourage imports and supplies of meal and other foodstuffs to markets.[192] In December 1799, the Paisley Town Council abolished customs on meal brought to market.[193]

A new feature of the responses to unusual hardship in 1799–1801 was the establishment of public kitchens. Popularized by Count Rumford and the Society for Bettering the Conditions of the Poor, these were much favoured as a form of relief in this period throughout Britain. This was partly because they avoided the problem of interfering in the free market in meal and grain, but they also, unlike financial support, were seen as not encouraging dependency and idleness.[194] Public kitchens were established in Edinburgh, Leith, Dundee, Glasgow, Aberdeen, Forfar, Montrose, Stirling, Peterhead, Elgin, Kelso, Dunfermline and Banff, and no doubt many other places.[195] Usually soup kitchens were supplemented by wider relief measures, which similarly depended on the voluntary donations of a wide cross-section of urban society.[196] As in earlier periods of hardship, the churches held periodic extraordinary charitable collections (that is, in addition to the regular weekly collections) to raise additional funds for relief of the poor. In Edinburgh, in 1800, voluntary assessments were given up in favour of compulsory assessment, authorized by parliamentary statute, to raise funds for relief until 1802.

County elites created or encouraged similar schemes at parish level in the countryside. The Lanarkshire county elite raised £9,430 in 1800 to purchase grain from corn merchants to ensure a regular supply.[197] On the Carse of Gowrie, as occurred in 1796, local landowners organized their tenant farmers in a system designed to secure local supply of grain, a system which involved visiting farmers to get an account of the different types of grain they had on hand, and of the needs of every householder until the next harvest, as well as securing additional supplies of grain to make up the shortfalls financed by subscriptions from tenant farmers and landowners.[198] This was one part of a county-side scheme led by the Duke of Atholl as Lord Lieutenant, for which Atholl purchased 3,000 quarters of oats for distribution throughout the county.[199] Relief, in sum, was led by local authorities, but depended on the support of a broad cross-section of society.

There were other initiatives to protect sections of the population against suffering. Taking another lead from national (meaning British) responses to the shortages, various initiatives were launched in respect of the composition of flour used in baking bread, with the aim of producing cheaper loaves for the poor, while campaigns of economy were also launched which were designed to lessen use of oats and other foods among the propertied classes.[200] Friendly societies, which had grown rapidly in number in the final third of the eighteenth century, clubbed together to purchase grain from abroad for distribution to their members.[201] There were schemes to establish cooperative bakeries in competition with existing bakers. These schemes involved subscribers purchasing grain, again from abroad, and having it milled at their own expense. The aim was not merely to provide flour at lower prices, but also to drive prices down through additional competition to local millers and bakers.[202]

Shortages and high prices in 1799–1801 drew, therefore, a multifaceted response from elites and communities. Relief schemes were carefully coordinated and managed, so far as we can tell, and concerted; they were not short-lived or minimal responses. Authorities in many burghs were forced to arrange for peasemeal, barley and oatmeal to be purchased for inhabitants in each of three consecutive years from 1799 until 1801.[203] The landed proprietors of Renfrewshire subscribed between £5,000 and £6,000 in 1799 to purchase foreign grain, on which they lost £30 for every £100 subscribed, but this did not discourage them from establishing a new subscription in 1800.[204] In Glasgow, £117,000 was spent in 1801 in securing grain of various kinds, as well as 202 tonnes of potatoes; in the previous year £15,000 had been raised by subscription for the same purpose by the Town Council, Merchants' House, incorporated trades, and 'wealthy and respectable' citizens.[205] In Edinburgh £9,700 was raised in 1800, which enabled more than 4,000 families to be supported with money, provisions and coals.[206] Assuming a multiplier of four, this meant that 16,000 people were being helped, from a population of around 80,000. Public kitchens were in operation for long periods and provided relief to significant numbers of people. The Aberdeen public kitchen was in operation between 17 December 1800 and 17 September 1801. In early January 1800, the Edinburgh kitchen was distributing 3,000 meals daily, and this was before a second kitchen was opened which doubled the quantity made available. In Glasgow in July 1800, there were 9 public kitchens in operation distributing 3,147 meals daily.[207]

How should we portray these measures and their impact? Unsurprisingly, it was argued at the time that they revealed a benevolent attitude towards the poor on the part of the propertied, but this, of course, was a script from 'above'; from the recipients of relief we only have silence, although at least one contributor to the press cast doubts on the extent of support in the capital in 1801.[208] There is very little evidence too regarding the extent of the needs of the poor against which we might measure their alleviating effects, or regarding the effectiveness of support provided by other, more permanent mechanisms of relief – trades incorporations, friendly societies, poor funds and a growing number of voluntary societies and subscriptions targeted at specific sections of the populace. There was clearly great strain on these systems. In Aberdeen, the number of women on the pension list had averaged 178 over the previous five years, but by July 1800 stood at 311.[209] By late 1800 the funds of the Glasgow general sessions were said to be exhausted.[210] At the beginning of that year, the Cumberland Society of Paisley, a friendly society, had raised the allowances it paid to its members in need of assistance, reflecting the climbing food prices.[211] By the summer of 1801, in Aberdeen at least, funds for supplying meal and coals had run out, although the public kitchen continued to operate.[212]

Those who argue that these measures provide a strong explanation of the relative stability and quiescence of Scottish society in 1795–6 and 1799–1801 portray paternalism as a more pervasive force north of the border than south, and measures such as these as evidence of this fact.[213] One possible criticism of this view is that it tends to accept the elites' own evaluation of their efforts and identity. Paternalism may have remained a key aspect of landowners' conception of their relations to their tenants and labourers – indeed many traditional rituals of paternalism persisted, for example, celebration of major events in the lives of the local notability – but this would often sit alongside by the later eighteenth century canny commercialism and a very hard-headed attitude towards exploitation of property rights. This, in turn, entailed increasing intolerance of lower-class independence or actions, such as poaching and gleaning, which adversely affected their property and interests.[214] Commercialization was cumulatively attenuating the bonds of deference and hierarchy in society, although at what speed and to what degree is hard to measure. Schemes of relief were often reactive, a direct response to disturbance or threatened disturbance; to this extent, they were less paternalistic than pragmatic. The relief efforts on the Carse of Gowrie in the spring of 1800 followed a period of considerable tension and threatened violence caused by concerns about movement of grain out of the area through landowners selling to merchants.[215] In Edinburgh, one response to the disturbances there in late April–early May 1800 was for the Town Council to offer premiums to encourage farmers and dealers to bring their meal to the capital's market, and also to reiterate their indemnification of any losses suffered by individuals because of the actions of rioters.[216] In 1801, the Provost of Dundee, Alexander Riddoch, found himself with barley on his hands surplus to requirements, but was only prepared to sell it if the purchaser would undertake not to ship it from Dundee or its environs. Pragmatism dictated this restriction, as Riddoch made clear later in defending his actions, actions predicated on an awareness of how delicate public order could be in conditions such as those which obtained in 1800–1:

> To have allowed any part of this corn, or the meal produced from it, to have been carried away would have been highly impolitic; and if scarcity had afterwards occurred, the magistrates and council would have been subject to a situation most disagreeable. There is not a doubt that popular clamour and perhaps tumult, too common in such cases, would have burst forth against them. Your Lordships know how much it is the

duty of every magistrate and every judge to use the proper precautions to avert such tumult.[217]

Rarely were those in authority so unguarded in disclosing motivation, although this was, admittedly, in the context of Riddoch defending himself before the Court of Session, whom he evidently expected to be sympathetic to his construction of magistrates' responsibilities.

By the end of the eighteenth century, attitudes towards poverty were also hardening in Scotland, as in the rest of Britain, under the impact of evangelical religious currents and a growing body of criticism of indiscriminate charitable giving and an overly expansive poor law.[218] In the following century, popularized by Thomas Chalmers and other evangelicals, these harsher views were to spread very widely.[219] Their growing influence in 1799–1801 is precisely why soup kitchens were so popular. Recipients of soup who were deemed able to afford to do so were expected to pay for it, albeit at subsidized prices. As one newspaper declared of the Trongate soup kitchen in Glasgow: '[It] cherishes in the lower ranks a praise worthy independency of mind and a desire to do for themselves as far as is in their power'.[220] Such schemes also had the advantage for the elites of making recipients acutely aware of their dependency on elite benevolence, in that it was the subscribers who directly controlled, through a ticket system, access to relief and on what terms. The tendency towards closer scrutiny of the objects of relief was manifest in many of the relief schemes, and for the same reason. The Edinburgh subscription in 1800 for the relief of the poor boasted of the 'minuteness of inquiry into the circumstances of the poor, and extent of benefit in proportion to value which applicants receive'.[221] Not only could subscribers be assured that only worthy or deserving individuals would receive support, but in a form which was properly economical. Fuelled in significant measure by vivid images of popular anarchy and irreligion imprinted on the minds of the elites by the French Revolution, charity and the urge towards greater social control were on sharply convergent paths at the end of the eighteenth century.

It is also far from self evident that, as referred to in the introduction to this chapter, relief measures were so much different in scale and range than those attempted south of the border. Town councils in England knew very well the importance of maintaining supplies of grain to social order, and took steps to secure this in periods of shortage and high prices.[222] London saw very few food riots in the eighteenth century precisely because the authorities understood the importance of ensuring its markets were kept supplied with food at reasonable prices.[223] Almost all of the initiatives taken in this period to relieve hardship have their counterparts south of the border, and in some cases, as already alluded to, are probably best seen as aspects of a British-wide campaign of relief.[224]

In his work on England in this period, Wells also emphasized how far the notion of a 'moral economy' retained its force during this crisis, despite the influence of Smith's 'laissez faire' ideas. As referred to earlier, the courts, led by Kenyon, gave powerful support to this notion in 1800.[225] By contrast, Scotland's Court of Session came out in favour of the free circulation of grain in a much publicized case in 1801, Leishman versus the Magistrates and Council of Ayr. The decision gave support to the growing number of voices which insisted that the solution to the fear of famine was 'free trade' in grain, a prescription which was hardly offered practical guidance to magistrates facing the prospect of protest and empty markets, and which, partly for this reason, was far from accepted by all writers on the subject; even those who did so were compelled to acknowledge that extraordinary conditions might demand extraordinary measures.[226] Leishman was a grain dealer from Paisley who had his grain seized in early 1800 under warrant from the magistrates of Ayr and sold in the public market, which was then almost completely denuded of supply. The outcome of the case hinged on the view that the Ayr magistrates had wrongly interpreted the actions of a merchant, who was collecting and moving grain from Ayrshire to supply Paisley, as forestalling.[227] The judgement marked a step change in the judges' attitudes to the bread market. One newspaper reported that, in a unanimous decision:

> The judges said, that the circulation of grain ought to be as free as any other commodity; and this was particularly necessary during the present year, in order that these parts of the country might be supplied from the crop in other parts of Scotland – the Court also declared, that the abuse thrown out against meal dealers in the Sheriff Court of Ayr, was founded on gross ignorance; for that this description of men, instead of being prejudicial to the community, was highly useful.[228]

The implication of the decision was that magistrates, contrary to what Lord Swinton and many others had asserted in 1796, did not have the power to direct sales in public markets in the event of shortages. It was also in line with those commentators who argued that, under a commercial system, the definition of forestalling or regrating should be an extremely narrow one;[229] the 'moral economy' was beginning to crack under the weight of the new ideology of the 'free market'. Many efforts at relief in 1799–1801 were designed precisely not to interfere with the market, but to work with or through it. Grain was purchased through merchants and sold at current or market prices. As Riddoch described for Dundee in 1801: 'the magistrates never entertained the idea of purchasing grain to be sold in the public markets below the prices current at the time'.[230] Those who were able were expected to pay market prices for grain or bread; only those who on enquiry were deemed incapable were to be supported with subventions or donations of meal.

Where other differences exist, moreover, some of these may be explained in large measure by different institutional contexts as much as in terms of any difference in a sense of obligation to the poor. In England, the poor rate carried a substantial part of the burden of relieving the poor, which was not the case, at least to the same degree, north of the border, although a growing number of parishes became subject to assessment in this period, and poor rates rose in the later eighteenth century.[231] Instructive in this context is the adoption in rural areas in Scotland in 1800 of the so-called Speenhamland system from England, whereby wages of those in work were supplemented by relief payments, referred to briefly above. In many parishes in Scotland, the funds used to do this were not raised by compulsory assessments for poor relief, but by voluntary subscription.[232]

In one specific way, however, the notion of a paternalistic economy was perhaps more meaningful and substantial north of the border. Unlike in England, Scottish magistrates had a role to play in intervening in wage disputes, and might, in the interests of social order and justice, rule on the side of workers, as they did on several occasions in the later 1790s. It was a power which was only, for purely ideological reasons, destroyed by the Court of Session in 1812.[233] Yet even here the difference may not be as great as it first appears. As John Rule has pointed out, in the inflationary period of the French wars, employers in England recognized the claims of workers to higher wages, although when prices fell they looked for wages to fall also.[234] Even the Combination Acts (1799–1801), which did not apply in Scotland, did not prevent an expansion of union and strike activity south of the border in this period, and had greater symbolic than practical import.[235]

Scottish Quiescence: Other Causes

If patterns of paternalism (however defined) seem, therefore, to provide at best only a partial explanation of Scottish difference in 1799–1801 – and certainly one which is difficult to test in any meaningful way – it may be that we need to look elsewhere to explain the less turbulent, disordered conditions north of the border. It is to this search that we turn in the final part of this chapter.

Although this might be seen as much as a symptom than cause of the relative quiescence of the Scots in this period, there were, undeniably, fewer political tensions in this period in Scotland to fuel potential discontent, and less alienation from the current structures of power and authority. Evidence for this is admittedly very slim, but then this itself was a symptom of the relative lack of concern of those in power. In England in 1800–1, dearth was linked to renewed agitation for peace and, while protests may not have been primarily motivated by politics, anger and social tension were often expressed in political language. Posters and graffiti appeared containing radical and at times revolutionary overtones. Radicals were active in seeking to politicize the tensions and alienation. Revolutionary groups – the United Englishmen and United Irishmen – were active.[236] North of the border, the subterranean press, the graffiti, and the 'democratic offensive' are conspicuous by their near complete absence. The sole evidence of politicization comes from Paisley, Glasgow and Pollokshaws in the autumn of 1800, and it was a faint echo of what was taking place south of the border. Inflammatory placards appeared in Paisley in September 1800 calling on people to take direct action to secure food in terms which betrayed radical authorship. Calling for the names of 'Aristocrate' and 'Democrate' to be forgotten, the handbill urged direct action to destroy the 'dreadful & exorbitant monopoly of the necessarys of life' and the 'sett of despicable and hardened wretches' now 'endeavouring to starve and drive to misery and destruction the labourious part of the nation'. The origin of the current 'evils' was war; and the solution uniting to demand 'immediate peace'.[237] The appearance of the handbill followed an earlier disturbance in the town which had only been suppressed at the cost of severe injuries to several volunteers.[238] It was accompanied by anonymous threatening letters to farmers, millers and dealers in the neighbourhood of the town. William McDowall, who led a successful policing effort to prevent a second disturbance, declared: 'the spirit of 1794 has burst forth and politics is mixed with the present scarcity to excite the disaffected to tumult & insurrection'. The suspected author of the handbill was an Irishman who had supposedly left Ireland during the Rebellion of 1798 in 'very suspicious circumstances' and was commonly suspected of 'bad & seditious principles & conduct'.[239] No further evidence survives to illuminate conditions in and around Paisley at this time, although Robert Dundas was happy that the discontent had been effectively contained.[240] Even less is known about circumstances in Pollokshaws, although we do know that 'incendiary letters' were circulating, and it was believed by those in authority that the authors were 'persons inimical to our happy constitution'.[241] The United Scotsmen were still in existence in this period, but their survival and strength following the repression of 1797–8 are almost entirely hidden from view.[242] 'French principles' had a tenacious foothold in some of the weaving villages of Renfrewshire in this period, and, as we saw in a previous chapter, Paisley had been the site of a turbulent strain of 'Jacobin' radicalism in the early 1790s, and to this extent the existence of a political dimension to the disturbances is not in itself surprising. Perhaps what it striking is that there was not more of this in the west-central manufacturing regions in 1799–1801, and no sign of it at all, at least that has left any evidence, in Perthshire, Angus and Fife, where the United Scotsmen also established a significant presence in 1796–7.[243]

There was also, again in contrast to parts of England, no peace campaign of any sort to talk of north of the border in 1800–1. This was despite the efforts of the opposition Whigs, through their press vehicle, the *Scots Chronicle*, to stir one up. The paper contained frequent reports on the peace agitation in the Common Council of the City of London, led by Robert Waithman, and in the textile towns of the West Riding of Yorkshire suffering from a similar collapse of domestic and overseas demand as the Scottish linen and cotton industries.[244] On 23 December 1800, 'A True Loyalist', writing to the *Scots Chronicle*, called for petitions or addresses to the throne to dismiss the present ministers as the 'only means of restoring the blessings of PEACE and PLENTY to his exhausted, bleeding and starving country subjects'. The Berwick guildry petitioned for peace at the beginning of November 1800, but that was it. The Glasgow incorporation of weavers, meeting to decide on whether to petition, declared that there was no cause for such a petition, and expressed their disapprobation of the conduct of those who had moved for such a measure.[245]

If there was less political discontent to stir social tensions arising from dearth, it may also be that, as a smaller, much less populous country, Scotland was more adequately provided with regular troops and other forces to police potential disorder. This argument must not be pushed too far since had there been more disturbances these forces might well have been badly stretched, as occurred in 1797 during the anti-militia disturbances and as occurred in England in 1795–6 and again in 1799–1801. Nevertheless, together with heightened magisterial vigilance in watching over the marketplace, the appearance of force did deter disturbances, as occurred for example in 1800 in Dundee. There was seemingly no difficulty embodying special constables to prevent disorder in towns, reflecting how quickly the propertied elites tended to unite in support of public order in the face of disturbances throughout the later eighteenth century. In Paisley, for example, on 30 October 1800 the town council agreed 'in order to quiet the Town from the present disturbances and riots' to elect a group of constables.[246] The much-expanded Scottish volunteer numbers proved a generally reliable police force. This was true, for example, in Edinburgh and Leith where they were particularly numerous. In Ayr, the volunteers proved a useful support to regular forces during the disturbed autumn of 1800. In April 1799, in the absence of any regular soldiers nearby, Banffshire volunteers suppressed disturbances in Portsoy with 'equal spirit and prudence'. In Paisley in November 1800, William McDowall chose to rely solely on the Paisley volunteers to contain potential protests, while '400 respectable inhabitants' were also sworn in as constables and provided with batons. In his report to Portland, McDowall wrote: 'It is impossible for me to express how much I was gratified with the zeal & alacrity of the volunteers'.[247] There were a few notable exceptions to this rule. In 1800, Peterhead and Auchtermuty volunteers disobeyed orders when called upon to police potential or actual food protests. In Peterhead, many of the corps simply refused to muster when called upon to protect the shipping of a cargo of oatmeal in February, arriving instead in their work clothes and offering to return uniforms and arms. Interestingly, they made a distinction between protecting property in the town and supposedly assisting in the shipping of meal. Peterhead was one of the places which had seen disturbances in 1796 occasioned by the shipping of meal in a period of shortage, and no doubt their actions are further illustration of the strength of the continuing consensus at a popular level that such action was a violation of community norms. The Auchtermuty volunteers stated that dealing with rioters was simply not part of their duty.[248] Meanwhile, in the rural setting of Errol in Perthshire, volunteers were disarmed by women during the protests there in late 1801, and it was subsequently reported that many men had resigned from the corps, claiming that they could not pursue their vocations in peace and without fear from the violence of neighbours.[249] In this case, it was probably the lack of any significant social difference between the volunteers and the general populace, and their relative dispersal around the parish, which explains their sense of vulnerability. Again what is worth emphasizing, however, is that incidents of volunteer unreliability in internal policing were rare in Scotland in 1799–1801.

Volunteering may have had another, rather different importance in 1799–1801, as the source of wage supplements. As we saw in the previous chapter, 1797 saw a major expansion of volunteering in Scotland, which involved recruitment of large numbers of artisans and other members of the labouring classes into urban companies, and farmers and labourers in rural ones. That said, numbers of volunteers even after 1797 never accounted for more than small percentage of the population, so its economic significance should not be exaggerated.[250] The Scottish labouring classes also had other, traditional ways of responding to hardship short of protest or support for radical politics. One was recruitment into the armed forces, while another was emigration. In May 1801, the 'spirit of emigration' to America was said to be present in Dundee and its environs.[251]

In what was still a poorer, less economically advanced society, foods other than bread or indeed meal constituted a larger component of the diets of the labouring classes, notably potatoes, but also, in places close to the coast, fish. Diets among the lower orders were simpler north of the border, although not less nutritious, which also helps explain why there were few, if any, food protests in eighteenth-century Scotland focused on foods other than oats or oatmeal. To this extent, relying more heavily on soup and other substitute foods while oats and oatmeal were in short supply or very high in price was likely to cause less tension and unrest. Supplies of fish may have been abundant in 1800–1 on the east coast, and certainly in 1800 Parliament was looking at ways to encourage herring fishing in the Firth of Forth and the old issue of changing the salt laws had resurfaced to ensure cheaper and better salt for curing.[252] In Dundee in early 1801, weavers and shopkeepers were allegedly turning to fishing, and herring were selling at five a penny so abundant were they.[253] In rural areas, meanwhile, Scottish labourers were still paid in kind, or partly in kind, despite a transformation in the rural economy since the mid-century, a fact which shielded them from rises in food prices, and which probably explains why there was no Scottish equivalent to the incendiarism and hostile anonymous letters which afflicted southern and south-eastern counties of England in 1800–1.[254]

As Devine has emphasized, Scottish society, despite rapid economic change in the final third of the eighteenth century, remained in 1800 a considerably less urbanized and industrialized society than England.[255] As has been emphasized elsewhere in this book, most Scottish towns were relatively small and, within urban society, trades incorporations and freemasonry provided further links between social ranks, which could be mobilized in a period of stress. In rural parishes, farmers seem, in many cases, to have been happy or at least prepared to cooperate with efforts to secure grain for urban and semi-urban markets. This may, in turn, reflect the fact that many tenant farmers were farming on a relatively modest basis in many parts of the country, and certainly not on the scale of English tenant farmers in arable areas. In England, several people argued that a return to smaller-scale farming was required to disable manipulation of the market for food,[256] an argument that was largely inapplicable to Scotland, with the exception perhaps of parts of the Lothians. The social and cultural distance of many tenant farmers from the labouring classes was, while growing in this period, less than south of the border, and their susceptibility to landlord influence correspondingly greater. To this extent, what may have differed was not the impulse towards paternalist measures, but rather their efficacy. The relative power of the smaller, more cohesive landed elite was also greater, a theme which runs throughout this book. One symbol of this is the importance of the planned village in Scotland in the later eighteenth century. These semi-urban settlements, where much manufacturing was located, were closely controlled by landowners, who ultimately, through their factors, held the power of non-renewal of leases over the heads of their populations. There were certainly limits to their quiescence, as was dramatically illustrated in 1797 during the anti-militia riots, but there was a relationship between them and the landowner for which there was no equivalent in respect, say, of the semi-industrial villages of the West Midlands. One other group which was prominent in food disturbances south of the border were miners, as they had been throughout the eighteenth century. Yet the Scottish colliers were conspicuously absent from the disturbances north of the border in 1795–6 and again in 1799–1801. While this might several decades ago have been attributed to their serf status, at least before this was abolished in 1799, it is their relative independence as an occupational group which is now emphasized, and at least one historian has pointed out that they frequently took action on food prices and could be found as participants in food protests if these took place in their localities.[257] Part of the explanation for their quiescence in the 1790s may have been the effectiveness of the strike as a means to secure wage increases in a period of inflation. It is conceivable too that landowners on whose estates they were present were providing them with meal during the crisis months.

Finally, religion may provide a further key to the different *mentalité* of the Scottish labouring classes.[258] The Presbyterian churches were very active throughout the century in portraying the harvest as a key instrument of God's providential relationship to his people. Fast days were held in almost every year in response to good or poor harvests, either thanking God or calling on his future mercy. This obviously did not prevent waves of food disturbances at moments of hardship and shortage, but it did provide an extra framework of explanation for periods of shortage which was deeply embedded in Scottish society. There is no way of telling how influential this was in 1799–1801, although, unlike in 1795–6, the evidence of poor harvests was there to be seen in the fields. It would be foolish to exaggerate its importance, compared to the actions of farmers and magistrates, but equally it would be wrong to assume that it had no bearing on popular perceptions. As we have seen at various points in this book, the pulpit retained a crucial importance in Scottish society in this period as a means of disseminating messages; this was no longer the case, to the same degree at least, in many parts of England and Wales.

CONCLUSION

Scottish politics in this period can be seen as a variation on a common British narrative – one of radical weakness, divisions and failures and of loyalist and subsequently patriotic ascendancy – although what John Dinwiddy once termed the 'Dickinsonian consensus', after the seminal work on the period of H. T. Dickinson, has not gained universal acceptance.[1] This book has presented much evidence which would support this portrayal of Scotland in the 1790s, but which also indicates some of its important limitations. It has also sought to focus attention, however, on the novel varieties of political experience in this decade, at various different levels of society. The issue of stability is unavoidable for historians of this decade, but preoccupation with it has on occasion squeezed other, equally compelling themes to the margins of historical debate.

It has been argued that in the case of Ireland the politics of the 1790s represented the culmination of a series of reforming and radical initiatives dating from the 1770s, if not slightly earlier.[2] A similar argument has been made for England, although the connecting threads are not always as clear as they are sometimes represented, and the popular radicalism of the 1790s did represent something new in terms of its being a self-conscious attempt to usher into being a new type of politics involving a new class of citizen.[3] In Scotland, the route to popular politicization was different, and 1792 appears to present an even sharper disjuncture in this context. The precocity of the eighteenth-century politicization of the 'public sphere' (to use Tim Blanning's formulation) was an English phenomenon, not a British one.[4] Indeed, it is commonly argued that a precondition of the Enlightenment in Scotland was precisely this – the absence of political division and preoccupation with national politics after 1707. As we have seen (in Chapter 1), the case should not be overstated; but in broad terms Scottish political culture for the most of the eighteenth century had an intimacy, a close-knittedness, and a strength of focus on patronage and clientage which was unusual (but not unknown) in other parts of the British Isles. Symptomatic of this condition was the Stirling Port Club, founded in 1782, and which was in many ways a typical Scottish Enlightenment club. It had a limit of eleven members, who were drawn from the local ruling elite; its first praeses (president) was David Gourlay, the current Provost of the town. Its discussions ranged across moral, social, cultural and economic questions, but it also tackled matters of local policy – for example, poor relief, how best to encourage the development of the local economy, and aspects of urban improvement. It also discussed issues of national political significance, including parliamentary reform on two occasions – on both members were strongly opposed – the advantages and disadvantages of the Union – the former far outweighed the latter in the view of the meeting – proposed changes to the Corn Laws, and several questions regarding current British foreign policy, for example, the Anglo-French commercial treaty of 1786.[5]

The receptivity of the Scottish weavers, other artisans and lesser tradesmen to the message of the French Revolution and Thomas Paine does seem, nevertheless, to demand explanation beyond the immediate impact of the Revolution and the *Rights of Man*. The formation of radical societies in late 1792 might be seen as standing at the confluence of various streams which gathered strength from the 1770s and '80s, including burgh reform and a growing intensity and breadth of debate on public issues. At a deeper level, the relative independence and cultural and religious articulacy of weaving communities had been evident from the 1730s and '40s. Religion and politics, it is worth stressing, were not separate categories of thought and activity, and crucial to the process of politicization in later eighteenth-century Scotland was the issue of patronage in the established church. As in Ulster, the politics of liberty in the Scotland of the final third of the eighteenth century were, to a large degree, religious in inspiration; they were also a continuation of the struggle against 'popery' which electrified much of lowland Scotland between 1779–and 1781.[6] At the same time, religious notions of liberty were during the later eighteenth century increasingly being supplemented by more secular emphases. This was an aspect of what Ned Landsman has called, with reference to Glasgow and its environs, the 'Evangelical enlightenment', but it also reflected a tactical imperative in that a crucial goal was to mobilize support from the landed classes and the laity for parliamentary repeal of the Patronage Act of 1712.[7]

What the connections were between religious habits of thought and activity and radical politics in the 1790s remains ambiguous. Seceders were repeatedly and persistently labelled as disaffected in the 1790s, but, as has been argued at various points in this book, this may be more because they chose to stand aside from the loyalist counter-reaction of 1792–4 than because they were active members and supporters of radical societies, although some of them were. There were different tendencies within the Secession churches in the later eighteenth century, one of which was towards greater accommodation with the British state. It was this divergence which meant that Secession ministers who actively promoted the cause of the political status quo in the early 1790s could find themselves opposed by at least some within their churches. This happened to Alexander

Shanks of Jedburgh, author of a prominent loyalist work in 1793, who would a few years later be the subject of petty persecution for political reasons. Reacting to Shanks's plight, the ultra-loyal leader of the Moderates, George Hill, Principal of St Mary's College, St Andrews, complained to Robert Dundas:

> If the seceding ministers, to whom the county has been indebted for their support, shall find themselves in different parts of Scotland so uncomfortable, as to be obliged to demit, those who remain will find themselves under the necessity of taking a different line, and the Established clergy will be every where counter-acted, instead of being in many places assisted, by the ministers of the secession.[8]

Equally, however, dissenting ministers who preached in support of political reform could alienate sections of their flock, as appears to have happened to Patrick Hutchison, Relief minister in Paisley, in 1796. According to a letter in the *Glasgow Courier*, six of his congregation had left his church owing to his 'mixing in his discourses political things', including opposition to the war against revolutionary France.[9] The boundary, moreover, between the Secession churches and the established church was a fluid one, especially when viewed from the perspective of the laity.[10] The key religious division may well have been that between orthodox Calvinism and more 'polite' forms of Presbyterianism, although there were, as Liam McIlvanney has recently emphasized, different elements within the latter.[11] As we saw in Chapter 1, Thomas Muir's father was an opponent of patronage in the early 1780s. Muir himself was an elder in the church and staunchly orthodox. In 1790, he was a leading critic in the General Assembly of the Moderate Ayrshire minister William McGill, author of the *Practical Essay on the Death of Christ* (1786), which led to accusations of McGill having promulgated the doctrines of Socinianism and Arianism in opposition to the teaching laid down in the Westminster Confession.[12] Popular and Moderate ministers joined ranks after 1792 to combat the threat from revolutionary France and domestic radicalism, but whether this tells us much about shifts of opinion among the laity is debateable. Perhaps in the end what was important was less the specificities of theological and ecclesiological positions, than a restive, intensely literate religious subculture which provided the context for the developments of 1792. More broadly, the polemical theology which formed a staple element of the reading of many weaving and labouring communities kept alive a discourse about liberty which would have strong echoes in the radical ideology of the 1790s. As Ian McBride has emphasized in the context of Presbyterian Ulster in the later eighteenth century: 'The binary oppositions around which so much political discussion turned – such as liberty/slavery or virtue/corruption – were historically, and often conceptually, linked to the master opposition of Protestantism and popery'.[13] For much Presbyterian opinion, patronage represented 'popery'. That the anti-patronage agitation of the early 1780s emerged out of the intense, vocal anti-popery campaign of 1779–81 should, therefore, occasion no surprise.

Another of the threads which this book has sought to follow is the importance of location and community in politics in this period. Work on English radicalism in this period indicates how important local factors could be to radical fortunes in the 1790s, whether it be structures of local government; the existence of propertied reformers who could offer, initially at least, leadership and support to popular radical societies; the structure of the local economy; and the impact of the war on local economic fortunes.[14] Edinburgh's leadership of the radical campaign in 1792–4 was to prove a major source of weakness to radicalism nationally, reflecting the local importance of the luxury economy, the extent to which its key institutions were dominated by the Dundas interest, and the conservatism of its elites and ministers. The centre of gravity of radical politics in Scotland was shifting westwards, where it would remain during the industrial era, but the 1790s marked in this context a moment of transition. Places of popular radical strength tended to share, not surprisingly, common characteristics throughout the British Isles. The most obvious was the presence of a relatively independent labouring class. The spread of radicalism also naturally tended to follow channels carved out by local and regional economic relationships. On Tayside, for example, Dundee and Perth formed key nodal points in a nexus of relationships which joined these towns to smaller burghs and industrial villages throughout their economic hinterlands, which in Dundee's case stretched across the Tay into Fife. It was a similar story in respect of Glasgow and Paisley, or indeed Stirling. Another important variable, already referred to, seems to have been local religious culture. The geography of radicalism maps fairly well onto the geography of the anti-popery and anti-patronage agitations of the late 1770s and early '80s. If the outlines are fairly clear, however, the detail often remains elusive. Not all places which were active in opposing patronage in the early 1780s went on to be sites of radical strength in the early 1790s. Greenock might be one such place. We also know relatively little about conditions in this period in the industrial villages of Fife, although it was there that the United Scotsmen seem to have gained a relatively strong presence in 1796–7; these villages were also sites of fierce and relatively well-organized protest against the implementation of the Militia Act in the late summer of 1797. Similarly, conditions in the industrial villages of the west and west-central lowlands are only occasionally revealed in the extant sources. Paisley and Stirling, to cite two places where popular radicalism developed a significant presence, deserve more detailed examination that it has been possible to give them here. Perth is sometimes regarded as a radical town in the 1790s, but this may simply reflect the fact that developments there are relatively well documented.

The moderation of Scottish radicalism has been much emphasized in recent years, not least in the published and unpublished work of John Brims.[15] This book has presented evidence that more ideologically extreme currents of radicalism, strongly influenced by Paine's *Rights of Man* and events in France, and by the experience of repression after early 1793, took a hold in many communities in parts of lowland Scotland, although they never found consistent or strong direction and leadership, and by mid-1794 had collapsed as an open force under the impact of official hostility, pressure from 'above' of various kinds of an intensity and pervasiveness which is often quickly passed over, and adverse circumstances (the economic downturn in 1793, the radicalization and escalating violence of the revolution in France).

The salient issue might be what happened to this ebullition of political talk and activity after 1794. Most obviously, it left behind groups of radicals who would join the Society of the United Scotsmen in 1796–7, although the emergence of this body also reflected the exportation (or rather expulsion) of insurrectionary politics and radicalism from an Ireland trapped in an escalating cycle of violent reaction and counter-reaction. Perhaps more common was its retreat into private spaces – for example, weaving shops – which are largely immune to the historian's gaze. The tantalizing evidence from the *Scots Chronicle* (cited in Chapter 5) of popular reading societies springing up in the mid–1790s, concentrated in and around Paisley and in other western manufacturing districts, suggests another route taken by this political energy and activity. A link between radical politics and popular enlightenment is traceable also through the Dundee bookseller Edward Leslie. Leslie, it will be recalled, was active in radical politics in the early 1790s, surfacing in the Fyshe Palmer trial, and was in the later 1790s an agent for the *Scots Chronicle* and also in communication with Alexander Leslie, the Edinburgh radical bookseller with links to Daniel Isaac Eaton and metropolitan radical publishing circles. In the 1800s he can be found selling cheap books. He was also closely involved in the Dundee Rational Society (1809–21), which held lectures on scientific subjects, and which established a museum of scientific curiosities and instruments, and a modest library of British and European Enlightenment scholarship. Membership of the society seems to have comprised younger tradesmen and artisans.[16] In 1820, Edward Leslie's name would be given as the person to receive subscriptions for a service of plate for the current heroine of the radicals, Queen Caroline.[17]

One of the most striking features of the glimpses we are afforded of surviving Scottish radical circles in the later 1790s is the tenacity with which some radicals appear to have maintained their faith in revolutionary France.[18] This was at a moment, it is worth stressing, when enthusiasm for France and French support was becoming much less common in British and some Irish radical circles, and misgivings were increasingly being expressed about the French role as 'liberators' of Europe.[19] It is almost certain that these advanced radicals were a tiny, isolated minority, many of whom, it seems, espoused an internationalist, deistical republicanism. As we saw in Chapter 5 whether the United Scotsmen ever had much coherence as a body, or whether its members had clear, uniform goals, apart from radical reform of parliament, is debateable, although the evidence on this is difficult to interpret. Quite a few former members of the radical societies of 1792–3 probably found their way into volunteer companies in 1797–8, and not necessarily only as a form of pragmatic adjustment to changed conditions. Popular opinion and mood shifted very abruptly during the 1790s. An effusion of patriotic spirit in early 1797 followed considerable alienation from the conduct and continuation of the war in 1795–6. Such shifts and volatility are not always easy to explain, but they were an intrinsic part of the character of politics in the 1790s.

What of those who actively opposed radicalism – the loyalists? From a British perspective it is the *limitations* surrounding the Scottish loyalist counter-reaction to the rise of domestic radicalism in 1792 which are striking. There was no Scottish equivalent to the wave of Tom Paine burnings in England in the winter of 1792–3 or the multitude of English loyalist societies which were founded during the same period. Any explanation of these differences must include the very different nature of Scottish political culture, but they were also symptomatic of the starkness of the political division which opened up so suddenly in much of lowland society in late 1792. Political debate appeared to polarize overnight between a labouring class intoxicated by talk of 'liberty' and elites deeply fearful of this contagion. From late 1792, active propertied reformers were very thin on the ground in Scotland. Part of the explanation for this is the climate of repression created by the actions of the High Court presided over by the fiercely reactionary Braxfield. But it also reflected the large gap which existed or came to exist between rational reform and popular radicalism. While by no means a specifically Scottish pattern, the divide may well have been wider than south of the border, reflecting the relative weakness of political reform traditions in Scottish political culture in the later eighteenth century. John Millar may have been an articulate and persistent opponent of Pitt and his conduct of the war; he was also an honorary member of the Whig Association of the Friends of the People; but he seems to have maintained his distance from the Scottish Friends of the People after late 1792, although his son, John Craig Millar, was a member of the Edinburgh Society of the Friends of the People. Millar's natural allies in reform politics were not radicals, but moderate reformers and advanced Whigs.[20] Another example might be James Wodrow, the Ayrshire minister. Initially a supporter of the Friends of the People, he was a proponent of moderate reform and opponent of the war against revolutionary France.[21] In style as well as substance, however, his political vision was very different from that of the popular radicals.

In September 1794, he declared, in terms which reflected directly his apprehensions about the activities of popular radicals:

> I apprehend nothing does more service to a good cause than moderation, & the wisdom which is peaceable gentle & easily intreated, & nothing hurts it more than intemperate zeal which generally issues in strife confusion & every evil work.[22]

Popular radicals were, in stirring up resistance to the authorities among the people, in Wodrow's eyes doing 'incredible hurt to the cause of Liberty & reformation'.[23] The acute fear of the 'mob' in this period among the elites can, as elsewhere in the British Isles, be explained in terms of reactions to the excesses and violence of revolutionaries in France in 1792–4, and a conviction that British radicals, whatever they said they were, were, in fact, Jacobin revolutionaries in all but name. But in Scotland, the values of order and subordination formed a central part of Enlightenment discourse and the narratives of economic progress which were shaped within and by this broad intellectual and cultural context.

If loyalism in Scotland in 1792–4 was, therefore, a less popular and populist phenomenon than south of the border, the patriotic mobilizations of the later 1790s attracted altogether broader and deeper support from within society. Loyalism and defensive patriotism shared certain features, unsurprisingly since there was overlap between them in terms of organization and personnel, and the latter did to some degree mutate from the former. Some of the structures of loyalism may have remained in place, in some form, into the later 1790s.[24] In both, ministers of the established church were prominent. The Kirk proved a powerful and keen auxiliary of the authorities throughout the decade, maintaining a close watch on not just the morals but the political outlook of the Scottish people. Direction from the centre and the elites is readily discernable in both loyalist and patriotic initiatives, although there was much more of a spontaneous element to the latter as we saw in Chapter 5. These are similarities of form, however, rather than essence, and it is the differences which are more significant.

The main threat which produced the expression and organization of loyalism was fear of domestic disaffection, a fear which persisted in Scotland into 1794 and which strongly influenced the raising of volunteer forces in the spring of that year. In the later 1790s, to a greater degree perhaps than in England, the threat to the political and social status quo was external not internal, although the United Scotsmen did emerge briefly in 1797–8 to remind contemporaries of the contagion of domestic disaffection. There was no panic about this, however, and a round of further repression from late 1797 and early 1798 dealt relatively quickly and effectively with this menace. The contrast between 1792–3 and the opening months of 1797, and even more perhaps 1798, was marked, and not lost on contemporaries, especially in regions which had seen a significant radical presence in the earlier period, for example, parts of Perthshire, Ayrshire or Renfrewshire. Patriotism, unlike loyalism, increasingly embraced opposition Whigs, religious dissenters and a sizeable element of the lower orders. This political and social inclusiveness, which was common to the patriotic reaction in the rest of Britain, was also a factor which limited its role as an integrative force in society. The effusions of patriotic spirit may also have presented something of an illusion, in that they helped to disguise the depth of contemporary disenchantment with the war and its effects, which by the end of the decade was compounded by the exceptional distress which resulted from the poor harvests and trade depression of 1799–1801.[25]

In some respects, the authorities in Britain were very fortunate that the moments of greatest threat to the political and social status quo tended not to coincide with economic downturns and poor harvests. The sharp economic downturn in 1793 did not, for example, coincide with a poor harvest.[26] It also seems to have weakened the radicals rather than drawn further strength to them, combining with repression to produce fairly rapid demoralization among the radical societies. In 1795–6, climbing food prices helped stimulate a radical revival in London and a few others places south of the border. The 'bread' crisis of 1795–6 was almost certainly less severe in Scotland than in England since, as we saw in Chapter 6, the oat harvest was less adversely affected than wheat. What occurred in 1795–6 was, in fact, an English crisis which spread to Scotland as agents from England searched for additional grain supplies from Scotland, and corn merchants and others in Scotland sought to profit from the soaring prices south of the border. The mood among many of the labouring classes in 1795–6 may well have been restive and discontented, but radicals were too demoralized and cowed by repression to take advantage on their own of these conditions. On the other hand, the opposition Whigs, almost certainly in alliance with radicals, did manage to mobilize significant opposition to the war and Pitt's Gagging Acts, a fact which is sometimes passed over very quickly by historians.

If the authorities had some good luck, therefore, the ruling elites mostly maintained their nerve throughout the strains of the decade. More than that, they very actively and assiduously supported the maintenance of order and loyal and later patriotic initiatives. Dundas's new system of lords lieutenant worked very effectively as an agency of local government, supported by the Kirk and local elites. The lords lieutenant appear to have performed their responsibilities diligently, although the effectiveness of the system as a whole has important structural explanations – notably, the close-knit nature of the Scottish ruling elite, but also its relative power and influence in society. Those historians who have argued that the quiescence of the Scottish population in 1799–1801 owed much to the efficiency of elites and the agents of local government and their willingness to intervene in the marketplace to protect the interests and well-being of the bulk of the population may be correct, although there has been tendency to present these reflexes (probably wrongly) as a more pervasive feature of Scottish society than south of the border. It was not so much that paternalism was a stronger disposition or force in Scottish society but that it may have been more effective, although there is no simple way of proving this. On the other hand, patterns of land ownership, and even more the relatively small-scale nature of farming in many areas, did create conditions conducive to this. Farmers from different parts of the country appear to have been willing to participate in schemes to release grain into local markets at prices which were made affordable to the lower orders, usually by means of a subscription. Only more detailed work on the operation of the grain market in Scotland in the later eighteenth century will confirm this conclusion, however, and it was certainly not a universal tendency.

The final theme which has been traced in this book is the strengthening dynamic towards fuller political integration with the rest of Britain, which was in operation from later 1770s, if not slightly earlier. The increasing focus on Parliament as a legislative body in Scotland in the later eighteenth century was a very important element in this development, as were, closely linked to this, changes in modes of parliamentary and public lobbying. The press was a powerful integrative force, through its promotion of a political narrative and discussion focused on events and personalities at Westminster. The Pantheon Society, the Edinburgh debating society which emerged in 1773, was a direct successor to the Robinhood Society, a parliamentary debating club, the speakers in which assumed the roles of Westminster parliamentarians.[27] When the Stirling Port Club, referred to above, chose to debate the adequacy of the peace terms agreed between Britain and France in 1783, they decided to postpone the discussion until they had had an opportunity 'of seeing [i.e. reading] the Debates in Parliament upon it'.[28] Through print, debates about social and economic reform and policy were changing in nature, becoming part of a public sphere defined by its transparency and accessibility to a widening cross-section of society, but also the importance of its connections to and interactions with a British public sphere focused on London. This was partly the wider significance of the lobbying activities and debates surrounding the Corn Laws from the early 1770s or the campaign to abolish the slave trade which had such a remarkable impact in Scotland in 1792. In early 1792, William Dickson, visiting Scotland for the London Committee for the Abolition of the Slave Trade, noted in his journal of his visit: 'Paisley and Kilm[arnoc]k people wish to correspond with London rather than Ed[inburg]h or Glasgow Comm[itt]ees'.[29] Radicalism itself was an important contributory factor to deeper political integration, containing within it strong impulses towards the adoption of a strategy of 'union', but also because it further reinforced a sense of 'Britishness' or 'Anglo-Britishness' in Scottish society at the end of the eighteenth century, as, in their different ways and to a no lesser extent, did loyalism and patriotism. The pattern of relationships and British outlook established by the reformers and radicals of the 1790s, south as well as north of the border, would be repeated by radicals in the nineteenth century.[30]

Equally significant in the longer term, however, may have been the ways in which the development of Scottish political culture was not frozen by political reaction in the 1790s. As Linda Colley has argued in a British context, this owed a great deal to the effects of the patriotic mobilizations during the French revolutionary and Napoleonic wars.[31] Volunteer troops were organized along democratic lines. Officers were often elected, and considerable care was often taken in relation to rules about the transparency and accountability of decision-taking and the management of finances.[32] The impact of such things in Scotland may have been all the greater because it was taking place in a society in which the normal structures of politics were closed. Women seem very rarely to have been part of the public sphere in eighteenth-century Scotland, although women from the labouring classes were important actors in food riots, as they were in several of the anti-militia riots in 1797.[33] Associations and clubs tended to meet in taverns and were male-only gatherings.[34] There were a few exceptions. Both the Pantheon Society and its breakaway, the Lycaeum Debating Society, admitted women to their debates, as did the Dundee Speculative Society; although they appear to have been unusual in so doing.[35] As elsewhere in the Britain, during the 1790s and later the Napoleonic Wars women achieved a new public visibility owing to their participation in patriotic initiatives and demonstrations – for example, as subscribers to patriotic donations or producing and handing colours to volunteer regiments in 1794–5 and again in 1797–8. No doubt, women of all social ranks were present too at the many reviews of volunteer troops. That said, most loyalist and patriotic initiatives were directed and dominated by men.[36] Farmers were another group strongly affected by patriotic initiatives, often forming the bulk of the membership of the rural volunteer companies established in 1797–8. The later eighteenth century saw a growing number of farmers' societies formed, which provided the basis for a more independent voice on, for example, the matter of taxation.[37] Patriotism provided a potent rhetorical tool with which to stake their claims for fuller recognition. On 17 March 1798, 'A Midlothian Farmer *& Volunteer*' (my emphasis) wrote to Henry Dundas complaining about a new tax on agricultural horses. The crux of his case was this was an additional burden on a class on whom had come to rest the task of defending the nation, as well as supporting its population. Farmers merited better treatment in recognition of this role.[38] Within towns, the 1790s saw a marked upswing in the development of a more sophisticated, complex urban culture, the lineaments of which would only become even clearer in the first two decades of the nineteenth century. One indicator of the quickening of change was the large number of subscription libraries founded in the 1790s.[39] Commercial circulating libraries, reading rooms and other venues for newspaper readership almost certainly also continued to grow in number, although evidence for this is inevitably impressionistic. The number of books and other works published in Edinburgh and Glasgow grew markedly.[40] Charitable bodies grew in number, most of which were organized as subscriber democracies and on transparent, accountable lines. In Aberdeen and Glasgow, intense debates, at the heart of which was the issue of political accountability, continued throughout the 1790s regarding police bills. In 1792, the 'citizens' of Glasgow published their own scheme for establishing a new system of police, while in 1799 what were said to be a 'great number of respectable inhabitants' petitioned the Council to apply for an act of parliament to achieve the same end.[41] In short, the development of the urban public sphere did not retreat or collapse in the 1790s, but in various ways only deepened and gathered further momentum. This is one explanation of why liberal forces in Scottish society were able to regroup so quickly after 1800. The political order presided over, at the top, by Henry and Robert Dundas, and in towns by closed, narrow oligarchies, survived into the early nineteenth century, not least because it was more flexible and open than it is sometimes portrayed. By 1800, however, the outlines of a new political and cultural order were taking shape, one which was underpinned by a broader series of social and economic changes in urban and rural society. It would be a political world and culture in many ways more strongly British in character than the one it replaced, but which in other ways remained distinct and distant from its southern neighbour.[42]

NOTES

The following abbreviations are used throughout the notes:

AP	Atholl Papers, Blair Castle
BL	British Library
Cal. M.	*Caledonian Mercury*
DARC	Dundee Records and Archives Centre, Dundee
ECA	Edinburgh City Archives
Edin. A.	*Edinburgh Advertiser*
Edin. E.	*Edinburgh Evening Courant*
Edin. G.	*Edinburgh Gazetteer*
Edin. H.	*Edinburgh Herald*
EUL	Edinburgh University Library
Glas. C.	*Glasgow Courier*
HMC	Historical Manuscripts Commission
Howell, *State Trials*	T. B. Howell and T. J. Howell, *A Complete Collection of State Trials*, 33 vols (London: Bagshaw, Longman, 1809–28)
Laing MSS	Historical Manuscripts Commission, *Report on the Laing Manuscripts Preserved in the University of Edinburgh*, 2 vols (London: HMSO, 1914–25)
NA	National Archives, Kew
NAS	National Archives of Scotland
NLS	National Library of Scotland
NRAS	National Register of Archives for Scotland
ODNB	*The Oxford Dictionary of National Biography*
PKCA	Perth and Kinross County Archives, Perth
Scots C.	*Scots Chronicle*
SL	Signet Library, Edinburgh, Court of Session Papers
W-KC	Wodrow-Kenrick Correspondence, Dr Williams's Library, London

Introduction

1. L. M. Cullen, 'Scotland and Ireland, 1600–1800: Their Role in the Evolution of British Society', in R. A. Houston and I. D. Whyte (eds), *Scottish Society 1500–1800* (Cambridge: Cambridge University Press, 1989), pp. 226–44, on p. 241. See also H. W. Meikle, *Scotland and the French Revolution* (Glasgow: J. Maclehose and Sons, 1912); T. M. Devine, 'The Failure of Radical Reform in Scotland in the Late 18th Century: The Social and Economic Context', in T. M. Devine (ed.), *Conflict and Stability in Scottish Society, 1700–1850* (Edinburgh: John Donald Publishers Ltd, 1990), pp. 51–64; M. Fry, *The Dundas Despotism* (Edinburgh: Edinburgh University Press, 1992), ch. 5; E. W. McFarland, *Ireland and Scotland in the Age of Revolution* (Edinburgh: Edinburgh University Press, 1994); J. S. Shaw, *The Political History of Eighteenth-Century Scotland* (Basingstoke: Macmillan, 1999), ch. 7.

2. T. C. Smout, *A History of the Scottish People* (London: Collins, 1969), p. 417.

3. For comment on this, see B. Harris, 'Introduction', in B. Harris (ed.), *Scotland in the Age of the French Revolution* (Edinburgh: John Donald, 2005), pp. 2–3.

4. E. Vincent Macleod, 'Scottish Responses to the Irish Rebellion of 1798', in T. Brotherstone, A. Clark and K. Whelan (eds), *These Fissured Isles: Ireland, Scotland and British History, 1798–1848* (Edinburgh: John Donald, 2005), pp. 123–40.

5. T. M. Devine, *The Scottish Nation, 1700–2000* (London: Allen Lane, 1999), p. 210.

6. W. H. Fraser, *Scottish Popular Politics: From Radicalism to Labour* (Edinburgh: Polygon, 2001), p. 20.

7. Henry Dundas to William Pitt, Arniston, 12 November 1792, NA, PRO 30/8/157, Part 1, fols 132–41.

8. See N. Murray, *The Scottish Handloom Weavers 1790–1850: A Social History* (Edinburgh: John Donald, 1978), esp. pp. 18–23. Murray estimates that numbers of handloom weavers rose from *c.* 25,000 in 1780 to *c.* 45,000 in 1790 and *c.* 58,000 ten years later.

9. Henry Mackenzie to William Pitt, 23 December 1793, NA, PRO 30/8/154/2.

10. Devine, 'The Failure of Radical Reform in Scotland'.

11. It is only fair to point out that Professor Devine acknowledges the importance of 'situational' factors in his *The Scottish Nation*, pp. 203–18.

12. For example, William Playfair, George Chalmers, John Sinclair and Patrick Colquhoun.

13. *Fresh Intelligence from the Coffee House* (Edinburgh, 1777).

14. As called for in the *Edinburgh Weekly Journal*, 25 April 1798.

15. This is also emphasized in a wider British context by J. Cookson, *The British Armed Nation 1793–1815* (Oxford: Clarendon Press, 1997) and A. Gee, *The British Volunteer Movement 1794–1814* (Oxford: Clarendon Press, 2003), esp. ch. 4. See also relevant comment on this, and the distinction in this respect to be drawn between loyalism and defensive patriotism, in D. Eastwood, 'Patriotism and the English State in the 1790s', in M. Philp (ed.), *The French Revolution and British Popular Politics* (Cambridge: Cambridge University Press, 1991), pp. 146–68, on pp. 157–62.

16. Although see E. Vincent, 'The Responses of Scottish Churchmen to the French Revolution, 1789–1802', *Scottish Historical Review*, 73 (1994), pp. 191–215; E. Vincent, 'A City Invincible? Edinburgh and the War against Revolutionary France', *British Journal of Eighteenth Century Studies*, 23 (2000), pp. 153–66.

17. These are the issues for 4–7 December 1792 (in the Mitchell Library, Glasgow) and 11–14 December 1792 (at NAS, GD 99/229/9).

18. M. Durey, '*With the Hammer of Truth*': *James Thomson Callender and American Early National Heroes* (Charlottesville, VA, and London: University Press of Virginia, 1990), p. 29. The full title of the pamphlet is *The Political Progress of Britain; or, an Impartial Account of the Principal Abuses in the Government of this Country, from the Revolution in 1688. The Whole Tending to Prove the Ruinous Consequences of the Popular System of War and Conquest. 'The World's Mad Business'. Part First* (Edinburgh: Robertson and Berry, 1792).

19. McFarland, *Ireland and Scotland in the Age of Revolution*, p. 154; Devine, *The Scottish Nation*, p. 210.

20. The phrase 'pugnaciously persistent' is Andrew Noble's from his 'Displaced Persons: Burns and the Renfrew Radicals', in Harris (ed.), *Scotland in the Age of the French Revolution*, pp. 196–225, on p. 214.

21. Report on Perth Friends of the People, [late 1792], NAS, RH 2/4/64, fols 341–3.

22. *Glas. C.*, 3, 5 December 1793; Robert to Henry Dundas, Edinburgh, 6 December 1793, NAS, RH 2/4/73, fols 25–3; George Paterson to Robert Dundas, 11 March 1793, where Paterson writes: 'Johnstons Newspaper has been discharged from the coffee house, by a vote, nearly unanimous, of the members & subscribers belonging to that ancient seat of Democracy & Republicanism', EUL, Laing Papers, II, 500, fols 248–9.

23. But see private letter from Dundee, 24 November 1792, where the writer observes, 'There is a house opened here with a voluminous sign The Constitutional Tap Room. It is patronized by people who ought to know better', NAS, RH 2/4/207, fols 369–71.

24. John Russell, Glasgow, to William Skirving, 26 October 1793 NAS, Court of Justiciary Papers, JC 26/280, bundle 1. Russell notes that the charge for the reading room, which promised newspapers and 'new' political pamphlets, was 10s. per annum.

25. Meikle, *Scotland and the French Revolution*.

26. L. Colley, 'Whose Nation? Class and National Consciousness in Britain 1750–1830', *Past and Present*, 113 (1986), pp. 97–117, on pp. 112–13.

27. J. Brims, 'The Scottish "Jacobins", Scottish Nationalism and the British Union', in R. A. Mason (ed.), *Scotland and England 1286–1875* (Edinburgh: John Donald, 1987), pp. 247–65; J. Brims, 'The Covenanting Tradition and Scottish Radicalism in the 1790s', in T. Brotherstone (ed.), *Covenant, Charter and Party: Traditions of Revolt and Protest in Modern Scottish History* (Aberdeen: Aberdeen University Press, 1989), pp. 50–62; G. Pentland, 'Patriotism, Universalism and the Scottish Conventions, 1792–1794', *History*, 89 (2004), pp. 340–60; A. Murdoch, 'Scotland and the Idea of Britain in the Eighteenth Century', in T. M. Devine and J. R. Young (eds), *Eighteenth-Century Scotland: New Perspectives* (East Linton: Tuckwell Press, 1999), pp. 106–20.

28. On this, see B. Harris, 'Scottish-English Connections in British Radicalism in the 1790s', in T. C. Smout (ed.), *Anglo-Scottish Relations from 1603 to 1900* (Oxford: Oxford University Press, 2005), pp. 189–212.

29. Lord Daer to Edward Grey, Edinburgh, 17 January 1793, in E. Hughes, 'The Scottish Reform Movement and Charles Grey 1792–94: Some Fresh Correspondence', *Scottish Historical Review*, 35 (1956), pp. 26–41, on pp. 33–7.

30. Minute Book of the Society for Constitutional Information, NA, TS 11/962.

31. For a comparative discussion of this, see J. Smyth, *The Making of the United Kingdom 1660–1800* (Harlow: Longman, 2001), esp. ch. 8. For a somewhat different interpretation, however, see J. Graham, *The Nation, the Law, and the King: Reform Politics in England 1789–1799*, 2 vols (Lanham, MD: University Press of America, 2000).

32. H. T. Dickinson, *The Politics of the People in Eighteenth Century Britain* (Basingstoke: Macmillan, 1994), ch. 7.

33. See, inter alia, ibid., ch. 8; R. R. Dozier, *For King, Constitution and Country: The English Loyalists and the French Revolution* (Lexington, KY: University Press of Kentucky, 1983); F. O'Gorman, 'The Paine Burnings of 1792–1793', *Past and Present*, 193 (2006), pp. 111–53.

34. Diary of George Ramsay, NAS, Steel-Maitland Papers, GD 193/1/1.

35. Journal of the Revd MacDonald, St Andrews University, Special Collections, Playfair Papers, MS Dep 14, fols 45–6. Why Ayr and Dumfries were included is not entirely clear since they were not strong centres of radicalism in the early 1790s. This may, however, be related to disturbances which occurred in both places during the 'bread crisis' of 1795–6.

36. For the most recent contribution to this debate, see N. Rogers, 'The Sea Fencibles, Loyalism and the Reach of the State', in M. Philp (ed.), *Resisting Napoleon: The British Response to the Threat of Invasion 1797–1815* (Aldershot: Ashgate, 2006), pp. 41–59.

37. James Wodrow to William Kenrick, 19 April 1797, W-KC, 24.157 (213).

38. For a recent critical discussion of this idea, see A. Randall, *Riotous Assemblies: Popular Protest in Hanoverian England* (Oxford: Oxford University Press, 2006), ch. 9.

39. St Andrews University, Special Collections, MS Dep 14, fol. 25.

40. See the extremely valuable discussion of this in M. Philp, 'The Fragmented Ideology of Reform', in Philp (ed.), *The French Revolution and British Popular Politics*, pp. 50–77.

1 The Eighteenth-Century Roots of Scottish 'Jacobin' Politics

1. See especially Dickinson, *The Politics of the People*, ch. 7; J. E. Bradley, *Religion, Revolution and English Radicalism: Non-Conformity in Eighteenth-Century Politics and Society* (Cambridge: Cambridge University Press, 1990), esp. the conclusion; J. Stevenson, 'Popular Radicalism and Popular Protest 1789–1815', in H. T. Dickinson (ed.), *Britain and the French Revolution 1789–1815* (Basingstoke: Macmillan, 1989), pp. 61–81, on p. 71.

2. Although see J. Beckett, 'Responses to War: Nottingham in the French Revolutionary and Napoleonic Wars, 1793–1815', *Midland History*, 12 (1997), pp. 71–84; M. N. Fishman-Cross, 'The People and the Petition, 1775–1780', *Midland History*, 14 (1999), pp. 114–28; K. Navickas, 'Redefining Loyalism, Radicalism and National Identity: Lancashire under the Threat of Napoleon, 1798–1812' (unpublished DPhil thesis, University of Oxford, 2005).

3. J. Money, *Experience and Identity, Birmingham and the West Midlands, 1760–1800* (Manchester: Manchester University Press, 1977), ch. 9.

4. This emerges from Albert Goodwin's accounts of the rise of radicalism in Norwich, Sheffield and Manchester in his *The Friends of Liberty: The English Democratic Movement in the Age of the French Revolution* (London: Hutchinson, 1979), ch. 5.

5. M. Elliott, 'Ireland and the French Revolution', in Dickinson (ed.), *Britain and the French Revolution*, pp. 83–101, esp. p. 84.

6. See, for example, J. R. Hill, *From Patriots to Unionists: Dublin Civic Politics and Irish Protestant Patriotism, 1660–1840* (Oxford: Clarendon Press, 1997), chs 3, 4; A. T. Q. Stewart, *A Deeper Silence: The Hidden Origins of the United Irishmen* (London: Faber, 1993); B. Harris, *Politics and the Nation: Britain in the Mid-Eighteenth Century* (Oxford: Oxford University Press, 2002), ch. 5.

7. S. Small, *Political Thought in Ireland 1776–1798: Republicanism, Patriotism and Radicalism* (Oxford: Oxford University Press, 2002), chs 2–4.

8. Meikle, *Scotland and the French Revolution*, chs 1, 2; McFarland, *Ireland and Scotland in the Age of Revolution*, chs 1, 2.

9. Most famously in R. R. Palmer, *The Age of Democratic Revolution*, 2 vols (Princeton, NJ: Princeton University Press, 1959–64); and J. Godechot, *France and the Atlantic Revolution of the Eighteenth Century, 1770–1799* (New York: Free Press, 1971).

10. J. Phillips, 'Popular Politics in Unreformed England', *Journal of Modern History*, 52 (1980), pp. 599–625.

11. At the 1774 general election, the total Scottish electorate may well have numbered no more than 478, comprising 428 county electors and just 50 burgh electors (P. Jupp, *The Governing of Britain, 1688–1848: The Executive, Parliament and the People* (London: Routledge, 2006), p. 235).

12. The phrase is used by William Ferguson in his 'Dingwall Burgh Politics and the Parliamentary Franchise in the Eighteenth Century', *Scottish Historical Review*, 38 (1959), pp. 89–108, on p. 91.

13. T. Oldfield, *History of the Original Constitution of Parliaments, from the time of the Britons to the Present Day ... To which is Added the Present State of Representation* (London: G. G. and J. Robinson, 1797), p. 491.

14. For one such example, see North Ayrshire Library, Irvine Town Council Minutes, entries for 9 November 1756, 5 February 1757.

15. R. H. Scott, 'The Politics and Administration of Scotland 1725–48' (unpublished PhD thesis, University of Edinburgh, 1981), pp. 296–7, 392; W. Ferguson, 'The Electoral System in the Scottish Counties Before 1832', in D. Sellar (ed.), *The Stair Society, Miscellany II*, Stair Society Publications, 35 (Edinburgh: Stair Society, 1984), pp. 261–94; D. Brown, '"Nothing but Struggalls and Coruption": The Commons Elections in Scotland in 1774', in C. Jones (ed.), *The Scots and Parliament* (Edinburgh: Edinburgh University Press for the Parliamentary History Yearbook Trust, 1996), pp. 100–19; R. M. Sunter, *Patronage and Politics in Scotland 1707–1832* (Edinburgh: John Donald, 1986).

16. See Ferguson, 'Dingwall Burgh Politics'; Sunter, *Patronage and Politics in Scotland*, part 3.

17. On this, see ibid., esp. ch. 1; B. Harris, 'The Scots, the Westminster Parliament, and the British State in the Eighteenth Century', in J. Hoppit (ed.), *Parliaments, Nations and Identities in Britain and Ireland 1660–1850* (Manchester: Manchester University Press, 2003), pp. 124–45; B. Harris, 'Parliamentary Legislation, Lobbying and the Press in Eighteenth-Century Scotland', in J. Peacey (ed.), *The Print Culture of Parliament 1600–1800* (Edinburgh: Edinburgh University Press, 2007), pp. 76–95.

18. Ferguson, 'Dingwall Burgh Politics', p. 100.

19. Dempster to Robert Graham of Fintry, 8 June 1790, NAS, Graham of Fintry Papers, GD 151/11/8.

20. Riddoch to Graham of Fintry, 10 September 1793, and Duke of Atholl to Graham of Fintry, 3 October 1793, NAS, Graham of Fintry Papers, GD 151/11/33, 151/11/3.

21. See especially F. O'Gorman, 'Campaign Rituals and Ceremonies: The Social Meaning of Elections in England 1780–1860, *Past and Present*, 135 (1992), pp. 79–115.

22. Brown, '"Nothing but Struggalls and Coruption"', p. 100. The low numbers also reflected the fact that county rolls were subject to revision at the annual Michaelmas head courts and the last revision before an election could be decisive.

23. This was true even of Perthshire, which had one of the largest county electorates. See, for example, journal by Lt Col. James Murray of journeys and visits undertaken by him in connection with election campaign of 7 May to 17 June 1773, AP, 54 (4), 156.

24. Figures derived from M. E. Craig, *The Scottish Periodical Press, 1750–1789* (Edinburgh: Oliver & Boyd, 1931); H. Barker, *Newspapers, Politics and English Society 1695–1855* (Harlow: Longman, 2000), pp. 29–30.

25. W. R. MacDonald, 'The *Aberdeen Journal* and the *Aberdeen Intelligencer* 1752–7', *Bibliotheck*, 5 (1969), pp. 204–6; W. R. MacDonald, 'Aberdeen Periodical Publishing 1786–91', *Bibliotheck*, 6 (1970), pp. 1–12.

26. In July 1790, Andrew Shirref was exploring the possibility of producing a new weekly paper (*Aberdeen Journal*, 3 July 1790). For a later attempt, see 'Proposals of the *Aberdeen Courier*, 1796', Aberdeen University Library, MS 3017/10/28/1.

27. R. H. Carnie, 'Provincial Periodical Publishing in Eighteenth-Century Scotland' (unpublished paper, Dundee University, n.d.).

28. I. D. Whyte, 'Urbanization in Eighteenth-Century Scotland', in Devine and Young (eds), *Eighteenth-Century Scotland*, pp. 176–94, esp. pp. 188–9.

29. On this, see the comments in B. Harris, 'Towns, Improvement and Cultural Change in Georgian Scotland: The Evidence of the Angus Burghs, c.1760–1820', *Urban History*, 33 (2006), pp. 195–212.

30. There is no systematic modern study of the role of speculative freemasonry in eighteenth-century Scotland. This comment is based on data which I have collected on membership of various lodges in Angus burghs in this period.

31. A. Murdoch, 'Politics and the People in the Burgh of Dumfries, 1758–1760', *Scottish Historical Review*, 70 (1991), pp. 151–71.

32. These disputes had been an important feature of the previous century as some crafts struggled against declining status and political influence. On this, see M. Lynch, 'Continuity and Change in Urban Society, 1500–1700', in Houston and Whyte (eds), *Scottish Society*, pp. 85–117.

33. A major research project begun in November 2007 on the Scottish burghs between *c.* 1745 and 1820, led by myself and involving Professors Chris Whatley and Charles McKean of the University of Dundee, and very generously supported financially by the Arts and Humanities Research Council, should help to fill this gap.

34. See Dundee University Museum and Archives Services, Kloc, Topographical Collections, Forfarshire, vol. 1, state of the conjoined processes, David Hodge, and others, against Provost James Low of Montrose and others, 1778.

35. *Cal. M.*, 20 November 1773; C. Wyvill, *Political Papers, Chiefly Respecting the Attempt by the County of York, and Other Considerable Districts, Commenced in 1779 and Continued During Several Subequent Years, to Effect a Reformation of the Parliament of Great Britain*, 6 vols (York: W. Blanchard, 1794–1802), vol. 3, p. 31. The freedom of the town was, in fact, forfeited in 1773 owing to acts of bribery and corruption at a recent parliamentary election. It was restored by the Privy Council in 1781 under a new system of election by the guildry and the trades incorporations.

36. Dundee University Museum and Archives Services, Kloc 941.31T675, Forfarshire Topographical Collections, vol. 1, The petition and complaint of the magistrates and town council of Brechin, in behalf of the community, 25 November 1769.

37. M. F. Richardson, *Autobiography of Mrs Fletcher of Edinburgh; with Letters and other Family Memorials* (Edinburgh: Edmonston and Douglas, 1875), 'Memoir of Archibald

Fletcher, Advocate, With a Sketch of the Political Feeling in Edinburgh from 1791 to 1815. By his Widow', pp. 366–7.

38. For Crosbie, see further below, pp. 35, 37.
39. D. F. Fagerstrom, 'Scotland and the American Revolution', *William and Mary Quarterly*, 11 (1954), pp. 252–75.
40. *London Chronicle*, 23–5 January 1776.
41. Wodrow to Kenrick, 19 September and 1 October 1775, and 16 March 1778, W-KC, 24.157 (54), (58), (60).
42. *Cal. M.*, 3 January, 25 March and 4 April 1778.
43. William Hutchison to the Earl of Buchan, 4 November 1792, EUL, Gen 1736, fol. 17. Hutchison may well have been the Cowgate apothecary who was treasurer to the Edinburgh citizens in favour of burgh reform in 1783 (Wyvill, *Political Papers*, vol. 3, p. 17).
44. Report on Edinburgh radical societies, 19 June 1793, NAS RH 2/4/71, fols 257–9.
45. *Cal. M.*, 8 January 1783.
46. I. R. Christie, *Wilkes, Wyvill and Reform. The Parliamentary Reform Movement in British Politics, 1760–1785* (London: Macmillan, 1962), pp. 160–3, 173, 190, 198, 211.
47. E. C. Black, *The Association: British Extra-Parliamentary Political Organization, 1769 to 1793* (Cambridge, MA: Harvard University Press, 1963), ch. 5. The Stirling merchant company chose to delay a petition in 1783 until the fate of Pitt's reform proposals was known (Wyvill, *Political Papers*, vol. 3, pp. 11–12).
48. On the motivations behind county reform, see especially J. Dwyer and A. Murdoch, 'Paradigms and Politics: Manners, Morals and the Rise of Henry Dundas, 1770–1784', in J. Dwyer, R. A. Mason and A. Murdoch (eds), *New Perspectives on the Politics and Culture of Early Modern Scotland* (Edinburgh: John Donald, 1982), pp. 210–48.
49. Shaw, *The Political History of Eighteenth-Century Scotland*, p. 28; W. Ferguson, *Scotland, 1689 to the Present* (Edinburgh: Oliver & Boyd, 1968).
50. Several recent accounts of the politics surrounding the Union have emphasized the popular dimension to the debates. See especially C. A. Whatley, *The Scots and the Union* (Edinburgh: Edinburgh University Press, 2006), esp. chs 7, 8; K. Bowie, *Scottish Public Opinion and the Anglo-Scottish Union, 1699–1707* (London: Royal Historical Society, 2007); J. Stephen, *Scottish Presbyterians and the Act of Union 1707* (Edinburgh: Edinburgh University Press, 2007).
51. On this, see Ferguson, *Scotland*, p. 137; R. A. Houston, *Social Change in the Age of Enlightenment: Edinburgh 1660–1760* (Oxford: Clarendon Press, 1994), ch. 5.
52. B. Harris, 'Political Protests in the Year of Liberty, 1792' in Harris (ed.), *Scotland in the Age of the French Revolution*, pp. 49–78, on p. 58.
53. For the existence of this press, see especially Bowie, *Scottish Public Opinion and the Anglo-Scottish Union*, ch. 1.
54. ECA, McLeod Collection, D, 107, item 45. For other cases, see D, 103, item 51 (1732); D, bundle 92, item 77 (1720).
55. NLS, Crawford MB 1392. Five hundred copies of this handbill appear to have been printed.
56. See Scott, 'The Politics and Administration of Scotland', p. 388.
57. Currently, the scale of this activity is unknown, but it can be traced through a variety of sources – booksellers' records, press advertisements, and the colophons of pamphlets which indicate their publishing history. In 1784, the stock of James Sibbald's circulating library included recently-published political pamphlets (*Cal. M.*, 27 March and 28 April 1784).

58. Complaint to baillies by procurator fiscal against Thomas Miller, apprentice to Andrew Miller, wheel wright in Edinburgh and Catherine Beg, spouse to said Andrew Miller, 13 July 1747, ECA, McLeod Collection, D 104, item 35.

59. Harris, *Politics and the Nation*, esp. p. 162.

60. Quoted in R. B. Sher, *The Enlightenment and the Book: Scottish Authors and their Publishers in Eighteenth-Century Britain, Ireland and America* (Chicago, IL, and London: University of Chicago Press, 2006), p. 406, n. 11.

61. J. S. Shaw, *The Management of Scottish Society 1707–1764* (Edinburgh: Donald, 1983).

62. Quoted in J. Carter, 'British Universities and Revolution, 1688–1718', in P. Dukes and J. Dunkley (eds), *Culture and Revolution* (London and New York: Pinter, 1990), pp. 8–21, on p. 15.

63. Shaw, *The Management of Scottish Society*, pp. 89–90.

64. Scott, 'The Politics and Administration of Scotland', pp. 399, 537, 542.

65. On colonial American urban politics, see especially G. B. Nash, 'The Transformation of Urban Politics 1700–1765', *Journal of American History*, 60 (1973), pp. 605–32.

66. NLS, Tweeddale Papers, MS 7046, fol. 22.

67. NLS, Tweeddale Papers, MS 7045, fol. 92.

68. *Great Britain's Memorial, Containing a Collection of Instructions, Representations, &c of the Freeholders and other Electors of Great Britain* (London: J. Watson, 1741), pp. 20, 21, 23, 30, 33, 36.

69. See, for example, *Extract from a Letter Wrote by a Scots Gentleman at London, to a Member of the Commons Council at Edinburgh, upon the Subject of the Ensuing Election, of a Member to Serve in Parliament for that City* (Edinburgh, 1741).

70. See especially the resolution of the merchants' company issued during the election which was published in *Cal. M.*, 1 April 1761. See also *Wednesday, April 1 1761. To the Citizens of Edinburgh* (Edinburgh, 1761); *Considerations on the Edinburgh Election* (Edinburgh, 1761).

71. A. Murdoch, 'The Importance of Being Edinburgh: Management and Opposition in Edinburgh Politics, 1746–1780', *Scottish Historical Review*, 62 (1983), pp. 1–16.

72. As referred to above, the issue of the role of the trades had periodically surfaced during the preceding decades, most recently in the aftermath of the so-called 'Dysdale Bustle', when the Council had sought to impose a minister, John Drysdale, in one the city's churches. The history of issue is summarized in *Answers for the Right Honourable John Dalrymple, Lord Provost of the City of Edinburgh, and others; to the Petition of James Stoddart, esq., late Old Provost, and James Stirling, esq., late one of the Baillies of the said City, and others* (Edinburgh, 1778).

73. *Edin. A.*, 19–22 August 1777.

74. *A Letter to James Stoddart, Esq* (Edinburgh, 1777), p. 4. See also *A Dream* (1777), which also drew the parallel between Stoddart and Wilkes as part of an attack on the former's new-found Patriot credentials.

75. *Common Sense. A Letter to the Fourteen Incorporations of Edinburgh* (Edinburgh, 1777).

76. *A Letter to James Stoddart*, pp. 5–6; *To the D. of B.* ([1777?]), North Riding Record Office, Northallerton, Zetland Papers, ZNK X 1/3/40. For the sensitivity of this issue among the urban population, see especially C. A. Whatley, *Scottish Society 1707–1830: Beyond Jacobitism, Towards Industrialisation* (Manchester: Manchester University Press, 2000), esp. ch. 4.

77. On the 1780 election, see, for example, *A Letter to the Author of Calumny Dectected* (Edinburgh, 1780); *An Address to the Citizens of Edinburgh upon the Nature of the Present*

Sett of the City and the Necessity of its being Speedily Reformed (Edinburgh, 1780); *To the Public* (Edinburgh, 1780); *A Short Account of the Elections at Edinburgh* (Edinburgh, 1780); *To the Inhabitants of Edinburgh* (Edinburgh, 1780).

78. *Cal. M.*, 10, 19 January, 18 February and 7 March 1778; *The History of the Rise, Opposition to, and Establishment of the Edinburgh Regiment* (Edinburgh, 1778). The proposal to raise the regiment seems to have been made originally by Sir John Dalrymple.

79. Thomas to Lawrence Dundas, Edinburgh, 15 November 1777, North Riding Record Office, Zetland Papers, ZNK, X 1/2/308.

80. Thomas to Lawrence Dundas, Edinburgh, 31 October 1777, ibid., ZNK X 1/2/302.

81. Murdoch, 'The Importance of Being Edinburgh', p. 13.

82. The poll election in 1746 was required because the Council had been unable to conduct the normal elections in the previous year owing to the occupation of the city by the Jacobite army; but also because the Duke of Cumberland believed that the old council had done too little to oppose the Jacobites (Scott, 'The Politics and Administration of Scotland', p. 516).

83. See above, p. 19.

84. For the Revolution Club, see Harris, *Politics and the Nation*, p. 187; EUL, List of Members of the Revolution Club at Edinburgh, ([prior to 1766]), CD. 8. 37.

85. For the Free Citizens, see Hill, *From Patriots to Unionists*, esp. pp. 144–5, 155–6.

86. See especially ibid., chs 3–6. The national political importance of figures such as Napper Tandy has recently been emphasized by Danny Mansergh in *Grattan's Failure: Parliamentary Opposition and the People in Ireland 1779–1800* (Dublin: Irish Academic Press, 2005), esp. pp. 51–67. For London politics, see especially N. Rogers, *Whigs and Cities: Popular Politics in the Age of Walpole and Pitt* (Oxford: Clarendon Press, 1989); J. Sainsbury, *Disaffected Patriots: London Supporters of Revolutionary America 1769–1782* (Kingston: McGill-Queen's University Press, 1987); L. S. Sutherland, 'The City of London in Eighteenth Century Politics', in R. Pares and A. J. P. Taylor (eds), *Essays Presented to Sir Lewis Namier* (London: Macmillan, 1956), pp. 49–74; J. R. Dinwiddy, 'The Patriotic Linen Draper: Robert Waithman and the Revival of Radicalism in the City of London, 1795–1818', in J R. Dindwiddy, *Radicalism and Reform in Britain, 1780–1850* (London: Hambledon Press, 1992), pp. 63–85.

87. As also noted in Sher, *The Enlightenment and the Book*, p. 147, n. 117, whose list comprises Francis Hutcheson, often viewed as the 'father' of the Scottish Enlightenment and a key influence on 'patriot' politics in Ireland and the North American colonies; the intemperate writer and historian Gilbert Stuart; John Millar, Professor of Civil Law at the University of Glasgow; William Ogilvie, the Aberdeen professor and advocate of land reform; Thomas Reid, who followed Adam Smith as the Professor of Moral Philosophy at Glasgow; William Smellie, the Edinburgh printer and compiler of the *Encyclopedia Britannica*; John Pinkerton, the denigrator of the Celts; and several others, including Robert Burns and John Moore, the physician, travel writer and novelist. The list is not exhaustive, and we can add several others, including Dugald Stewart, the Professor of Moral Philosophy at the University of Edinburgh; James Dunbar, the Aberdeen writer on moral philosophy and follower of Reid; Dr Robert Anderson, the first biographer of Tobias Smollett; and John Maclaurin, Lord Dreghorn, and his son, also called John.

88. Duke of Montrose to Campbell, 20 May 1800, Mitchell Library, Glasgow, Campbell of Succoth Papers, TD 219/6/301. See also 'A General View of the State of Parties in Glasgow Colllege', 294B.

89. Meikle, *Scotland and the French Revolution*, p. 71.

90. J. W. Cairns, '"Famous as a School for Law, as Edinburgh ... for Medicine": Legal Education in Glasgow, 1761–1801', in A. Hook and R. B. Sher (eds), *The Glasgow Enlightenment* (East Linton: Tuckwell Press with Eighteenth-Century Scottish Studies Society, 1995), pp. 133–62; K. Holcomb, 'Thomas Reid in the Glasgow Literary Society', in ibid., pp. 95–110.

91. Cairns, '"Famous as a School for Law"', p. 145.

92. 16 March 1778, W-KC, 24.157 (60).

93. Meikle, *Scotland and the French Revolution*, p. 5; *Cal. M.*, 3 March 1784; Wodrow to Kenrick, 15 April 1784, W-KC, 24.157 (74). Millar took similar action in 1789 in an attempt to prevent an address from Lanarkshire during the Regency Crisis in support of Pitt (D. E. Ginter, *Whig Organization in the General Election of 1790* (Berkeley, CA: University of California Press, 1967), p. 35).

94. A list of members of the society is included in *The Dundee Register of Merchants and Trades* (Dundee, 1783), pp. 41–2.

95. Small was one of two Dundee ministers who were disciplined by the local Presbytery and General Assembly for failing to insist that new elders subscribe to the Westminster Confession. James Wodrow was to report that the real motivation behind this rebuke was suspicion of Small arising from his previous 'intimacy' with the radical martyr of 1793, Thomas Fyshe Palmer. Interestingly, his case in the General Assembly was supported by the opposition Whigs, the Earl of Lauderdale and Henry Erskine (Wodrow to Kenrick, 12 July 1800, W-KC, 24. 157 (227)).

96. Wellgate Library, Dundee, Lamb Collection, 316 (6), Minute Book of the Dundee Public Library; *Regulations and Catalogue of the Dundee Public Library* (Dundee, 1807), 8 (16).

97. *Edin. A.*, 27–31 August and 31 August–1 September 1790.

98. NAS, RH 2/4/209, fol. 3; RH 2/4/68, fols 96–9; petition of John Morthland Ag.t Inner House interlo.r, 20 June 1800, NAS, Court of Session Papers, unextracted processes, CS 230 1/6/10/12, which refers to trips Morthland made to the north-east to collect debts owed to and raise funds for the *Scots Chronicle*. In Perth, he was told of a letter from a Mr Jobson, a Dundee merchant, which expressed a wish to provide money for the paper. Since there were quite a few Jobsons in Dundee in the later eighteenth century, we cannot be absolutely certain that David was the author of this letter, although it seems very likely.

99. See Chapter 5, below, pp. 165–6.

100. J. Crawford, 'Reading and Book Use in 18th-Century Scotland', *Bibliotheck*, 19 (1994), pp. 23–43, on p. 37.

101. *ODNB* entry for Tytler; J. Fergusson, *Balloon Tytler* (London: Faber and Faber, 1972).

102. See especially C. Kidd, *Subverting Scotland's Past: Scottish Anglo-Whig Historians and the Creation of an Anglo-British Identity, 1689–c.1830* (Cambridge: Cambridge University Press, 1993).

103. J. G. A. Pocock, *Barbarism and Religion: Volume Two, Narratives of Civil Government* (Cambridge: Cambridge University Press, 1999), chs. 16–19; C. Kidd, 'The Ideological Significance of Robertson's *History of Scotland*', in S. J. Brown (ed.), *William Robertson and the Expansion of Empire* (Cambridge: Cambridge University Press, 1997), pp. 122–44; N. K. Hargreaves, 'National History and "Philosophical" History: Character and Narrative in William Robertson's History of Scotland', *History of European Ideas*, 26 (2000), pp. 19–33. But see also, for a slightly different reading of Robertson's *History of Scotland During the Reigns of Queen Mary and King James VI* (1759), A. Du

Toit, 'Unionist Nationalism in the Eighteenth Century: William Robertson and James Anderson', *Scottish Historical Review*, 85 (2006), pp. 305–32.

104. J. G. A. Pocock, *The Discovery of Islands: Essays in British History* (Cambridge: Cambridge University Press, 2005), p. 110.

105. See especially R. L. Emerson, 'Lord Bute and the Scottish Universities, 1760–1792', in K. W. Schweizer (ed.), *Lord Bute: Essays in Reinterpretation* (Leicester: Leicester University Press, 1988), pp. 147–79; R. L. Emerson, 'Politics and the Glasgow Professors, 1690–1800', in Hook and Sher (eds), *The Glasgow Enlightenment*, pp. 21–39; R. L. Emerson and P. Wood, 'Science and Enlightenment in Glasgow, 1690–1802' in C. W. Withers and P. Wood (eds), *Science and Medicine in the Scottish Enlightenment* (East Linton: Tuckwell Press, 2002), pp. 79–142.

106. Sher, *The Enlightenment and the Book*, esp. ch. 3.

107. Durey, *'With the Hammer of Truth'*.

108. E. H. Gould, 'American Independence and Britain's Counter Revolution', *Past and Present*, 154 (1997), pp. 107–41, on p. 128.

109. A. Ferguson, *Principles of Moral and Political Science*, 2 vols (Edinburgh: A. Strahan and T. Cadell, and W. Creech, 1792), vol. 2, p. 474.

110. Ibid., vol. 2, p. 498–9.

111. For the nature of Millar's reformism, see especially Cairns, '"Famous as a School for Law"', pp. 144–6; D. Winch, *Riches and Poverty: An Intellectual History of Political Economy in Britain 1750–1834* (Cambridge: Cambridge University Press, 1996), pp. 191–7.

112. As emphasized in Bernard Bailyn's classic study *The Ideological Origins of the American Revolution* (Cambridge, MA: Belknap Press of Harvard University Press, 1967).

113. See, inter alia, M. Brown, 'Alexander Carlyle and the Shadows of Enlightenment', in Harris (ed.), *Scotland in the Age of the French Revolution*, pp. 226–46; C. Kidd, 'The Kirk, the French Revolution and the Burden of Scottish Whiggery', in N. Aston (ed.), *Religious Change in Europe, 1650–1914: Essays for John McManners* (Oxford: Clarendon Press, 1997), pp. 213–34; Vincent, 'The Responses of Scottish Churchmen to the French Revolution'.

114. Kidd, 'The Kirk, the French Revolution, and the Burden of Scottish Whiggery', p. 224.

115. H. Mitchell, *A Short Apology for Apostasy* (Glasgow, 1797), p. 5.

116. James Bradley identifies thirteen pro-Americans among Popular ministers (J. E. Bradley, 'The Religious Origins of Radical Politics in England, Scotland and Wales, 1662–1800', in J. E. Bradley and D. K. Van Kley (eds), *Religion and Politics in Enlightenment Europe* (Notre Dame, IN: University of Notre Dame Press, 2001), pp. 187–253, on p. 219).

117. Ibid., p. 219. For Nisbet, see also S. Miller, *Memoir of the Rev. Charles Nisbet* (New York: R. Carter, 1840).

118. R. K. Donovan, 'The Popular Party of the Church of Scotland and the American Revolution', in R. B. Sher and J. R. Smitten (eds), *Scotland and America in the Age of the Enlightenment* (Edinburgh: Edinburgh University Press, 1990), pp. 46–65.

119. J. R. McIntosh, *Church and Theology in Enlightenment Scotland: The Popular Party, 1740–1800* (East Linton: Tuckwell Press, 1998), pp. 155–60.

120. Wodrow to Kenrick, 16 March 1778, W-KC, 24.157 (60); Mitchell Library, TD 1/1070, Letter Book of Alexander Wilson, 1775–8.

121. J. Erskine, *The Fatal Consequences and the General Sources of Anarchy. A Discourse on Isaiah, XXIV, 1–5* (Edinburgh, 1793).

122. C. Kidd, 'Conditional Britons: The Scots Covenanting Tradition and the Eighteenth Century British State', *English Historical Review*, 474 (2002), pp. 1147–76.

123. Ibid., p. 1174.
124. A. Bruce, *A Serious View of the Remarkable Providences of the Times* (Glasgow: J. Ogle, 1795).
125. Kidd, 'The Kirk, the French Revolution, and the Burden of Scottish Whiggery', p. 230; A. Bruce, *A Brief Statement and Declaration of the Genuine Principles of Seceders Respecting Civil Government; the Duty of Subjects; and National Reformation: And a Vindication of their Conduct in Reference to Some Late Plans and Societies for Political Reform; and the Public Dissentions of the Time* (Edinburgh: J. Ogle, 1799); *The Principal Difference between the Religious Principles of those Commonly Called the Anti-Government Party, and of other Presbyterians, Especially those of the Secession in Scotland; on the Head of Magistracy, Briefly Stated* (Edinburgh: J. Guthrie, 1797).
126. Bruce, *A Brief Statement and Declaration*, esp. pp. 56–7.
127. J. McKerrow, *History of the Secession Church* (Glasgow: A. Fullerton, 1841), pp. 448–59. Bruce opposed holding a day of thanksgiving in 1788 in commemoration of 1688 on the grounds that ecclesiastically-sanctioned celebrations of secular events violated true Presbyterian principles (A. Bruce, *Annus Secularis: or The British Jubilee* (Edinburgh: M. Gray, 1788)).
128. For the latter, see R. B. Sher, 'Witherspoon's *Dominion of Providence* and the Scottish Jeremiad Tradition', in Sher and Smitten (eds), *Scotland and America*, pp. 44–64.
129. Bruce, *A Serious View of the Remarkable Providences of the Times*.
130. McKerrow, *History of the Secession Church*, pp. 271–3, 344–7.
131. A. Gib, *The Present Truth, A Display of the Secession-Testimony*, 2 vols (Edinburgh, 1774), vol. 1, pp. 292–342; McKerrow, *History of the Secession Church*, pp. 184–5.
132. Ibid., pp. 199–207; Harris, *Politics and the Nation*, pp. 150–9.
133. J. Seed, '"A Set of Men Powerful Enough in Many Things": Rational Dissent and Political Opposition in England, 1770–1790', in K. Haakonssen (ed.), *Enlightenment and Religion: Rational Dissent in Eighteenth Century Britain* (Cambridge: Cambridge University Press, 1996), pp. 140–68.
134. As Kidd notes of the 'qualified loyalty' espoused by the Associate Synod: 'defensive [as opposed to offensive] arms, however loosely defined, presumably remained a legitimate option for Seceders, who acknowledged only the "lawful commands" of the defective state' (Kidd, 'The Kirk, The French Revolution and the Burden of Scottish Whiggery', p. 217).
135. McKerrow, *History of the Secession Church*, pp. 372–6. The burghers approved a loyal address to the Crown in 1798.
136. Ibid., pp. 375–7.
137. See esp I. R. McBride, *Scripture Politics: Ulster Presbyterians and Irish Radicalism in the Late Eighteenth Century* (Oxford: Clarendon Press, 1998); Sher, *The Enlightenment and the Book*, p. 550.
138. C. Hay, *James Burgh, Spokesman for Reform in Hanoverian England* (Washington, DC: University Press of America, 1979). For Murray, see Bradley, *Religion, Revolution and English Radicalism*, esp. pp. 128–30.
139. N. C. Landsman, 'Liberty, Piety and Patronage: The Social Context of Contested Clerical Class in Eighteenth-Century Glasgow', in Hook and Sher (eds), *The Glasgow Enlightenment*, pp. 214–26. See also R. K. Donovan, *No Popery and Radicalism: Opposition to Roman Catholic Relief in Scotland, 1778–1782* (New York and London: Garland, 1987), esp. pp. 310–11.

140. See especially C. G. Brown, 'Protest in the Pews: Interpreting Presbyterianism and Society in Fracture During the Scottish Economic Revolution', in Devine (ed.), *Conflict and Stability in Scottish Society*, pp. 83–105; R. B. Sher and A. Murdoch, 'Patronage and Party in the Church of Scotland 1750–1800', in N. MacDougall (ed.), *Church, Politics and Society: Scotland 1408–1929* (Edinburgh: John Donald, 1983), pp. 197–220.

141. Landsman, 'Liberty, Piety and Patronage'; R. B. Sher, 'Moderates, Managers and Popular Politics in mid-Eighteenth Century Edinburgh: The Drysdale Bustle of the 1760s', in Dwyer et al. (eds), *New Perspectives on the Politics and Culture of Early Modern Scotland*, pp. 179–209.

142. *Edin. A.*, 13–16 April 1790; *A Seasonable Address to the Citizens of Glasgow* (Glasgow, 1762), p. 18.

143. Tweedale to Craigie, 13 March 1742, NAS, GD 1/609/2, fol. 3.

144. S. J. Brown, 'William Robertson (1721–1793) and the Scottish Enlightenment', in Brown (ed.), *William Robertson and the Expansion of Empire*, pp. 7–35, on p. 27.

145. McIntosh, *Church and Theology*, ch. 4.

146. Ibid., pp. 142–7.

147. See especially *Glasgow Mercury*, 1782–3.

148. The main source for the old society is the pamphlet *A Speech Addressed to the Provincial Synod of Glasgow and Ayr, Met at Ayr, 14th April 1784, by one of the Members of the Court, Upon Patronage* (Edinburgh, 1784).

149. Notice in *Glasgow Mercury*, 21–8 March 1782, entitled 'Reformation Interest'. This makes it clear that the society had emerged from a series of ad hoc meetings in the city among opponents of patronage, which had been taking place for 'some time'. See also notices in *Glasgow Mercury*, 1–5 May, 12–19 June, 21–8 August and 30 October–1 November 1783.

150. Notice in *Glasgow Mercury*, 20–7 June 1782.

151. Notice in *Glasgow Mercury*, 12–19 June 1783.

152. Circular of New Committee in Glasgow for Abolishing Patronage, 1 July 1783, endorsed in pen in the Earl of Buchan's hand 'circular from Mr Muir merchant in Glasgow, father of the unfortunate Advocate', EUL, Gen 1736.

153. Donovan, *No Popery and Radicalism, passim*. Donovan particularly emphasizes the role of propaganda and novel forms of organization in the anti-Catholic agitation of 1778–82, and the degree to which this agitation drew on the support of trades incorporations and journeymen friendly societies.

154. See, for example, *Edin. A.*, 11–14 February, 21–5 March, 19–23 September, 21–4 October and 24–8 October 1783.

155. See, for example, *A Collection of Letters on Patronage and Popular Election* (Edinburgh: W. Coke, 1783); *The Progress and Present State of the Laws of Patronage in Scotland* (Edinburgh, 1783).

156. Notice in *Edin. A.*, 25–8 February 1783.

157. Sher and Murdoch, 'Patronage and Party in the Church of Scotland'.

158. A. Crosbie, *Thoughts of a Layman Concerning Patronage and Presentations* (Edinburgh: W. Gray, 1769), p 15.

159. Mitchell Library, Glasgow, TD 209/1, Book of the General Session of Glasgow, fols 14–15, 46–7.

160. *A Collection of Letters*, pp. 1–2.

161. John, Lord Maclaurin, *Considerations on the Right of Patronage* (Edinburgh, 1766), p. 26.

162. NAS, Minutes of the Synod of Angus and Mearns, CH2/12/9/124. fol. 123.
163. *An Address to the People of Scotland on Ecclesiastical and Civil Liberty* (Edinburgh, 1782), pp. 16–17.
164. *The Progress and Present State of the Laws of Patronage*, esp. pp. 32, 34; *A Collection of Letters*, pp. 35, 58.
165. J. Snodgrass, *An Effectual Method for Recovering our Religious Liberties, Addressed to the Elders of the Church of Scotland* (Glasgow: James Duncan, 1770), p. 5.
166. *The Progress and Present State of the Laws of Patronage*, pp. 36, 38.
167. Crosbie, *Thoughts of a Layman Concerning Patronage and Presentations*, p. 16.
168. A. Bruce, *The Patron's A.B.C., or The Shorter Catechism* (Glasgow: J. Duncan, 1771), pp. 14–15.
169. *Patronage Demolished, and the Rights of the Christian People Restored* (Edinburgh, 1769), pp. 6–8, 13, 24, quoted in Bradley, 'The Religious Origins of Radical Politics', p. 213.
170. Ibid., p. 218.
171. See also *Tracts Concerning Patronage, By Some Eminent Hands* (Edinburgh: W. Gray, 1770), p. 183.
172. *An Inquiry into the Principles of Ecclesiastical Patronage and Presentation* (Edinburgh, 1783), p. 75.
173. Notice in *Glasgow Mercury*, 20–7 June 1782.
174. *A Collection of Letters*, p. 39.
175. Notice in *Glasgow Mercury*, 21–8 August 1783.
176. Brown, 'Protest in the Pews', pp. 100–1.
177. Quoted in Bradley, 'The Religious Origins of Radical Politics', p. 219.
178. *A Speech Addressed to the Provincial Synod of Glasgow and Ayr*, p. 6.
179. As evident in *Scotland's Opposition to the Popish Bill. A Collection of all the Declarations and Resolutions, Published by the Different Counties, Cities, Towns, Parishes, Incorporations, and Societies, throughout Scotland* (Edinburgh, 1780).
180. N. C. Landsman, 'Evangelists and their Hearers: Popular Interpretation of Revivalist Preaching in Eighteenth-Century Scotland', *Journal of British Studies*, 28 (1989), pp. 120–49, esp. pp. 136–7.
181. On this, see especially T. C. Smout, 'Born again at Cambuslang: New Evidence on Popular Religion and Literacy in Eighteenth-Century Scotland', *Past and Present*, 97 (1982), pp. 114–27.
182. Mitchell Library, TD 217/1, Personal Memoirs of John Scot of Heatheryknow, Old Monkland.
183. For a useful summary of existing work on this, see Crawford, 'Reading and Book Use', pp. 24–9.
184. Kidd, 'Conditional Britons', pp. 1160–1.
185. NAS, St Andrew's Commissary Court Records, CC3/4/28, pp. 3873–7.
186. Crawford, 'Reading and Book Use', p. 27.
187. *The Statistical Account of Scotland, 1791–1799, vol. 10, Fife*, ed. J. Sinclair, new intro. R. G. Cant (Wakefield: EP Publishing, 1978), pp. 48–9.
188. Noble, 'Displaced Persons'.
189. Crawford, 'Reading and Book Use', p. 26.
190. Kidd, 'Conditional Britons, p. 1161.
191. See especially Landsman, 'Evangelists and their Hearers', pp. 145–6; W. H. Fraser, *Conflict and Class: Scottish Workers 1700–1838* (Edinburgh: John Donald, 1988), esp. chs 1–4; Whatley, *Scottish Society*, ch. 5.

192. See relevant comment in C. A. Whatley, 'Roots of 1790s Radicalism: Reviewing the Economic and Social Background', in Harris (ed.), *Scotland in the Age of the French Revolution*, pp. 23–48, on pp. 36–42.

193. *Glasgow Mercury*, 18 March 1779.

194. P. Kelly, 'British and Irish Politics in 1785', *English Historical Review*, 90 (1975), pp. 536–63, on p. 543.

195. S. Drescher, *Capitalism and Antislavery: British Mobilization in Comparative Perspective* (London: Macmillan, 1986), esp. p. 80.

196. William Dickson, 'Diary of a Visit to Scotland, 5th Jan–19 Mar 1792 on Behalf of the Committee for the Abolition of the Slave Trade', Friends House, Temp MSS Box 10/14.

197. *Dumfries Weekly Magazine*, 12 April 1773.

198. *Dumfries Weekly Magazine*, 16 March 1773.

199. For the role of the Provost of Glasgow in orchestrating the opposition at the Convention of Royal Burghs, see *Dumfries Weekly Magazine*, 6 May 1777.

200. *Dumfries Weekly Magazine*, 3 June 1777; *Scots Magazine*, 39 (1777), pp. 569–75.

201. *Considerations on our Corn Laws and the Bill Proposed to Amend Them* (Aberdeen and Edinburgh: C. Elliot, 1777), p. 15.

202. *Dumfries Weekly Magazine*, 13 May 1777; *Edin. E.*, 3 May 1777.

203. *Dumfries Weekly Magazine*, 13 May 1777.

204. For minutes of the meeting of the 'landed interest' in Edinburgh, at which representatives from thirteen counties were apparently present, see *Aberdeen Weekly Journal*, 8 December 1777.

205. *Cal. M.*, 21 January 1778.

206. *Cal. M.*, 29 March 1791.

207. For preliminary comment on the extent of this debate, see Harris, 'Parliamentary Legislation, Lobbying and the Press', pp. 86–7.

208. PKCA, 59/24/2/31; B59/34/82; B59/34/83.

209. See, for example, S. Nenadic, 'Political Reform and the "Ordering" of Middle-Class Protest', in Devine (ed.), *Conflict and Stability in Scottish Society*, pp. 65–82.

210. *Cal. M.*, 20, 25, 27 and 30 May, 1, 3, 6, 17 and 20 June and 1 July 1778.

211. As one contemporary who lived close to Edinburgh, and was a regular visitor to the capital, noted in his journal for 1792: '... so the journeymen carpenters, masons and all your operatives that have the strength [word obscure in MS] youth and labour are forming clubs where Payne on the Rights of Man are read and spoken upon like Texts of Scripture' (NLS, Saltoun Papers, MS 17765, fol. 108).

212. *Glasgow Mercury*, 27 June–4 July and 11–18 July 1782.

213. See, for example, Wyvill, *Political Papers*, vol. 3, pp. 18–20, Patrick Barron, Esq., President of the Committee of Aberdeen, to Thos. McGrugar, Esq, Secretary of the Committee at Edinburgh, 12 November 1782, where Barron declares: 'The grievances of which the Burgesses of Scotland complain, are those of a very respectable part of the BRITISH PEOPLE to a BRITISH HOUSE of COMMONS, where distinctions, long since obsolete, are unknown'.

214. Harris, 'Parliamentary Legislation, Lobbying and the Press', pp. 90–1.

215. E. Vincent Macleod, 'The Scottish Opposition Whigs and the French Revolution', in Harris (ed.), *Scotland in the Age of the French Revolution*, pp. 79–98; D. J. Brown, 'The Government of Scotland under Henry Dundas and William Pitt', *History*, (1998), pp. 265–79, esp. pp. 269–70.

2 Newspapers, the French Revolution and Public Opinion

1. See, inter alia, I. R. Christie, 'James Perry of the Morning Chronicle', in I. R. Christie, *Myth and Reality in Late Eighteenth-Century British Politics* (Berkeley, CA: University of California Press, 1970), pp. 334–58; J. Black, *The English Press 1621–1861* (Stroud: Sutton, 2001), chs 4, 8; M. J. Smith, 'English Radical Newspapers in the French Revolutionary Era, 1790–1803' (unpublished PhD thesis, University of London, 1979); N. J. Curtin, *The United Irishmen: Popular Politics in Ulster and Dublin 1791–1798* (Oxford: Clarendon Press, 1994), ch. 8.
2. *Glasgow Advertiser*, 20 January 1793.
3. J. King, *Mr King's Apology* (1798), p. 29, quoted in Smith, 'English Radical Newspapers', p. 287.
4. On this, see especially Barker, *Newspapers, Politics and English Society*, ch. 2; B. Harris, *Politics and the Rise of the Press: Britain and France 1620–1800* (London: Routledge, 1996), ch. 1.
5. Quoted in Smith, 'English Radical Newspapers', p. 162.
6. See, for example, R. Heron, *Observations Made in a Journey through the Western Counties of Scotland in the Autumn of 1792*, 2nd edn, 2 vols (Perth: W. Morison, 1799), vol. 1, pp. 111–12, 143–9, vol. 2, pp. 232–4, 285–6, 393, 421–2; *The Statistical Account of Scotland, 1791–1799, vol. 10, Fife*, pp. 48–9.
7. See Chapter 1, above, pp. 38–9.
8. Harris, *Politics and the Rise of the Press*, p. 11.
9. See, for example, I. Hampsher-Monk, 'Civic Humanism and Parliamentary Reform: The Case of the Society of the Friends of the People', *Journal of British Studies*, 18 (1979), pp. 70–89; H. T. Dickinson, *Liberty and Property: Political Ideology in Eighteenth-Century Britain* (London: Weidenfeld and Nicolson, 1977), pp. 237–69; B. Weinstein, 'Popular Constitutionalism and the London Corresponding Society', *Albion*, 34 (2002), pp. 37–57.
10. For comment on this, see also Philp, 'The Fragmented Ideology of Reform', pp. 57–61.
11. A useful methodological discussion is M. Peters, 'Historians and the Eighteenth-Century Press: A Review of Possibilities and Problems', *Australian Journal of Politics and History*, 24 (1988), pp. 37–50.
12. A full list of such individuals would be a long one, and would include several very well-known names – James Perry, Daniel and Peter Stuart – as well as a host of much less well-known ones. One radical of this period who carved out a role for himself in the London press after fleeing repression in Scotland in 1794 was George Ross, who became a member of the London Corresponding Society. In the later 1790s, he was the publisher of several radical papers, including the *Telegraph*, a paper which had links to the London Corresponding Society.
13. Harris, *Politics and the Rise of the Press*, pp. 8–9.
14. Relevant figures are reproduced in M. Harris, 'The Structure, Ownership and Control of the Press, 1620–1780', in J. Curran, G. Boyce and P. Wingate (eds), *Newspaper History from the Seventeenth Century to the Present Day* (London: Constable for the Press Group of the Acton Society, 1978), pp. 82–97, on p. 90.
15. Notice in *Glas. C.*, 1 April 1794. For contemporary observation on the rise of the subscription coffee room as an important aspect of Scottish urban culture, see J. Lettice, *Letters on a Tour through Various Parts of Scotland in the Year 1792* (London: T. Cadell, 1794), pp. 454–5.

16. *Glas. C.*, 2 December 1794. The cost of an annual subscription to the room was 15*s.*, but non-subscribers could gain access for a charge of 2*d.* per visist.

17. A. Campbell, *A Journey from Edinburgh through Parts of North Britain*, 2 vols (London: T. N. Longman and O. Rees, 1802), vol. 1, p. 368.

18. Christie, 'James Perry of the Morning Chronicle'. See also the revised entry on Perry by Hannah Barker in the *ODNB*.

19. L. Werkmeister, 'Robert Burns and the London Daily Press', *Modern Philology*, 63 (1966), pp. 322–35.

20. See, for example, *Edin. H.*, 3 September 1794.

21. *Morning Chronicle*, 2 and 5 December 1793. They also appeared in pamphlet form and were widely circulated north and south of the border.

22. *Morning Chronicle*, 7 February 1793.

23. For further discussion of Macleod's involvement in reform politics in this period, see Chapter 3, below, pp. 93–4.

24. *Morning Chronicle*, 26 February 1793.

25. *Morning Chronicle*, 18 September 1793.

26. See, for example, *Morning Chronicle*, 9, 16 and 19 August, 7, 18, 20 and 27 September, 11 October, 15 and 21 November 1793, and 1 January 1794.

27. See below, p. 69.

28. BL, Add. MSS 51,572, fol. 5.

29. It was, for example, still being taken in 1798 by the Paisley subscription coffee room (R. Brown, *The History of Paisley, From the Roman Period down to 1884*, 2 vols (Paisley: Cook, 1886), vol. 2, p. 61).

30. John [Buchanan?] of [Auchlesstrie?], Cambusmond, to the Duke of Atholl, 27 September 1794, AP, 59 (1), 318.

31. *Cambridge Intelligencer*, 24 January 1801. Another Scottish reader of the paper was James Wodrow (W-KC, 24.157 (195), where he notes that he is receiving the paper every Monday).

32. Smith, 'English Radical Newspapers', pp. 171–2.

33. Ibid., pp. 177, 179.

34. Ibid., pp. 14, 60–1.

35. *The Second Report from the Committee of Secrecy of the House of Commons* (London: J. Debrett, 1794), appendix, letter from Thomas Hardy, secretary of the London Corresponding Society to Maurice Margarot and Joseph Gerrald, 8 November 1793, where Hardy notes: 'I would have sent you the Courier, but they informed me that they sent several to the coffee-houses and taverns in Edinburgh; for that reason I thought it unnecessary'.

36. *Sheffield Iris*, 3 July 1795. For the *Chester Chronicle*, see Smith, 'English Radical Newspapers', p. 176. On 17 February 1797, a Glasgow correspondent wrote of this paper's 'very extensive circulation among the friends of humanity'.

37. Smith, 'English Radical Newspapers', p. 177.

38. Ibid., ch. 2.

39. *Albion*, 18 November 1800.

40. Subject to repeated prosecution, Macleod spent 3½ years in Newgate before being pardoned in mid 1804. He died a year later in Edinburgh.

41. Anonymous letter, Edinburgh, 26 October 1790, ECA, McLeod Collection, D, 44, item 7.

42. It was a similar story in relation to the English provincial press, for which, see especially H. Barker, *Newspapers, Politics and Public Opinion in Late Eighteenth Century England* (Oxford: Clarendon Press, 1998).

43. See Dickinson, *Liberty and Property*, pp. 232–40.

44. On this, see especially T. C. Smout, 'Problems of Nationalism, Identity and Improvement in Later Eighteenth-Century Scotland', in T. M. Devine (ed.), *Improvement and Enlightenment* (Edinburgh: John Donald Publishers Ltd, 1989), pp. 1–21.

45. Harris, 'Political Protests in the Year of Liberty'.

46. C. Emsley, 'The "London Insurrection" of 1792: Fact, Fiction or Fantasy?', *Journal of British Studies*, 17 (1978), pp. 66–86; J. Mori, 'Responses to Revolution: The November Crisis of 1792', *Bulletin of the Institute of Historical Research*, 69 (1996), pp. 284–305.

47. *Glas. C.*, 26 January, 24 March, 19 July 1792.

48. See, for example, *Glas. C.*, 5, 17, 21, 24, 28 and 31 January, 4, 14, 18 and 23 February, 1, 3, 6, 8, 10, 13, 15, 18, 20, 22, 24 and 31 March, 3 April 1792.

49. *Glas. C.*, 4 October 1792.

50. *Glas. C.*, 16 October, 1792.

51. *Glas. C.*, 19 May 1792. For the circulation of the *Rights of Man*, see Chapter 3, below, pp. 79–80.

52. *Glas. C.*, 26 May 1792.

53. *Glas. C.*, 26 May (Manchester Constitutional Society), 24 April, 19 July, 11 December (Glasgow Society for Borough Reform, 5 May (Whig Association of the Friends of the People), 7 August, 15 December (Scottish Friends of the People), 23 July, 20 and 30 October (Associated Friends of the Constitution and of the People), 5 November, 29 December (United Societies of Paisley associated for Parliamentary Reform). Other papers to find space for such resolutions included the *Glasgow Mercury*, the *Caledonian Mercury* and, most strikingly of all, the *Edinburgh Evening Courant*, for which see *Edin. E.*, 31 March, 16, 19 and 26 July, 6 August, 1 and 10 September, 4, 13 and 27 October, 3 and 24 November, 1, 6, 8, 13 and 15 December 1792.

54. For contemporary comment on the paper's success, see H. Arnot, *The History of Edinburgh* (Edinburgh: W. Creech, 1779), p. 267.

55. *Edin. A.*, 27–30 April 1790.

56. *Edin. A.*, 25–8 May and 10–14 December 1790.

57. In early November 1790, Peter Hill was advertising the arrival by coach of 'a few copies of Burke's Reflections' (*Edin. A.*, 9–12 November 1790). Subsequent booksellers' advertisements indicate a strong demand for Burke's work north of the border.

58. *Edin. A.*, 5–9 November 1790 and 18–21 February 1791.

59. *Edin. A.*, 29 July–2 August, 22–6 July, 29 November–1 December and 9–13 December 1791.

60. *Edin. A.*, 2–5 and 19–23 August, 4–8 and 22–5 November 1791.

61. *Edin. A.*, 14–17 August, 31 August–4 September, 7–11, 11–14, 14–18 and 18–21 September 1792.

62. See *Edin. A.*, 30 November–4 December 1792.

63. See B. Harris, 'Scotland's Newspapers, the French Revolution and Domestic Radicalism, c.1789–1794', *Scottish Historical Review*, 84 (2005), pp. 38–62, on p. 47.

64. The singular nature of its stance was noted in *The Historical Register, or Edinburgh Monthly Intelligencer*, July 1791, p. 37.

65. See the comment on this in B. Harris, 'The Press, Newspaper Fiction and Literary Journalism, 1707–1918', in S. Manning (ed.), *The Edinburgh History of Scottish Literature*,

Volume Two: Enlightenment, Britain and Empire (1707–1918) (Edinburgh: Edinburgh University Press, 2007), pp. 308–16, on p. 311.

66. Files of the *Edinburgh Herald* for 1790–6 were sold by the Signet Library to the National Library of Scotland in 1996. The volume for 1792 is currently missing.
67. *Edin. H.*, 25 and 30 March, 1 and 5 April 1790.
68. *Edin. H.*, 5, 8 and 10 November 1790.
69. *Edin. H.*, 22 November 1790. For other items critical of Burke's *Reflections*, see also issues for 15, 17 and 19 November 1790.
70. *Edin. H.*, 12 January 1791.
71. *Edin. H.*, 11 April 1791.
72. *Edin. H.*, 27 May 1791.
73. *Edin. H.*, 8 July 1791.
74. *Edin. H.*, 8, 10, 12, 15 and 22 August 1792.
75. *Edin. H.*, 22 August 1791.
76. *Edin. A.*, 16–19 April and 2–5 July 1793, 10–13 June 1794.
77. *Edin. A.*, 2–5 April 1793.
78. See Harris, 'Scotland's Newspapers, the French Revolution and Domestic Radicalism'.
79. This was originally entitled the *Kelso Chronicle*.
80. *Edin. A.*, 12–15 March 1793; *Edin. H.*, 6 March 1793.
81. *Glas. C.*, 1 December 1792, 'To the Inhabitants of the West of Scotland'; 8 December 1792, 'Copy of a Letter from a Weaver of Anderston, near Glasgow to Captain Johnston, Newswriter in Edinburgh'; 11 December 1792, 'To the Manufacturers, Mechanics and Labouring People of Scotland'; 13 December 1792, 'To the People of Scotland'; 20 December 1792, 'The Paisley Weaver's Letter to his Neighbours and Fellow Tradesmen', 'To Mr Hugh Bell, President of the Friends of the People'.
82. *Glas. C.*, 10 April 1793.
83. See Chapter 3, below, p. 88.
84. *Edin. A.*, 10–13, 13–17 and 17–20 June 1793; *Glas. C.*, 20, 23 and 27 May, 19 and 26 June 1794; *Aberdeen Weekly Journal*, 26 May, 9 and 23 June 1793; *Edin. H.*, 13, 16 and 18 June, 5 July 1794. On 21 May, the *Edinburgh Herald* provided the summary conclusions of the report, highlighted by being printed in capitals.
85. *Edin. A.*, 20–3 May 1794. See also *Aberdeen Weekly Journal*, 26 May and 9 June 1794.
86. *Dumfries Weekly Journal*, 21 October 1794. Similar accounts were published in *Glas. C.*, 21 October 1794; and *Aberdeen Weekly Journal*, 21 October 1794.
87. *Edin. H.*, 1 November 1794; *Glas. C.*, 1 November 1794. The confession was also disseminated very widely in pamphlet form.
88. This was an especially significant feature of the coverage of the trials in the *Edinburgh Herald*. See especially the issues of 10 and 12 November 1794, for the reaction to the acquittal of Thomas Hardy.
89. See, for example, the account of the trial of Margarot in *Edin. A.*, 14–17 January 1794; see also *Edin. H.*, 13 and 15 January 1794.
90. *Dumfries Weekly Journal*, 27 May and 3 June 1794.
91. This also reflected, of course, the role of the opposition Whigs, especially William Adam, in taking up the issues of the sentencing of Muir and Fyshe Palmer at Westminster during the parliamentary session of 1793–4. Letters on the outcome of the trials made a frequent appearance in the *Morning Chronicle*, a number of which, unsurprisingly, were from Scottish correspondents (*Morning Chronicle*, 6, 7, 18, 20 and 27 September, 4, 7, 11, 18 and 29 October, 4 and 9 December 1793, 28 February 1794).

92. *Dumfries Weekly Journal*, 5 February and 19 March 1793, 4 February 1794; *Glas. C.*, 5 and 10 January and 16 February 1793, 30 January and 3 May 1794.

93. *Dumfries Weekly Journal*, 8 April 1794; *Aberdeen Weekly Journal*, 21 April, 19 May and 9 June 1794; *Edin. H.*, 17 March 1794. This was also printed as a cheap pamphlet.

94. *Edin. A.*, 18–21 June and 2–5 July 1793.

95. See, for example, *Glas. C.*, 30 September and 8 November 1794.

96. See, for example, *Dumfries Weekly Journal*, 12 March, 6 August and 27 December 1793, 28 January, 29 April, 6, 20 and 27 May, 17 June and 22 July 1794.

97. See, for example, *Glas. C.*, 23 March 1793. The *Glasgow Courier* also reported favourably (see 30 April and 4 May) on ministerial efforts to shore up liquidity through the issuing of exchequer bills. Glasgow was by far the major recipient of such support in Scotland.

98. On this, see especially Whatley, 'Roots of 1790s Radicalism', pp. 25–6.

99. N. Douglas, *Thoughts on Modern Politics* (London: Button, 1793), p. 198, n.

100. *Glas. C.*, 2 August 1794.

101. *Glas. C.*, 30 December 1794.

102. Robert Allan, Edinburgh, to John Moore, 2 December 1792, BL, Reeves Papers, Add. MSS 16, 920, fols 39–40.

103. B. Harris, 'Print and Politics', in Harris (ed.), *Scotland in the Age of the French Revolution*, pp. 164–95, on pp. 181–2.

104. In April 1792 Sibbald was requesting that the terms of the Bankruptcy Act be altered to include the *Edinburgh Herald* among those papers in which bankruptcy notices were obliged to be placed. The existing beneficiaries of the requirement were the *Caledonian Mercury* and the *Edinburgh Evening Courant*. Dundas was unwilling to make any change at that time, presumably because he did not wish to alienate the conductors of these papers at a time when he hoped for their support (Henry Mackenzie to Robert Dundas, 14 April 1792, enclosing a letter of James Sibbald to Mackenzie of 11 April 1792, EUL, Laing Papers, II, 500, 182–3).

105. Robert to Henry Dundas, 12 December 1792, NAS, RH 2/4/66, fols 313–15; accounts of money imprest into the hands of John Pringle, Sheriff Depute of the County of Edinburgh, for secret services, the first dated June 1793 and covering the period 8 February–15 June 1793, the second dated April 1794 and covering activities from the winter of 1792 to April 1794, EUL, Laing Papers, II, 500, 566.

106. Ibid.

107. NAS, Court of Justiciary Papers, JC 26/280.

108. See especially K. Schweizer and R. Klein, 'The French Revolution and Developments in the London Daily Press to 1793', in K. Schweizer and J. Black (eds), *Politics and the Press in Hanoverian Britain* (Lewiston, NY: E. Mellon Press for Bishop's University, 1989), pp. 171–86.

109. Smith, 'English Radical Newspapers', p. 212. According to Smith, this scheme of supporting 'respectable country papers' lasted until 1806.

110. For Brown, see the voluminous correspondence involving him in EUL, Laing Papers, II, 500, especially Robert to Henry Dundas, 25 February 1794, where Robert notes that he is 'endeavouring to employ [Brown] to good purpose', 554; memorandum for Mr Dundas from the Lord Advocate, April 1794, 566. Brown received a pension or allowance of £150 in the first year and £100 thereafter.

111. *Dundee Repository of Political and Miscellaneous Information* (1793–4); [W. Brown], *Look Before Ye Loup: or, A Healin' Sa' for the Crackit Crowns of Country Politicians, by Tam Thrum, an Auld Weaver* (Edinburgh, 1793); [W. Brown], *Look Before Ye Loup. Part*

Second: or anither Box of Healin' Sa' for the Crackit Crowns of Country Politicians, by Tam Thrum, an Auld Weaver (Edinburgh, 1794).

112. EUL, Laing Papers, II, 500, 566.

113. The *Herald and Chronicle* lasted for only two years. Brown went on to edit the *Edinburgh Weekly Chronicle* from 1798.

114. As hinted in various memoranda by Brown about his business affairs (see, for example, EUL, Laing Papers, II, 500, 607, 674, 678, 849, 880).

115. William McConnell to Robert Dundas, Wigton, 26 August 1797, EUL, Laing Papers, II, 500, 1309.

116. Henry Mackenzie to George Chalmers, [1793], NLS, 'Scott and Contemporaries', MS 786, fols 73–4.

117. Allan Maconockie to Robert Dundas, Glasgow, 12 October 1792, NAS, RH 2/4/64, fols 369–70; Henry Dundas to William Pitt, 12 November 1792, NA, 30/8/157, part 1, fols 132–41.

118. In the event, Mennons's co-accused, Smith, did not appear at the trial in early 1793 and was duly outlawed. The diet was adjourned and the matter not proceeded with (Howell, *State Trials*, vol. 23, p. 36).

119. Robert to Henry Dundas, 9 December 1792, NAS, RH 2/4/66, fols 254–8; see also Chapter 4, below, p. 119.

120. Harris, 'Print and Politics'.

121. Only one issue is known to survive for this period, that for 1 March 1793 (to be found at NLS, 7.59).

122. See Chapter 5, below, p. 182.

123. See, for example, *Edin. A.*, 23–6 April and 13–17 September 1793, 15–18 April and 27 June–1 July 1794.

124. The two extant issues are those of 4–7 December (in the Mitchell Library, Glasgow) and of 11–14 December (at NAS, GD 99/229/9).

125. For Robertson and Berry, see Harris, 'Print and Politics', p. 168.

126. For the former, see *A Letter to Mr Hugh Bell, Chairman of the Convention of Delegates* (Edinburgh, [late 1792?]).

127. Ibid., p. 4.

128. See Chapter 5, below, p. 163.

129. For Johnston's political views, see Chapter 3, below, p. 99. *Edin. G.*, 22 January and 23 February 1793.

130. *Edin. G.*, 30 November 1792.

131. Henry Dundas to Evan Nepean, 24 November 1792, NAS, RH 2/4/65, fols 48–53, authorizing the interception of letters to the Glasgow reformer Col. William Dalrymple, the MP for Invernesshire and Whig reformer Norman Macleod, and Johnston; Robert to Henry Dundas, 9 December 1792, RH 2/4/66, fols 254–8.

132. Howell, *State Trials*, vol. 23, pp. 7–25.

133. NAS, RH 2/4/70, fol. 82.

134. *Edin. G.*, 15 October 1793.

135. *Edin. G.*, 5 November 1793.

136. The number of advertisers fell very rapidly to just a handful in any issue by early 1793.

137. See Chapter 3, below, pp. 90–1.

138. See NAS, RH 2/4/73, fol. 185r, for the report of the anonymous spy, J.B., on the motion in the third convention to support the paper. The matter was remitted to the Edinburgh monthly committee. See also ibid., fols 220–6, for the further motion in the British

convention to support the paper and the referral of the issue to a committee, and fols 238–42 for the outcome. See also 'Report of the committee appointed to take into consideration the proper measures for supporting the Gazetteer', 'Plan for Supporting the Gazetteer submitted to the Consideration of the Friends of the People' and 'Minute of the Second Meeting of the Committee Relative to the Gazetteer, Edin, 27 November 1793', NAS, JC 26/280, bundle 6.

139. *Edin. G.*, 10 December 1793. See also the issue for 7 January 1794.

140. The item appeared in the issue for 10 December 1793. Entitled 'An Extraordinary Instance of Public Spirit in A Cobler [*sic*] of Messina', it described an instance of a private individual executing justice on corrupt rulers, asking 'What if the cobler of Messina should revive?'

141. A. Scott, *Reasons Justifying the Departure of A. Scott* (Edinburgh, 1794). Scott was later arrested in London, but released on agreeing to act as a government spy (NA, TS 11/956/3501; HO 42/33).

142. See especially *Edin. G.*, 25 December 1792, where the paper declared under the 'Edinburgh' heading: 'In bestowing our praise on these momentous events, we hope that our readers will not consider us blind to the excesses which have been committed ...'.

143. NAS, JC 26/280, bundle 1, item 24.

144. Quoted in *Edin. G.*, 15 January 1794.

145. See, for example, *Glas. C.*, 4 August 1796.

146. See, for example, *Edin. A.*, 15 and 19 April and 11 October 1796, 6 January, 12 May and 29 September 1797.

147. George Hill, St Mary's College, St Andrews, to Robert Dundas, 2 March 1797, EUL, Laing Papers, II, 500, 1033.

148. Alexander Brown to James Ferguson of Kilmundy, [1797], NLS, Ferguson of Kilmundy Papers, MS 9050, 113.

149. Vincent Macleod, 'The Scottish Opposition Whigs and the French Revolution'.

150. Petition of John Johnston, 1800; process of damages ag.t John Morthland Esq & John Johnston; and petition for John Morthland ag.t Inner House interlo.r of date 20 June 1800, NAS, Court of Session Papers, CS 230, 1/6/10/12. Other figures involved included Sir John Henderson and Andrew Stirling. Lauderdale was another victim of the Dundas hegemony in 1796, losing his seat in the Lords as a representative peer, but continuing his prominent opposition to Pitt and his policies through involvement in the politics of the City of London and the press. The foundation of the *Scots Chronicle* was very much in line with this change in political strategy.

151. The paper also relentlessly puffed the efforts of the Whig opposition in Parliament.

152. See *Scots C.*, 17 and 28 February, 17, 24, 28 and 31 March, 4, 12, 14, 21 and 25 April, 2, 9 and 26 May 1797. Other important pamphlets which were extracted in the paper in the first half of 1797 were Lauderdale's *Thoughts on Finance* (1797) and William Morgan's *An Appeal to the People of Great Britain, on the Present Alarming State of the Public Finances, and of Public Credit* (1797).

153. See Chapter 5, below, pp. 153–4.

154. Answer for John Cadell Esq of Cockenzie, NAS, CS 230, 1/6/10/12.

155. Declaration of William Morris, 5 November 1797, NAS, JC 26/294.

156. Letter from Brown to Archibald Campbell of Clathick, enclosed in letter from Cambell to Robert Dundas, 16 March 1796, EUL, Laing Papers, II, 500, 849; Sir William Murray to Robert Dundas, 15 September 1797, 1479–80.

157. As suggested in EUL, Laing Papers, II, 500, 849.

158. Petition from John Morthland, NAS, CS 230, 1/6/10/12.
159. John Morthland to Robert Dundas, 10 October 1797, EUL, Laing Papers, II, 500, 1573.
160. Process of damages ag.t John Morthland Esq. & John Johnston, NAS, CS 230, 1/6/30/12.
161. See *Scots C.*, 10 February 1797, where it was noted that costs outweighed profits and that the paper was, therefore, currently dependent on 'pecuniary indemnification'. See also petition for John Morthland ag.t Inner House interlo.r of date 20 June 1800, NAS, CS 230, 1/6/10/12, where it was noted that the paper was established with 'no expectancy or desire for profit'.
162. H. T. Dickinson, 'Popular Loyalism in Britain in the 1790s', in E. Hellmuth (ed.), *The Transformation of Political Culture: England and Germany in the Late Eighteenth Century* (Oxford: Oxford University Press, 1990), pp. 503–34, on p. 527.
163. Quoted in D. Clare, 'The Growth and Importance of the Newspaper Press in Manchester, Liverpool, Sheffield and Leeds, between 1780 and 1800' (unpublished MA thesis, University of Manchester, 1960), pp. 126–7.
164. Smith, 'English Radical Newspapers', pp. 7–8.
165. As discussed in ibid., ch. 5.
166. J. Cookson, *The Friends of Peace: Anti-War Liberalism in England 1793–1815* (Cambridge: Cambridge University Press, 1982), esp. ch. 4.
167. See J. Seed, 'Gentlemen Dissenters: The Social and Political Meaning of Rational Dissent in the 1770s and 1780s', *Historical Journal*, 28 (1995), pp. 299–325.
168. See especially Buchan to Wyvill, 29 May 1797, in Wyvill, *Political Papers*, vol. 6, pp. 284–91.
169. For example, Alexander Geddes, who wrote for the *Analytical Review*. Geddes is currently the subject of research by Dr Gerard Carruthers of the University of Glasgow.
170. Brown, 'The Government of Scotland under Henry Dundas and William Pitt', esp. pp. 273–4.
171. R. Morison to Bell and Bradfute, Perth, 10 May 1794, NLS, Dep 317.
172. See, for example, notices of the Glasgow Circulating Library (*Glas. C.*, 15 June 1793).
173. Wodrow to Kenrick, 30 May 1792, W-KC, 24.157 (174).

3 'The True Spirit of Liberty'

1.   On the 'Anglo-British' identity of Scottish radicalism in this period, see Brims, 'The Scottish "Jacobins", Scottish Nationalism and the British Union'; Brims, 'The Covenanting Tradition and Scottish Radicalism'; Pentland, 'Patriotism, Universalism and the Scottish Conventions'.
2.   For comparison between the Scottish Claim of Right and the English Bill of Rights, see T. Harris, 'Reluctant Revolutionaries? The Scots and the Revolution of 1688–89', in H. Nenner (ed), *Politics and the Political Imagination in Late Stuart Britain: Essays Presented to Lois Green Schwoerer* (Rochester, NY: University of Rochester Press, 1997), pp. 97–117.
3.   For further comment on the small numbers of spies and informers used by the authorities, see Chapter 4, below, pp. 118–19.
4.   The phrase 'practical political imagination' is used by Günther Lottes in his essay 'Radicalism, Revolution and Political Culture: An Anglo-French Comparison', in Philp (ed.), *The French Revolution and British Popular Politics*, pp. 78–98, on p. 89.

5. J. Brims, 'From Reformers to "Jacobins": The Scottish Association of the Friends of the People', in Devine (ed.), *Conflict and Stability in Scottish Society*, pp. 31–50, on pp. 31–2. The Edinburgh Friends of the People were established at a meeting on 26 July, while the Perth Friends of the People were founded on 14 August. The first reform society to appear was the Glasgow Society for Effecting Constitutional and Parliamentary Reform, on 23 July. Apart from its establishment, however, nothing further is known of this society.

6. Notice of meeting of burgh reformers in Edinburgh, dated 27 July, in *Edin. E.*, 6 August 1792. See also Archibald Fletcher to Robert Graham of Gartmore, 17 June 1792, in which Fletcher describes Dundas's bill as a 'mere deception', NAS, Letters and Papers to Robert Graham of Gartmore, GD 22/1/315/55.

7. For the debates among the burgh reformers in July, see the notices placed in the *Edin. A.*, 3–7 August 1792.

8. The English total would be at least double if it included divisions of the London Corresponding Society.

9. *Edin. E.*, 29 November 1792.

10. William Pulteney to [William Pitt?], 16 November 1792, NA, PRO 30/8/169, fols 211–12.

11. Robert Watt to Robert Dundas, Edinburgh, 21 September 1792, NAS, RH 2/4/64, fols 318–19.

12. Harris, 'Scotland's Newspapers, the French Revolution and Domestic Radicalism'. See also Chapter 2, above.

13. B. D. Bonnyman, 'Agricultural Improvement in the Scottish Enlightenment: The Third Duke of Buccleuch, William Kier and the Buccleuch Estates, 1751–1812' (unpublished PhD thesis, University of Edinburgh, 2004), pp. 217–18. I am very grateful to Dr Bonnyman for giving me a copy of this thesis to read.

14. Harris, 'Political Protest in the Year of Liberty', pp. 62–8.

15. M. Ozouf, *Festivals and the French Revolution* (Cambridge, MA: Harvard University Press, 1988).

16. Anon. to Alexander Todd, 15 December 1792, NAS, RH 2/4/67, fol. 438; David Smyth to Henry Dundas, 24 November 1792, RH 2/4/65, fol. 86.

17. Brims, 'From Reformers to "Jacobins"', p. 37.

18. For the influence of the *Rights of Man* in England and Ireland, see D. Dickson, 'Paine and Ireland', in D. Dickson, D. Keogh and K. Whelan (eds), *The United Irishmen: Republicanism, Radicalism, and Rebellion* (Dublin: Lilliput Press, 1993), pp. 135–50; G. Claeys, *Thomas Paine: Social and Political Thought* (Boston, MA, and London: Unwin Hyman, 1989).

19. See advertisement placed by John Elder, Thomas Brown and J. J. Fairbairn in the *Edinburgh Evening Courant* for 19 April, which included Part 2 of the *Rights of Man* for 3s. 6d. Joel Barlow's *Advice to the Privileged Orders* was being sold at the same price. See also advertisement placed by Alexander Guthrie in same paper on 21 April.

20. *Edin. E.*, 7 May 1792.

21. *Edin. A.*, 25–9 March and 15–19 June 1792. Wollstonecraft's *Vindication* cost 6s., putting it well beyond the pockets of people below the prosperous middling ranks.

22. Macleod to Charles Grey, Edinburgh, 30 November 1792, in Hughes, 'The Scottish Reform Movement and Charles Grey', pp. 31–3.

23. Letter from Paine to the Society for Constitutional Information, 18 May 1792, Minute Book of the Society for Constitutional Information, NA, TS 11/962, fols 74v.–75r.

24. NA, TS 11/3495.

25. *Edin. A.*, 24–7 July 1792. Thomson was also responsible for the short-lived pro-reform weekly publication *The Political Review of Edinburgh Periodical Publications*, sold at 1½*d.*

26. See notices in *Edin. E.*, 30 August, 15 and 22 September 1792.

27. Wodrow to Kenrick, 9 October 1792, W-KC, 24.157 (176). In May, Wodrow had observed that Paine's 'books' were being imported from Ireland 'almost for nothing, & have had a wonderful spread' (24.157 (174), Wodrow to Kenrick, 30 May 1792). See also James [?] to Robert Dundas, Stonehaven, 29 November 1792, NAS, RH 2/4/65, fols 158–9, for the circulation of the 6*d.* edition of the *Rights of Man* in Stonehaven in the north-east.

28. *Edin. G.*, 23 November 1792. Other cheap radical works he was distributing included copies of Paine's *Common Sense* at 30*s.* per 100 copies; the *Letter from M Condorcet to a Magistrate of Switzerland – To Which is Added a Letter from Thomas Paine to the People of France* (3*d.* or 5*s.* per 100); and the *Dialogue Between the Governors and the Governed* (1*d.* or 6*s.* per 100). In September, Elder was also distributing free copies of *The Declaration of the Associated friends of the People at Edinburgh* (*Edin. E.*, 15 September 1792). See also declaration of John Elder, bookseller and stationer, North Bridge Street, 19 December 1792, NAS, JC 26/269, where Elder stated that he had imported 'many copies' of the *Rights of Man* from London, which he had sold in Edinburgh and around the country, as well as 'many copies' of a cheap edition printed in Edinburgh.

29. Sir William Maxwell to Robert Dundas, 19 November 1792, NAS, RH 2/4/65, fol. 55.

30. Meikle, *Scotland and the French Revolution*, p. 88.

31. See advertisement for this issue in *Edin. E.*, 21 July 1792.

32. Meikle says this periodical, founded to advocate reform in July 1791, was, from its tenth issue, published in two parts, one of which was much more extreme than the other. The more extreme version went under the full title the *Historical Register, or Universal Monthly Intelligencer* (Meikle, *Scotland and the French Revolution*, p. 88). The National Library of Scotland, however, has a copy of number 11 of the periodical (ABS. 4.87.9 (1–2)), with the original subtitle, which is clearly radical in its political sympathies. The copy is bound together with Paine's *Letter to the Right Honourable Mr Secretary Dundas*, which was given free with the periodical. The colophon indicates that the issue was printed for Cornelius Elliot and sold by H. D. Symonds, the London radical bookseller.

33. For Tytler in exile, see J. Quinn, *Soul on Fire: A Life of Thomas Russell* (Dublin: Irish Academic Press, 2002), pp. 126–7, 128, 226. Two years later Tytler left Ireland for the United States.

34. Allan Maconockie to Robert Dundas, Glasgow, 12 October 1792, NAS, RH 2/4/64, fols 369–70.

35. J. Brims, 'The Scottish Democratic Movement in the Age of the French Revolution' (unpublished PhD thesis, University of Edinburgh, 1983), pp. 180–1, 188, 191.

36. Paisley sent four delegates to the first convention, but seven to the second; Stirling sent six delegates to the first convention; and Kilmarnock two from seven societies.

37. See B. Harris, 'Popular Politics in Angus and Perthshire in the Seventeen-Nineties', *Historical Research*, 210 (2007), pp. 518–44, on p. 524.

38. Meikle, *Scotland and the French Revolution*, p. 241.

39. W. Murray to Robert Dundas, 15 April 1793, EUL, Laing Papers, II, 500, 295–6.

40. *The Statistical Account of Scotland, 1791–1799, vol. 11, South and East Perthshire, Kinross-Shire*, ed. J. Sinclair, new intro. B. Lenman (Wakefield: EP Publishing, 1976), p. 212.

41. Harris, 'Popular Politics in Angus and Perthshire', pp. 520–1.

42. Andrew Dundas to Henry Dundas, 13 May 1793, EUL, Laing Papers, II, 500, 355.

43. John Fyffe to Robert Graham, Commissioner of Excise, Dundee, 25 November 1792, NAS, RH 2/4/207, fol. 409.

44. David Smyth, Sheriff Depute, Perth, to Col. Allan Macpherson, 4 May 1793; Andrew McWhannel to Macpherson, 17 May 1793; Macpherson to David Smyth, 21 May 1793, Newton Castle, Blairgowrie, Macpherson of Clunie Papers, bundle 95.

45. William Murray of Ochtertyre to Robert Dundas, 20 November 1797, *Laing MSS*, vol. 2, p. 635. In the same letter, Murray also described Auchterarder and Dunning as 'democratick' nests.

46. See Chapter 5, below.

47. Sir John Wedderburn of Balindean to the Duke of Atholl, 4 September 1794, AP, 59 (1), 298.

48. For England, see Goodwin, *The Friends of Liberty*, ch. 5.

49. Howell, *State Trials*, vol. 23, pp. 139, 143–5.

50. Report on Perth Friends of the People, NAS, RH 2/4/64, fols 341–3, where the 'leading men' are identified as merchants, a surgeon, a dyer, a minister, a shoemaker and a writer (lawyer); G. Penny, *Traditions of Perth* (Perth: Dewar, 1836), p. 66.

51. See J. Drummond to David Blair, Edinburgh, 21 February 1786, NLS, MS 3288, where the author notes that George had succeeded his brother Andrew, and had married a Miss Kelly Stuart of Edinburgh, bringing her to Rosemount, which was described as 'very handsomely furnished'.

52. David Smyth to Henry Dundas, 18 December 1792, NAS, RH 2/4/67, fol. 442. Meliss was still actively supporting the 'cause of liberty' in October 1793, proposing to the third general convention of Scottish radicals, through Robert Sands, that members of the Friends of the People should donate 1*d.* a week to raise funds for the movement (Minute Book of the Third General Convention of the Scottish Friends of the People, NAS, JC 26/280, fol. 18).

53. NAS, Paterson of Castle Huntly Papers, GD 508/9/35/2.

54. NAS, RH 2/4/68, fols 96–9.

55. See George Dempster, Dunnichen, to William Pulteney, December 1792, NAS, RH 2/4/66, fols 202–3.

56. Robert Watt to Robert Dundas, 21 September 1792, NAS, RH 2/4/64, fols 318–19.

57. Harris, 'Popular Politics in Angus and Perthshire', p. 530.

58. NAS, RH 2/4/64, fols 369–70.

59. E. P. Dennison, D. Ditchburn and M. Lynch (eds), *Aberdeen Before 1800: A New History* (East Linton: Tuckwell Press, 2002), pp. 280–4. The debates surrounding police reform can be followed in the pages of the *Aberdeen Journal* for the first half of the 1790s.

60. Murdoch, 'The Importance of Being Edinburgh'.

61. See R. B. Sher, *Church and University in the Scottish Enlightenment: The Moderate Literati of Edinburgh* (Edinburgh: Edinburgh University Press, 1985). The powerful support which the capital's ministers provided the ruling elites in 1792–3 is partly described in the contemporary journal of Edinburgh burgess Andrew Armstrong (Edinburgh Central Library, Andrew Armstrong Journal, 1789–93, DA 1861.789).

62. See especially Whyte, 'Urbanization in Eighteenth Century Scotland', pp. 190–2; N. Phillipson, *The Scottish Whigs and the Reform of the Court of Session 1785–1830* (Edinburgh: Stair Society, 1990), pp. 34–6. Phillipson suggests that the capital's society was never more aristocratic in tone and substance than in the final third of the eighteenth century.

63. NAS, JC 26/280, unfoliated bundle.

64. Meikle, *Scotland and the French Revolution*, p. 270.

65. Taylor, East Linton, to William Skirving, 22 October 1793, NAS, JC 26/280, bundle 1, item 39. See also resolutions of the town council, merchants, university, clergy and principal gentlemen resident in St Andrews, NAS, RH 2/4/67, fols 508–9, which declared the signatories' intention not to employ 'any tradesman or other person whatever who discovers principles adverse to the spirit of our resolutions'.

66. J. Dickson, Dunfermline, to William Skirving, 31 October 1793, NAS, JC 26/280, bundle 1, item 59. For Culross, see T. McCleish to unknown, [late 1792 or 1793?], item 73.

67. Thomas McCliesh, Edinburgh, to George Mealmaker, [1797], NAS, JC 26/281.

68. Known Edinburgh societies are: the Original Association; Lawnmarket; Potterow; the Operative Society; Canongate, nos 1 and 1; Cowgate; New Town; New Town and Calton; Water of Leith; Portsburgh; Black Friars Wynd; and New Society.

69. Heron, *Observations Made in a Journey*, vol. 1, p. 148. The Methven anti-burgher minister John Wilson was a leading figure in Perth radical circles, as was assistant burgher minister Jedidiah Aikman. For Wilson's prominence, see Patrick Moir to William Scott, 19 January 1793, NAS, RH 2/4/68, fol. 231.

70. Sir Alex Douglas to Robert Graham of Fintry, 9 January 1795, EUL, Laing Papers, II, 500, 609.

71. For Alexander Christie's role in Montrose politics, see NLS, Correspondence of Alexander Christie, Provost of Montrose, MS 3701–3. For MacFarlane, see Susan Bean to Robert Graham of Fintry, 17 March 1793, NAS, Graham of Fintry Papers, GD 151/11/3. Another anti-burgher minister who was a delegate to the second general convention was James Robertson of Kilmarnock.

72. McIntosh, *Church and Theology*, p. 32.

73. James Playfair to William Creech, 17 April 1784, NAS, Dalguise Muniments, RH 4/26/1.

74. *History of the Town of Dundee, with the Present State of its Situation ... also the Religious Principles, Literature and Population of its Inhabitants* (Dundee, 1804), p. 127.

75. On Small, see Chapter 1 above, p. 26.

76. Petition to the magistrates anent Mr Sangster using seditious expressions, 1 March 1794, declaration of Alex Waterson [with respect to same], [1794?], PKCA, PE 51/25. See also James Peddie to William Pulteney, 26 December 1792, NAS, RH 2/4/67, fols 475–6, in which the author, defending the Burgher seceders, noted that the opinions of the members of their church varied, but that only one minister (unnamed) had given 'public countenance to reforming associations'.

77. The first Unitarian church in Scotland was founded in 1782 by William Christie, who dominated the St Cyrus Society of the Friends of the People. Other Unitarian churches existed in 1792 in Edinburgh, Arbroath, Montrose, Newburgh, Dundee and Glasgow, where in May 1792 Fyshe Palmer was evidently preaching (on which, see Wodrow to Kenrick, 30 May 1792, W-KC, 24.157 (174)).

78. Whatley, *Scottish Society*, pp. 169–70.

79. Heron, *Observations Made in a Journey*, vol. 1, p. 393.
80. *A General History of Stirling: Containing a Description of the Town, and Origin of the Castle and Burgh* (Stirling, 1794), pp. 165–7; *The Statistical Account of Scotland, 1791–1799, vol. 9, Dunbartonshire, Stirlingshire and Clackmannanshire*, ed. J. Sinclair, new intro. I. M. M. Macphail (Wakefield, EP Publishing, 1978), p. 630.
81. For Ulster, see especially McBride, *Scripture Politics*, pp. 195–201.
82. James Smithson, Selkirk, to William Skriving, 29 April 1793, NAS, JC 26/280, bundle 1, item 7. Smithson also referred to the dependency of local 'burghers' (i.e. townsfolk) and of farmers being under the influence of the nobility and gentry.
83. Taylor, East Linton, to William Skirving, 22 October 1793, NAS, JC/280, bundle 1, item 39, which noted that no society had been yet formed at East Linton, although it also declared that one would be established 'in due time before the Petition goes off to London'. Other places where radicals failed to form societies, probably for the same reason, included Bo'ness and Bathgate (Stephen Gibson, Linlithgow, to William Skirving, 28 October 1793, JC 26/280, bundle 1, item 52).
84. Mrs Hamilton to unknown, 16 July 1792, ECA, Correspondence of Andrew Haliburton, 1780–1793, unfoliated. For the East Linton meeting on 14 July, see notice in *Edin. A.*, 24–7 July 1792.
85. See Brims, 'The Scottish Democratic Movement', pp. 206–7. For an example of this pressure in operation, see Lord Ruthven, Melville House, to [Robert Dundas?], 29 December 1792, NAS, RH 2/4/67, fols 520–1.
86. J. H. Treble, 'The Standard of Living of the Working Class', in T. M. Devine and R. Mitchison (eds), *People and Society in Scotland: Volume 1, 1760–1830* (Edinburgh: John Donald with the Economic and Social History Society of Scotland, 1988), pp. 188–226.
87. See various notices about new, increased prices owing to higher wages paid to and shortages of journeymen placed by the 'incorporation of tailors and staymakers in Perth' (*Edin. E.*, 21 June 1792) and the 'master weavers of household cloth, within town and suburbs of Dundee' (ibid., 1 October 1792).
88. Heron, *Observations Made in a Journey*, vol. 1, pp. 111–12. Heron traced the source of this independence not just to high wages, but also to the fact that wages were paid weekly.
89. Fraser, *Conflict and Class*, esp. ch. 4.
90. On this, see Whatley, 'Roots of 1790s Radicalism'.
91. NAS, RH 2/4/209, fol. 32.
92. Brims, 'The Scottish Democratic Movement', p. 395.
93. James Waterson, Paisley, to William Skirving, 8 July 1793, NAS, JC 26/280, bundle 1, item 15.
94. For comment and reports on this, see, for example, Thomas Elder to Robert Dundas, 7 September 1793, NAS, RH 2/4/72, fol. 43; John Pringle to Robert Dundas, 8 September 1793, fol. 48–9; reports of 'J.B.', 4, 6 September 1793, fols 50v.–52, 52v.–55.
95. James Brown, Glasgow, to William Skirving, 24 October 1793, NAS, JC 26/280, bundle 1, item 45; John Russell, Glasgow, to William Skirving, 26 October 1793, item 50. It is significant, in this context, that the *Glasgow Courier*'s anti-radical correspondent 'Asmodeus' gave up his attacks on local 'democrats' in early October. These were collected together and published in pamphlet form as *Asmodeus, or Strictures on the Glasgow Democrats in a Series of Letters* towards the end of October.

96. James Waterson to William Skirving, 18 October 1793, NAS, JC 26/280, bundle 1, item 38.

97. William Christie to William Skirving, 24 October 1793, NAS, JC 26/280, bundle 1, item 43.

98. Andrew Mercer, Dunfermline, to William Skirving, 26 September 1793, NAS, JC 26/280, bundle 1, item 27.

99. Minute Book, NAS, JC 26/280, fol. 4. Two of the three names under the Perth delegate are scored out, suggesting that Robert Sands may have been the only one to actually attend.

100. The Friends of the Constitution to William Skirving, 25 October 1793, NAS, JC 26/280, bundle 2, item 16.

101. James Mitchell to [Robert Dundas?], 19 November 1793, NAS, RH 2/4/71, fol. 204v.

102. Thomas Watt, West Barns near Dunbar, to William Skirving, 26 October 1793, NAS, JC 26/280, bundle 1, item 449.

103. William Scott to Robert Dundas, 30 October 1793, NA, PRO 30/8/176, fols 67–8.

104. Brims, 'From Reformers to "Jacobins"', p. 43.

105. Ibid., p. 44.

106. See below, pp. 102–3.

107. Whatley, 'Roots of 1790s Radicalism', p. 25.

108. *Glas. C.*, 23 March, 30 April and 4 May1793.

109. Predictably, there were strong exchanges about the number and authenticity of signatories, and the circumstances under which their support had been gained. See, for example, *Glas. C.*, 13 and 16 July 1793. The Glasgow petition was presented to Parliament by the Earl of Lauderdale.

110. R. Saville, *Bank of Scotland: A History, 1695–1995* (Edinburgh: Edinburgh University Press, 1996), esp. pp. 198–201.

111. Gilbert Hamiton to Henry Dundas, 3 May 1792, EUL, Laing Papers, II, 500, 335–6.

112. Saville, *Bank of Scotland*, p. 201.

113. *Glas. C.*, 1 August and 23 November 1793.

114. John Dunlop, Glasgow, to [Henry Dundas?], 3 December 1793, NA, PRO 30/8/131, fols 94–6.

115. *Glas. C.*, 21 and 28 November 1793.

116. *Glas. C.*, 14 December 1793.

117. As suggested by 'A Journeyman Calico Printer', in *Glas. C.*, 28 November 1793. As an avowedly loyalist piece of propaganda, scepticism must be maintained regarding the extent of this practice, but the point was not refuted, at least in print.

118. John Dunlop to [Henry Dundas?], 3 December 1793, NA, PRO 30/8/131, fols 94–6.

119. W-KC, 24.157 (183). See also his letter of 12 November (24.157 (189)), where he notes the continuing pressure on the banks and credit and the lack of any upturn in the cotton industry.

120. See James Lapslie to Robert Dundas, 6 December 1793, NAS, RH 2/4/73, fols 268–73, where Lapslie writes: 'The weavers in my parish at this moment are more sober, industrious and better behaved people when making fourteen pence p day than twelve months ago when they made three shillings – Their wives and families share more of their wages, now the Publicans share less'.

121. Quoted in Brims, 'From Reformers to "Jacobins"', p. 40.

122. James Mitchell to Robert Graham of Fintry, 23 December 1793, NAS, GD 151/11/26.

123. For Sands, see Harris, 'Introduction', in Harris (ed.), *Scotland in the Age of the French Revolution*, p. 6.
124. Other occupations represented were tailor, baker, watchmaker, bookseller, schoolmaster, wright, mason, nurseryman, reed-maker, town drummer, cotton spinner, leather merchant, cheesemonger, apprentice writer, printer, type-founder, goldsmith, lapidary, hatter, stocking-maker, cooper, hairdresser, leather-cutter, cow feeder, cork-cutter, grocer, ale-seller, rectifier of spirits, tobacconist, ham seller and fishmonger.
125. This is a key theme of the work of John Brims; see especially 'From Reformers to "Jacobins"'.
126. Philp, 'The Fragmented Ideology of Reform', esp. pp. 74–5.
127. Harris, 'Scottish-English Connections in British Radicalism', p. 193.
128. For the Whig Association, see E. A. Smith, *Lord Grey 1764–1845* (Oxford: Clarendon Press, 1990), ch. 2.
129. N. Macleod, *Two Letters from Norman M'Leod, Esq MP to the Chairman of the Friends of the People at Edinburgh* (1793). The Edinburgh edition was printed for and sold by Alexander Scott from the office of the *Edinburgh Gazetteer*. A London edition, entitled *Letters to the People of North Britain ... By Norman McLeod, Member of the Scotch Convention, and MP*, was published by James Ridgway, and sold at 1*d*. or 7*s*. per 100 copies. For other letters, see intelligence respecting the societies in Edinburgh, NAS, RH 2/4/209, fols 31–2. On 30 November 1792, Macleod spoke to a convention of Edinburgh radicals.
130. Macleod to William Skirving, 11 May 1793, NAS, JC 26/280, bundle 1, item 8.
131. Minute Book, NAS, JC 26/280, fol. 19.
132. He withdrew, for example, his franking privilege as an MP from the *Edinburgh Gazetteer* shortly after the suppression of the British convention (*Edin. G.*, 10 December 1793).
133. L. Stewart, 'Putting on Airs: Science, Medicine and Polity in the Late Eighteenth Century', in T. Levere and G. L'e Turner (eds), *Discussing Chemistry and Steam: The Minutes of a Coffee House Philosophical Society 1780–1787* (Oxford: Oxford University Press, 2002), pp. 236–7.
134. Hughes, 'The Scottish Reform Movement and Charles Grey', pp. 33–7.
135. NAS, RH 2/4/209, fol. 33.
136. Hughes, 'The Scottish Reform Movement and Charles Grey', pp. 29–30.
137. James Duncan, Jr, to the Earl of Buchan, 23 November 1792, EUL, Gen 1736, 27.
138. See, inter alia, J. R. Dinwiddy, 'Conceptions of Revolution in the English Radicalism of the 1790s', in Hellmuth (ed.), *the Transformation of Political Culture*, pp. 535–60.
139. Philp, 'The Fragmented Ideology of Reform', p. 56.
140. Brims, 'From Reformers to "Jacobins"', p. 38.
141. Appendix A, 'Minutes of the Proceedings of the First General Convention of the Delegates from the Societies of the Friends of the People Throughout Scotland ...', in Meikle, *Scotland and the French Revolution*, pp. 239–73.
142. See especially the discussion of this in J. Brims, 'Scottish Radicalism and the United Irishmen', in Dickson, Keogh and Whelan (eds), *The United Irishmen*, pp. 151–66, on pp. 156–9; McFarland, *Ireland and Scotland in the Age of the French Revolution*, pp. 79–88; Meikle, *Scotland and the French Revolution*, pp. 107–9.
143. Ibid., pp. 239–73.
144. Ibid., pp. 239–73. Fyshe Palmer, who was a regular attender at the general committee of the Edinburgh Friends of the People, seems to have been a consistent advocate of a more forward posture by the Friends of the People, for which see the report by J.B. on

the general committee meeting of the Society of the Friends of the People, January 1793, NAS RH 2/4/68, fols 250–4.

145. Quoted in Brims, 'From Reformers to "Jacobins"', pp. 36–7. See also copies of letters from William Peddie to Robert Purves, 21 and 30 November 1792, NAS, RH 2/4/68, fols 70–4.

146. NAS, RH 2/4/64, fols 341–3.

147. John Dunlop to Robert Dundas, Glasgow, 27 October 1793, NAS, RH 2/4/72, fols 84–5.

148. Meikle, *Scotland and the French Revolution*, p. 239.

149. Ibid., p. 272.

150. Ibid., p. 272.

151. Ibid., p. 270; J. Barrell, *Imagining the King's Death: Figurative Treason, Fantasies of Regicide, 1793–1796* (Oxford: Oxford University Press, 2000), p. 147.

152. Howell, *State Trials*, vol. 23, pp. 197–8.

153. Meikle, *Scotland and the French Revolution*, pp. 251, 258.

154. See above, pp. 79–80.

155. Minute Book of the Society for Constitutional Information, NA, TS 11/962, fol. 94r.

156. Ibid., fol. 92. See also fol. 82r.

157. Ibid., fol. 128v.

158. Ibid., fol. 139. The society's resolution arising from the letter and the account of the proceedings it furnished were also to be 'published in the newspapers'.

159. Hardy to Daer, 14 July 1792, BL, Add. MS 27,817, fol. 15.

160. Harris, 'Scottish-English Connections in British Radicalism', pp. 197–9.

161. Copy of a private letter from Hardy to Daer, 8 September 1792, BL, Add. MSS 27,814, fol. 184.

162. M. Thale (ed.), *Selections from the Papers of the London Corresponding Society, 1792–1799* (Cambridge: Cambridge University Press, 1983), pp. 31, 35, 44, 54.

163. See advertisement placed by Guthrie in *Edin. E.*, 30 April 1792.

164. *The Second Report from the Committee of Secrecy of the House of Commons*, copy of a letter from the editors of the *Patriot* to the secretary of the London Corresponding Society, Sheffield, 15 October 1792, in M. T. Davis (ed.), *The London Corresponding Society, 1792–1799*, 6 vols (London: Pickering & Chatto, 2002), vol. 6, pp. 69–70.

165. Harris, 'Scottish-English Connections in British Radicalism', p. 200.

166. Meikle, *Scotland and the French Revolution*, p. 255.

167. Johnston to Hardy, 31 October 1792, NA, TS 11/965/3510A.

168. Notice of meeting of a convention of delegates in and around Edinburgh, 21 November, in *Edin. G.*, 23 November 1792.

169. Meikle, *Scotland and the French Revolution*, pp. 267–8.

170. Howell, *State Trials*, vol. 23, pp. 7–25.

171. Report on Edinburgh radicals by J.B., 19 June 1793, NAS, RH 2/4/70, fols 257–9.

172. Minute Book, NAS, JC 26/280, fols 25, 84.

173. Johnston to Skirving, 6 November 1793, in Howell, *State Trials*, vol. 23, p. 71.

174. Robert to Henry Dundas, 28 October 1793, NAS, RH 2/4/72, fols 86–8.

175. John Elder to Robert Dundas, 7 September 1793, NAS, RH 2/4/72, fol. 43. On 6 September Elder gave an order that people were only to be admitted to see Muir once during the day, and that no more than two at a time should do so. Four additional watchmen were also put at the disposal of the jailers.

176. Minute Book, NAS, JC 26/280, fols 6–7, 11.

177. List of persons who have called on Palmer since his confinement with the date of each call, Perth, 14 September to November 1793, NAS, RH 2/4/73, fols 228–30.

178. Barrell, *Imagining the King's Death*, p. 148.

179. Minute Book, NAS, JC 26/280, fol. 51.

180. Barrell, *Imagining the King's Death*, p. 151.

181. The Society for Constitutional Information also elected Henry Redhead Yorke as a delegate, but he did not travel to Edinburgh. During the convention, Brown was adopted as delegate by the Leeds Constitutional Society and Margarot by the United Societies at Norwich.

182. For the idea of the emergency convention, elaborated by Sinclair, see Barrell, *Imagining the King's Death*, pp. 154–5.

183. Minute Book, NAS, JC 26/280, fol. 50.

184. Letter to William Skirving, Dundee, 14 November 1793, NAS, JV 26/280/2, item 31.

185. Brims, 'From Reformers to "Jacobins"', pp. 43–4.

186. Minute Book, NAS, JC 26/280, fols 19–21, 24.

187. NAS, JC 26/280, bundle 5, item 8.

188. NAS, JC 26/280, bundle 2, item 18.

189. See especially resolutions of the Edinburgh general committee, 5 September 1793, NAS, JC 26/280, unfoliated bundle.

190. NAS, JC 26/280, bundle 2, item 16.

191. Calder, Cromarty, to Skirving, 4 September 1793, NAS, JC 26/280, bundle 1, item 22.

192. 'Hints on the Question of Union Suggested by Class No. 3', NAS, JC 26/280, loose papers.

193. The best recent discussion of this plot is to be found in Barrell, *Imagining the King's Death*, ch. 9.

194. James Paton, Sheriff Clerk of Perthshire, to Lord Methven, 9 January 1794, NAS, RH 2/4/74, fols 62–3.

195. Declaration of William Wedderspoon and David Buist relative to some persons writing on the bridge, 24 April 1794, PKCA, B59/32/109.

196. Susan Bean to Robert Graham of Fintry, 3 and 29 March, 2 June 1794, NAS, GD 151/11/3.

197. Wodrow to Kenrick, 31 March 1794, W-KC, 24.157 (189).

198. Undated, but part of a letter of 21 August 1794, as endorsed on the back, W-KC, 24.157 (193).

199. On 1 November, at the third convention, James Mitchell of Paisley presented a motion, which was adopted, for petitioning the King against the war. Mitchell 'drew a lively picture of the poor in support of the motion' (Minute Book, NAS, JC 26/280, fol. 31). See also NAS, RH 2/4/73, fol. 184v.

200. *Glas. C.*, 10 December 1793.

201. 'Accompt of Allan Maconochie Esq, Advocate & Sheriff Depute of Renfrewshire to Robert Walkinshaw, Sheriff Clerk, 1794', NAS, Sheriff Court Papers, SC 58/22/72. This document is marked 'sedition'.

202. Harris, 'Introduction', in Harris (ed.), *Scotland in the Age of the French Revolution*, p. 7.

203. Harris, 'Scottish-English Connections in British Radicalism', pp. 202–3.

204. Thale (ed.), *Selections from the Papers of the London Corresponding Society*, p. 177. This individual may well have been James Kennedy, who fled Edinburgh to London following his arrest after the exposure of the so-called Watt or Pike Plot.

205. James Mitchell to Robert Graham of Fintry, Dundee, 23 December 1793, NAS, GD 151/11/26.

206. J.B. to William Scott, 9 February 1794, NLS, Melville Papers, MS 6, fols 147–8.

207. Petition of James Miller, procurator fiscal to the magistrates of Perth, 19 April 1794, PKCA, BE 51/25.

208. 'The present internal state of the County of East Lothian, 28 May 1794', NLS, MS 7099, fols 2–4. Concern about the King's birthday as the possible date for a radical attack on the authorities was voiced elsewhere, for which, see Archibald Campbell to Robert Dundas, 25 May 1794, NAS, RH 2/4/76, fol. 52.

209. Barrell, *Imagining the King's Death*, pp. 254–5, 259.

210. Report by J.B., 21 March 1794, NLS, Melville Papers, MS 351, fol. 15, refers to provincial conventions in Glasgow, Perth and Fife to elect delegates.

211. James Mitchell to Robert Graham of Fintry, 23 December 1793, NAS, GD 151/11/26.

212. Second declaration of Walter Miller, 28 April 1794, PKCA, PE 51/25.

213. Meikle, *Scotland and the French Revolution*, pp. 145, 147; printed proclamation by Provost Thomas Elder and Sheriff James Clerk, 14 April 1794, NAS, Craighall of Rattray Papers, GD 385/23/3; Robert Dundas to James Clerk, 19 April 1794, GD 385/23/4; memorial for Donald Maclean, writer in Edinburgh, NLS, Material relating to Edinburgh Theatre Riot, 1794, MS 1567, esp. fols 8–18. This memorial was an answer to a charge of assault and claim for damages amounting to £500 by a student of medicine at the university, one Joseph Mason, a carpenter from Wiltshire.

214. Declaration of George Mealmaker, 18 June 1794, NAS, RH 2/4/76, fols 129–33; declaration of John Sinclair, 11 June 1794, fols 123–7.

215. See above, note 4. See also Dickinson, 'Popular Loyalism in Britain', esp. p. 503.

216. Meikle, *Scotland and the French Revolution*, pp. 268–9.

217. Resolutions of the Edinburgh general committee, 5 September 1793, NAS, RH 2/4/72, fols 63–4; JC 26/280, unfoliated bundle.

218. Minute Book, NAS, JC 26/280, fol. 23.

219. Meikle, *Scotland and the French Revolution*, p. 261.

220. Ibid., pp. 256–7.

221. Ibid.

222. On the issue of indebtedness, see Skirving to the Laurieston Society, 16 October 1793, NAS, JC 26/280, bundle 1, item 36.

223. Minute Book, NAS, JC 26/280, fols 14–15. Masters were to pay 1s. per half year, and servants in employment 6d. Similar sums were to be paid on entry by new members. The first collection was to have been one month after the end of the convention. Societies were also to open up public subscriptions to receive donations.

224. Minute Book, NAS, JC 26/280, fols 32, 60; RH 2/4/73, fol. 185v.

225. 'Plan of the Internal Government of the Society of the Friends of the Constitution and of the People [Glasgow]', NAS, RH 2/4/64, fols 371–2.

226. James Waterson, Paisley, to William Skirving, 8 July 1793, NAS, JC 26/280, bundle 1, item 15; resolutions of Fife societies met on 15 October 1793, bundle 2, item 16; printed letter from the convention of Edinburgh delegates proposing a general convention, 21 November 1792, bundle 1, item 7.

227. See NAS, RH 2/4/209, fols 3–23.

228. See Chapter 2, above.

229. Meikle, *Scotland and the French Revolution*, p. 266.

230. See Chapter 2, above, p. 64; *Edin. G.*, 26 November, 3 and 10 December 1793.

231. NAS, JC 26/280, bundle 1, item 16.

232. Minute Book, NAS, JC 26/280, fol. 33; RH 2/4/73, fol. 185r; JC 26/280, bundle 1, item 29.

233. See Chapter 2, above, p. 66.

234. Printed letter from Skirving to societies, 21 May 1793, NAS, JC 26/280, bundle 1, item 28.

235. 24 October 1793, NAS, JC 26/280, bundle 1, item 45.

236. NAS, JC 26/280, bundle 5, item 2.

237. Minute Book, NAS, JC 26/280, fols 10–11, 12, 17, 20.

238. Minute Book, NAS, JC 26/280, fols 4, 10–11.

239. Davis (ed.), *The London Corresponding Society*, vol. 3, pp. 125–6.

240. In the Scottish context, see Harris, 'Print and Politics', p. 171. For examples of written handbills, see Susan Bean to Robert Graham of Fintry, 19 December 1792, 19 April 1793, NAS, GD 151/11/3.

241. Reports on meetings of the Friends of the People in Edinburgh, NAS RH 2/4/70, fols 35–43. See also fol. 82 for Johnston's refusal also to print Palmer's anti-war resolutions in the *Edinburgh Gazetteer*.

242. This debate has produced a very extensive literature, but see, inter alia, J. Smyth, *The Men of No Property: Irish Radicals and Popular Politics in the Late Eighteenth Century* (Basingstoke: Macmillan, 1992); Curtin, *The United Irishmen*.

243. NA, TS 11/962, fols 126v.–127r.

244. Minute Book, NAS, JC 26/280, fols 24–6.

245. NAS, JC 26/280, unfoliated bundle.

246. Brims, 'The Scottish Democratic Movement', p. 55.

247. Minute Book, NAS, JC 26/280, fol. 7; proposal of John Mitchell of Strathaven to have law of patronage included in list of grievances, JC 24/280/5, item 40; similar proposal by Alex. Bremner, item 18.

248. Minute Book, NAS, JC 26/280, fol. 32.

249. Smyth, *The Men of No Property*, p. 89.

250. Report by J.B., 21 June 1793, NAS, RH 2/4/71, fols 275–8.

251. McBride, *Scripture Politics*, p. 200.

252. Wodrow to Kenrick, 22 January 1794, W-KC, 24.157 (187i).

253. James Peddie to William Pulteney, 26 December 1792, NAS, RH 2/4/67, fols 475–6.

254. *Glas. C.*, 9 September 1794.

4 Checking the Radical Spirit

1. See Harris, 'Political Protests in the Year of Liberty', p. 58. This was despite considerable rewards, respectively 100 and 50 guineas, from the Town Council and Merchants' Company for discovery of the ringleaders and instigators (*Edin. E.*, 9 June 1792).

2. John Pringle to Henry Dundas, 5 July 1792, NAS, Melville Papers, GD 51/5/6.

3. Between 1 May and the end of August, 76 addresses from Scotland were published in the government journal of record, the *London Gazette*. The majority of these came from local authorities (burgh authorities or counties) or presbyteries.

4. See Chapter 3, above, pp. 79–80.

5. These letters are to be found at NAS, RH 2/4/64 & 65. The phrase 'emissaries of sedition' was used by Sir William Maxwell of Springkell (RH 2/4/65, fol. 54).

6.   Allan Maconockie to Robert Dundas, 12 October 1792, NAS, RH 2/4/64, fols 369–70.
7.   George Home to Patrick Home, 25 November and 3 December 1792, NAS, Home of Wedderburn Papers, GD 267/1/16.
8.   Harris, 'Political Protests in the Year of Liberty', p. 65; *Glas. C.*, 13 November 1792, extract of a letter from Perth, 12 November; *Edin. G.*, 16 November 1792, extract of a letter from Perth, to the editors of the *Gazetteer*, 6 November.
9.   J. Mori, *William Pitt and the French Revolution, 1785–1795* (Edinburgh: Keele University Press, 1997), p. 127.
10. Report on Commons debate on King's speech to Parliament, *Edin. A.*, 14–18 December 1792. Thomas Erskine also sought to ridicule the notion of a Scottish insurrection at a meeting of the Friends to the Liberty of the Press in December, for a report on which, see *Edin. G.*, 28 December 1792.
11. Dundas to Pitt, 12 November 1792, NA, 30/8/157, part 1, fols 132–41.
12. Only Aberdeen was not a centre of radical strength; it was presumably included because of the sailors' strike of the autumn of 1792. There was also a minor radical protest in the city in early December (George Auldjo, Provost of Aberdeen, to Lord Adam Gordon, 5 December 1792, NAS, RH 2/4/66, fol. 66).
13. Dundas to Pitt, 22 November 1792, NA, 30/8/157, part 1, fols 142–9.
14. J. Ehrman, *The Younger Pitt: The Reluctant Transition* (London: Constable, 1983), p. 195. Ehrman says this new policy reflected experience at Birmingham during the 'Church and King' riots there in the previous year.
15. Barrell, *Imagining the King's Death*.
16. Fsyhe Palmer was, of course, English by birth.
17. See Barrell, *Imagining the King's Death*, ch. 6.
18. John Bruce on practice of Parliament in modifying the Bill of Rights, 1794, NLS, Melville Papers, MS 642, 103, fols 40–53. Bruce later carried out research for Portland and Dundas on the effects of the Union on Scotland, later used by Dundas as the basis of his famous parliamentary speech on Anglo-Irish union.
19. Richard Ford, Whitehall, to Robert Dundas, 27 June 1794, EUL, Laing Papers, II, 500, 578.
20. See, inter alia, Lord Cockburn, *An Examination of the Trials for Sedition which have hitherto occurred in Scotland*, 2 vols (1888; New York: A. M. Kelley, 1970); Christina Bewley, *Muir of* Huntershill (Oxford, 1981); Meikle, *Scotland and the French Revolution*, pp. 128–36, 144; B. D. Osborne, *Braxfield: The Hanging Judge?: The Life and Times of Justice-Clerk Robert McQueen of Braxfield* (Glandaurel: Argyll, 1997); Brims, 'The Scottish Democratic Movement', pp. 428–31, 444, 448; A. L. Wold, 'The Scottish Government and the French Threat, 1792–1802' (unpublished PhD thesis, University of Edinburgh, 2003), ch. 3.
21. See, for example, L. Colley, *Britons: Forging the Nation 1707–1837* (New Haven, CT, and London: Yale University Press, 1992), ch. 7.
22. Accompt of money imprest in the hands of John Pringle, Esquire, His Majesty's Sheriff Depute of the County of Edinburgh, on Account of secret services, 15 June 1793, EUL, Laing Papers, II, 500, 404–5; memorandum for Mr Dundas from Lord Advocate, April 1794, 566; secret service funds, September 1793–January 1794, 569.
23. See my entry on Watt in the *ODNB*. At Watt's trial for treason in 1794, Robert Dundas testified that, following enquiries into his character, his services had been used, and he had come to Dundas's house in George Square under cover of darkness on several occa-

sions with information. In March 1793, however, he had written a letter asking for a payment of £1,000 supposedly for two persons who had crucial intelligence to divulge. Pitt and Henry Dundas had been shown this letter, but had decided not to come forward with the money. Instead, he was paid £30, which Watt said he was already obliged to pay to his prospective informants, and had not been heard of again after July of that year.

24. Robert Dundas to Robert Graham of Fintry, December 1792, NAS, Graham of Fintry Papers, GD 151/11/12; John Fyffe, 'Intrepid', Plymouth Sound, to Robert Dundas, 31 December 1794, EUL, Laing Papers, II, 500, 532; John Fyffe, 'Powerful', Spithead, 30 August 1797, 1358.

25. James Mitchell to Robert Graham of Fintry, 23 December 1793, NAS, Graham of Fintry Papers, GD 151/11/26.

26. NAS, GD 151/11/3. Bean appears to have supported ministerial interest from the 1780s. On 29 March 1794, Bean admitted: 'I have no meeting of that class of people in my house as they know too well that I do not favour their party but I hear it from some that has access to their private entertainments'. Bean was paid £30 from secret service accounts at end of 1793 (Robert Dundas to Robert Graham of Fintry, where Dundas notes that, 'We can afford £30 to the Old Wife ...', NAS, Graham of Fintry Papers, GD 151/11/12) The 'Old Wife' was almost certainly Susan Bean.

27. For Jamieson, see Meikle, *Scotland and the French Revolution*, p. 186. The authorities did, however, have an informant in Perth in 1797, for which, see Chapter 5, below, p. 158.

28. See NAS, RH 2/4/65, fols 48–53.

29. Robert Dundas to Henry Dundas, 9 December 1792, NAS, RH 2/4/66, fols 254–8, in which Robert writes that he has 'procured a considerable number of the Caledonian Chronicle and the whole of the Gazetteer'. He also remarks that the remaining issues of the former will be sent by post the next day.

30. Charles Long to Robert Dundas, 21 October and 10 November 1792, NAS, Arniston Papers, RH 4/15/5, fols 74–5. For the earlier eighteenth century, see M. Harris, *London Newspapers in the Age of Walpole: A Study in the Origins of the Modern English Press* (London and Toronto: Associated University Presses, 1987), pp. 136–7.

31. NAS, RH 2/4/64, fol. 333.

32. Henry Dundas, Melville Castle, to William Pitt, 22 November 1792, NA, 30/8/157, part 1, fols 142–9; Robert Dundas to Henry Dundas, 9 December 1792, RH 2/4/66, fols 254–8. Mennons was arrested and bailed in December. Smith failing to turn up for the trial in early February, the prosecutor chose not to proceed against Mennons alone, and the sitting was adjourned.

33. Scott, *Reasons Justifying the Departure*.

34. Robert Dundas to the Duke of Atholl, 21 April 1798, AP, 59 (5) 65. Dundas informed Atholl that he was going to try to prepare something for the current parliamentary session and to this end was consulting with the Lord Chancellor and his colleagues in the Court of Session. Another radical who fled on bail rather than facing his chances in court was the Edinburgh bookseller Alexander Leslie.

35. See above, note 20.

36. C. Bewley, *Muir of Huntershill* (Oxford: Oxford University Press, 1981), pp. 67, 70. Muir did not challenge the relevancy of the indictment either.

37. Muir's closing speech to the jury lasted three hours. Margarot delivered a similar speech lasting even longer (four hours), which was mocked in the loyal press both for its tediousness and its inflammatory content (see, for example, *Edin. H.*, 15 January 1794). For a wider discussion of the court's role as a political platform, see M. T. Davis, "'The Impartial

Voice of Future Times Will Rejudge Your Verdict": Discourse and Drama in the Trials of the Scottish Political Martyrs of the 1790s', in J. Paisana (ed.), *Hélio Osvaldo Alves: O Guardador de Rios* (Braga: Centro de Estudos Humanísticos, 2005), pp. 65–78. One might ask, however, given the outcome of other political trials in this period, whether any approach would have yielded different results.

38. See Meikle, *Scotland and the French Revolution*, p. 132, n. 3. The jurors in Muir's trial were all members of the Edinburgh loyalist group the Goldsmiths' Hall Association.

39. *Glas. C.*, 31 January 1793.The speech was widely reported in the Scottish press.

40. Memorandum to Mr Dundas about Muir's trial, NLS, Melville Papers, MS 3011, fols 49–51.

41. Quoted in Wold, 'The Scottish Government and the French Threat', p. 97.

42. *Aberdeen Weekly Journal*, 17 March 1794.

43. Phillipson, *The Scottish Whigs*, esp. p. 79, n. 49.

44. No statutory legislation had been passed in Scotland for the crime of sedition, as opposed to the crime denoted as 'leasing-making'; nor were there relevant precedents from case law.

45. Meikle, *Scotland and the French Revolution*, pp. 150–1; Fry, *The Dundas Despotism*, p. 171.

46. See, for example, *Aberdeen Weekly Journal*, 24 March 1794.

47. For Muir's representation to the opposition Whigs in London, see NAS, RH 2/4/209, fol. 32.

48. Hughes, 'The Scottish Reform Movement and Charles Grey', pp. 37–8.

49. Davis, '"The Impartial Voice of Future Times Will Rejudge Your Verdict"', p. 74.

50. NAS, RH 2/4/73, fols 282–4.

51. Fyshe Palmer was also in touch with the Society for Constitutional Information.

52. The chair was taken by the Lord President, Ilay Campbell.

53. See Chapter 3, above, p. 89.

54. NAS, RH 2/4/72, fols 43, 48–9.

55. Robert Small, Dundee, to William Adam, 8 April 1794, cited in Vincent Macleod, 'The Scottish Opposition Whigs and the French Revolution', p. 99, n. 56.

56. This phrase was used by George Lawson, Burgher Professor of Divinity and minister of Selkirk. Quoted in Brims, 'The Convenanting Tradition and Scottish Radicalism', p. 53.

57. John to Robert Richardson, 28 March 1794, PKCA, Richardson of Pitfour Papers, MS 101, bundle 8.

58. See Robert to Henry Dundas, 6 December 1793, NAS, RH 2/4/73, fols 250–3.

59. See Harris, 'Print and Politics', p. 181.

60. See the report of the event widely published in the press (*Aberdeen Weekly Journal*, 21 October 1794).

61. NAS, RH 2/4/209, fol. 44.

62. Capt. Maclean, Perth, to unknown, 16 December 1792, NA, 30/8/154/2. Alexander Riddoch, Provost of Dundee, was opposed to calling in the troops to the town during the political disturbances of November 1792, but was apparently overruled by the authorities in Edinburgh (Robert Dundas to Robert Graham of Fintry, 21 November 1792, NAS, GD 151/11/12).

63. In 1794, for example, Beith unsuccessfully sought a bill of suspension from the Court of Session against the billeting of soldiers on private inhabitants. There were several cases involving Edinburgh and its suburbs, for which see, inter alia, petition for James Sandison and others anent the billeting of soldiers, 1795, ECA, Mcleod Collection, D, 143,

item 5; petition for the commissioners of Crosscausway and the ballies of Canongate anent quartering of soldiers, 1796, D, 120, item 43.

64. NAS, RH 2/4/209, fols 42–3; RH 2/4/64, fols 250–1; RH 2/4/72, fols 84–5, 92; RH 2/4/73, fol. 262. See also James Andrew to Thomas Dundas, Linlithgow, 18 November 1794, North Riding Record Office, Northallerton, Zetland Papers, ZNK X 2/1/1242, for a similar call in relation to Linlithgow and converting Linlithgow Palace into barracks.

65. Duke of Atholl to Robert Graham of Fintry, 26 January 1793, NAS, GD 151/11/8; George Paterson, Castle Huntly, to Robert Dundas, 21 January 1793, NLS, MS 14,838, fols 88–91; Robert Dundas to Henry Dundas, 23 January 1793, fol. 92.

66. See below, pp. 139–40.

67. English figures are those cited by Dickinson in his 'Popular Loyalism in Britain', p. 519.

68. *Edin. H.*, 2 January 1793; Chief Magistrate, Cupar, to Robert Dundas, 3 January 1793, NAS, RH 2/4/68, fols, 63–4.

69. Dickinson, 'Popular Loyalism in Britain', pp. 529–30; N. Rogers, *Crowds, Culture and Politics in Georgian Britain* (Oxford: Clarendon Press, 1998), ch. 6.

70. Brims, 'The Scottish Democratic Movement', p. 352.

71. For this tendency, see Phillipson, *The Scottish Whigs*, p. 34.

72. NA, 30/8/157, fols 174–81. Dundas also talked of having several writers in government pay.

73. John Freeling to unknown, 28 December 1792, BL, Add. MS 16,920, fols 144–7.

74. Charles Long to Robert Dundas, 21 October and 10 November 1792, NAS, Arniston Papers, RH 4/15/5, fols 74–5.

75. James Sibbald to [Robert Dundas?], 10 February 1792, EUL, Laing Papers, II, 500, 178–9; Henry Mackenzie to Robert Dundas, 14 April 1792, 182–3.

76. M. Duffy, 'William Pitt and the Origins of the Loyal Association Movement', *Historical Journal*, 39 (1986), pp. 943–62. For earlier contributions to this discussion, see Ehrman, *The Younger Pitt*, pp. 229–33; A. Mitchell, 'The Association Movement of 1792', *Historical Journal*, 4 (1961), pp. 56–77; D. E. Ginter, 'The Loyalist Association Movement of 1792–3 and British Public Opinion', *Historical Journal*, 9 (1966), pp. 179–90; Dickinson, 'Popular Loyalism in Britain', p. 517, n. 30.

77. Dundas to Pitt, 30 November 1792, NA, 30/8/157, fols 174–81. A revised declaration, in which Pitt and Grenville had a heavy role, was published in the London press on 26 November. Both sets of resolutions were widely reprinted in the Scottish press.

78. Henry Mackenzie to George Chalmers, [1793], NLS, MS 786, fols 73–4.

79. Dundas to Pitt, 30 November 1792, NA, 30/8/157, part 1, fols 174–81; Dundas to Pitt, 22 November 1792, 30/8/157, part 1, fols 142–9.

80. For Wauchope's role, see especially NAS, GD 158/2625, fols 72, 73, 82.

81. NAS, RH 2/4/66, fols 313–14.

82. See the entry on Pulteney in *ODNB*.

83. For Campbell's political views, see Harris, 'Popular Politics in Angus and Perthshire', p. 534.

84. For some preliminary comment on this, which emphasizes Mackenzie's role in erasing the radical Burns from public view, see Noble, 'Displaced Persons', pp. 198–200.

85. For links to Pitt, see Mackenzie to Pitt, 13 May 1792, 23 and 25 December 1793, NA, Chatham Papers, 30/8/ 154/2. For the link to Chalmers, see Henry Mackenzie to George Chalmers, [1793?], NLS, MS 786, fols 73–4.

86. *Edin. G.*, 5 March 1793.

87. Admission made in a letter to George Chalmers, written in 1793 (NLS, MS 786, fols 73–4).
88. Mackenzie to Pitt, Edinburgh, 13 February 1788, NA, 30/8/157, fols 215–16.
89. See Robert Heron to Robert Dundas, 22 February 1798, EUL, Laing Papers, II, 500, 1820–2; note from David Hume, Archibald Campbell and John Wauchope regarding William Brown's efforts to 'repress the Democratic Doctrines circulated in 1793', 16 March 1798, 1889.
90. See above, note 3.
91. *Glas. C.*, 29 December 1792.
92. Dickinson, 'Popular Loyalism in Britain', p. 520, citing BL, Add. MSS 16924, fols 128–9.
93. *Edin. A.*, 18–21 December 1792.
94. *Edin. A.*, 15–19 February and 1–5 March 1793. The Dundee Club resolutions were signed by several local gentry, ministers, officials and wealthy merchants such as John Jobson, James Small, and former Provost Alexander Pitcairn and his two sons.
95. The resolutions included many of the wealthiest merchants. Leading local opposition Whigs who signed the resolutions included Dr Robert Stewart, Revd Robert Small and Dr John Willison. All three were expelled from the Dundee Club for being 'democrates'.
96. *Glas. C.*, 22 January 1793; *Edin. H.*, 7 January 1793.
97. John Dunlop to Henry Dundas, Glasgow, 11 December 1792, NAS, GD 51/5/6, fol. 7. This letter makes it clear that the Glasgow resolutions had followed a meeting between Dundas and Dunlop at Melville Castle. See also *Glas. C.*, 11 December 1792, where it was reported that while several members of the Trades House had supported a reform amendment, this had been dropped so as not to 'clog' the resolutions. See also *Edin. E.*, 15 December 1792.
98. *Glas. C.*, 20 December 1793; Gilbert Hamilton to Robert Dundas, 15 December 1792, NAS, RH 2/4/66, fol. 327.
99. For these links, see Harris, 'Parliamentary Legislation, Lobbying, and the Press', pp. 89–90; D. J. Hamilton, *Scotland, the Caribbean and the Atlantic World, 1750–1820* (Manchester: Manchester University Press, 2005).
100. In 1789, for example, the Glasgow Town Council voted thanks of the town to Pitt for his stance during the Regency crisis (John Dunlop to William Pitt, 1 February 1789, NA, 30/8/13/76). The letter also refers to a conversation between Pitt and Dunlop in July in which Pitt invited Dunlop to communicate directly with him rather than via a secretary.
101. For Colquhoun's efforts to avert meetings of the LCS in Shoreditch in 1795, see NA, 30//8/124, part 2, fols 199–200.
102. *Edin. G.*, 5 February 1793.
103. Kenneth Mackenzie to [Robert Dundas?], 3 January 1793, NAS, RH 2/4/68, fol. 60.
104. Anonymous report on the Perth Friends of the People, [late 1792], NAS, RH 2/4/64, fols 341–3.
105. *Edin. A.*, 28 December–1 January 1793. Such steps appear to have quite common; the Renfrew county address, for example, was lodged in the principal town or village in each parish for signing.
106. Anonymous memorandum on Scottish radicalism, [late 1792], NAS, RH 2/4/209, fols 3-23. See also Sir David Carnegie, Kinnaird, to Robert Graham of Fintry, 8 February

1793, NAS, GD 151/11/5, where Carnegie writes: 'many country people were shy of signing our Declaration on the idea that they would be carried off for soldiers & sailors'.

107. David Johnson of Lathrisk to Robert Dundas, 16 December 1792, EUL, Laing Papers, II, 500, 217–18.

108. NAS, JC 26/280, bundle 1, item 7.

109. *Edin. A.*, 1–4 January 1793.

110. NAS, RH 2/4/209, fols 2–23; *Edin. A.*, 18–21 December 1792.

111. *Glas. C.*, 25 December 1792.

112. See above, note 95.

113. Meikle, *Scotland and the French Revolution*, p. 109.

114. *Glas. C.*, 15 December 1792.

115. George Paterson to Robert Dundas, 21 January 1793, NLS, Melville Papers, MS 14,838, fols 88–91.

116. *Ten Minutes Reflection on the Late Events in France, Recommended by a Plain Man to his Fellow Citizens* (Edinburgh, 1792), pp. 13–54 (at NLS, R 251 f).

117. Harris, 'Print and Politics', p. 179.

118. See Charles Long to Robert Dundas, 21 October 1792, NAS, Arniston Papers, RH 4/15/5, fol. 74, where Long writes: 'Could you without any trouble send me a few copies of the Letters of Publicola they are the best written of any thing I have yet seen – I want to get them publish'd in our Newspapers'.

119. Harris, 'Print and Politics', p. 108.

120. *Edin. H.*, 14 January 1793.

121. Henry Mackenzie to William Pitt, 23 December 1793, NA, 30/8/154/2.

122. NLS, MS 786, fols 73–4.

123. Mackenzie to Pitt, 23 December 1793, NA, 30/8/154/2. Extracts of Young's *The Example of France* appeared in *Edin. H.*, 13 and 22 March 1793.

124. John Wauchope to the Earl of Marchmont, 11 December 1793, NAS, GD 158/2625, fol. 82, where Wauchope writes: 'It was thought publishing the Names and Designations of the motely [*sic*] group, would have satisfied them of their insignificance. But as it had not that effect it became necessary for the Civil Power to interfere. An Investigation as to their proceedings is at present making which I hope will lead to the Punishment that the Promoters of that business merit' (*Edin. H.*, 2, 7 December 1793).

125. *Edin. H.*, 6 March 1793.

126. *Glas. C.*, 1, 8, 11, 13 and 20 December 1792.

127. Gilbert Hamilton to Robert Dundas, 15 December 1792, NAS, RH 2/4/66, fol. 327. See also John Orr to Robert Dundas, Glasgow, 29 July 1793, NAS, RH 2/4/71, fol. 366, where he notes that £40 has been spent by the Lord Provost on 'constitutional publications'.

128. Harris, 'Scotland's Newspapers, the French Revolution and Domestic Radicalism', pp. 61–2.

129. *Edin. H.*, 15 February and 6 March 1793.

130. Harris, 'Print and Politics', pp. 184–5.

131. Claud Boswell to John Moore, 6 January 1793, BL, Add. MS 16,924, fols 43–4.

132. John Wauchope to Robert Graham of Fintry, 13 February 1793, NAS, GD 151/11/39.

133. Andrew McWhannel to Col. Allan Macpherson, Blairgowrie, 17 May 1793, Newton Castle, Macpherson of Clunie Papers.

134. Document marked 'Thanks to the Committee of the Edinburgh Constitutional Association', 1794, ECA, Convention of Royal Burghs, Moses Collection, SL 30/244.

135. George Paterson to Robert Dundas, 11 March 1793, EUL, Laing Papers, II, 500, 248–9.
136. *Edin. H.*, 14 January 1793.
137. Archibald Neilson to Robert Graham of Fintry, 31 January 1793, NAS, GD 151/11/30; David Johnson of Lathrisk to Robert Dundas, 16 December 1792, EUL, Laing Papers, II, 500, 217–18.
138. Archibald Neilson to Robert Graham of Fintry, Dundee, 11 January 1793, NAS, GD 151/11/30.
139. *The Correspondence of James Boswell with James Bruce and Andrew Gibb, Overseers of the Auchinleck Estate*, ed. N. P. Hankins and J. Strawhorn (Edinburgh: Edinburgh University Press, 1998), pp. 169–71.
140. John Fyffe to Robert Graham of Fintry, 26 November 1792, NAS, GD 151/11/15.
141. George Dempster to Robert Graham of Fintry, 7 March 1793, NAS, GD 151/11/8; Mackenzie to Pitt, 23 December 1793, NA, 30/8/154/2.
142. On this theme, see especially Mackenzie to Pitt, 23 December 1793, NA, 30/8/154/2; Wodrow to Kenrick, 7 March 1793, W-KC, 24.157 (179).
143. *Edin. G.*, 4 January 1793.
144. Quoted in Brims, 'The Scottish Democratic Movement', p. 358.
145. On Young, see Chapter 1, above, p. 31.
146. *Edin. H.*, 15 March 1793.
147. Harris, 'Print and Politics', p. 183.
148. B. Harris and C. A. Whatley, '"To Solemnize his Majesty's Birthday": New Perspectives on Loyalism in George II's Britain', *History*, 83 (1998), pp. 397–419. Queen Charlotte's birthday (16 January) was also widely signalized by celebrations. See, for example, *Edin. A.*, 18–22 January 1793 for celebrations on that day at Crail, Fife. See also *Aberdeen Weekly Journal*, 27 January 1794, for similar celebrations in the following year at Banff and Fochabers in the north-east. Edinburgh City Council issued proclamations for illuminating windows on 14 June 1794, for Howe's victory over the French fleet on 1 June; on 13 April 1795, for the marriage of the Prince of Wales and the capture and destruction of the French navy in the Mediterranean; on 5 October 1798, for Nelson's victory at the Battle of the Nile; and again in 1798 for Admiral Duncan's victory at Camperdown (miscellaneous proclamations, 1791–1860, ECA, Mcleod Collection, D, 138, item 152).
149. See especially C. A. Whatley, 'Royal Day, People's Day: The Monarch's Birthday in Scotland, c.1660–1860', in R. Mason and N. MacDougall (eds), *People and Power in Scotland: Essays in Honour of T. C. Smout* (Edinburgh: John Donald, 1992), pp. 170–88; C. A. Whatley, '"The Privilege which the Rabble have to be Riotous": Carnivalesque and the Monarch's Birthday in Scotland', in I. Blanchard (ed.), *Labour and Leisure in Historical Perspective: Papers Presented at the 11th International Economic History Congress, Milan 1994* (Stuttgart: Franz Steiner Verlag, 1994), pp. 89–100.
150. See, for example, Proclamation against Rioters on 4 June 1795, ECA, Mcleod Collection, D, 138, item 152, miscellaneous proclamations, 1791–1860; motion (accepted) for economy in public entertainments, 18 April 1798, D, 147, item 23.
151. *Edin. H.*, 9 June 1794; ECA, SL1/1/122, Edinburgh Town Council Minutes, September 1793–May 1794, entry for 31 May 1794.
152. Copy of part of letter from Sheriff Depute of Perthshire, 4 June 1794, NLS, Lynedoch Papers, MS 3595, fol. 230.
153. William Scott to Robert Dundas, 20 January 1794, EUL, Laing Papers, II, 500, 540.

154. K. J. Logue, *Popular Disturbances in Scotland 1780–1815* (Edinburgh: John Donald, 1979), pp. 143–4. For the incident in Dundee, see W. Duncan, *The True Briton: Containing Poems, Curious, Moral and Political; (chiefly in the Scots Language)* (Dundee, 1796), pp. 49–63.

155. Henry Dundas to the Lord Advocate of Scotland, 28 March 1794, NAS, Craighall of Rattray Papers, GD 385/20, item 1; circular entitled 'Whitehall' which included provisions of the 'Plan of an augmentation', no. 23; Henry Dundas, Whitehall, to the Duke of Atholl, 14 May 1794, AP, 59 (1), 182, explaining the object of appointing lords lieutenant for counties in Scotland. The last letter made it clear that the internal defence plan was aimed against any who might 'cooperate' with a foreign power in the event of an invasion or otherwise disturb the public peace. The main burden of defence against the foreign enemy was to be assumed by the new fencible regiments raised from 1793.

156. Cookson, *The British Armed Nation*, pp. 24–7.

157. NAS, Buccleuch Papers, GD 224/676/1/1.

158. Provost James Ramsay, Perth, to the Duke of Atholl, 14 November 1794, AP, 59 (1), 365.

159. *Aberdeen Weekly Journal.* 16 September 1794.

160. Aberdeen's town council agreed to allow the freedom of the city to all volunteers recommended and received into the Battery company forming in the city (*Aberdeen Weekly Journal*, 30 September 1794).

161. *Edin. H.*, 7 and 14 June, 7 July 1794. For a similar offer made by the farmers of Kirkliston and Abercorn, and also refused, see NAS, GD 224/676/12, fol. 17.

162. Sir David Carnegie to Robert Graham of Fintry, 24 May 1794, NAS, GD 151/11/5; *Edin. H.*, 2 August 1794.

163. *Edin. H.*, 17 May 1794. Johnston of Alva's motion in favour of a militia was defeated by 32 votes to 23. A further amendment that extraordinary measures were not warranted was defeated by 29 votes to 14.

164. Most counties agreed to raise companies of volunteer cavalry usually funded by a subscription on landowners. Rosshire, Aberdeenshire, and Banff agreed to raise troops of infantry. Several counties, including Wigtonshire and Kirkudbright, had offers of raising cavalry companies rejected. Kinkardine established a standing committee for internal defence and agreed to arm, if necessary, but took no further steps at this stage.

165. Figure cited in NAS, GD 224/676/1/4.

166. Letter Book of the Royal Aberdeen Volunteers, 1795–1802, fols 7–8, NLS, MS 9363.

167. James Ramsay to the Duke of Atholl, 18 November 1794, AP, 59 (1) 370.

168. Meikle, *Scotland and the French Revolution*, p. 154, n. 2.

169. NAS, GD 224/676/1/1.

170. NAS, GD 224/676/1/4.

171. Angus Archives, Montrose Town Council Minutes 1771–1794, M1/1/9, entries for 13 August and 17 September 1794; Montrose Town Council Minutes 1794–1817, M1/1/10, entry for 27 September 1795.

172. See, for example, Gee, *The British Volunteer Movement*; Eastwood, 'Patriotism and the English State', pp. 157–61.

173. Copies of declaration and resolutions of the Stirling volunteers, NAS, GD 224/676/1/3. For a similar declaration subscribed to by the Angus volunteer cavalry, see *Edin. H.*, 2 August 1794.

174. Offer dated 23 September 1795, PKCA, PE 66, bundle 6.

175. Archibald Campbell of Clathick, Edinburgh, to the Duke of Atholl, 18 November 1794, AP, 59 (1) 371.
176. Meikle, *Scotland and the French Revolution*, p. 154.
177. Private instructions to the deputy lieutenants relative to the extraordinary officers of the peace in Perthshire; private instructions to the deputy lieutenants relative to the ordinary constables in Perthshire, Newton Castle, Macpherson of Clunie Papers, bundle 93. See also Archibald Campbell of Clathick to the Duke of Atholl, 25 June 1794, AP, 59 (1), 240.
178. Ibid.
179. George Drummond of Blair Drummond to the Duke of Atholl, 10 July 1794, AP, 59 (1), 255.
180. George Haldane of Gleneagles to the Duke of Atholl, 18 July 1794, AP, 59 (1), 259.
181. Newton Castle, Macpherson of Clunie Papers, bundle 93; Andrew Macpherson, Blair-gowrie, to the Duke of Atholl, 10 November 1794, AP, 50 (1) 361.
182. See, for example, Sir John Wedderburn of Balindean to the Duke of Atholl, 4 September 1794, AP, 59 (1), 298, reporting on response in parishes of Inchture, Kinnaird, Abernyte and Errol.
183. 'The present internal state of the county of East Lothian, 28 May 1794', NLS, MS 7099, fols 2–4.
184. Report from a deputy lieutenant for West Lothian, 1794, North Riding Record Office, Northallerton, Zetland Papers, ZNK X 2/1/1258.
185. NLS, MS 7099, fols 2–4.
186. Drummond of Blair Drummond to the Duke of Atholl, 4 December 1794, AP, 59 (1) 387.
187. Alexander Murray, Ayton House, to the Duke of Atholl, 2 December 1794, AP, 59 (1) 384.
188. John Ramsay, Ochtertyre, to Lt Col. Murray, 22 November 1794, AP, 59 (1) 375.
189. Wedderburn to the Duke of Atholl, 22 August 1794, AP, 59 (1), 283. See also Wedderburn to the Duke of Atholl, 4 September 1794, 59 (1), 298; George Paterson, Castle Huntly, to the Duke of Atholl, 5 and 9 September 1794, 59 (1), 299, 59 (1), 301.
190. Sir William Ramsay, Bamff House, by Coupar Angus, to the Duke of Atholl, 21 September 1794, AP, 59 (1), 311; Stirling of Garden to the Duke of Atholl, 8 October 1794, 59 (1), 329.
191. See Chapter 1 above, p. 30.
192. James Morison to Mr Alexander Hutton, Dunkeld, 30 July 1794, Dundee University Museum and Archive Services, Glassite Papers, MS9/4/2, fol. 16.
193. Stewart of Ardvorlich to the Duke of Atholl, 30 October 1794, AP, 59 (1), 351; Campbell to the Duke of Atholl, 24 October 1794, 59 (1), 342.
194. Notice in *Edin. H.*, 27 December 1794; plan for preserving the public peace within the county of Midlothian, North Yorkshire County Record Office, ZNKX 2/1/1259.
195. List of persons enrolled as peace officers, 1794, PKCA, B59/24/11/27.
196. Wauchope to the Earl of Marchmont, 28 January 1793, NAS, GD 158/2625. fol. 73.
197. See William Murray, Inverness, to Robert Dundas, 15 April 1793, EUL, Laing Papers, II, 500, 295–6, in which the author speaks of 'too many of my brother country gentlemen [being] in a silly conceited state of security ...'.
198. See Gee, *The British Volunteer Movement*, esp. chs 2, 7.
199. Duncan, *The True Briton*, preface.

200. See, for example, 'Warning by the Presbytery of Glasgow to the People under their Charge', in *Glas. C.*, 9 February 1793; 'Pastoral Admonition by the Synod of Glasgow and Ayr, 9 April', in *Glas. C.*, 12 April 1794. Several presbyteries also issued resolutions at the end of 1793 expressing their repugnance for the French National Convention and British convention of radicals which had met in Edinburgh (*Glas. C.*, 31 December 1793).
201. See, for example, *Edin. H.*, 22 March 1794.
202. See, for example, reports of loyal sermons on fast days in *Edin. H.*, 1 March 1794.
203. *Edin. A.*, 4–5 June and 8–12 November 1793, 6–10 June 1794.
204. *Admonition and Information Respecting the Profanation of the Lord's Day* (1794).
205. L. Leneman, *Sin in the City: Sexuality and Social Control in Urban Scotland 1660–1780* (Edinburgh: Scottish Cultural Press, 1998), introduction.
206. See Chapter 1, above, esp. pp. 14–25.

5 Volunteers, the Militia and the United Scotsmen, 1797–8

1. For the very different contemporary views, see Susan Clerk to Miss Adam, Edinburgh, 12 September 1797, NAS, GD 5486/18/47; Mr Taylor to William Forbes of Callendar, Edinburgh, 30 August 1797, Falkirk District Archives, Falkirk, Forbes of Callendar Papers, GD 171/616.
2. See the Duke of Hamilton and Brandon to the Duke of Portland, 30 August 1797, *Laing MSS*, vol. 2, pp. 616–17; the Duke of Hamilton to Robert Dundas, 2 September 1797, ibid., vol. 2, pp. 620–1; Robert Dundas to the Duke of Atholl, 1 September 1797, AP, 59 (4), 384.
3. *Edin. A.*, 30 December–3 January and 3–6, 6–10 and 10–13 January 1797; *Dumfries Weekly Journal*, 24 January 1797. The Royal Edinburgh Volunteers made their offer on 2 January. This was quickly followed by similar offers by the Royal Glasgow Volunteers, the Leith Volunteers, the Royal Perth Volunteers, the Dundee Volunteers, the Royal Aberdeen Volunteers and the Royal Dumfries Volunteers.
4. Several volunteer companies also offered from the end of January to serve anywhere in Great Britain in the event of an invasion. The first such offer seems to have come from the Moidart and Culloden Company of Volunteers in Invernesshire (*Edin. A.*, 24–7 January 1797).
5. The address appeared in *Edin. A.*, 10–13 January 1797; *Herald and Chronicle*, 14 January 1797; *Edin. E.*, 12 January 1797.
6. Sir John Wedderburn to the Duke of Atholl, 20 January 1797, AP, 59 (4), 10. See also George Paterson, Castle Huntly, to the Duke of Atholl, 3 February 1797, 59 (4), 23.
7. *Edin. A.*, 27–31 January 1797.
8. *Edin. A.*, 3–6 January 1797; *Herald and Chronicle*, 7 January 1797; *Edin. E.*, 5 January 1797.
9. Return of strength of the 1st regiment of the Royal Glasgow Volunteers, 4 September 1798, NRAS 2177, Papers of the Dukes of Hamilton and Brandon, bundle 2156.
10. *Herald and Chronicle*, 21 January 1797.
11. *Herald and Chronicle*, 23 January 1797.
12. *Edin. A.*, 24–7 January 1797.
13. The resolutions were widely printed in the press. See, for example, *Edin. A.*, 17–21 February 1797; *Dumfries Weekly Journal*, 21 February 1797.

14. The Renfrewshire county meeting took place on 3 March; Fife, 7 March; Aberdeenshire, 10 March; Elgin and Forres, 13 March; Kinkardine, 14 March; Banff, 15 March; Wigton, 22 March; Roxburghshire, 29 March; Perthshire, 30 March; Invernesshire, 7 April; and Dumfriesshire and Stewartry of Kirkudbright, 11 April.

15. See notice in *Dumfries Weekly Journal*, 28 March 1797.

16. *Edin. E.*, 25 March 1797.

17. For Maxwell, see *Herald and Chronicle*, 23 March 1797.

18. As hinted at in Hope Steuart, George Square, Edinburgh, to the Duke of Atholl, 13 February 1797, AP, 59 (4), 39. One Robert Dundas of Blair Castle, Culross, reported to the Duke of Atholl that he was willing to grant rent relief to tenants who came forward to enrol as volunteers (Dundas to Atholl, 25 February 1797, 59 (4), 63).

19. The Duke of Atholl to Henry Dundas, 2 February 1797, AP, 59 (4), 18.

20. The Duke of Atholl to the Duke of Portland, 20 February 1797, AP, 59 (4), 44. See also the Duke of Atholl to the Duke of Portland, 27 February 1797, 59 (4), 67.

21. Mungo Murray of Lintrose to the Duke of Atholl, 28 February 1797, AP, 59 (4), 71.

22. Minutes of a meeting of members of the Atholl Club, at Moulinearn, 21 February 1797, AP, 59 (4), 51.

23. Meeting referred to in William McDonald, Edinburgh, to the Duke of Atholl, 24 February 1797, AP, 59 (4), 61. See also Archibald Campbell of Clathick to the Duke of Atholl, 59 (4), 73, endorsed as March, but more likely to have been written in February since meeting was in that month.

24. George Paterson, Castle Huntly, to the Duke of Atholl, 21 February 1797, AP, 59 (4), 48. See also George Paterson to the Duke of Atholl, 7 April 1797, 59 (4), 137.

25. The Duke of Portland to the Duke of Atholl, 17 April 1797, AP, 59 (4), 173.

26. *Herald and Chronicle*, 28 January 1797.

27. *Herald and Chronicle*, 25 February 1797.

28. AP, 59 (4), 24. For a similar offer from the postmasters of Aberdeen, see *Aberdeen Weekly Journal*, 28 February 1797.

29. *Edin. E.*, 25 March 1797.

30. *Dumfries Weekly Journal*, 4 April 1797.

31. See, for example, *Aberdeen Weekly Journal*, 28 March 1797 for such an offer from the fishermen of Buckie.

32. *Edin. A.*, 28 February–3 March 1797.

33. James Stedman, Whinfield, to unknown, 7 March 1797, NAS, Kinross House Papers, GD 29/2113/1.

34. Letter dated 18 February 1797, NLS, Letter Book of the Royal Aberdeen Volunteers, 1795–1802, fols 9–10, MS 9363.

35. Ilay Campbell to [Robert Dundas?], 14 January 1797, NAS, RH 2/4/80, fol. 3.

36. The Earl of Eglinton to Henry Dundas, Eglinton Castle, 28 February 1797, NAS, Melville Papers, GD 51/1/881.

37. Ibid. See also the Earl of Eglinton to Robert Dundas, 12 March 1797, EUL, Laing Papers, II, 500, 1162.

38. The Earl of Eglinton to Henry Dundas, 11 January 1798, NAS, RH 2/4/83, fol. 93; see also, for similar comments, same to same, 26 January 1798, NAS, GD 51/1/899.

39. Patrick Crichton to the Duke of Buccleuch, 21, 23, 24 and 28 February 1797, NAS, Buccleuch Papers, GD 224/676/2.

40. See NAS, GD 224/676/1, fol. 15, for a draft of the handbill. The Certificate of the Condition of Service in the 2nd battalion of the 2nd regiment of the Royal Edinburgh

Volunteers also contained the following declaration: 'As the Officers of this Battalion are all of them Gentlemen settled in Edinburgh, and engaged in Professions, and who have no purpose of becoming Soldiers, but only to lend their assistance for the Defence of their Native Country against Invasion; you may be assured, that the above Conditions will be inviolably observed; and that you can, on no Pretence whatsoever, be called on for any Service other than what is above specified' (ECA, McLeod Collection, D, 21, item 21).

41. David [Burns?] to the Duke of Buccleuch, Musselburgh, 7 March 1797, NAS, GD 224/676/2.
42. 12 April 1797, AP, 59 (4), 151.
43. 21 April 1797, AP, 59 (4), 163.
44. *Scots C.*, 24–8 February 1797.
45. *Scots C.*, 3–7 March 1797.
46. See, for example, *Scots C.*, 24–8 February 1797. See also below, p. 178.
47. NAS, GD 224/676/1/26.
48. This was not true of all – for example, companies formed in burghs which had not seen a company formed in 1794–5. For a list of the Dalkeith Company of Volunteers, formed in 1797, see NAS, GD 224/376/16D, E. Yeomanry cavalry companies formed in this period typically comprised better-off tenant farmers and members of the gentry.
49. James McDowall to the Duke of Hamilton, 1 March 1797, NRAS 2177, bundle 2154; officers of the 2nd battalion of the 2nd regiment of the Royal Edinburgh Volunteers to the Duke of Buccleuch, 10 February 1798, NAS, GD 224/674/4/D, where they note that the battalion is 'made up of the lower and working classes of the people'.
50. 'A private of the Royal Edinburgh Volunteers' to the Duke of Buccleuch, Edinburgh, 20 February 1797, NAS, GD 224/676/2.
51. Muster roll of the Edinburgh Royal Highland Volunteers, 24 December 1799, ECA, McLeod Collection, bundle 328.
52. James Brodie, Lieutenant, Nairnshire Volunteers, to Henry Dundas, 30 January 1798, NAS, RH 2/4/83, fol. 67.
53. A 'loyal subject' to Henry Dundas, February 1798, NAS, GD 51/1/902.
54. 31 March 1797, AP, 59 (4), 128. Another who wished to see 'a very strong declaration by way of Test' to weed out 'democrats' was Paterson of Castle Huntly (12 April 1797, 59 (4), 151).
55. James McDowall to the Duke of Hamilton, 29 March 1797, NRAS 2177, bundle 2154. See also same to same, 1 March 1797, bundle 2156.
56. The Duke of Buccleuch, Dalkeith House, to Henry Dundas, 25 March 1797, NAS, GD 51/1/882.
57. The Earl of Eglinton to Henry Dundas, 11 January 1798, NAS, RH 2/4/83, fol. 93. A few months later, a party of Girvin volunteers, escorting Irishmen taken on the coast to Ayr, was fired upon. Eglinton reported that it was suspected that 'some of the Irish in the volunteer corps at Ayr' were responsible (GD 51/5/264/36).
58. NAS, GD 224/676/16C.
59. In Perth, for example, the 1st and 2nd battalions of the Royal Perth Volunteers took turns on alternate days in guarding the prison and the town during the height of the anti-militia disturbances owing to the dispatch of regular soldiers to other places to quell protests (James Paton to the Duke of Atholl, Perth, 31 August 1797, AP, 59 (4), 375). On 5 September, the 1st regiment of the Royal Edinburgh Volunteers announced its readiness to march to any part of Midlothian to aid the magistrates in the 'suppression

of all Riots, Tumults, and disorders which might happen and in enforcing obedience to lawful authority' (NAS, GD 224/676/6). See also below, p. 168.

60. See especially the copy of memorial and representation for 116 Royal Paisley Volunteers to the Duke of Portland, submitted 26 November 1799, ECA, McLeod Collection, C, 366.

61. See, for example, minutes of meeting of tenants, tradesmen and other inhabitants of the parish of Newbattle, held at Newbattle, 2 March 1797, NAS, GD 224/676/1/20.

62. See, for example, James Stewart of Dowally, Perth, to the Duke of Atholl, 21 March 1797, AP, 59 (4), 111; George Paterson, Castle Huntly, to the Duke of Atholl, 16 March 1797, 59 (4), 100. See also the notice issued by the Duke of Gordon, the Lord Lieutenant of Aberdeenshire (*Aberdeen Weekly Journal*, 30 March 1797).

63. J. R. Western, 'The Formation of the Scottish Militia in 1797', *Scottish Historical Review*, 34 (1955), pp. 1–18.

64. William Stewart of Ardvorlich to the Duke of Atholl, 8 May 1797, AP, 59 (4), 187.

65. The Duke of Montrose to Henry Dundas, 2 February 1797, NAS, GD 51/1/878. In light of this refusal, Montrose had felt compelled, owing to the cost and trouble already undergone by the new volunteers to learn their exercise, to increase the size of the existing Stirling volunteer companies from 50 to 70.

66. *Edin. A.*, 9–12, 12–16 and 16–19 May 1797.

67. *Edin. A.*, 9–12 May 1797.

68. The Duke of Atholl to the Duke of Portland, 11 April 1797, AP, 59 (4), 147. For a similar warning, see Andrew Wauchope to the Duke of Buccleuch, Niddrie, 16 April 1797, NAS, GD 224/676/1.

69. For comment on the lack of success in penetrating radical designs, see Robert Dundas to John King, 2 August 1797, NAS, RH 2/4/80, fol. 140; William Scot to [Henry Dundas?], 16 August 1798, fol. 148. The examination of suspects in detention revealed similarly little, for which see John Orr to Robert Dundas, 9 May 1798, RH 2/4/84, fol. 216.

70. The Earl of Eglinton to Robert Dundas, 12 March 1797, EUL, Laing Papers, II, 500, 1162.

71. The Earl of Eglinton to Robert Dundas, 10 May 1797, NAS, GD 51/5/29. Scrutiny of alleged oath-taking in the west extended to Greenock (David Hutcheson to the sheriff of Renfrewshire, Greenock, 25 June 1797, 114–15).

72. Robert Dundas to the Duke of Portland, 6 and 9 May 1797, NAS, RH 2/4/84, fol. 212, 2/4/80, fols 67–8. The watch at Portpatrick was resumed in June (Robert Dundas to the Duke of Portland, 24 June 1797, fols 108–9; Robert Dundas to Charles Greville, 7 July 1797, fol. 122).

73. For doubts about Jamieson's utility as an informer, see especially Robert Dundas to John King, 11 August 1798, NAS, RH 2/4/84, fol. 214; Robert Dundas to the Duke of Portland, 22 November 1797, RH 2/4/82, fol. 244.

74. William Scot to Robert Dundas, 22 July 1797, NAS, GD 51/5/30; excerpt of letter to Scot, 19 July 1797, 30/2. Scot received another report from Perth on 13 August (fols 150–2) of a meeting which took place on the anniversary of the fall of the monarchy in France (10 August). There was no mention of 'uniting' at this meeting.

75. John Caw, Jr, to the Duke of Atholl, Perth, 1 September 1797, AP, 59 (4), 383.

76. A. Warrender to Robert Dundas, 7 October 1797, EUL, Laing Papers, II, 500, 1569–70.

77. See especially the descriptions of radicalism in Perth and Dundee contained in, respectively, letters from Robert Sands and George Mealmaker to the London Corresponding Society from the autumn of 1795 (Davis (ed.), *The London Corresponding Society*, vol. 2, pp. 132–3; Thale (ed.), *Selections from the Papers of the London Corresponding Society*, pp. 308, 333). In 1796, a group of radicals met in Kilmarnock on the anniversary of the acquittal of Thomas Hardy. The press report of this meeting noted that a 'good many' from the 'country' had attended the meeting, which had involved the customary toasts and songs (*Scots C.*, 11 November 1796, extract of a letter from Kilmarnock, 8 November 1796).

78. See especially R. Wells, *Insurrection: The British Experience 1795–1803* (Gloucester: Sutton, 1983), *passim*.

79. McFarland, *Ireland and Scotland in the Age of Revolution*, esp. chs 5–7; E. W. McFarland, 'Scottish Radicalism in the Later Eighteenth Century: 'The Social Thistle and Shamrock'', in Devine and Young (eds), *Eighteenth-Century Scotland*, pp. 275–97.

80. McFarland, *Ireland and Scotland in the Age of Revolution*, p. 158.

81. See *Resolutions and Constitution of the Society of United Scotsmen* (n.d.). A copy can be found at AP, 59 (4), 383a.

82. McFarland, *Ireland and Scotland in the Age of Revolution*, p. 139. For further mention of Irish delegates, see declaration of William Reid, 22 April 1798, NAS, Craighall of Rattray Papers, GD 385, bundle 39, fol. 6; Robert Carmichael, Portpatrick, to Robert Dundas, 12 June 1798, NAS, RH 2/4/84, fols 336–7; Colonel James Durham to Robert Dundas, 14 September 1797, *Laing MSS*, vol. 2, pp. 628–9.

83. William Scot to Henry Dundas, 22 July 1797, NAS, GD 51//5/30.

84. Howell, *State Trials*, vol. 26, p. 1154.

85. Examination of James Jarvie, cotton spinner at Thornliebank, 13 April 1798, NAS, RH 2/4/84, fols 210–11.

86. Quoted in Wells, *Insurrection*, p. 72.

87. William Murray to Robert Dundas, 20 November 1797, *Laing MSS*, vol. 2, p. 635.

88. Thomas Kennedy to Robert Dundas, 13 May 1798, EUL, Laing Papers, II, 500, 1959.

89. See Robert Carmichael to the Duke of Portland, Portpatrick, 12 June 1797, NAS, RH 2/4/84, fols 336–7; Robert Dundas to the Duke of Portland, 15 and 24 June 1797, fols 347–8, 366–7. For continued official concern about the influx of the Irish, see the Earl of Eglinton to Henry Dundas, 5 April 1799, NAS, GD 51/5/44.

90. See especially McFarland, *Ireland and Scotland in the Age of Revolution*, p. 160, where McFarland writes: 'The impression is that radical developments also possessed a greater *internal* momentum than elsewhere on the British mainland'.

91. For Cameron, see below, pp. 173–4. For Grey, see NAS, JC 26/294.

92. McFarland, *Ireland and Scotland in the Age of Revolution*, p. 161.

93. State of the investigation anent the Societies of United Scotsmen in Cupar &c, NAS, GD 20/7/222.

94. For the Falkland meeting, see report in *Scots C.*, 25 August 1797. For the Freuchie meeting, see Claud Boswell, Sheriff of Fife, to [Robert Dundas?], 8 September 1797, NAS, RH 2/4/81, fols 97–9.

95. Harris, 'Scottish-English Connections in British Radicalism', p. 204.

96. This scrutiny extended to interception of mail or items he was dispatching to London from Scotland. For which, see Robert Dundas to John King, 26 June and 14 July 1797, NAS, RH 2/4/80, fols 116–17, 130; James McDowall to [the Duke of Portland?], 13 July 1797, fol. 132.

97. BL, Francis Place Papers, Add. MS 27,815, fols 74–5.

98. Thomas McCliesh to George Mealmaker, Edinburgh, 20 July 1797, NAS, JC 26/281.

99. BL, Add. MS 27,815, fols 74–5; Thale (ed.), *Selections from the Papers of the London Corresponding Society*, pp. 370, 381.

100. Petition of Alexander Leslie to the Lord Justic Clerk and Lords Commissioners of Justiciary for Scotland, 2 April 1798, Minute Book of the High Court of Justiciary, 30 October 1797–25 July 1799, entry for 28 May 1798, NAS, JC 26/293. Leslie had been called previously on 14 and 21 May. He was admitted to bail on 2 April.

101. These can be found at NAS, JC 26/293.

102. *Scots C.*, 18 March 1796.

103. As revealed in 'Excerpts of sales taken from the day book of Alexander Leslie', NAS, JC 26/293.

104. For Galloway, see Chapter 1, above, p. 6.

105. Andrew Scott, print-cutter, Avon printfield near Perth, to Alexander Leslie, 10 October 1797, NAS, JC 26/293.

106. NAS, JC 26/281.

107. Leslie to William Shaw, weaver, Kilsyth, 28 January 1797, NAS, JC 26/293.

108. NAS, JC 26/293/3.

109. NAS, JC 26/293.

110. NAS, JC 26/293.

111. See, for example, report of Archibald Jamieson, [May 1798?], NAS, RH 2/4/84, fols 226–7, which referred to radicals waiting 'in awful suspense the result' of the trials of Roger O'Connor and others in Maidstone for treasonable practices. Jamieson may, however, have been prone to exaggerating the importance of London connections, given his background. See also the examination of Jarvie, fols 210–11, which refers to talk of the Glasgow society planning to send delegates to London, Ireland and the north country. See evidence of Walter Brown, bleacher in Cupar, Fife, in Howell, *State Trials*, vol. 26, p. 1153, where Brown testifies: 'The system I was told, was, that all through England were to rise in one day, and all who held places, if they resisted, were to be dispatched ... They also said they had about 100,000 of the army now in England engaged ....' Since Brown turned King's evidence, he may have been exaggerating to justify his stance.

112. See advertisements in *Scots C.*, 3 March and 11 April 1797.

113. *Scots C.*, 17 February and 17 March 1797. On 16 March, the Court of Session granted an interdict prohibiting the sale of the pamphlet since the proprietor was going to bring actions for damages against the printers and publishers of spurious editions.

114. Declaration of William Morris, 5 November 1797, NAS, JC 26/294.

115. Sir William Murray to Robert Dundas, 15 September 1797, EUL, Laing Papers, II, 500, 1479–80. See also Archibald Campbell of Clathick to Robert Dundas, 16 October 1797, 1600.

116. See Chapter 2 above, pp. 48–9; Brown, *The History of Paisley*, vol. 2, p. 61.

117. See, for example, *Scots C.*, 14 April 1797.

118. Vincent Macleod, 'The Scottish Opposition Whigs and the French Revolution', p. 88.

119. There were also petitions from the nine incorporated trades of Dundee; the incorporation of hammermen in Edinburgh; the inhabitants of the borough and parish of Rutherglen; the magistrates, counsellors and burgesses of the burgh of Haddington; and the burgh of Kirkudbright. The Edinburgh petition was allegedly signed by 11,000 people. Attempts to move for petitions by members of the burgh of Linlithgow and St Mary's Chapel, Edinburgh, were defeated (*Scots C.*, 21 and 28 April 1797).

120. Susan Clerk to Miss Adam, 7 March 1797, NAS, GD 5486/18/44.
121. Wells, *Insurrection*, p. 74.
122. *Resolutions and Constitution of the Society of United Scotsmen*; Sands to the paper, Perth, 20 January 1798, *Scots C.*, 26 January 1798. See also David Couston's declaration that the oath he took on being sworn in as a member of the United Scotsmen in Glasgow was 'to persist in a Parliamentary Reform without regard to hopes of fears of rewards or punishments ...' (NAS, JC 26/294).
123. Howell, *State Trials*, vol. 26, pp. 1135–64.
124. *Scots C.*, 14 April 1797.
125. James McDowall to the Duke of Portland, Glasgow, 21 November 1797, NAS, RH 2/4/82, fol. 240.
126. *Scots C.*, 27 January 1797.
127. *Scots C.*, 26 May 1797.
128. Declaration of William Morris, 1797, NAS, JC 26/294.
129. *Scots C.*, 20, 24 and 31 January, 10 and 24 February, 4 April, 19 and 30 May, 7 July 1797. Around 50 societies were referred to in total, the majority of them in the west and west-central areas of lowland Scotland.
130. *Scots C.*, 19 May 1797.
131. John Orr, Glasgow, to Robert Dundas, 18 November 1797, NAS, RH 2/4/82, fols 237–8.
132. Evidence of Robert Bain, weaver in Coupar Angus, Howell, *State Trials*, vol. 26, p. 1154.
133. *Scots C.*, 27 January 1797.
134. Loudon McAdam to Robert Dundas, Muirkirk, 29 September 1797, EUL, Laing Papers, II, 500, 1499–500.
135. *Scots C.*, 10 February 1797.
136. Western, 'The Formation of the Scottish Militia'.
137. For the widespread view that such a measure would provoke intense opposition, see, inter alia, copy of a letter from John Rutherford to the Duke of Buccleuch, 21 February 1797, NAS, GD 51/1/879; the Earl of Eglinton to Henry Dundas, 28 February 1797, 881.
138. Henry Dundas to the Duke of Montrose, 15 November 1796, NAS, GD 51/1/876/2. For his continued adherence to this view, see Henry Dundas to Robert Dundas, 7 March 1798, *Laing MSS*, vol. 2, pp. 646–9.
139. Logue, *Popular Disturbances in Scotland*, p. 77.
140. Henry Dundas, Walmer Castle, to Alex Dirom, 7 August 1797, NAS, GD 51/1/888/2.
141. Logue, *Popular Disturbances in Scotland*, pp. 78–100. For Abernethy, see Alexander Murray to the Duke of Atholl, Ayton House, 19 August 1797, AP, 59 (4), 318; Robert Dundas to the Duke of Atholl, 20 August 1797, 59 (4), 319, where Dundas notes that he had expected trouble, but that this was the first which had been reported; the Duke of Atholl to Col. Murray of Ayton, 21 August 1797, 59 (4), 323.
142. The Duke of Atholl to the Duke of Portland, 19 September 1797, NAS, RH 2/4/82, fols 164–7.
143. Unrest in Angus was confined to a few parishes close to Arbroath, for which see Peter Rankin, sheriff-substitute of Forfar, to Hugh Warrender, crown agent, Arbroath, 24 August 1797, *Laing MSS*, vol. 2, p. 613.
144. For Caithness, see report in the *Aberdeen Weekly Journal*, 26 September 1797; for Banff, Elgin and Ross, see Robert Dundas to the Duke of Portland, 20 September 1797, NAS,

RH 2/4/82, fol. 175; for Kinkardine, see James Strachan to Robert Dundas, Stonehaven, 8 September 1797, fol. 127; Robert Dundas to Henry Dundas, 13 September 1797, GD 51/5/32.

145. For the situation in and around Culross, Perthshire, see Sir Charles Preston, Culross, to the Duke of Atholl, 7 September 1797, AP, 59 (4), 421.

146. Logue, *Popular Disturbances in Scotland*, pp. 85–94.

147. See above, note 1. See also relevant comment in Susan Clerk to Miss Adam, 12 September 1797, NAS, GD 5486/18/47; Mr Taylor, Edinburgh, to William Forbes of Callendar, 30 August 1797, Falkirk District Archives, Forbes of Callendar Papers, GD 171/616/18.

148. *Scots C.*, 8, 12 and 19 September 1797.

149. See, for example, James Henderson to William Forbes of Callendar, 3 September 1797, Falkirk District Archives, Forbes of Callendar Papers, GD 171/626/17, which refers to a meeting of delegates of seven neighbouring parishes to be held on Denny Muir; Hyndford to the Duke of Hamilton, 29 August 1797, NRAS 2177, bundle 2153, which refers to a meeting at Carluke on the evening before a planned district meeting at Lanark; the Earl of Fife, Mar Lodge, to Henry Dundas, 19 September 1797, NAS, GD 51/1/891/1, refers to a meeting of five parishes on Deeside which individuals were allegedly forced to attend under threat of having their houses burned down; Mr Lapslie to Robert Dundas, Campsie, 28 August 1797, EUL, Laing Papers, II, 500, 1328–33, refers to several 'tumultuous meetings' and dispatch of delegates between parishes; petition of John Fairservice, labourer, Muirkirk, [1797], 1493.

150. Compare, for example, the reports of the disturbances at Selkirk on 21 August, where the sheriff was forced to relinquish lists of men eligible for the ballot under threat of having his house fired, the lists were burnt in the streets, and several members of the gentry were attacked and forced to flee on horseback, with the much more peaceable behaviour of a mob which sought to compel a Mr Ferguson of Raith to sign an undertaking not to implement the Act (*Scots C.*, 1 September 1797; *Aberdeen Weekly Journal*, 19 September 1797). See also the contemporary comment on this in extract declaration of Hope Stewart, Esq., of Ballechin, 22 September 1797, NAS, Crown Precognitions, AD 14/1/1.

151. For Dundee, see Lord Douglas to Robert Dundas, 3 September 1797, EUL, Laing Papers, II, 500, 1406.

152. For a description of his approach, see William McDowall to Robert Dundas, Castle Semple, 26 August 1797, EUL, Laing Papers, II, 500, 1313–14.

153. See below, pp. 170–1.

154. See especially the verdict of the Duke of Buccleuch, the Lord Lieutenant, in Buccleuch to [Henry Dundas?], 23 September 1797, NAS, RH 2/4/82, fol. 183; Buccleuch to the Duke of Portland, 8 September 1797, RH 2/4/81, fol. 89; Robert Dundas to the Duke of Portland, 9 September 1797, fol. 93. See also *Aberdeen Weekly Journal*, 12 September 1797, for the conduct of district meetings at Canonmills and Dalkeith.

155. Edinburgh volunteers, for example, were very active in policing meetings in and around the capital. The Perth and Coupar Angus volunteers offered their services to the Duke of Atholl for policing anti-militia disturbances in Perthshire, but they were required to remain in these places to guard them and to allow the regular soldiers to be deployed where there was unrest (19 September 1797, NAS, RH 2/4/82, fols 164–71). For contemporary comment on their limitations as a police force, see, for example, David Staig to Sir Robert Grierson, 28 August 1797, EUL, Laing Papers, II, 500, 1332; Lord Garlies to the Duke of Portland, 2 September 1797, NAS, RH 2/4/81, fol. 11, where Garlies

writes that the long delays in sending arms had rendered the volunteers 'at present nearly nugatory'.

156. See especially William Cunninghame to Robert Dundas, 25 August 1797, EUL, Laing Papers, II, 500, 1299–301, which refers to the special constables in the parish of Stewarton giving up their batons. For other examples of similar refusals to act, see Alexander Fechney to the Duke of Atholl, Perth, 20 and 24 August 1797, AP, 59 (4), 320, 330.

157. The Duke of Roxburgh, Fleurs Castle, to Robert Dundas, 2 September 1797, NAS, RH 2/4/81, fols 13–14. One reason why many volunteer companies were useless as forces to police potential protest in the autumn of 1797 was that those formed in the first half of 1797 had, in many cases, yet to receive arms from the government.

158. NAS, RH 2/4/81, fols 23–4; the Duke of Portland to Robert Dundas, 3 and 5 September 1797, EUL, Laing Papers, II, 500, 1417–20, 1435.

159. James Paton to the Duke of Atholl, Perth, 31 August 1797, AP, 59 (4), 375; Col Charles Rooke, Perth Barracks, to the Duke of Atholl, 12 September 1797, 59 (4), 451. See also the Duke of Hamilton's comments on the impact of the military in Lanarkshire (Hamilton to Robert Dundas, 4 September 1797, NAS, RH 2/4/81, fol. 65). See also the lack of military in Aberdeenshire in September (NAS, RH 2/4/81, fols 95–6), and the similar situation in Ayrshire parishes (RH 2/4/83, fol. 93). See also John Hay, Edinburgh, to unknown, 16 September 1797, NAS, GD 504/9/79/1, which noted that there were 'troops in every district south of the Forth'; the Duke of Hamilton to Lord Adam Gordon, 19 September 1797, NRAS 2177, bundle 2155, on the role of two troops of Norfolk Light Dragoons in maintaining order at a district meeting at Cadder, Lanarkshire.

160. See especially the Earl of Crauford to Robert Dundas, 3 September 1797, EUL, Laing Papers, II, 500, 1404.

161. See, inter alia, George Buchan Hepburn, Smeaton near Haddington, to Henry Dundas, 8 September 1797, NAS, GD 51/5/31; John Robertson, minister at Little Dunkeld, to the Duke of Atholl, 31 August 1797, AP, 59 (4), 374.

162. Forbes of Callendar to the Duke of Montrose, 2, 4, 7 and 28 September 1797, Falkirk District Archives, Forbes of Callendar Papers, GD 171/626/15, 22, 26, 36.

163. The Duke of Hamilton to Robert Dundas, 2 September 1797, *Laing MSS*, vol. 2, p. 620.

164. For examples of schoolmasters subjected to severe intimidation, see, inter alia, William Barclay to Charles Stirling, Bishopsbridge, 22 August 1797, EUL, Laing Papers, II, 500, 1283; the Earl of Eglinton to Robert Dundas, Ayr, 9 September 1797, 1453; W. Macdonald and John Drummond to the Duke of Atholl, St Martins, 23 August 1797, AP, 59 (4), 328; William Graham to the Duke of Atholl, Orchill, 29 August 1797, 59 (4), 359.

165. The Duke of Montrose to William Forbes of Callendar, 29 September 1797, Falkirk District Archives, Forbes of Callendar Papers, GD 171/38.

166. For examples of this, see John Gordon, William Copland, William Douglas and Walter S Laurie, deputy lieutenants, to Robert Dundas, 23 August 1797, *Laing MSS*, vol. 2, p. 612; Peter Rankin sheriff-substitute of Forfar, to Hugh Warrender, crown agent, 24 August 1797, ibid., vol. 2, p. 613; John Bannatyne to the Duke of Hamilton, 29 August 1797, ibid.; Allan Lockhart to the Duke of Hamilton, 29 August 1797, ibid., vol. 2, p. 617; copy of a letter from Allan Macpherson to the Duke of Atholl, Blairgowrie, 29 August 1797, EUL, Laing Papers, II, 500, 1338–41; Dr Thomas Bisset, Logierait, to unknown, 7 September 1797, AP, 59 (4), 423.

167. John Brown to the Duke of Hamilton, 2 September 1797, *Laing MSS*, vol. 2, pp. 618–19. For good examples of the determination of crowds and their signal defiance of entreaties by authorities to desist from opposing implementation of the Act, see William Oliver to Robert Dundas, Jedburgh, August 1797, EUL, Laing Papers, II, 500, 1311–12; NAS, RH 2/4/81, fol. 53, extract of a letter from David Staig, Dumfries, 4 September 1797, where the author notes that, 'There is not one of your Grace's Deputies who has not been threatened with certain distruction [*sic*]'.
168. See especially Logue, *Popular Disturbances in Scotland*, esp. pp. 114–15.
169. For contemporary comment on this aspect of the Act, see J. H. Cochrane to the Duke of Hamilton, Edinburgh, 18 April 1798, NRAS 2177, bundle 2153.
170. See, for example, Callendar House, GD 171/626/13, Stirlingshire militia proclamation, 29 August 1797.
171. Copy of declaration subscribed to by the parishioners of Blair Atholl and Struan, 12 September 1797, AP, 59 (4), 459.
172. Another source of 'popular prejudice' against the Act in this region was highlanders' aversion to having their names fixed to the door of the kirk. Hitherto, this had been associated with an individual being found guilty of moral misconduct. (NAS, RH 2/4/82, fols 164–71.)
173. *Scots C.*, 8 September 1797.
174. Callendar House, GD 171/626/13. See also George Buchanan Hepburn to Robert Dundas, 4 September 1797, EUL, Laing Papers, II, 500, 1423–4, which refers to concerns in East Lothian that the militia ballot would not include the 'sons of lords & lairds'.
175. For this dimension to the protests, see also Logue, *Popular Disturbances in Scotland*, p. 105. For the English protests in 1757, see especially Rogers, *Crowds, Culture and Politics*, ch. 2.
176. See, for example, Henry Veitch to the Duke of Queensberry, 31 August 1797, NAS, RH 2/4/81, fols 55–7; extract of the declaration of Thomas Ferguson, weaver, Ballychandy, near Mullinearn, Logierait, AD 14/1/2, where Ferguson testifies that before the mobs of 4 and 5 September 'he heard that by the Militia Act as soon as people's names were put on the church doors they might be sent to the East Indies or out of the country'.
177. See, for example, General Maxwell to Forbes of Callendar, 28 August 1797, Falkirk District Archives, Forbes of Callendar Papers, GD 171/626/9, referring to the distribution of a handbill prior to district meeting in Falkirk on 15 September. The said handbill is to be found at 626/13. See also minute of meeting of deputy lieutenants of Lanarkshire, Glasgow, 23 August 1797, EUL, Laing Papers, II, 500, 1289; William McDowall to Robert Dundas, Castle Semple, 26 August 1797, 1313–14; factor to the Duke of Montrose to Robert Dundas, Glasgow, 29 August 1797, 1345; Alexander Murray to the Duke of Atholl, Ayton, 23 August 1797, AP, 59 (4) 327, where Murray asks if the Duke approves of his suggestion that an explanatory leaflet be printed and distributed; James Paton to the Duke of Atholl, Perth, 25 August 1797, 59 (4) 334; Col. Andrew Macpherson to the Duke of Atholl, Blairgowrie, 26 August 1797, 59 (4) 338; Sir John Wedderburn to the Duke of Atholl, Ballindean, 28 August 1797, 59 (4), 348; George Paterson, Castle Huntly, to the Duke of Atholl, 28 August 1797, 59 (4), 350.
178. David Staig to Robert Dundas, 4 September 1797, EUL, Laing Papers, II, 500, 1429–30; the Duke of Portland to the Duke of Hamilton, 3 September 1797, NRAS 2177, bundle 1433; Robert Dundas to the Duke of Atholl, 31 August and 2 September 1797, AP, 59 (4), 370, 388. On 28 August, Portland had written to the Duke of Atholl recommending printing and circulating cautionary notices explaining the Act but also warning

that resistance to its implementation would be punished (the Duke of Portland to the Duke of Atholl, 28 August 1797, AP, 59 (4), 246). The Duke of Roxburgh had by the beginning of September received a copy of the West Lothian notice on the Act from the Duke of Buccleuch and another one sent by Robert Dundas. However, a local address, drawn up by Sir Gilbert Elliot, had already been printed and distributed to ministers to read to their congregations. The address was also fixed to the doors of the kirks. Copies of the Militia Act were sent to ministers and schoolmasters in order to allay suspicions of the 'common people' regarding extracts which might be misleading. See the Duke of Roxburgh to Robert Dundas, Fleurs, 3 September 1797, EUL, Laing Papers, II, 500, 1421–2.

179. *Scots C.*, 25 August 1797.

180. Wold, 'The Scottish Government and the French Threat', p. 188. In fact, Rutherglen was probably not the first parish to institute such a subscription. Callender in Perthshire was raising a fund at least by the third week in August (John Buchanan to the Duke of Atholl, Cambusmore, 22 August 1797, AP, 59 (4), 325).

181. John Baird to William Forbes of Callendar, 13 December 1797, Falkirk District Archives, Forbes of Callendar Papers, GD 171/625/40.

182. Loudon Macadam, Muirkirk, to Robert Dundas, 29 September 1797, EUL, Laing Papers, II, 500, 1499–1500. For a similar observation from elsewhere, see Susan Clerk to Miss Adam, 12 September 1797, NAS, GD 5486/18/47.

183. James Baillie to the Duke of Hamilton, Edinburgh, 7 February 1800, NRAS 2177, bundle 1443.

184. See, for example, John Robertson, Little Dunkeld, to the Duke of Atholl, 23 September 1797, AP, 59 (4), 513; James Stewart of Dowally, Dowally, to the Duke of Atholl, 23 September 1797, 59 (4), 514; David Campbell of Glenlyon, Glenlyon House, to the Duke of Atholl, 23 September 1797, 59 (4), 515.

185. See especially Robert Dundas to Henry Dundas, 13 September 1797, NAS, GD 51/5/32; Robert Allan to Robert Dundas, 12 September 1797, GD 51/5/32/2. Other, similar companies were established elsewhere.

186. Robert Dundas to the Duke of Portland, 7 February 1798, NAS, RH 2/4/81, fols 75–9. In the 10th regiment of the North British Militia, for example, of 685 men enlisted between 1798 and 1802, as many as 72.1 per cent were substitutes (Wold, 'The Scottish Government and the French Threat', pp. 340–53). For comment on the role of substitutes in enabling the initial embodiment of the militia, see Sir William Murray of Ochtertyre to the Duke of Atholl, 16 May 1798, AP, 59 (5), 93; Sir Charles Preston to the Duke of Atholl, Culross, 17 May 1798, 59 (5), 95; James Stobie to the Duke of Atholl, Marlehall, 20 May 1798, 59 (5), 97; Andrew Clephane to James Loch, Kirkness, 15 May 1798, NAS, GD 268/42/1.

187. Henry Veitch to the Duke of Queensberry, 31 August 1797, NAS, RH 2/4/81, fols 55–7.

188. Robert Grierson to unknown, 29 August 1797, EUL, Laing Papers, II, 500.

189. Patrick Murray of Ochtertyre to Robert Dundas, [September 1797], EUL, Laing Papers, II, 500, 1455–6.

190. See, for example, the Duke of Roxburgh to Henry Dundas, 2 September 1797, NAS, RH 2/4/81, fols 13–14; Henry Dundas to the Duke of Portland, 4 September 1797, fols 35–40, where Dundas noted that 'Jacobinism is to a certain extent at the bottom of it' and also referred to role being played by 'flagitious emissaries'.

191. The Duke of Montrose to Robert Dundas, 7 September 1797, EUL, Laing Papers, II, 500, 1444–5. See also Montrose to Robert Dundas, 7 September 1797, NAS, RH 2/4/81, fol. 78, where Montrose emphasizes the role, as he had been informed, in weaving villages of 'the set of men who were active with Muir &c'; Montrose to Robert Dundas, 5 October 1797, NAS, RH 2/4/82, fols 293–7.

192. William McDowall to Robert Dundas, 3 September 1797, EUL, Laing Papers, 11, 500, 1413–14, refers to a schoolmaster of Cumbernauld being forced into a 'long political exile'.

193. Threatening letter to William Cunningham of Lainshaw, 21 August 1797, *Laing MSS*, vol. 2, pp. 614–15.

194. R. H. Lindsay to the Earl of Eglinton, 22 August 1797, ibid., vol. 2, p. 612.

195. The Earl of Eglinton to Robert Dundas, Ayr, 9 September 1797, EUL, Laing Papers, II, 500, 1453. See also Eglinton to the Duke of Portland, 11 January 1798, NAS, RH 2/4/81, fol. 93.

196. George Buchanan Hepburn to Robert Dundas, 4 September 1797, EUL, Laing Papers, II, 500, 1423–4.

197. Logue, *Popular Disturbances in Scotland*, p. 113.

198. Col. Charles Rooke to General Lord Adam Gordon, 12 September 1797, *Laing MSS*, vol. 2, p. 628; particulars communicated from Perth very lately, [end 1797], ibid., vol. 2, pp. 639–40; Logue, *Popular Disturbances in Scotland*, p. 112. For Cameron's radical political views, see especially examination of Robert Menzies, tenant at Rashieley in the Parish of [Auchlingaven?], Perth, 13 October 1797, NAS, AD 14/1/10.

199. Lord Fife, Rothiemay, to Henry Dundas, 23 April 1798, NAS, GD 51/1/903/3.

200. Extract of the declaration of Robert Low, portioner of Chapeltown of Tullymett, in the parish of Logierait, NAS, AD 14/1/1.

201. Extract of the precognition anent the riots that took place at Ballnakielly &c, 1797, Robert Robertson, schoolmaster of the parish of Muline, NAS, AD 14/1/2.

202. Logue, *Popular Disturbances in Scotland*, pp. 113–14.

203. *Dumfries Weekly Journal*, 16 January 1798; *Scots C.*, 19 and 26 January 1798.

204. See Thomas Hardy to unknown, March 1814, BL, Add. MS 27,818, fol. 169. There is some doubt surrounding the circumstances of Cameron's flight and whether it was with the connivance of the authorities.

205. See John King to the Solicitor General, 28 March 1801, NAS, GD 385, bundle 39, item 18, marked 'secret'.

206. Lord Adam Gordon to the Duke of Hamilton, 18 October 1797, NRAS 2177, bundle, 2154.

207. See, for example, Lord Home to the Duke of Portland, 7 September 1797, NAS, RH 2/4/82, fol. 19; the Duke of Buccleuch to the Duke of Portland, 23 September 1797, fol. 183; the Duke of Montrose to Robert Dundas, 5 October 1797, fols 193–7; the Duke of Montrose to Robert Dundas, 2 September 1797, *Laing MSS*, vol. 2, pp. 621–2. The desire to secure quick prosecutions seems to have contributed to the first trials failing, in that several people had to be acquitted owing to lack of evidence (Archibald Campbell of Clathick, Edinburgh, to the Duke of Atholl, 19 October 1797, AP, 59 (4), 536).

208. NAS, RH 2/4/82, fol. 205. See also Archibald Campbell of Clathick, Edinburgh, to the Duke of Atholl, 26 October 1797, AP, 59 (4), 540, where Campbell writes that he will 'not be sorry to that spirit which [excites? MS unclear at this point] break forth into action, being persuaded that without some bloodshed there will not be a decisive check given to the progress of democracy in this country'.

209. Narrative of the proceedings at Tranent, on Tuesday the 29th of August [1797], NAS, RH 2/4/81, fols 49–50.

210. See especially George Buchanan Hepburn to Robert Dundas, 4 September 1797, EUL, Laing Papers, II, 500, 1423–4; NLS, MS 7099, fol. 32, Lord Tweeddale to the Duke of Portland, 10 September 1797. The authorities later acknowledged that the deaths of two individuals could not be defended, and that one would warrant a charge of murder if the guilty party could be identified. A general meeting of the lord lieutenant and deputies lieutenant for the County of Haddington, which took place at Haddington on 7 September, quickly voted its thanks to the Cinque Port and Pembrokeshire Cavalry for their actions at Tranent (Sir James Stewart, Inveresk, to the Duke of Hamilton, 13 September 1797, NRAS 2177, bundle 1441).

211. For conviction about the effectiveness of the policy of explanation, see, for example, James McDowall to the Duke of Hamilton, 5 September 1797, NRAS 2177, bundle 2153; Robert Dundas to the Duke of Hamilton, 3 September 1797, NRAS 2177, bundle 2153.

212. See, for example, Andrew Clephane, Kirkness, to James Loch, 15 May 1798, NAS, GD 268/42/1; George Paterson, Castle Huntly, to Henry Dundas, 10 June 1798, GD 51/1/946. For the continued persecution of schoolmasters, see Dr William Porteous to Robert Dundas, 21 February 1798, *Laing MSS*, vol. 2, p. 643; William Hutchison, Auchterarder, to Robert Dundas, 17 January 1798, EUL, Laing Papers, II, 500, 1775. For hints that opposition to the militia continued in some places into the final month of 1797, see Mungo Murray of Lintrose, Lintrose, to the Duke of Atholl, 1 December 1797, AP, 59 (4), 543.

213. Circular letter from Henry Dundas to lords lieutenant, 12 April 1798, NRAS 2177, bundle 2154; plan for encouraging associations &c, for the general defence, 6 April 1798, NAS, GD 46/6/46 (1).

214. Letters to the Duke of Hamilton, Glasgow, 8 June and 9 July 1798, NRAS 2177, bundle 2155; Capt. Cunningham Corbett, of the 1st Company of the Glasgow Armed Association, to the Duke of Hamilton, 1 September 1797, bundle 2156.

215. Baillie David Black, Biggar, to the Duke of Hamilton, 21 May 1798, NRAS 2177, bundle 1441.

216. Paterson, Castle Huntly, to Henry Dundas, 10 June 1798, NAS, GD 51/1/946. See also Lord Kinnaird and George Paterson to the Duke of Atholl, 14 May 1798, AP, 59 (5), 84; George Paterson to the Duke of Atholl, 14 May 1798, 59 (5), 86; George Paterson to the Duke of Atholl, 3 June and 3 December 1798, 59 (5), 114, 215.

217. Angus Archives, B/15/10, Brechin Admissions Register 1710–1830, entry for 5 February 1799. The admission register records the names of 105 volunteers from 26 occupations.

218. The Duke of Montrose, Buchanan, to Henry Dundas, 9 May 1798, NAS, GD 51/1/939. For hints, however, of continued difficulties and non-cooperation from lesser officials in the parish of Falkirk, see GD 171/659/6. In Stirlingshire, embodiment was aided by payment of bounties to balloted men or those who provided substitutes (Callendar House, GD 171/661/22).

219. George Paterson, Castle Huntly, to the Duke of Atholl, 18 June 1798, AP, 59 (5), 133; Sir John Wedderburn to the Duke of Atholl, Balindean, 18 June 1798, 59 (5), 134. Kinnaird and his son had also lent their firm support to the implementation of the Militia Act in the previous year (George Paterson, Castle Huntly, to the Duke of Atholl, 7 September 1797, 59 (4), 425).

220. For Scottish volunteer numbers in 1801, see NA, PRO, WO 13/65/26. For relevant comment on volunteering in the Highlands, see J. M. Bumstead, *The People's Clearance: Highland Emigration to British North America 1770–1815* (Edinburgh: Edinburgh University Press, 1982), p. 157; Cookson, *The British Armed Nation*, pp. 142–3.
221. The policy change was announced in a circular letter from the Duke of Portland, 23 January 1798 (NRAS 2177, bundle 1433).
222. James Brodie to Henry Dundas, 30 January 1798, NAS, GD 51/1/900/2; memorial of the field officers and captains of the 1st battalion of the 2nd regiment of Royal Edinburgh Volunteers, 906; memorial for the officers of the Royal Edinburgh Volunteer Artillery Company, 907/2; officers of the 2nd battalion of the 2nd regiment of the Royal Edinburgh Volunteers to the Duke of Buccleuch, 10 February 1798, GD 224/676/4/D; memorial for the officers of the Midlothian Royal Volunteer Artillery Company, 13 February 1798, GD 224/676/4/C.
223. Patrick Crichton to the Duke of Buccleuch, 5 February 1798, NAS, GD 224/676/4.
224. See especially Robert Dundas to the Duke of Portland, 10 February 1798, NAS, RH 2/4/83, fols 126–9. In this letter, Dundas particularly emphasized information he had received about the disaffected at Dundee using news of the decision to 'inflame' the minds of the volunteers. The information from Dundee was contained in a pseudonymous letter, for which see 'A Loyal Subject', Dundee, to Henry Dundas, February 1798, GD 51/1/902. See also Alex Chalmers, Capt. of the Culross Company of Volunteers, to Henry Dundas, 10 February 1798, GD 51/1/908; William McDowall to the Duke of Portland, 26 January 1798, NAS, RH 2/4/83, fol. 61.
225. Henry Dundas took credit for this decision, for which see Henry to Robert Dundas, Wimbledon, 17 February 1798, EUL, Laing Papers, II, 500, 1808–12, where Henry writes, 'I have got matters put right relative to the proposed retrenchment of the shilling ....'
226. See especially James McDowall to the Duke of Hamilton, 29 May 1798, NRAS 2177, bundle 2153, where McDowall writes: 'I am much obliged to your Grace for the letter respecting the volunteers not being taken as substitutes for the militia which will have a good effect'.
227. John Davie to the Earl of Morton, 12 July 1798, NAS, GD 150/2366, fol. 6. See also Capt. Maitland to the Duke of Buccleuch, 17 February 1797, GD 224/676/3, where Maitland writes of offers made by farmers in the parish of Kirkliston to form troops of volunteer cavalry but on condition that 'no more of their time [be] taken up by exercise (at least during the busy season of the year) than is just sufficient to teach them the usefull parts of it'.
228. William McDowall to Henry Dundas, 3 June 1798, NAS, GD 51/1/944/1.
229. The Duke of Montrose to Forbes of Callendar, 10 August 1798, Falkirk District Archives, Forbes of Callendar Papers, GD 171/625/40, GD 171/643/4/1.
230. NAS, GD 51/5/34.
231. Susan Clerk to Miss Adams, [1798], NAS, GD 5486/18/50; Faculty of Advocates to the Duke of Portland, Edinburgh, 6 February 1798, RH 2/4/81, fol. 118.
232. Angus Archives, Forfar Town Council Minutes, 1793–1807, F/1/1/7, entry for 22 February 1798.
233. George Paterson to Robert Dundas, Bath, 2 March 1798, EUL, Laing Papers, II, 500, 1833–4.
234. James Stobie to the Duke of Atholl, Marlehall, 26 March 1798, AP, 59 (5), 38.

235. The Earl of Cassilis to Robert Dundas, Cassilis House, 21 April 1798, EUL, Laing Papers, II, 500, 1917–18.

236. *Dumfries Weekly Journal*, 9 October 1798.

237. See, for example, George Farquhar to the Duke of Atholl, Edinburgh, 3 and 23 March 1798, AP, 59 (5), 26, 35.

238. Tweeddale to Henry Dundas, 4 March and 4 April 1798, NLS, Yester Papers, MS 14,828, fols 48–9.

239. Minutes of meeting regarding the Stirlingshire voluntary contribution for the defence of the country, 16 March 1798, Falkirk District Archives, GD 171/639/1. Printed copies of these minutes were circulated to deputy lieutenants and Justices of the Peace for distribution to the clergy. For similar efforts in Perthshire, see George Farquhar to the Duke of Atholl, Edinburgh, 30 March 1798, AP, 59 (5), 40.

240. Hyndford to Hamilton, 18 March 1798, NRAS 2177, bundle 2154.

241. Cochrane to Hamilton, 7 April 1798, NRAS 2177, bundle 2154.

242. James Johnstone to Andrew Macpherson, 18 April and May 1798, Newton Castle, Macpherson of Clunie Papers, box 93.

243. Lord Meadowbank to Robert Dundas, 27 April 1798, *Laing MSS*, vol. 2, pp. 655–6.

244. NAS, GD 224/676/16. In 1797, Seceders in Dalkeith had been willing to join the volunteers, but wanted to be excluded from any obligation to take an oath of allegiance (George Whytock to the Duke of Buccleuch, 4 March 1797, GD 224/676/2).

245. See, for example, Henry Butter of Pitlochry, John Stewart of Ballnakillie, Henry Balneavis of Edradour and Alexander Fergusson of Balyoukan to the Duke of Atholl, Mouline, 31 May 1798, AP, 59 (5), 109; Sir William Ramsay to the Duke of Atholl, 2 July 1798, 59 (5), 152; the Duke of Atholl to the Duke of Portland, 12 August 1798, 59 (5), 176; the Duke of Portland to the Duke of Atholl, Whitehall, 24 August 1798, 59 (5), 183.

246. Colley, *Britons: Forging the Nation*.

247. Memorandum on the Linlithgowshire Royal Volunteers, 15 March 1797, NAS, GD 224/676/1, fol. 17.

248. For further comment on this, see Harris, 'Parliamentary Legislation, Lobbying and the Press', pp. 87–8.

249. Monthly pay lists and returns of the Inchture volunteers, 1799, PKCA, Kinnaird Papers, MS 100, bundle 288.

250. For a dispute of this kind in Kirkaldy in 1797, which seems to have been shaped also by opposition to the ruling elite in the burgh, see Claud Boswell to Walter Fergus, 10 August 1797, EUL, Laing Papers, II, 500, 1243; Walter Fergus to Robert Dundas, Kirkaldy, 11 August 1797, 1744; George Morgan to Robert Dundas, Kirkaldy, 11 July 1797, 1253–4. See also Capt. Plenderleath and the officers of the Midlothian Royal Volunteer Artillery Company to the Duke of Buccleuch, 29 January 1798, NAS, GD 224/676/4/B, calling on Buccleuch as Lord Lieutenant to take over responsibility for appointing officers rather than by election to avoid disputes and divisions; see also 676/6, 676/7, 696/16/B, C.

251. See NA, HO 50/46, esp. the Duke of Montrose to Henry Dundas, 6 November 1799.

252. PKCA, PE 66, bundle 3.

253. *Scots C.*, 28–31 March 1797.

254. George Hill, St Mary's College, St Andrews, to Robert Dundas, 2 March 1797, EUL, Laing Papers, II, 500, 1033.

255. William McKenzie to Henry Dundas, Paisley, 23 June 1799, NA, HO 50/46.

256. Notes of concern about arming the disaffected were still heard in 1798, but they were rare. See, for example, Sir William Murray of Ochtertyre to the Duke of Atholl, 16 June 1798, AP, 59 (5), 130.

257. See, for example, examination of James Jarvie, cotton spinner at Thornliebank, 13 April 1798, NAS, RH 2/4/84, fols 219–11.

258. McFarland, *Ireland and Scotland in the Age of Revolution*, p. 168.

259. For Kennedy in 1797–8, see *Scots C.*, 2 January 1798, narrative of experience by James Kennedy, 31 December 1797; report of Archibald Jamieson, [spring 1798], NAS, RH 2/4/84, fols 218–19; and the same, May 1798, fols 226–7, which noted that Kennedy had 'Gone north to lie quiet'.

260. Campbell, *A Journey from Edinburgh*, vol. 1, p. 368.

261. McFarland, *Ireland and Scotland in the Age of Revolution*, pp. 162–7.

262. Whatley, 'Roots of 1790s Radicalism', esp. pp. 39–40.

263. See Robert Dundas to the Duke of Atholl, 30 August and 1 September 1797, AP, 59 (4), 368, 384; Robert to Henry Dundas, 13 September 1797, NAS, GD 51/5/32; Robert Dundas to the Duke of Portland, 20 September 1797, RH 2/4/82, fol. 175.

264. See above, note 175.

265. George Paterson, Castle Huntly, to the Duke of Atholl, 10 September 1797, AP, 59 (4), 437.

266. William McConnell to Robert Dundas, Wigton, 26 August 1797, EUL, Laing Papers, II, 500, 1309; William McDowall to Robert Dundas, Castle Semple, 26 August 1797, 131–4.

267. George Douglas to Robert Dundas, Springwoodpark, 30 August 1797, EUL, Laing Papers, II, 500, 1360; the Duke of Roxburgh to Robert Dundas, Fleurs, 3 September 1797, 1421–2; the Duke of Roxburgh to Robert Dundas, Fleurs, 7 September 1797, 1446.

268. David Staig to Robert Dundas, 13 September 1797, EUL, Laing Papers, II, 500, 1469–70.

269. Lord President to Robert Dundas, 14 September 1797, EUL, Laing Papers, II, 500, 1477–8.

270. Sir John Menzies, Castle Menzies, to the Duke of Atholl, 11 September 1797, AP, 59 (4), 448.

271. The Duke of Atholl to the Duke of Portland, 20 May 1799, *Laing MSS*, vol. 2, pp. 676–8.

272. For Douglas, see Chapter 3, above, pp. 111–12.

6 Bread, Dearth and Politics, 1795–1801

1. The paragraph below draws heavily on Whatley, 'Roots of 1790s Radicalism'.

2. Observations on the State of the Cotton and Silk Manufactures at Glasgow and Paisley – October 8th and the Woollen Manufacture at Leeds, October 17th 1793, NAS, Melville Castle Papers, GD 51/16/82.

3. Edinburgh Central Library, Andrew Armstrong Journal 1789–93, fol. 348.

4. Petition of carters, 3 June 1793, PKCA B59/26/4/16, bundle 8.

5. John to Robert Richardson, 11 August 1793, PKCA, Richardson of Pitfour Papers, MS 101, bundle 45.

6. [William?] Scott, Dundee, to Capt. Robert Stewart of Fincastle, 19 June 1795, AP, 59 (2), 147.

7.   See, for example, J. Donaldson, *General View of the Agriculture of the Carse of Gowrie* (London, 1794), pp. 21–2. See also Mary Snodgrass to Mrs Buchanan, 6 March 1798, NAS, Court of Session Papers, CS 96/2319, for a complaint that it was impossible, owing to the general demand for labour, to get servants in and around Irvine, Ayrshire, except on the 'most extravagant terms'.

8.   Treble, 'The Standard of Living of the Working Class'.

9.   A. J. S. Gibson and T. C. Smout, *Prices, Food and Wages in Scotland, 1550–1780* (Cambridge: Cambridge University Press, 1995), p. 225.

10. See Harris, 'Political Protests in the Year of Liberty', pp. 62–8; Logue, *Popular Disturbances in Scotland*, pp. 148–53.

11. Robert Dundas to Henry Dundas, 25 December 1792, NLS, Melville Papers, MS 6, fols 59–60.

12. PKCA, B59/24/12/45; Edinburgh Central Library, Andrew Armstrong Journal, fol. 319. A subscription for supplying the poor with coal at lower prices was begun in the capital at this time.

13. Fry, *The Dundas Despotism*, p. 166.

14. R. Wells, *Wretched Faces: Famine in Wartime England 1763–1803* (Gloucester: Sutton, 1988), esp. pp. 315–39.

15. Compare ibid. and J. Stevenson, *Popular Disturbances in England 1700–1870* (London: Longman, 1979), esp. pp. 187–8.

16. J. Dinwiddy, 'Intepretations of Anti-Jacobinism', in Philp (ed.), *The French Revolution and British Popular Politics*, pp. 38–49, on pp. 47–8.

17. Logue, *Popular Disturbances in Scotland*, ch. 1.

18. See especially Wells, *Wretched Faces*, part 2; J. Bohstedt, *Riots and Community Politics in England and Wales* (Cambridge, MA: Harvard University Press, 1983); A. Booth, 'Food Riots in the North-West of England 1790–1801', *Past and Present*, 77 (1988), pp. 88–122.

19. See especially Devine, 'The Failure of Radical Reform in Scotland'; Fraser, *Conflict and Class*, ch. 4.

20. *Glas. C.*, 18 October 1800.

21. See especially D. Hay, 'The State and the Market in 1800: Lord Kenyon and Mr Waddington', *Past and Present*, 162 (1999), pp. 101–62; D. Hay, 'Moral Economy, Political Economy and Law', in A. Randall and A. Charlesworth (eds), *Moral Economy and Popular Protest: Crowds, Conflict and Authority* (Basingstoke: Macmillan, 2000), pp. 93–122.

22. R. Mitchison, 'The Movements of Scottish Corn Prices in the Seventeenth and Eighteenth Centuries', *Economic History Review*, new series, 18 (1965), pp. 278–91, on p. 289.

23. An Account of the Number of Quarters in Each Year That These Ports were Open in the Several Counties for the Importation of Oats & Oatmeal Since the Commencement of the Act of 13th Geo III, North Riding Record Office, Northallerton, Zetland Papers, ZNK X 2/1/1027; Answers for George Charles, Esq, Provost and Peter McTaggart and Thomas McClelland, Baillies of the Burgh of Ayr ... 6 March 1800, SL, 415:9, p. 15. These imports into Ayr and Irvine were in addition to grain brought from Galloway and via Greenock.

24. This phrase appears in Answers for George Charles, SL, 415:9, p. 14.

25. L. M. Cochrane, *Scottish Trade with Ireland in the Eighteenth Century* (Edinburgh, 1985), p. 97, cited in Whatley, 'Roots of 1790s Radicalism', p. 35.

26. *Cal. M.*, 13 July 1795.

27. E. P. Thompson, 'The Moral Economy of the English Crowd in the Eighteenth Century', *Past and Present*, 50 (1971), pp. 76–136.
28. See J. Erskine, *An Institute of the Law of Scotland*, 3rd edn, 2 vols (Edinburgh: Bell and Bradfute, 1793), vol. 2, p. 765.
29. David Staig, Dumfries, to Robert Dundas, 27 December 1795, NAS, GD 51/5/226/1.
30. For similar observations about the 'culture of the market' in England, see A. Randall, A. Charlesworth, R. Sheldon and D. Walsh, 'Markets, Market Culture and Popular Protest in Eighteenth-Century Britain and Ireland', in A. Randall and A. Charlesworth (eds), *Markets, Market Culture and Popular Protest in Eighteenth-Century Britain and Ireland* (Liverpool: Liverpool University Press, 1996), pp. 1–24, on p. 15.
31. Petition of Henry Band, baker and corn dealer in Edinburgh, 1 September 1796, and Answers for James Clerk, Esq, Advocate, Sheriff Depute of the County of Edinburgh, & William Scott, Procurator Fiscal of that county, defenders to the petition of Henry Band ... 17 January 1797, SL, 371:7. The early 1790s saw a proposal for the establishment of a weekly market for wheat and barley in the capital, to match the one for oats and oatmeal. On this, see ECA, McLeod Collection, D, 69, item 82. For complaint about the lack of a regular grain market in the capital, see *Aberdeen Weekly Journal*, 26 August 1801.
32. For contemporary comment on this, see Col. W. Fullarton, *A Letter Addressed to the Right Hon. Lord Carrington, President of the Board of Agriculture* (London: J. Debrett, 1801); R. Frame, *Considerations on the Interest of the County of Lanark* (Glasgow, 1799).
33. The debates and controversies generated by changes to the Corn Laws, proposed as well as actual, were very extensive, but see, inter alia, G. S. Keith, *Tracts on the Corn Laws of Great Britain* (1792); J. Girvin, *An Investigation of the Practice of the Sheriffs, Commissioners of the Customs and Merchants, under the Present Corn Laws* (Glasgow: J. and W. Shaw, 1787); *Considerations on our Corn Laws*; *Third Report of a Committee of the Chamber of Commerce and Manufactures in Glasgow, Relative to the Corn Laws* (Glasgow, 1790). See also Chapter 1, above, pp. 40–2.
34. See below, p. 216.
35. North Circuit Minute Book, May 1753–April 1754, case of Alexander Livingstone v. James Smith, pp. 74–9, NAS, High Court Records, JC 11/18; H. Colquhoun to Henry Pelham, 19 April 1752, University of Nottingham, Department of Manuscripts and Special Collections, Newcastle (Clumber) Papers, NeC 2144/1.
36. Petition of James Coutts, merchant in Edinburgh, March 1753, Edinburgh Central Library, qYDA 1822 1723, also includes copy of a letter from William Maitland to Mr Dickie, WS, 16 March 1753.
37. See Whatley, *Scottish Society*, esp. p. 203.
38. DARC, Dundee Town Council Minute Book, vol. 11, entries for 2 March 1771, 6 January 1772, pp. 1767–79.
39. Between October and November 1782, for example, the Lord Provost of Perth wrote to 25 farmers and landowners requesting meal to supply the town's market (PKCA, B59/24/15/51).
40. *Act of the Town Council of Edinburgh, for Encouraging the Importation of Grain to the Port of Leith, at Edinburgh, the nineteenth day of December, one thousand, seven hundred and forty* (Edinburgh, 1740). For a similar example, see Draft advertisement by the magistrates and town council of Perth, 1778, PKCA, B59/24/15/39.
41. *Glasgow Mercury*, 19–26 December 1782.

42. Trades incorporations also customarily bought grain in bulk for distribution to their members (A. M. Smith, *The Nine Trades of Dundee* (Dundee: Abertay Historical Society, 1995), pp. 52–3).

43. A. E. Whetstone, *Scottish County Government in the Eighteenth and Nineteenth Centuries* (Edinburgh: John Donald, 1981), p. 55.

44. R. Mitchison, *The Old Poor Law in Scotland: The Experience of Poverty, 1574–1845* (Edinburgh: Edinburgh University Press, 2000), esp. pp. 80, 100–1. The shortages lasted in Shetland for three years (1782–5). For the relief effort, see sketch of a computation upon the quantity of victual necessary to maintain the inhabitants of Shetland for a twelve month, * by what means they have been maintained from July 1784, to July 1785, being the third year of famine in these islands, Shetland Archives, Sumburgh Papers, D8/150.

45. S. Brown, '"A Just and Profitable Commerce": Moral Economy and the Middle Classes in Eighteenth Century London', *Journal of British Studies*, 31 (1993), pp. 305–32.

46. Thompson, 'The Moral Economy of the English Crowd'; Hay, 'The State and the Market in 1800'.

47. R. Boyd, *The Office, Powers and Jurisdiction of His Majesty's Justices of the Peace, and Commissioners of Supply for Scotland*, 2 vols (Edinburgh: William Creech, 1794), vol. 1, pp. 210–23.

48. Quoted in Answers for George Charles, Esq, Provost and Peter McTaggart and Thomas McClelland, Baillies for the Burgh of Ayr ..., 6 March 1800, SL, 415:9, p. 8.

49. Ibid., p. 9.

50. Petition of James Beattie of Davington, John Wightman of Craighaugh, and Thomas Bell of Crurie, 10 June 1802, SL, 445:15, p. 2.

51. Bakers of Edinburgh & Sprott v. Wardlaw, 1803, SL, 458:17.

52. See M. L. Stavert, *The Guildry Incorporation of Perth, 1200–2002* (Perth: National Register of Archives, 2003).

53. See below, pp. 210–11. This broad pattern, of activism being concentrated in periods of shortage and high prices, seems to have been followed south of the border, for which see Randall et al., 'Markets, Market Culture and Popular Protest', pp. 11–17; Hay, 'Moral Economy, Political Economy and Law', pp. 100–1. In England, Lord Mansfield's opposition to cases against forestalling and regrating seems to have deterred magistrates from pursuing such actions in the 1770s and '80s, fearing that cases would be brought before the Court of King's Bench on a writ of certiorari.

54. Police memorandums by John Hutton, superintendent, 1793–4–5–6, EUL, Laing Papers, III, 552, vol. 1, fol. 11.

55. EUL, Laing Papers, III, 552, fols 77, 78.

56. EUL, Laing Papers, III, 552, fol. 102.

57. EUL, Laing Papers, III, 552, fols 129–31.

58. PKCA, B59/22/14, Perth Bread Price Regulation Book, 26 July 1763–27 September 1809.

59. George Farquhar to the Duke of Atholl, 2 February 1795, AP, 59 (2), 21.

60. EUL, Laing Papers, III, 552, fol. 119.

61. Wells, *Wretched Faces*, p. 290.

62. *Dumfries Weekly Journal*, 3 February 1795.

63. *Aberdeen Weekly Journal*, 7 July 1800.

64. DARC, Dundee Town Council Minute Book, vol. 13, 1793–1805, entry for 10 February 1795. By March, 1,500 individuals in the town were being supported with money, meal and coals (*Cal. M.*, 14 March 1795).

65. Names of those in receipt of meal, coal and money, 1795, ECA, McLeod Collection, D129, item 209.

66. *Cal. M.*, 5 March 1795.

67. Wells, *Wretched Faces*, pp. 36–7, 39–46.

68. State of crops, 1795, to the Duke of Atholl, 16 November 1795, PKCA, b59/38/6/217/2.

69. Archibald Campbell of Clathick, Edinburgh, to the Duke of Atholl, 15 February 1796, AP, B 59 (3), 23.

70. Rough draft made by the Duke of Atholl of a letter on the 'state of grain' in Perthshire, 1795, AP, B 59 (2), 261.

71. *Cal. M.*, 14 December 1795.

72. *Cal. M.*, 23 July 1795.

73. John Glas to Provost James Ramsay, 17 August 1795, PKCA, B59/24/15/56.

74. Petition from the magistrates and town council of Perth to the Lords of the Privy Council on the present scarcity, 29 December 1795, PKCA, B59/24/15/58.

75. Circular letter from the Duke of Portland, Whitehall , to the Duke of Atholl as Lord Lieutenant of Perthshire, 11 July 1795, AP, B 59 (2), 167; printed copy of engagement entered into by Privy Council and others, B 59 (2), 168.

76. Wells, *Wretched Faces*, chs 11, 12.

77. *Dumfries Weekly Journal*, 4 August 1795. For similar sets of resolutions passed by a county meeting in the county of Linlithgow, see *Cal. M.*, 3 August 1795. In Roxburghshire, it was resolved that there was no 'sufficient reason' for either 'alarm or apprehension', however, the high prices and 'wants of their neighbours to the south' made it desirable that people practise the 'greatest frugality and oeconomy in consumption of all kinds of grain' (*Cal. M.*, 8 August 1795), For Aberdeenshire, see *Aberdeen Weekly Journal*, 11 August 1795.

78. DARC, Dundee Town Council Minute Book, vol. 13, entry for 5 August 1795.

79. Ibid., entries for 20 August and 29 September 1795.

80. John Dudgeon to Lord Provost anent the different payments of oats & oatmeal, 30 June 1795, ECA, McLeod Collection, D, 129, item 207; minute of meeting called by the Lord Provost to consider response to possible shortages, 21 July 1795, and of resolution reached by the Common Council on 5 August with respect to the authorisation of credit, item 206.

81. Angus Archives, Montrose Town Council Minute Book, 1794–1817, M1/1/10, entry for 18 August 1795. Dumfries Town Council only began purchasing meal in December 1795 (Dumfries and Galloway Archives, RB2/1/59, Dumfries Meal Accounts, 1795–7).

82. *Cal. M.*, 7 May 1796.

83. Petition of Henry Band, baker and corn dealer in Edinburgh, 1 September 1796, SL, 371:7.

84. Answers for Messrs William Watson and son of Warrenhouse, in the County of Northumberland, merchants, and Thomas Cranstoun, Writer to the Signet, their Attorney, Pursuers; the Two Petitions of Alexander Garden, Tacksman of the Mill of Ardlethan, in the County of Aberdeen; and of William Strachan, Baker in the City of Aberdeen, Defenders, 6 April 1797, SL, 372:11.

85. Logue, *Popular Disturbances in Scotland*, p. 35; *Cal. M.*, 24 August 1795; *Aberdeen Weekly Journal*, 25 August 1795.
86. Logue, *Popular Disturbances in Scotland*, p. 30. In Berwick in March, a crowd took corn from the carts of a merchant, but was persuaded to return it (*Cal. M.*, 2 April 1796).
87. Ewart Library, Dumfries, Diary of William Grierson, entries for 12–15 March 1796.
88. It is significant that no special measures were, for example, taken in this period to procure grain in Paisley.
89. For which, see Whatley, *Scottish Society*, pp. 207–9; S. G. E. Lythe, 'The Tayside Meal Mobs, 1772–3', *Scottish Historical Review*, 46 (1967), pp. 26–36.
90. Ewart Library, Diary of William Grierson, entry for 14 March 1796.
91. *Cal. M.*, 21 and 28 April 1796.
92. J. Murray to the Earl of Mansfield, 11 December 1795, Scone Palace, Perth, Mansfield Papers, Box 111, bundle 1; Logue, *Popular Disturbances in Scotland*, p. 46.
93. DARC, Dundee Town Council Minute Book, vol. 13, entries for 11, 18 February 1796, 27 November 1797.
94. Provost James Ramsay to the Duke of Atholl, 27 January 1796, AP, B59 (3), 12. Other burghs which purchased quantities of oats and oatmeal in early 1796 because of new fears about scarcity included Forfar (Angus Archives, Forfar Town Council Minutes, 1793–1807, F1/1/7, pp. 64, 64–5, 67, 97–8) and Montrose (Angus Archives, M1/1/10, entry for 6 January 1796).
95. Dr John McLagan to Provost James Ramsay, 4 February 1796, PKCA, B59/24/15/64.
96. Memorandum regarding grain supplies, 1796, PKCA, B59/24/15/71.
97. Logue, *Popular Disturbances in Scotland*, p. 30.
98. *Cal. M.*, 17 March 1796.
99. *Cal. M.*, 2 April 1796.
100. *Scots C.*, 29 April 1796. From Ayrshire, James Wodrow noted the high and continuing fluctuations in grain prices in May 1796 (Wodrow to Kenrick, Stevenston, 14 May 1796, W-KC, 24.157 (207)).
101. *Cal. M.*, 2 May 1796.
102. Angus Archives, M1/1/10, entry for 9 May 1796.
103. *Cal. M.*, 28 April 1796; Wodrow to Kenrick, 20 October 1796, W-KC, 24.157 (210).
104. Logue, *Popular Disturbances in Scotland*, pp. 143–4.
105. Ibid., p. 143.
106. Proclamation, 26 April 1796, ECA, McLeod Collection, D138, item 152.
107. South, criminal letters against John Rodger and others; declaration of John Rodger, 21 August 1795, NAS, Court of Justiciary Papers, 1795.
108. Letter from Archibald Campbell to the commanding officer of the Royal Perth Volunteers, 22 August, in *Cal. M.*, 24 August 1795.
109. Ibid.
110. Harris, 'Political Protests in the Year of Liberty', pp. 56–8. On 29 October 1795, Perth's billet master stated that over the preceding 12 months, between 1,000 and 1,300 soldiers had been billeted on the town, and since the previous February another 10,000 or so had passed through en route (PKCA, B59/26/5/54, bundle 6).
111. See, for example, PKCA, B59/32/54, Perth Burgh Court Processes, bundles 2, 3; B59/26/4/16, bundles 6, 9. See also petition by Alexander Robertson against Donald McKenzie, 23rd Batallion of the Breadalbane Fencibles, 13 November 1795, B59/32/68.

112. Precognition of witnesses in relation to a riot upon the streets of this burgh on 22 crt. about seven o'clock at night, Perth, 23 November 1793, PKCA, PE51/20/42. Alcohol seems to have contributed to the fracas on this occasion.

113. General Alexander Mackay, Deputy Adjutor General to Provost James Ramsay, Edinburgh, 20 August 1795, PKCA, B59/32/104.

114. Proclamation concerning quarrels and disturbances between the 31st Regiment of Dragoons and the Inhabitants of Perth, 30 September 1795, PKCA, B59/32/111.

115. Letter to Lord Adam Gordon, 26 October 1795, PKCA, B59/32/111/3.

116. Duncan, *The True Briton*, preface.

117. James Anderson to Lord Kinnaird, 15 February 1795, PKCA, Kinnaird Papers, MS 100, bundle 9.

118. *Edinburgh Magazine*, 31 (1795), 319; Thomas Donaldson, Dundee, to Henry Dundas, 5 February 1795, NAS, GD 51/5/6/13.

119. Notice in *Cal. M.*, 3 December 1795.

120. Meikle, *Scotland and the French Revolution*, p. 159; *Cal. M.*, 30 November 1795.

121. NLS, Misc. Letters, Mrs William Gibson Letters, MS 3017, fols 6, 10, 14.

122. Wodrow to Kenrick, 15 January and 9 December 1795, W-KC, 24.157 (197), (204).

123. Wells, *Wretched Faces*, pp. 268–73.

124. Logue, *Popular Disturbances in Scotland*, p. 46.

125. *Cal. M.*, 24 August 1795; the Provost and magistrates to Major Sharp [commanding officers of the Royal Perth Volunteers], 25 August 1795, PKCA, B59/32/109.

126. James Anderson to Lord Kinnaird, 3–9 May 1795, PKCA, MS 100, bundle 10.

127. DARC, Dundee Town Council Minute Book, vol. 13, entry for 23 October 1794.

128. David Staig, Dumfries, to Robert Dundas, 27 December 1795, NAS, Melville Castle Papers, GD 51/5/226/1.

129. John Dunlop, Port Glasgow, to [Robert Dundas?], 18 March 1796, NAS, GD 51/5/229.

130. Rough draft of letter from the Duke of Atholl to [the Duke of Portland?], 1795, AP, 59 (2), 261; copy of a report by the Duke of Atholl to the Secretary of State as to the amount of crops in that county for 1795, 59 (3), 2; James Ramsay, Provost of Perth, to the Duke of Atholl, 27 January 1796, 59 (3), 12.

131. PKCA, B59/24/15/58.

132. The Duke of Atholl to the Duke of Portland, 12 February 1796, AP, 59 (3) 22.

133. The Duke of Atholl, draft of instructions to deputy lieutenants, February 1796, AP, 59 (3), 31. See also Archibald Campbell of Clathick, Edinburgh, to the Duke of Atholl, 15 February 1796, 59 (3), 23.

134. *Dumfries Weekly Journal*, 31 October and 10 November 1795.

135. See, for example, *Cal. M.*, 10 August 1795. Scots would also have read Kenyon's remarks in English newspapers.

136. *Cal. M.*, 21 April 1796.

137. *Cal. M.*, 19 March, 28 and 30 April and 2, 12 and 19 May 1796. See also the earlier resolution of the Edinburgh City Council against forestalling (*Cal. M.*, 10 March 1796).

138. Regulations proclaimed on 16 March, in *Cal. M.*, 19 March 1796.

139. See *Cal. M.*, 2 June, 29 September, 3, 8 and 13 October and 7 November 1796; James Clerk to Robert Dundas, 27 September 1796, EUL, Laing Papers, II, 500; Hints in Consideration of the Proposed Plan of Selling Corn by Weight, 1796, 1067.

140. G. B. Hepburn, *Observations on the Bill for the Sale of Corn by Weight* (Edinburgh: W. Creech, 1796), p. 41.

141. Petition of Robert Alexander in Cloakston, 26 November 1800, SL, 148:44.

142. NAS, RH 2/4/86, fols 181–2, 183.

143. Petition of James Twaddle, farmer in Spittal, and James Taylor, farmer in Boghead, 27 May 1801, SL, 429:49. The Highland Society was concerned about the danger of relying on unsound seed corn, as had occurred in 1783, for which see 'Address from the Highland Society ... 20 January 1800' (*Cal. M.*, 10 February 1800).

144. NLS, MS 9050, fol. 229.

145. *Scots C.*, 12–15 August 1800.

146. *Glas. C.*, 2 October 1800, where it was reported from Dundee that the average heat had been a third higher than in any summer during the previous twenty years.

147. For reports of price falls in several places, see *Scots C.*, 15–19 and 19–22 August 1800.

148. *Scots C.*, 24–8 October 1800.

149. As reported in *Scots C.*, 30 December–2 January 1801.

150. Mitchison, 'The Movements of Scottish Corn Prices', p. 285. In Orkney crisis conditions appear to have endured until 1804 (Whatley, 'Roots of 1790s Radicalism', p. 27).

151. Logue, *Popular Disturbances in Scotland*, p. 26; Mitchison, 'The Movements of Scottish Corn Prices', p. 285.

152. *Scots C.*, 29 April–2 May 1800.

153. Answers for Thomas Stewart, merchant in Leith to the petition of William Rattray and William Alexander, 24 May 1802, p. 14, SL, 441:50–1.

154. Logue, *Popular Disturbances in Scotland*, p. 31.

155. Representation of the Lord Provost and Magistrates of the City of Glasgow to the Lord Commissioners of HM Treasury, 16 February 1800, NLS, MS 5390, fol. 350.

156. Answers for George Charles, Esq., Provost, and Peter McTaggart and Thomas McClelland, Baillies of the Burgh of Ayr, for themselves and the Magistrates and Council of the said Burgh, as representing the Community thereof, to the Petition of Thomas Leishman, grain dealer in Paisley, 6 March 1800, SL, 415:9.

157. Extract of a letter from Perth, 29 March, in *Scots C.*, 1–14 April 1800; extract of a letter from Dundee, 5 April, in *Scots C.*, 4–8 April; extract of a letter from Dundee, 29 April, in *Scots C.*, 29 April–2 May.

158. *Scots C.*, 29 April–2 May 1800.

159. William Kerr, general post offices, Edinburgh, to Francis Freeling, 1 May 1800, NAS, RH 2/4/86, fols 209–10; James Clerk, Sheriff Depute of Edinburgh to Robert Dundas, 30 April and 4 May 1800, fols 219–20v., 221.

160. Memorial for George Harper, merchant in Leith, 21 May 1803, ECA, McLeod Collection, D147, item 85.

161. *Scots C.*, 1–4 July 1800; *Aberdeen Weekly Journal*, 7 July 1800.

162. Logue, *Popular Disturbances in Scotland*, p. 31; *Aberdeen Weekly Journal*, 8 September 1800, under Edinburgh heading 4 September; *Glas. C.*, 30 August 1800.

163. Logue, *Popular Disturbances in Scotland*, p. 31; William McDowall to the Duke of Portland, 5 November 1800, NAS, RH 2/4/86, fols 272–3; *Glas. C.*, 21, 25 and 30 October and 1 November 1800.

164. *Aberdeen Weekly Journal*, 20 April 1801.

165. Charles Hope, Lord Advocate, to the Duke of Portland, 24 June 1801, NAS, RH 2/4/87, fols 79–80.

166. *Aberdeen Weekly Journal*, 9 December 1801 [Arbroath]; Logue, *Popular Disturbances in Scotland*, p. 31.

167. Ibid., p. 3; NAS, Journal of Adjournment, Edinburgh 1801–4, JC 4/2, entry for 14 December 1801.

168. Extract of a letter from Dundee, 3 February, in *Aberdeen Weekly Journal*, 9 February 1801.

169. H-Q, Patrick Orr to W. Adam, 21 February 1801, National Register of Archives, Scotland, Adam of Blair Adam Papers, General Correspondence, 1801, 0063.

170. *Dundee Weekly Advertiser*, 15 May 1801. See also *Aberdeen Weekly Journal*, 16 December 1801, for the continued depressed state of the local linen industry at the end of the year.

171. *Aberdeen Weekly Journal*, 13 April 1801.

172. Extract of a letter from Glasgow, 3 May, in *Scots C.*, 2–5 May 1800. See also, for very similar comments, extract of a letter from a merchant in Glasgow, 19 September, in *Scots C.*, 19–23 September 1800.

173. *Glas. C.*, 25 July 1800. See also *Glas. C.*, 29 and 31 July, 1, 3, 5, 9, 14, 16, 21, 26 and 30 August and 4 September 1800. For other examples, see *Aberdeen Weekly Journal*, 4, 11 and 18 August and 29 September 1800.

174. *Glas. C.*, 5 November 1800.

175. Petition of the Friendly Societies in the Burgh of Dumfries, 29 October 1800, NAS, RH 2/4/86, fols 251–2.

176. *Glas. C.*, 5 and 8 November 1800.

177. *Scots C.*, 21–4 October 1800.

178. See, for example, *Aberdeen Weekly Journal*, 4 August 1800; *Glas. C.*, 10 and 19 July 1800.

179. See, for example, *Glas. C.*, 23, 25, 28 and 30 October and 1 November 1800.

180. *Scots C.*, 1–4 April 1800.

181. Resolutions of meeting, 1 July 1800, of those who suffered either in persons or property in the meal mobs in the course of the year 1800, or on Thursday the 23 day of June last ..., ECA, McLeod Collection, D147, item 85.

182. See below, p. 216.

183. *Glas. C.*, 25 October 1800.

184. *Glas. C.*, 15 November 1800. See also the series of prosecutions launched by Renfrewshire justices of the peace, who appear to have been especially active (*Glas. C.*, 11 February 1800; *Edin. A.*, 10–14 and 24–8 January 1800).

185. NAS, RH 2/4/86, fol. 182.

186. See, for example, *Edin. A.*, 7–11 and 11–14 February 1800; *Scots C.*, 1–5 August 1800.

187. Quoted in Wells, *Wretched Faces*, p. 86.

188. See above, note 19.

189. *Scots C.*, 29 April–2 May 1800. For other subscriptions and schemes to import meal and other types of grain, see, inter alia, Renfrewshire County Archives, Paisley Town Council Minutes, P1/1/23, xix, entry for 1 December 1800; *Glas. C.*, 6 September 1800, where it was reported that James Grant had purchased meal and grain to the value of £7,000 for estates in Strathspey and Urquhart and was selling it at considerably below prime cost. See also below, p. 213.

190. Mitchison, *The Old Poor Law in Scotland*, pp. 130–1. For a similar example from 1796, see proposals of Lord Kinnaird and George Paterson of Castle Huntly for the relief of the 'distressed' in the Carse of Gowrie, 4 and 5 March 1796, PKCA, MS 100, bundle 35.

191. Letter book of the first Strathmore or Stormont Volunteers, 1798–1800, letter for 9 May 1800, Newton Castle, Macpherson of Clunie Papers. For other examples, see, for example, *Aberdeen Weekly Journal*, 16 and 23 February 1801.

192. NAS, RH 2/4/86, fol. 205, 207 [Edinburgh]; Renfrewshire County Archives, Paisley Town Council Minutes, P1/1/23, xix, entry for 26 August 1800; DARC, Dundee Town Council Minute Book, vol. 13, entry for 16 June 1801.

193. Renfrewshire County Archives, Paisley Town Council Minutes, P1/1/23, xix, entry for 6 December 1799.

194. See, for example, letter from Rumford to Dr Majendie, at Windsor, 5 December 1799, reprinted in *Edin. A.*, 7–10 January 1800; *Aberdeen Weekly Journal*, 3 January 1800.

195. *Glas. C.*, 25 October 1801 [Elgin]; 28 October 1801 [Musselburgh]; 27 December 1801 [Perth]; *Edin. A.*, 14–17 January 1800 [Stirling]; 31 December–3 January 1800 [Leith]; 17–21 January 1800 [Montrose, Forfar]; 22–5 February [Kelso]; Renfrewshire County Archives, Paisley Town Council Minutes, P1/1/23, xix, entries for 3 February and 27 November 1800; *Aberdeen Weekly Journal*, 27 January 1800 [Glasgow, Forfar, Montrose]; 31 March 1800 [Banff]; 14 April 1800 [Peterhead]; 14 October 1801 [Aberdeen]; *Glas. C.*, 2 January 1800 [Dunfermline].

196. See, for example, Renfrewshire County Archives, Paisley Town Council Minutes, P1/1/23, entry for 27 November 1800; *Aberdeen Weekly Journal*, 31 March, 14 April 1800.

197. *Glas. C.*, 6 December 1800.

198. Robert Cranstoun to Lord Kinnaird, 28 February, 5 April, 4 May and 16 June 1800, PKCA, MS 100, bundles 35, 36.

199. The Duke of Atholl to Lord Kinnaird, 30 April 1800, PKCA, MS 100, bundle 36.

200. See, for example, Address from the Lord Provost, Magistrates and Sherrif to the Public, 25 April 1800, NAS, RH 2/4/86, fol. 203; *Edin. A.*, 10–14 and 14–17 January 1800; *Glas. C.*, 28 January, 6 February and 11 November 1800.

201. See, for example, *Glas. C.*, 25 October 1800 [Dumfries friendly societies]; 11 November 1800 [Glasgow friendly societies]; *Edin. A.*, 24–8 January 1800 [Edinburgh friendly societies].

202. *Glas. C.*, 30 September 1800 [Stirling society]; *Aberdeen Weekly Journal*, 1 June 1801 [Anderston, Glasgow].

203. Angus Archives, Forfar Town Council Minutes 1793–1807, F1/1/7, entries for 28 August 1799, 20 March, 21, 23 and 28 April and 15 May 1800, 22 January and 2 March 1801.

204. *Letter from an Inhabitant of Paisley to his Fellow Townsmen* (Paisley, 1800), p. 2.

205. *Memorial for the Lord Provost, Magistrates and Town Council of the City of Glasgow, 11 March 1803* (Glasgow, 1803).

206. *Scots C.*, 25–8 November 1800.

207. *Aberdeen Weekly Journal*, 3 January 1800 and 14 October 1801; *Scots C.*, 27 July 1800.

208. Letter from 'Anti-Evil' on the 'Miserable State of the Poor in Edinburgh', *Scots C.*, 13–17 February 1801.

209. *Aberdeen Weekly Journal*, 7 July 1800.

210. *Glas. C.*, 28 November 1800.

211. *Glas. C.*, 4 January 1800.

212. *Aberdeen Weekly Journal*, 15 July 1801.

213. See, for example, W. H. Fraser, 'Patterns of Protest', in Devine and Mitchison (eds), *People and Society in Scotland*, pp. 268–91, on pp. 275–6; Devine, *The Scottish Nation*, esp. p. 218.

214. Whatley, *Scottish Society*, pp. 150–1. See also Bonnyman, 'Agricultural Improvement in the Scottish Enlightenment', esp. chs 6, 7.

215. Robert Cranstoun to Lord Kinnaird, 28 February 1800, PKCA, MS 100, bundle 35.
216. NAS, RH 2/4/86, fols 205, 207.
217. Petition of Lord Provost Riddoch to the Sheriff Depute, 21 May 1801, NAS, Court of Session Papers, CS229/R5/27.
218. There is no agreement among historians about the timing of this shift, or series of shifts, but it seems indisputable that in a Scottish context change accelerated and became more pervasive in the final decade of the century.
219. S. J. Brown, *Thomas Chalmers and the Godly Commonwealth in Scotland* (Oxford: Oxford University Press, 1982).
220. *Glas. C.*, 8 May 1800. See also 'A Friend to Soup Kitchens', in *Glas. C.*, 8 July 1800.
221. *Edin. A.*, 26–31 January 1800.
222. See the essays by Poole, Renton and Thwaites in Randall and Charlesworth (eds), *Markets, Market Culture and Popular Protest*.
223. Brown, '"A Just and Profitable Commerce"'. The bread assize continued to operate in London until 1822 (J. Stevenson, 'The "Moral Economy" of the English Crowd: Myth and Reality', in A. Fletcher and J. Stevenson (eds), *Order and Disorder in Early Modern England* (Cambridge: Cambridge University Press, 1985), pp. 218–38, on p. 230.
224. Wells, *Wretched Faces*, ch. 4.
225. Ibid., esp. p. 86.
226. See, for example, A. Dirom, *An Inquiry into the Corn Laws and Corn Trade of Great Britain, and their Influence on the Prosperity of the Kingdom* (Edinburgh: William Creech, 1796), esp. p. 19; *Third Report of the Chamber of Commerce and Manufactures in Glasgow*, pp. 12–13; Girvin, *An Investigation of the Practice of the Sheriffs*, pp. 21, 37–8, 40; Skene Keith, *Tracts on the Corn Laws of Great Britain*, pp. 7–8.
227. Answers for George Charles, Esq., Provost ..., SL, 415:9, p. 17.
228. *Aberdeen Weekly Journal*, 17 March 1800.
229. See, for example, Boyd, *The Office, Powers and Jurisdiction of His Majesty's Justices of the Peace*, vol. 1, pp. 218–19; Hepburn, *Observations on the Bill for the Sale of Corn*, p. 43.
230. Answers for Alexander Riddoch Esquire to the Condescence for Messrs MacKenzie and Lindsay (1802), NAS, CS 229/25/27, p. 27. A similar concern was evident earlier, for example in Aberdeenshire in 1782, when the 'charitable and well-disposed' were urged not to sell meal at below market price (Resolutions of the Proprietors and Principal Inhabitants of the County of Aberdeen, 23 December 1782, PKCA, B59/24/15/52).
231. According to Mitchison, the 'expansive tendency' of the Scottish Poor Law reached its peak n this period (Mitchison, 'The Poor Law', in Devine and Mitchison (eds), *People and Society in Scotland*, pp. 252–67, on p. 256).
232. See, for example, *Edin. A.*, 31 December–2 January 1800, for the example of the parish of Corstorphine.
233. Fraser, *Conflict and Class*, chs 4, 5.
234. J. Rule, *The Experience of Labour in Eighteenth-Century Industry* (London: Croom Helm, 1981), pp. 177–8.
235. Stevenson, *Popular Disturbances in England*, pp. 189–93.
236. Wells, *Wretched Faces*, esp. ch. 9.
237. Copy of handbill, NAS, RH 2/4/86, fol. 280.
238. Precognition respecting rioters, November 1800, NAS, SC58/22/95, Paisley Sheriff Court Processes, 1801, bundle.
239. William McDowall to the Duke of Portland, Paisley, 16 November 1800, NAS, RH 2/4/86, fols 283–5.

240. Robert Dundas to the Duke of Portland, Edinburgh, 15 November 1800, NAS, RH 2/4/86, fols 281–2.
241. *Glas. C.*, 1 November 1800.
242. Wells, *Insurrection*, p. 235.
243. Although see Ayrshire Archives, Dick Institute, Kilmarnock, Kilmarnock Town Council Minute Book, BK/1/1/2/2, entry for 30 October 1800, in which, following reports of 'inflammatory and seditious hand bills lately posted in the burgh', the Council called for 'the decent and well disposed inhabitants' to support magistrates and the volunteer forces in the town. There was also a call for a meeting of special constables. I owe this reference to David Barrie.
244. See, for example, *Scots C.*, 14–17 October and 4–7 November 1800, 13–16 and 20–3 January 1801.
245. *Scots C.*, 7–11 and 18–21 November 1800.
246. Renfrewshire County Archives, Paisley Town Council Minutes, P1/1/23, xix, entry for 30 October 1800.
247. NAS, RH 2/4/86, fols 283–5.
248. Gee, *The British Volunteer Movement*, pp. 235, 239, 242.
249. Ibid., p. 247.
250. See Chapter 5, above, p. 175.
251. *Dundee Weekly Advertiser*, 15 May 1801.
252. For comment on the abundance and cheapness of herring in Edinburgh in 1800, see George Farquhar to the Duke of Atholl, 7 February 1800, AP, B48 (1), 13.
253. *Scots C.*, 13–16 January 1801.
254. T. M. Devine, 'Social Responses to Agrarian Improvement: The Highland and Lowland Clearances in Scotland', in Houston and Whyte (eds), *Scottish Society*, pp. 148–68, esp. p. 167. The only incidents of 'fire raising' in rural Scotland in this period took place on the Carse of Gowrie in 1801.
255. Devine, 'The Failure of Radical Reform in Scotland', p. 57.
256. See, for example, Revd J. Malham, *The Scarcity of Grain Considered* (Salisbury: J. Easton, 1800), *passim*.
257. C. A. Whatley, 'How Tame were the Scottish Lowlanders during the Eighteenth Century?', in Devine (ed.), *Conflict and Stability in Scottish Society*, pp. 1–30, on p. 15.
258. Although see the cautionary words of Whatley on this general theme in his *Scottish Society*, pp. 164–70.

Conclusion

1. Dinwiddy, 'Interpretations of Anti-Jacobinism', p. 38; Dickinson, *The Politics of the People*, chs 7, 8.
2. See, for example, McBride, *Scripture Politics*, esp. introduction. See also, for a similar perspective, Smyth, *The Men of No Property*.
3. See especially Dickinson, *The Politics of the People*; Bradley, *Religion, Revolution and English Radicalism*. But see also Dinwiddy, 'Interpretations of Anti-Jacobinism'.
4. T. Blanning, *The Pursuit of Glory: Europe 1648–1815* (London: Allen Lane, 2007), p. 332.
5. NLS, Minutes of the Stirling Port Club, Acc 7862, no. 3.
6. Donovan, *No Popery and Radicalism*.

7. N. C. Landsman, 'Presbyterians and Provincial Society: The Evangelical Enlightenment in the West of Scotland, 1740–1775', in J. Dwyer and R. B. Sher (eds), *Sociability and Society in Eighteenth-Century Scotland* (Edinburgh: Mercat Press, 1993), pp. 194–209.

8. George Hill to Robert Dundas, 31 July 1795, EUL, Laing Papers, II, 500, 692. See also enclosed letter from Thomas Somerville to George Hill, Jedburgh, 24 July 1795.

9. *Glas. C.*, 3 January 1796. See also issues of the same paper for 21 and 28 January 1796.

10. See the observations on this made by James Wodrow in 1784 (Wodrow to Kenrick, 15 April 1784, W-KC, 24.157 (74)).

11. L. McIlvanney, *Burns the Radical: Poetry and Politics in Late Eighteenth-Century Scotland* (East Linton: Tuckwell Press, 2002), ch. 5.

12. Wodrow to Kenrick, 22 January 1794, W-KC, 24.157 (187, i). On the McGill case more generally, see McIntosh, *Church and Theology*, pp. 152–3.

13. McBride, *Scriptural Politics*, p. 9.

14. See, inter alia, Goodwin, *The Friends of Liberty*; J. Barrell, *The Spirit of Despotism: Invasions of Privacy in the 1790s* (Oxford: Oxford University Press, 2006), ch. 1; Money, *Experience and Identity*; J. Stevenson, *Artisans and Democrats: Sheffield and the French Revolution 1789–97* (Sheffield: Sheffield History Pamphlets, 1989).

15. Most notably, Brims, 'Scottish Radicalism and the United Irishmen'; Brims, 'From Reformers to "Jacobins"'; Brims, 'The Scottish Democratic Movement'.

16. Catalogue of Effects of the Dundee Rational Institution, to be sold by public roup, 1821, Lamb Collection, Wellgate Library, Dundee. The library comprised 134 volumes. See also *Dundee, Perth and Cupar Advertiser*, 21 April 1809, 14 December 1810 and 28 January and 24 February 1814.

17. *Dundee, Perth and Cupar Advertiser*, 1 December 1820.

18. William Scot to [Henry Dundas?], Perth, 13 August 1797, report of a meeting of Perth radicals on the fifth anniversary of the deposition of Louis XVI, NAS, RH 2/4/80, fols 150–2.

19. See Dinwiddy, 'Conceptions of Revolution', pp. 554–5; Curtin, *The United Irishmen*, pp. 262–4.

20. In 1800 Millar cooperated with the Revd Christopher Wyvill, veteran of the Yorkshire Association and moderate reformer, on a Glasgow edition of the latter's pamphlet *The Secession from Parliament Vindicated* (Wyvill, *Political Papers*, vol. 6, pp. 95–7, 98–100 100–2, 102–4, 104–5, 105–7).

21. Wodrow to Kenrick, 30 May 1792, 2 January 1793 and 16–21 June 1794, W-KC, 24.157 (174), (178), (191, i).

22. Wodrow to Kenrick, 10 September 1794, W-KC, 24.157 (195).

23. Ibid.

24. In February 1797, Gilbert Innes of Stow, who had been a member of the Goldsmiths' Hall Association publications committee, wrote to the Duke of Buccleuch: 'Our committee for publication has been at work & your Grace will observe the Newspapers teeming with loyalty & Patriotism' (Innes of Stow to the Duke of Buccleuch, 28 February 1797, NAS, Buccleuch Papers, GD 224/676/2).

25. The existence of this feeling formed a prominent theme in the diary entries for these years of William Grierson, a resident of Dumfries (Ewart Library, Diary of William Grierson, 1794–1808). See also *Letters of John Ramsay of Ochtertyre 1799–1812*, ed. B. L. H. Horn, Publications of the Scottish History Society (Edinburgh: Scottish History Society, 1966), p. 15, where Ramsay notes, on 8 July 1800, that people's thoughts were 'gloomy and perplexed with famine and greed at home and indignant at the triumphs

of our enemies ...'; Andrew Clephane to James Loch, 11 April 1801, NAS, Papers of the Loch Family of Drylaw, GD 268/42/6.

26. For contemporary observation on this, see Henry Mackenzie to William Pitt, 23 December 1793, NA, PRO 30/8/154/2.

27. J. A. Fairley, 'The Pantheon: An Old Edinburgh Debating Society', *Book of the Old Edinburgh Club*, 1 (1908), pp. 47–75, on p. 49.

28. NLS, Acc. 7863, no. 3, entry for 22 February 1783.

29. William Dickson, 'Diary of a Visit to Scotland, 5th Jan–19 Mar 1792 on Behalf of the Committee for the Abolition of the Slave Trade', entry for 24 January, Friends House, London, Temp MSS, Box 10/14.

30. See, inter alia, M. Chase, *Chartism: A New History* (Manchester: Manchester University Press, 2007); G. Pentland, 'Scotland and the Creation of a National Reform Movement, 1830–1832', *Historical Journal*, 48 (2005), pp. 999–1023.

31. Colley, *Britons: Forging the Nation*, chs 6, 7.

32. See, for example, additional regulations for the Royal Perth Volunteer Regiment, ([1795/6?]); minutes of general meeting, 5 May 1796; votes for officers and committee of the Royal Perth Volunteers, 1795, PKCA, PE 66, bundle 3.

33. On this, see especially Whatley, *Scottish Society*, pp. 197–200.

34. See H. A. Cockburn, 'An Account of the Friday Club Written by Lord Cockburn, Together with Notes on Certain Other Social Clubs in Edinburgh', *Book of the Old Edinburgh Club*, 3 (1910), pp. 105–78.

35. Fairley, 'The Pantheon', pp. 72, 75. The role of women was envisaged as adding to the popularity of the occasion, but also as a civilizing influence on the speakers.

36. See, for example, list of 'gentlemen ... desired to meet' with the magistrates at the Council Chambers to open a subscription for a 'voluntary aid to Government at the present critical period', 12 February 1798, PKCA, B59/25/2/171.

37. For brief comment on this, see Harris, 'Parliamentary Legislation, Lobbying and the Press', pp. 87–8.

38. NAS, Melville Castle Papers, GD 51/5/250.

39. Thirty-seven subscription libraries were founded in Scotland in the 1790s, compared to around fifteen before 1790. The rate of growth further quickened in the first two decades of the nineteenth century. The role of the subscription library is a major focus in a recent PhD thesis by Mark R. M. Towsey ('Reading the Scottish Enlightenment: Libraries, Readers and Intellectual Culture in Provincial Scotland, c.1750–c.1820' (unpublished PhD thesis, University of St Andrews, 2007)).

40. T. Munck, *The Enlightenment: A Comparative Social History 1721–1794* (London: Arnold, 2000), p. 92.

41. 'Scheme for Regulating the Police of the City of Glasgow: Suggested by the general sense of the citizens that some such regulations are absolutely necessary; and which, it is hoped, may form the ground of a plan of Police, as agreeable to the views of all parties, as the nature of that necessary establishment will permit', Glasgow, 1792, Glasgow University Library, Mu24-y.1; Glasgow City Archives, Mitchell Library, Glasgow, C1/1/44, Glasgow Town Council Minute Book, entry for 7 November 1799. I owe these references to David Barrie.

42. See especially I. G. C. Hutchison, 'Anglo-Scottish Political Relations in the Nineteenth Century c.1815–1914', in Smout (ed.), *Anglo-Scottish Relations from 1603 to 1900*, pp. 247–66; K. Robbins, *Nineteenth-Century Britain: England, Scotland, and Wales, the Making of a Nation* (Oxford: Oxford University Press, 1989), ch. 4.

WORKS CITED

Manuscript Sources

Aberdeen University Library, Special Collections

Angus Archives, Restenneth
 Brechin Admissions Register 1710–1830
 Forfar Town Council Minutes
 Montrose Town Council Minutes

Ayrshire Archives, Dick Institute, Kilmarnock
 Kilmarnock Town Council Minute Book

Blair Castle, Blair
 Atholl Papers

British Library
 Francis Place Papers
 Reeves Papers

Dr Williams's Library, London
 Wodrow-Kenrick Correspondence [microfilm copy]

Dumfries and Galloway Archives
 Dumfries Meal Accounts

Dundee Archives and Records Centre
 Dundee Town Council Minute Book

Dundee University Museum and Archives Services
 Glassite Papers (MS9/4/2).
 Topographical Collections, Forfarshire

Edinburgh Central Library
 Andrew Armstrong Journal, 1789–93

Edinburgh City Archives
 Convention of Royal Burghs, Moses Collection
 Correspondence of Andrew Haliburton, 1780–93
 Edinburgh Town Council Minutes
 McLeod Collection

Edinburgh University Library
    Gen 1736, material relating to the Earl of Buchan
    Laing Papers
    List of Members of the Revolution Club at Edinburgh

Ewart Library, Dumfries
    Diary of William Grierson, 1794–1808 [copy]

Falkirk District Archives, Callendar House, Falkirk
    Forbes of Callendar Papers

Friends House, London
    William Dickson, Diary of a Visit to Scotland, 1792

Mitchell Library, Glasgow
    Book of the General Session of Glasgow
    Campbell of Succoth Papers
    Glasgow Town Council Minute Book
    Letter Book of Alexander Wilson
    Personal Memoirs of John Scot of Heatheryknow, Old Monkland.

The National Archives, Kew
    Chatham Papers
    Minute Book of the Society for Constitutional Information

National Archives of Scotland, General Register House
    Arniston Papers [microfilm copy]
    Buccleuch Papers
    Craighall of Rattray Papers
    Crown Precognitions
    Dalguise Muniments [microfilm copy]
    Graham of Fintry Papers [microfilm copy]
    Home Office Papers (Scotland) [photocopies]
    Home of Wedderburn Papers
    Journal of Adjournment, Edinburgh 1801–4
    Justiciary Court Papers
    Kinross House Papers
    Letters and Papers to Robert Graham of Gartmore
    Melville Castle Papers
    Minutes of the Synod of Angus and Mearns
    Papers of the Earls of Glasgow (Crawford Priory).
    Papers of the Loch Family of Drylaw
    Paterson of Castle Huntly Papers
    Steel-Maitland Papers
    John Wauchope, W.S., Edinburgh, to Marchmont, 1780–93

National Archives of Scotland, West Register House
    Court of Session Papers
    North Circuit Minute Book
    Sheriff Court Papers
    Paisley Sheriff Court Processes, 1801
    St Andrew's Commissary Court Records

National Library of Scotland, Edinburgh
    Bell and Bradfute Papers
    Correspondence of Alexander Christie, Provost of Montrose
    Ferguson of Kilmundy Papers
    Mrs William Gibson Letters
    Letter Book of the Royal Aberdeen Volunteers, 1795–1802.
    Lynedoch Papers
    Material relating to East Lothian, 1794
    Material relating to Edinburgh Theatre Riot, 1794
    Melville Papers
    Minutes of the Stirling Port Club
    Misc. Letters
    Saltoun Papers
    'Scott and Contemporaries'
    Tweeddale Papers
    Yester Papers

National Register of Archives, Scotland
    Adam of Blair Adam Papers
    Papers of the Dukes of Hamilton and Brandon

Newton Castle, Blairgowrie
    Macpherson of Clunie Papers

North Ayrshire Library
    Irvine Town Council Minutes

North Riding Record Office, Northallerton
    Zetland Papers

Perth and Kinross County Archives
    Kinnaird Papers
    Miscellaneous Perth Burgh Records
    Perth Bread Price Regulation Book
    Perth Burgh Court Processes
    Richardson of Pitfour Papers

Renfrewshire County Archives
    Paisley Town Council Minutes

St Andrews University, Special Collections
    Playfair Papers

Scone Palace, Perth
    Mansfield Papers

Shetland Archives
    Sumburgh Papers

Signet Library, Edinburgh
    Court of Session Papers

University of Nottingham, Department of Manuscripts and Special Collections
    Newcastle (Clumber) Papers

Wellgate Library, Dundee
    Catalogue of Effects of the Dundee Rational Institution, to be sold by public roup, 1821
    Minute Book of the Dundee Public Library

Newspapers and Periodicals

Aberdeen Weekly Journal

Albion

Caledonian Mercury

Cambridge Intelligencer

Dumfries Weekly Magazine

Dumfries Weekly Journal

Dundee Repository of Political and Miscellaneous Information (1793–4).

Edinburgh Advertiser

Edinburgh Evening Courant

Edinburgh Gazetteer

Edinburgh Herald

Edinburgh Magazine

Edinburgh Weekly Journal

Glasgow Advertiser

Glasgow Courier

Glasgow Mercury

Herald & Chronicle

The Historical Register, or Edinburgh Monthly Intelligencer

London Chronicle

Morning Chronicle

The Political Review of Edinburgh Periodical Publications (1792).

Scots Chronicle

Scots Magazine

Sheffield Iris

Printed Primary Sources

Act of the Town Council of Edinburgh, for Encouraging the Importation of Grain to the Port of Leith, at Edinburgh, the nineteenth day of December, one thousand, seven hundred and forty (Edinburgh, 1740).

Admonition and Information Respecting the Profanation of the Lord's Day (Edinburgh, 1794).

An Address to the Citizens of Edinburgh upon the Nature of the Present Sett of the City and the Necessity of its being Speedily Reformed (Edinburgh, 1780).

An Address to the People of Scotland on Ecclesiastical and Civil Liberty (Edinburgh, 1782).

Answers for the Right Honourable John Dalrymple, Lord Provost of the City of Edinburgh, and others; to the Petition of James Stoddart, esq., late Old Provost, and James Stirling, esq., late one of the Baillies of the said City, and others (Edinburgh, 1778).

Arnot, H., *The History of Edinburgh* (Edinburgh: W. Creech, 1779).

Asmodeus, or Strictures on the Glasgow Democrats in a Series of Letters (Glasgow, 1793).

Boswell, J., *The Correspondence of James Boswell with James Bruce and Andrew Gibb, Overseers of the Auchinleck Estate*, ed. N. P. Hankins and J. Strawhorn (Edinburgh: Edinburgh University Press, 1998).

Boyd, R., *The Office, Powers and Jurisdiction of His Majesty's Justices of the Peace, and Commissioners of Supply for Scotland*, 2 vols (Edinburgh: William Creech, 1794).

[Brown, W.], *Look Before Ye Loup: or, A Healin' Sa' for the Crackit Crowns of Country Politicians, by Tam Thrum, an Auld Weaver* (Edinburgh, 1793).

—, *Look Before Ye Loup. Part Second: or anither Box of Healin' Sa' for the Crackit Crowns of Country Politicians, by Tam Thrum, an Auld Weaver* (Edinburgh, 1794).

Bruce, A., *The Patron's A.B.C., or The Shorter Catechism* (Glasgow: J. Duncan, 1771).

—, *Annus Secularis: or The British Jubilee* (Edinburgh: M. Gray, 1788).

—, *A Serious View of the Remarkable Providences of the Times* (Glasgow: J. Ogle, 1795).

—, *A Brief Statement and Declaration of the Genuine Principles of Seceders Respecting Civil Government; the Duty of Subjects; and National Reformation: And a Vindication of their Conduct in Reference to Some Late Plans and Societies for Political Reform; and the Public Dissentions of the Time* (Edinburgh: J. Ogle, 1799).

Callender, J. T., *The Political Progress of Britain; or, an Impartial Account of the Principal Abuses in the Government of this Country, from the Revolution in 1688. The Whole Tending to Prove the Ruinous Consequences of the Popular System of War and Conquest. 'The World's Mad Business'. Part First* (Edinburgh: Robertson and Berry, 1792).

Campbell, A., *A Journey from Edinburgh through Parts of North Britain*, 2 vols (London: T. N. Longman and O. Rees, 1802).

Cockburn, H., *An Examination of the Trials for Sedition which have hitherto occurred in Scotland*, 2 vols (1888; New York: A. M. Kelley, 1970).

A Collection of Letters on Patronage and Popular Election (Edinburgh: W. Coke, 1783).

Common Sense. A Letter to the Fourteen Incorporations of Edinburgh (Edinburgh, 1777).

Considerations on our Corn Laws and the Bill Proposed to Amend Them (Aberdeen and Edinburgh: C. Elliot, 1777).

Considerations on the Edinburgh Election (Edinburgh, 1761).

Crosbie, A., *Thoughts of a Layman Concerning Patronage and Presentations* (Edinburgh: W. Gray, 1769).

Dirom, A., *An Inquiry into the Corn Laws and Corn Trade of Great Britain, and their Influence on the Prosperity of the Kingdom* (Edinburgh: William Creech, 1796).

Donaldson, J., *General View of the Agriculture of the Carse of Gowrie* (London, 1794).

Douglas, N., *Thoughts on Modern Politics* (London: Button, 1793).

A Dream (Edinburgh, 1777).

Duncan, W., *The True Briton* (Dundee, 1796).

The Dundee Register of Merchants and Trades (Dundee, 1783).

Erskine, J., *The Fatal Consequences and the General Sources of Anarchy. A Discourse on Isaiah, XXIV, 1–5* (Edinburgh, 1793).

Erskine, J., *An Institute of the Law of Scotland*, 3rd edn, 2 vols (Edinburgh: Bell and Bradfute, 1793).

Extract from a Letter Wrote by a Scots Gentleman at London, to a Member of the Commons Council at Edinburgh, upon the Subject of the Ensuing Election, of a Member to Serve in Parliament for that City (Edinburgh, 1741).

Ferguson, A., *Principles of Moral and Political Science*, 2 vols (Edinburgh: A. Strahan and T. Cadell, and W. Creech, 1792).

Frame, R., *Considerations on the Interest of the County of Lanark* (Glasgow, 1799).

Fresh Intelligence from the Coffee House (Edinburgh, 1777).

Fullarton, W., *A Letter Addressed to the Right Hon. Lord Carrington, President of the Board of Agriculture* (London: J. Debrett, 1801).

A General History of Stirling: Containing a Description of the Town, and Origin of the Castle and Burgh (Stirling, 1794).

Gib, A., *The Present Truth, A Display of the Secession-Testimony*, 2 vols (Edinburgh, 1774).

Girvin, J., *An Investigation of the Practice of the Sheriffs, Commissioners of the Customs and Merchants, under the Present Corn Laws* (Glasgow: J. and W. Shaw, 1787).

Great Britain's Memorial, Containing a Collection of Instructions, Representations, &c of the Freeholders and other Electors of Great Britain (London: J. Watson, 1741).

Hepburn, G. B., *Observations on the Bill for the Sale of Corn by Weight* (Edinburgh: W. Creech, 1796).

Heron, R., *Observations Made in a Journey through the Western Counties of Scotland in the Autumn of 1792*, 2nd edn, 2 vols (Perth: W. Morison, 1799).

Historical Manuscripts Commission, *Report on the Laing Manuscripts Preserved in the University of Edinburgh*, 2 vols (London: HMSO, 1914–25).

History of the Town of Dundee, with the Present State of its Situation ... also the Religious Principles, Literature and Population of its Inhabitants (Dundee, 1804).

The History of the Rise, Opposition to, and Establishment of the Edinburgh Regiment (Edinburgh, 1778).

Howell, T. B., and Howell, T. J., *A Complete Collection of State Trials*, 33 vols (1809–28).

To the Inhabitants of Edinburgh (Edinburgh, 1780).

An Inquiry into the Principles of Ecclesiastical Patronage and Presentation (Edinburgh, 1783).

Letter from an Inhabitant of Paisley to his Fellow Townsmen (Paisley, 1800).

A Letter to James Stoddart, Esq (Edinburgh, 1777).

A Letter to Mr Hugh Bell, Chairman of the Convention of Delegates (Edinburgh, [late 1792?]).

A Letter to the Author of Calumny Detected (Edinburgh, 1780.

Lettice, J., *Letters on a Tour through Various Parts of Scotland in the Year 1792* (London: T. Cadell, 1794).

Maclaurin, J., *Considerations on the Right of Patronage* (Edinburgh, 1766).

Macleod, N., *Two Letters from Norman McLeod, Esq MP to the Chairman of the Friends of the People at Edinburgh* (Edinburgh: Alexander Scott, 1793).

Malham, J., *The Scarcity of Grain Considered* (Salisbury: J. Easton, 1800).

Mealmaker, G., *The Moral and Political Catechism of Mankind* (Edinburgh, 1797).

Memorial for the Lord Provost, Magistrates and Town Council of the City of Glasgow, 11 March 1803 (Glasgow, 1803).

Miller, S., *Memoir of the Rev. Charles Nisbet* (New York: R. Carter, 1840).

Mitchell, H., *A Short Apology for Apostacy* (Glasgow, 1797).

Oldfield, T., *History of the Original Constitution of Parliaments, from the time of the Britons to the Present Day ... To which is Added the Present State of Representation* (London: G. G. and J. Robinson, 1797).

The Principal Difference between the Religious Principles of those Commonly Called the Anti-Government Party, and of other Presbyterians, Especially those of the Secession in Scotland; on the Head of Magistracy, Briefly Stated (Edinburgh: J. Guthrie, 1797).

The Progress and Present State of the Laws of Patronage in Scotland (Edinburgh, 1783).

To the Public (Edinburgh, 1780).

Ramsay, J., *Letters of John Ramsay of Ochtertyre 1799–1812*, ed. B. L. H. Horn, Publications of the Scottish History Society (Edinburgh: Scottish History Society, 1966).

Regulations and Catalogue of the Dundee Public Library (Dundee, 1807).

Resolutions and Constitution of the Society of United Scotsmen (n.d.).

Richardson, M. F., *Autobiography of Mrs Fletcher of Edinburgh; with Letters and other Family Memorials* (Edinburgh: Edmonston and Douglas, 1875).

The Second Report from the Committee of Secrecy of the House of Commons (London: J. Debrett, 1794).

Scotland's Opposition to the Popish Bill. A Collection of all the Declarations and Resolutions, Published by the Different Counties, Cities, Towns, Parishes, Incorporations, and Societies, throughout Scotland (Edinburgh, 1780).

Scott, A., *Reasons Justifying the Departure of A. Scott* (Edinburgh, 1794).

A Seasonable Address to the Citizens of Glasgow (Glasgow, 1762).

A Short Account of the Elections at Edinburgh (Edinburgh, 1780).

Skene Keith, G., *Tracts on the Corn Laws of Great Britain* (London: J. Murray; and Edinburgh: C. Elliot, 1792).

Snodgrass, J., *An Effectual Method for Recovering our Religious Liberties, Addressed to the Elders of the Church of Scotland* (Glasgow: James Duncan, 1770).

A Speech Addressed to the Provincial Synod of Glasgow and Ayr, Met at Ayr, 14th April 1784, by one of the Members of the Court, Upon Patronage (Edinburgh, 1784).

The Statistical Account of Scotland, 1791–1799, vol. 9, Dunbartonshire, Stirlingshire and Clackmannanshire, ed. J. Sinclair, new intro. I. M. M. Macphail (Wakefield, EP Publishing, 1978).

The Statistical Account of Scotland, 1791–1799, vol. 10, Fife, ed. J. Sinclair, new intro. R. G. Cant (Wakefield: EP Publishing, 1978).

The Statistical Account of Scotland, 1791–1799, vol. 11, South and East Perthshire, Kinross-Shire, ed. J. Sinclair, new intro. B. Lenman (Wakefield: EP Publishing, 1976).

Ten Minutes Reflection on the Late Events in France, Recommended by a Plain Man to his Fellow Citizens (Edinburgh, 1792).

Third Report of a Committee of the Chamber of Commerce and Manufactures in Glasgow, Relative to the Corn Laws (Glasgow, 1790).

Tracts Concerning Patronage, By Some Eminent Hands (Edinburgh: W. Gray, 1770).

Wednesday, April 1 1761. To the Citizens of Edinburgh (Edinburgh, 1761).

Wyvill, C., *Political Papers, Chiefly Respecting the Attempt by the County of York, and Other Considerable Districts, Commenced in 1779 and Continued During Several Subequent Years, to Effect a Reformation of the Parliament of Great Britain*, 6 vols (York: W. Blanchard, 1794–1802).

Secondary Sources

Bailyn, B., T*he Ideological Origins of the American Revolution* (Cambridge, MA: Belknap Press of Harvard University Press, 1967).

Barker, H., *Newspapers, Politics and Public Opinion in Late Eighteenth Century England* (Oxford: Clarendon Press, 1998).

—, *Newspapers, Politics and English Society 1695–1855* (Harlow: Longman, 2000).

Barrell, J., *Imagining the King's Death: Figurative Treason, Fantasies of Regicide, 1793–1796* (Oxford: Oxford University Press, 2000).

—, *The Spirit of Despotism: Invasions of Privacy in the 1790s* (Oxford: Oxford University Press, 2006).

Beckett, J., 'Responses to War: Nottingham in the French Revolutionary and Napoleonic Wars, 1793–1815', *Midland History*, 12 (1997), pp. 71–84.

Bewley, C., *Muir of Huntershill* (Oxford: Oxford University Press, 1981).

Black, E. C., *The Association: British Extra-Parliamentary Political Organization, 1769 to 1793* (Cambridge, MA: Harvard University Press, 1963).

Black, J., *The English Press 1621–1861* (Stroud: Sutton, 2001).

Blanning, T., *The Pursuit of Glory: Europe 1648–1815* (London: Allen Lane, 2007).

Bohstedt, J., *Riots and Community Politics in England and Wales* (Cambridge, MA: Harvard University Press, 1983).

Bonnyman, B. D., 'Agricultural Improvement in the Scottish Enlightenment: The Third Duke of Buccleuch, William Kier and the Buccleuch Estates, 1751–1812' (unpublished PhD thesis, University of Edinburgh, 2004).

Booth, A., 'Food Riots in the North-West of England 1790–1801', *Past and Present*, 77 (1988), pp. 88–122.

Bowie, K., *Scottish Public Opinion and the Anglo-Scottish Union, 1699–1707* (London: Royal Historical Society, 2007).

Bradley, J. E., *Religion, Revolution and English Radicalism: Non-Conformity in Eighteenth-Century Politics and Society* (Cambridge: Cambridge University Press, 1990).

—, 'The Religious Origins of Radical Politics in England, Scotland and Wales, 1662–1800', in J. E. Bradley and D. K. Van Kley (eds), *Religion and Politics in Enlightenment Europe* (Notre Dame, IN: University of Notre Dame Press, 2001), pp. 187–253.

Brims, J., 'The Scottish Democratic Movement in the Age of the French Revolution' (unpublished PhD thesis, University of Edinburgh, 1983).

—, 'The Scottish "Jacobins", Scottish Nationalism and the British Union', in R. A. Mason (ed.), *Scotland and England 1286–1875* (Edinburgh: John Donald, 1987), pp. 247–65.

—, 'The Covenanting Tradition and Scottish Radicalism in the 1790s', in T. Brotherstone (ed.), *Covenant, Charter and Party: Traditions of Revolt and Protest in Modern Scottish History* (Aberdeen: Aberdeen University Press, 1989), pp. 50–62.

—, 'From Reformers to "Jacobins": The Scottish Association of the Friends of the People', in Devine (ed.), *Conflict and Stability in Scottish Society*, pp. 31–50.

—, 'Scottish Radicalism and the United Irishmen', in Dickson, Keogh and Whelan (eds), *The United Irishmen*, pp. 151–66.

Brown, C. G., 'Protest in the Pews: Interpreting Presbyterianism and Society in Fracture During the Scottish Economic Revolution', in Devine (ed.), *Conflict and Stability in Scottish Society*, pp. 83–105.

Brown, D., '"Nothing but Struggalls and Coruption": The Commons Elections in Scotland in 1774', in C. Jones (ed.), *The Scots and Parliament* (Edinburgh: Edinburgh University Press for the Parliamentary History Yearbook Trust, 1996), pp. 100–19.

Brown, D. J., 'The Government of Scotland under Henry Dundas and William Pitt', *History* (1998), pp. 265–79.

Brown, M., 'Alexander Carlyle and the Shadows of Enlightenment', in Harris (ed.), *Scotland in the Age of the French Revolution*, pp. 226–46.

Brown, R., *The History of Paisley, From the Roman Period down to 1884*, 2 vols (Paisley: Cook, 1886).

Brown, S., '"A Just and Profitable Commerce": Moral Economy and the Middle Classes in Eighteenth Century London', *Journal of British Studies*, 31 (1993), pp. 305–32.

Brown, S. J., *Thomas Chalmers and the Godly Commonwealth in Scotland* (Oxford: Oxford University Press, 1982).

—, 'William Robertson (1721–1793) and the Scottish Enlightenment', in Brown (ed.), *William Robertson and the Expansion of Empire*, pp. 7–35.

— (ed.), *William Robertson and the Expansion of Empire* (Cambridge: Cambridge University Press, 1997).

Bumstead, J. M., *The People's Clearance: Highland Emigration to British North America 1770–1815* (Edinburgh: Edinburgh University Press, 1982).

Cairns, J. W., '"Famous as a School for Law, as Edinburgh ... for Medicine": Legal Education in Glasgow, 1761–1801', in Hook and Sher (eds), *The Glasgow Enlightenment*, pp. 133–62.

Carnie, R. H., 'Provincial Periodical Publishing in Eighteenth-Century Scotland' (unpublished paper, Dundee University, n.d.).

Carter, J., 'British Universities and Revolution, 1688–1718', in P. Dukes and J. Dunkley (eds), *Culture and Revolution* (London and New York: Pinter, 1990), pp. 8–21.

Chase, M., *Chartism: A New History* (Manchester: Manchester University Press, 2007).

Christie, I. R., *Wilkes, Wyvill and Reform. The Parliamentary Reform Movement in British Politics, 1760–1785* (London: Macmillan, 1962).

—, 'James Perry of the Morning Chronicle', in I. R. Christie., *Myth and Reality in Late Eighteenth Century British Politics* (Berkeley, CA: University of California Press, 1970), pp. 334–58.

Claeys, G., *Thomas Paine: Social and Political Thought* (Boston, MA, and London: Unwin Hyman, 1989).

Clare, D., 'The Growth and Importance of the Newspaper Press in Manchester, Liverpool, Sheffield and Leeds, between 1780 and 1800' (unpublished MA thesis, University of Manchester, 1960).

Cockburn, H. A., 'An Account of the Friday Club Written by Lord Cockburn, Together with Notes on Certain Other Social Clubs in Edinburgh', *Book of the Old Edinburgh Club*, 3 (1910), pp. 105–78.

Colley, L., 'Whose Nation? Class and National Consciousness in Britain 1750–1830', *Past and Present*, 113 (1986), pp. 97–117.

—, *Britons: Forging the Nation 1707–1837* (New Haven, CT, and London: Yale University Press, 1992),

Cookson, J., *The Friends of Peace: Anti-War Liberalism in England 1793–1815* (Cambridge: Cambridge University Press, 1982).

—, *The British Armed Nation 1793–1815* (Oxford: Clarendon Press, 1997).

Craig, M. E., *The Scottish Periodical Press, 1750–1789* (Edinburgh: Oliver & Boyd, 1931).

Crawford, J., 'Reading and Book Use in 18th-Century Scotland', *Bibliotheck*, 19 (1994), pp. 23–43.

Cullen, L. M., 'Scotland and Ireland, 1600–1800: Their Role in the Evolution of British Society', in Houston and Whyte (eds), *Scottish Society*, pp. 226–44.

Curtin, N. J., *The United Irishmen: Popular Politics in Ulster and Dublin 1791–1798* (Oxford: Clarendon Press, 1994).

Davis, M. T. (ed.), *The London Corresponding Society, 1792–1799*, 6 vols (London: Pickering & Chatto, 2002).

—, '"The Impartial Voice of Future Times Will Rejudge Your Verdict": Discourse and Drama in the Trials of the Scottish Political Martyrs of the 1790s', in J. Paisana (ed.), *Hélio Osvaldo Alves: O Guardador de Rios* (Braga: Centro de Estudos Humanísticos, 2005), pp. 65–78.

Dennison, E. P., D. Ditchburn and M. Lynch (eds), *Aberdeen Before 1800: A New History* (East Linton: Tuckwell Press, 2002).

Devine, T. M., 'Social Responses to Agrarian Improvement: The Highland and Lowland Clearances in Scotland', in Houston and Whyte (eds), *Scottish Society*, pp. 148–68.

— (ed.), *Conflict and Stability in Scottish Society, 1700–1850* (Edinburgh: John Donald Publishers Ltd, 1990).

—, 'The Failure of Radical Reform in Scotland in the Late 18th Century: The Social and Economic Context', in Devine (ed.), *Conflict and Stability in Scottish Society*, pp. 51–64.

—, *The Scottish Nation 1700–2000* (London: Allen Lane, 1999).

Devine, T. M., and R. Mitchison (eds), *People and Society in Scotland: Volume 1, 1760–1830* (Edinburgh: John Donald with the Economic and Social History Society of Scotland, 1988).

Devine, T. M., and J. R. Young (eds), *Eighteenth-Century Scotland: New Perspectives* (East Linton: Tuckwell Press, 1999).

Dickinson, H. T., *Liberty and Property: Political Ideology in Eighteenth-Century Britain* (London: Weidenfeld and Nicolson 1977).

— (ed.), *Britain and the French Revolution, 1789–1815* (Basingstoke: Macmillan, 1989).

—, 'Popular Loyalism in Britain in the 1790s', in Hellmuth (ed.), *The Transformation of Political Culture*, pp. 503–34.

—, *The Politics of the People in Eighteenth Century Britain* (Basingstoke: Macmillan, 1994).

Dickson, D., 'Paine and Ireland', in Dickson, Keogh and Whelan (eds), *The United Irishmen*, pp. 135–50.

Dickson, D., D. Keogh and K. Whelan (eds), *The United Irishmen: Republicanism, Radicalism, and Rebellion* (Dublin: Lilliput Press, 1993).

Dinwiddy, J. R., 'Conceptions of Revolution in the English Radicalism of the 1790s', in Hellmuth (ed.), *The Transformation of Political Culture*, pp. 535–60.

—, 'Intepretations of Anti-Jacobinism', in Philp (ed.), *The French Revolution and British Popular Politics*, pp. 38–49.

—, 'The Patriotic Linen Draper: Robert Waithman and the Revival of Radicalism in the City of London, 1795–1818', in J R. Dindwiddy, *Radicalism and Reform in Britain, 1780–1850* (London: Hambledon Press, 1992), pp. 63–85.

Donovan, R. K., *No Popery and Radicalism: Opposition to Roman Catholic Relief in Scotland, 1778–1782* (New York and London: Garland, 1987).

—, 'The Popular Party of the Church of Scotland and the American Revolution', in Sher and Smitten (eds), *Scotland and America*, pp. 46–65.

Dozier, R. R., *For King, Constitution and Country: The English Loyalists and the French Revolution* (Lexington, KY: University Press of Kentucky, 1983).

Drescher, S., *Capitalism and Antislavery: British Mobilization in Comparative Perspective* (London: Macmillan, 1986).

Duffy, M., 'William Pitt and the origins of the Loyal Association Movement', *Historical Journal*, 39 (1986), pp. 943–62.

Durey, M., *'With the Hammer of Truth': James Thomson Callender and American Early National Heroes* (Charlottesville, VA, and London: University Press of Virginia, 1990).

Du Toit, A., 'Unionist Nationalism in the Eighteenth Century: William Robertson and James Anderson', *Scottish Historical Review*, 85 (2006), pp. 305–32.

Dwyer. J., and A. Murdoch, 'Paradigms and Politics: Manners, Morals and the Rise of Henry Dundas, 1770–1784', in Dwyer et al. (eds), *New Perspectives on the Politics and Culture of Early Modern Scotland*, pp. 210–48.

Dwyer, J., R. A. Mason and A. Murdoch (eds), *New Perspectives on the Politics and Culture of Early Modern Scotland* (Edinburgh: John Donald, 1982).

Eastwood, D., 'Patriotism and the English State in the 1790s', in Philp (ed.), *The French Revolution and British Popular Politics*, pp. 146–68.

Ehrman, J., *The Younger Pitt: The Reluctant Transition* (London: Constable 1983).

Elliott, M., 'Ireland and the French Revolution', in Dickinson (ed.), *Britain and the French Revolution*, pp. 83–101.

Emerson, R. L., 'Lord Bute and the Scottish Universities, 1760–1792', in K. W. Schweizer (ed.), *Lord Bute: Essays in Reinterpretation* (Leicester: Leicester University Press, 1988), pp. 147–79.

—, 'Politics and the Glasgow Professors, 1690–1800', in Hook and Sher (eds), *The Glasgow Enlightenment*, pp. 21–39.

Emerson, R. L., and P. Wood, 'Science and Enlightenment in Glasgow, 1690–1802', in C. W. Withers and P. Wood (eds), *Science and Medicine in the Scottish Enlightenment* (East Linton: Tuckwell Press, 2002), pp. 79–142.

Emsley, C., 'The "London Insurrection" of 1792: Fact, Fiction or Fantasy?', *Journal of British Studies*, 17 (1978), pp. 66–86.

Fagerstrom, D. F., 'Scotland and the American Revolution', *William and Mary Quarterly*, 11 (1954), pp. 252–75.

Fairley, J. A., 'The Pantheon: An Old Edinburgh Debating Society', *Book of the Old Edinburgh Club*, 1 (1908), pp. 47–75.

Ferguson, W., 'Dingwall Burgh Politics and the Parliamentary Franchise in the Eighteenth Century', *Scottish Historical Review*, 38 (1959), pp. 89–108.

—, *Scotland, 1689 to the Present* (Edinburgh: Oliver & Boyd, 1968).

—, 'The Electoral System in the Scottish Counties Before 1832', D. Sellar (ed.), *The Stair Society, Miscellany II*, Stair Society Publications, 35 (Edinburgh: Stair Society, 1984), pp. 261–94.

Fergusson, J., *Balloon Tytler* (London: Faber and Faber, 1972).

Fishman-Cross, M. N., 'The People and the Petition, 1775–1780', *Midland History*, 14 (1999), pp. 114–28.

Fraser, W. H., *Conflict and Class: Scottish Workers 1700–1838* (Edinburgh: John Donald, 1988).

—, 'Patterns of Protest', in Devine and Mitchison (eds), *People and Society in Scotland*, pp. 268–91.

—, *Scottish Popular Politics: From Radicalism to Labour* (Edinburgh: Polygon, 2001).

Fry, M., *The Dundas Despotism* (Edinburgh: Edinburgh University Press, 1992).

Gee, A., *The British Volunteer Movement 1794–1814* (Oxford: Clarendon Press, 2003).

Gibson, A. J. S., and T. C. Smout, *Prices, Food and Wages in Scotland, 1550–1780* (Cambridge, 1995).

Ginter, D. E., 'The Loyalist Association Movement of 1792–3 and British Public Opinion', *Historical Journal*, 9 (1966), pp. 179–90.

—, *Whig Organization in the General Election of 1790* (Berkeley, CA: University of California Press, 1967).

Godechot, J., *France and the Atlantic Revolution of the Eighteenth Century, 1770–1799* (: Free Press, 1971).

Goodwin, A., *The Friends of Liberty: The English Democratic Movement in the Age of the French Revolution* (London: Hutchinson, 1979).

Gould, E. H., 'American Independence and Britain's Counter Revolution', *Past and Present*, 154 (1997), pp. 107–41.

Graham, J., *The Nation, The Law, and the King, Reform Politics in England, 1789–1799*, 2 vols (Lanham, MD: University Press of America, 2000).

Hamilton, D. J., *Scotland, the Caribbean and the Atlantic World, 1750–1820* (Manchester: Manchester University Press, 2005).

Hampsher-Monk, I., 'Civic Humanism and Parliamentary Reform: The Case of the Society of the Friends of the People', *Journal of British Studies*, 18 (1979), pp. 70–89.

Hargreaves, N. K., 'National History and "Philosophical" History: Character and Narrative in William Robertson's History of Scotland', *History of European Ideas*, 26 (2000), pp. 19–33.

Harris, B., *Politics and the Rise of the Press: Britain and France 1620–1800* (London: Routledge, 1996).

—, *Politics and the Nation: Britain in the Mid-Eighteenth Century* (Oxford: Oxford University Press, 2002).

—, 'The Scots, the Westminster Parliament, and the British State in the Eighteenth Century', in J. Hoppit (ed.), *Parliaments, Nations and Identities in Britain and Ireland 1660–1850* (Manchester: Manchester University Press, 2003), pp. 124–45.

—, 'Political Protests in the Year of Liberty, 1792', in Harris (ed.), *Scotland in the Age of the French Revolution*, pp. 49–78.

—, 'Print and Politics', in Harris (ed.), *Scotland in the Age of the French Revolution*, pp. 164–95.

— (ed.), *Scotland in the Age of the French Revolution* (Edinburgh: John Donald, 2005).

—, 'Scotland's Newspapers, the French Revolution and Domestic Radicalism, c.1789–1794', *Scottish Historical Review*, 84 (2005), pp. 38–62.

—, 'Scottish-English Connections in British Radicalism in the 1790s', in Smout (ed.), *Anglo-Scottish Relations from 1603 to 1900*, pp. 189–212.

—, 'Towns, Improvement and Cultural Change in Georgian Scotland: The Evidence of the Angus Burghs, c.1760–1820', *Urban History*, 33 (2006), pp. 195–212.

—, 'Parliamentary Legislation, Lobbying and the Press in Eighteenth-Century Scotland', in J. Peacey (ed.), *The Print Culture of Parliament 1600–1800* (Edinburgh: Edinburgh University Press, 2007), pp. 76–95.

—, 'Popular Politics in Angus and Perthshire in the Seventeen-Nineties', *Historical Research*, 210 (2007), pp. 518–44.

—, 'The Press, Newspaper Fiction and Literary Journalism, 1707–1918', in S. Manning (ed.), *The Edinburgh History of Scottish Literature, Volume Two: Enlightenment, Britain and Empire (1707–1918)*, (Edinburgh: Edinburgh University Press, 2007), pp. 308–16.

Harris, B., and C. A. Whatley, '"To Solemnize his Majesty's Birthday": New Perspectives on Loyalism in George II's Britain', *History*, 83 (1998), pp. 397–419.

Harris, M., 'The Structure, Ownership and Control of the Press, 1620–1780', in J. Curran, G. Boyce and P. Wingate (eds), *Newspaper History from the Seventeenth Century to the Present Day* (London: Constable for the Press Group of the Acton Society, 1978), pp. 82–97.

—, *London Newspapers in the Age of Walpole: A Study in the Origins of the Modern English Press* (London and Toronto: Associated University Presses, 1987).

Harris, T., 'Reluctant Revolutionaries? The Scots and the Revolution of 1688–89', in H. Nenner (ed.), *Politics and the Political Imagination in Late Stuart Britain: Essays Presented to Lois Green Schwoerer* (Rochester, NY: University of Rochester Press, 1997), pp. 97–117.

Hay, C., *James Burgh, Spokesman for Reform in Hanoverian England* (Washington, DC: University Press of America, 1979).

Hay, D., 'The State and the Market in 1800: Lord Kenyon and Mr Waddington', *Past and Present*, 162 (1999), pp. 101–62.

—, 'Moral Economy, Political Economy and Law', in A. Randall and A. Charlesworth (eds), *Moral Economy and Popular Protest: Crowds, Conflict and Authority* (Basingstoke: Macmillan, 2000), pp. 93–122.

Hellmuth, E. (ed.), *The Transformation of Political Culture: England and Germany in the Late Eighteenth Century* (Oxford: Oxford University Press, 1990).

Hill, J. R., *From Patriots to Unionists: Dublin Civic Politics and Irish Protestant Patriotism, 1660–1840* (Oxford: Clarendon Press, 1997).

Holcomb, K., 'Thomas Reid in the Glasgow Literary Society', in Hook and Sher (eds), *The Glasgow Enlightenment*, pp. 95–110.

Hook, A., and R. B. Sher (eds), *The Glasgow Enlightenment* (East Linton: Tuckwell Press with Eighteenth-Century Scottish Studies Society, 1995).

Houston, R. A., *Social Change in the Age of Enlightenment: Edinburgh 1660–1760* (Oxford: Clarendon Press, 1994).

Houston, R. A., and I. D. Whyte (eds), *Scottish Society 1500–1800* (Cambridge: Cambridge University Press, 1989).

Hughes, E., 'The Scottish Reform Movement and Charles Grey 1792–94: Some Fresh Correspondence', *Scottish Historical Review*, 35 (1956), pp. 26–41.

Hutchison, I. G. C., 'Anglo-Scottish Political Relations in the Nineteenth Century c.1815–1914', in Smout (ed.), *Anglo-Scottish Relations from 1603 to 1900*, pp. 247–66.

Jupp, P., *The Governing of Britain, 1688–1848: The Executive, Parliament and the People* (London: Routledge, 2006).

Kelly, P., 'British and Irish Politics in 1785', *English Historical Review*, 90 (1975), pp. 536–63.

Kidd, C., *Subverting Scotland's Past: Scottish Anglo-Whig Historians and the Creation of an Anglo-British Identity, 1689–c.1830* (Cambridge: Cambridge University Press, 1993).

—, 'The Ideological Significance of Robertson's *History of Scotland*', in Brown (ed.), *William Robertson and the Expansion of Empire*, pp. 122–44.

—, 'The Kirk, the French Revolution and the Burden of Scottish Whiggery', in N. Aston (ed.), *Religious Change in Europe, 1650–1914: Essays for John McManners* (Oxford: Clarendon Press, 1997), pp. 213–34.

—, 'Conditional Britons: The Scots Covenanting Tradition and the Eighteenth Century British State', *English Historical Review*, 474 (2002), pp. 1147–76.

Landsman, N. C., 'Evangelists and their Hearers: Popular Interpretation of Revivalist Preaching in Eighteenth-Century Scotland', *Journal of British Studies*, 28 (1989), pp. 120–49.

—, 'Presbyterians and Provincial Society: The Evangelical Enlightenment in the West of Scotland, 1740–1775', in J. Dwyer and R. B. Sher (eds), *Sociability and Society in Eighteenth-Century Scotland* (Edinburgh: Mercat Press, 1993), pp. 194–209.

—, 'Liberty, Piety and Patronage: The Social Context of Contested Clerical Class in Eighteenth-Century Glasgow', in Hook and Sher (eds), *The Glasgow Enlightenment*, pp. 214–26.

Leneman, L., *Sin in the City: Sexuality and Social Control in Urban Scotland 1660–1780* (Edinburgh, 1998).

Logue, K. J., *Popular Disturbances in Scotland 1780–1815* (Edinburgh: John Donald, 1979).

Lottes, G., 'Radicalism, Revolution and Political Culture: An Anglo-French Comparison', in Philp (ed.), *The French Revolution and British Popular Politics*, pp. 78–98.

Lynch, M., 'Continuity and Change in Urban Society, 1500–1700', in Houston and Whyte (eds), *Scottish Society*, pp. 85–117.

Lythe, S. G. E., 'The Tayside Meal Mobs, 1772–3', *Scottish Historical Review*, 46 (1967), pp. 26–36.

MacDonald, W. R., 'The *Aberdeen Journal* and the *Aberdeen Intelligencer* 1752–7', *Bibliotheck*, 5 (1969), pp. 204–6.

—, 'Aberdeen Periodical Publishing 1786–91', *Bibliotheck*, 6 (1970), pp. 1–12.

McBride, I. R., *Scripture Politics: Ulster Presbyterians and Irish Radicalism in the Late Eighteenth Century* (Oxford: Clarendon Press, 1998).

McFarland, E. W., *Ireland and Scotland in the Age of Revolution* (Edinburgh: Edinburgh University Press, 1994).

—, 'Scottish Radicalism in the Later Eighteenth Century: "The Social Thistle and Shamrock"', in Devine and Young (eds), *Eighteenth-Century Scotland*, pp. 275–97.

McIlvanney, L., *Burns the Radical: Poetry and Politics in Late Eighteenth-Century Scotland* (East Linton: Tuckwell Press, 2002).

McIntosh, J. R., *Church and Theology in Enlightenment Scotland: The Popular Party, 1740–1800* (East Linton: Tuckwell Press, 1998).

McKerrow, J., *History of the Secession Church* (Glasgow: A. Fullerton, 1841).

Mansergh, D., *Grattan's Failure: Parliamentary Opposition and the People in Ireland 1779–1800* (Dublin: Irish Academic Press, 2005).

Meikle, H. W., *Scotland and the French Revolution* (Glasgow: J. Maclehose and Sons, 1912).

Mitchell, A., 'The Association Movement of 1792', *Historical Journal*, 4 (1961), pp. 56–77.

Mitchison, R., 'The Movements of Scottish Corn Prices in the Seventeenth and Eighteenth Centuries', *Economic History Review*, new series, 18 (1965), pp. 278–91.

—, 'The Poor Law', in Devine and Mitchison (eds), *People and Society in Scotland*, pp. 252–67.

—, *The Old Poor Law in Scotland: The Experience of Poverty, 1574–1845* (Edinburgh: Edinburgh University Press, 2000).

Money, J., *Experience and Identity, Birmingham and the West Midlands, 1760–1800* (Manchester: Manchester University Press, 1977).

Mori, J., 'Responses to Revolution: The November Crisis of 1792', *Bulletin of the Institute of Historical Research*, 69 (1996), pp. 284–305.

—, *William Pitt and the French Revolution, 1785–1795* (Edinburgh: Keele University Press, 1997).

Munck, T., *The Enlightenment: A Comparative Social History 1721–1794* (London: Arnold, 2000).

Murdoch, A., 'The Importance of Being Edinburgh: Management and Opposition in Edinburgh Politics, 1746–1780', *Scottish Historical Review*, 62 (1983), pp. 1–16.

—, 'Politics and the People in the Burgh of Dumfries, 1758–1760', *Scottish Historical Review*, 70 (1991), pp. 151–71.

—, 'Scotland and the Idea of Britain in the Eighteenth Century', in Devine and Young (eds), *Eighteenth-Century Scotland*, pp. 106–20.

Murray, N., *The Scottish Handloom Weavers 1790–1850: A Social History* (Edinburgh: John Donald, 1978).

Nash, G. B., 'The Transformation of Urban Politics 1700–1765', *Journal of American History*, 60 (1973), pp. 605–32.

Navickas, K., 'Redefining Loyalism, Radicalism and National Identity: Lancashire under the Threat of Napoleon, 1798–1812' (unpublished DPhil thesis, University of Oxford, 2005).

Nenadic, S., 'Political Reform and the "Ordering" of Middle-Class Protest', in Devine (ed.), *Conflict and Stability in Scottish Society*, pp. 65–82.

Noble, A., 'Displaced Persons: Burns and the Renfrew Radicals', in Harris (ed.), *Scotland in the Age of the French Revolution*, pp. 196–225.

O'Gorman, F., 'Campaign Rituals and Ceremonies: The Social Meaning of Elections in England 1780–1860, *Past and Present*, 135 (1992), pp. 79–115.

—, 'The Paine Burnings of 1792–1793', *Past and Present*, 193 (2006), pp. 111–53.

Osborne, B. D., *Braxfield: The Hanging Judge?: The Life and Times of Justice-Clerk Robert McQueen of Braxfield* (Glandaurel: Argyll, 1997).

Ozouf, M., *Festivals and the French Revolution* (Cambridge, MA: Harvard University Press, 1988).

Palmer, R. R., *The Age of Democratic Revolution*, 2 vols (Princeton, NJ: Princeton University Press, 1959–64).

Penny, G., *Traditions of Perth* (Perth: Dewar, 1836).

Pentland, G., 'Patriotism, Universalism and the Scottish Conventions, 1792–1794', *History*, 89 (2004), pp. 340–60.

—, 'Scotland and the Creation of a National Reform Movement 1830–1832', *Historical Journal*, 48 (2005), pp. 999–1023.

Peters, M., 'Historians and the Eighteenth-Century Press: A Review of Possibilities and Problems', *Australian Journal of Politics and History*, 24 (1988), pp. 37–50.

Philp, M., 'The Fragmented Ideology of Reform', in Philp (ed.), *The French Revolution and British Popular Politics*, pp. 50–77.

— (ed.), *The French Revolution and British Popular Politics* (Cambridge: Cambridge University Press, 1991).

Phillips, J., 'Popular Politics in Unreformed England', *Journal of Modern History*, 52 (1980), pp. 599–625.

Phillipson, N., *The Scottish Whigs and the Reform of the Court of Session 1785–1830* (Edinburgh: Stair Society, 1990).

Pocock, J. G. A., *Barbarism and Religion: Volume Two, Narratives of Civil Government* (Cambridge: Cambridge University Press, 1999).

—, *The Discovery of Islands: Essays in British History* (Cambridge: Cambridge University Press, 2005).

Quinn, J., *Soul on Fire: A Life of Thomas Russell* (Dublin: Irish Academic Press, 2002).

Randall, A., *Riotous Assemblies: Popular Protest in Hanoverian England* (Oxford: Oxford University Press, 2006).

Randall, A., and A. Charlesworth (eds), *Markets, Market Culture and Popular Protest in Eighteenth-Century Britain and Ireland* (Liverpool: Liverpool University Press, 1996).

Randall, A., A. Charlesworth, R. Sheldon and D. Walsh, 'Markets, Market Culture and Popular Protest in Eighteenth-Century Britain and Ireland', in Randall and Charlesworth (eds), *Markets, Market Culture and Popular Protest*, pp. 1–24.

Robbins, K., *Nineteenth-Century Britain: England, Scotland and Wales, the Making of a Nation* (Oxford: Oxford University Press, 1989).

Rogers, N., *Whigs and Cities: Popular Politics in the Age of Walpole and Pitt* (Oxford: Clarendon Press, 1989).

—, *Crowds, Culture and Politics in Georgian Britain* (Oxford: Clarendon Press, 1998).

—, 'The Sea Fencibles, Loyalism and the Reach of the State', in M. Philp (ed.), *Resisting Napoleon: The British Response to the Threat of Invasion 1797–1815* (Aldershot: Ashgate, 2006), pp. 41–59.

Rule, J., *The Experience of Labour in Eighteenth-Century Industry* (London: Croom Helm, 1981).

Sainsbury, J., *Disaffected Patriots: London Supporters of Revolutionary America 1769–1782* (Kingston: McGill-Queen's University Press, 1987).

Saville, R., *Bank of Scotland: A History, 1695–1995* (Edinburgh: Edinburgh University Press, 1996).

Schweizer, K. W., and R. Klein, 'The French Revolution and Developments in the London Daily Press to 1793', in K. Schweizer and J. Black (eds), *Politics and the Press in Hanoverian Britain* (Lewiston, NY: E. Mellon Press for Bishop's University, 1989), pp. 171–86.

Scott, R. H., 'The Politics and Administration of Scotland 1725–48' (unpublished PhD thesis, University of Edinburgh, 1981).

Seed, J., 'Gentlemen Dissenters: The Social and Political Meaning of Rational Dissent in the 1770s and 1780s', *Historical Journal*, 28 (1995), pp. 299–325.

—, '"A Set of Men Powerful Enough in Many Things": Rational Dissent and Political Opposition in England, 1770–1790', in K. Haakonssen (ed.), *Enlightenment and Religion: Rational Dissent in Eighteenth Century Britain* (Cambridge: Cambridge University Press, 1996), pp. 140–68.

Shaw, J. S., *The Management of Scottish Society 1707–1764* (Edinburgh: Donald, 1983).

—, *The Political History of Eighteenth-Century Scotland* (Basingstoke: Macmillan, 1999).

Sher, R. B., 'Moderates, Managers and Popular Politics in mid-Eighteenth Century Edinburgh: The Drysdale Bustle of the 1760s', in Dwyer et al. (eds), *New Perspectives on the Politics and Culture of Early Modern Scotland*, pp. 179–209.

—, *Church and University in the Scottish Enlightenment: the Moderate Literati of Edinburgh* (Edinburgh: Edinburgh University Press, 1985).

—, 'Witherspoon's *Dominion of Providence* and the Scottish Jeremiad Tradition', in Sher and Smitten (eds), *Scotland and America*, pp. 44–64.

—, *The Enlightenment and the Book: Scottish Authors and their Publishers in Eighteenth-Century Britain, Ireland and America* (Chicago, IL, and London: University of Chicago Press, 2006).

Sher, R. B., and A. Murdoch, 'Patronage and Party in the Church of Scotland 1750–1800', in N. MacDougall (ed.), *Church, Politics and Society: Scotland 1408–1929* (Edinburgh: John Donald, 1983) pp. 197–220.

Sher, R. B., and J. R. Smitten (eds), *Scotland and America in the Age of the Enlightenment* (Edinburgh: Edinburgh University Press, 1990).

Small, S., *Political Thought in Ireland 1776–1798: Republicanism, Patriotism and Radicalism* (Oxford: Oxford University Press, 2002).

Smith, A. M., *The Nine Trades of Dundee* (Dundee: Abertay Historical Society, 1995).

Smith, E. A., *Lord Grey 1764–1845* (Oxford: Clarendon Press, 1990).

Smith, M. J., 'English Radical Newspapers in the French Revolutionary Era, 1790–1803' (unpublished PhD thesis, University of London, 1979),

Smout, T. C., *A History of the Scottish People* (London: Collins, 1969).

—, 'Born again at Cambuslang: New Evidence on Popular Religion and Literacy in Eighteenth-Century Scotland', *Past and Present*, 97 (1982), pp. 114–27.

—, 'Problems of Nationalism, Identity and Improvement in Later Eighteenth-Century Scotland', in T. M. Devine (ed.), *Improvement and Enlightenment* (Edinburgh: John Donald Publishers Ltd, 1989), pp. 1–21.

— (ed.), *Anglo-Scottish Relations from 1603 to 1900* (Oxford: Oxford University Press, 2005).

Smyth, J., *The Men of No Property: Irish Radicals and Popular Politics in the Late Eighteenth Century* (Basingstoke: Macmillan, 1992).

—, *The Making of the United Kingdom 1660–1800* (Harlow: Longman, 2001).

Stavert, M. L., *The Guildry Incorporation of Perth, 1200–2002* (Perth: National Register of Archives, 2003).

Stephen, J., *Scottish Presbyterians and the Act of Union 1707* (Edinburgh: Edinburgh University Press, 2007).

Stevenson, J., *Popular Disturbances in England 1700–1870* (London: Longman, 1979).

—, 'The "Moral Economy" of the English Crowd: Myth and Reality', in A. Fletcher and J. Stevenson (eds), *Order and Disorder in Early Modern England* (Cambridge: Cambridge University Press, 1985), pp. 218–38.

—, *Artisans and Democrats: Sheffield and the French Revolution 1789–97* (Sheffield: Sheffield History Pamphlets, 1989).

—, 'Popular Radicalism and Popular Protest 1789–1815', in Dickinson (ed.), *Britain and the French Revolution*, pp. 61–81.

Stewart, A. T. Q., *A Deeper Silence: The Hidden Origins of the United Irishmen* (London: Faber, 1993).

Stewart, L., 'Putting on Airs: Science, Medicine and Polity in the Late Eighteenth Century', in T. Levere and G. L'e Turner (eds), *Discussing Chemistry and Steam: The Minutes of a Coffee House Philosophical Society 1780–1787* (Oxford: Oxford University Press, 2002).

Sunter, R. M., *Patronage and Politics in Scotland 1707–1832* (Edinburgh: John Donald, 1986).

Sutherland, L. S., 'The City of London in Eighteenth Century Politics', in R. Pares and A. J. P. Taylor (eds), *Essays Presented to Sir Lewis Namier* (London: Macmillan, 1956), pp. 49–74.

Thale, M., (ed.), *Selections from the Papers of the London Corresponding Society, 1792–1799* (Cambridge: Cambridge University Press, 1983).

Thompson, E. P., 'The Moral Economy of the English Crowd in the Eighteenth Century', *Past and Present*, 50 (1971), pp. 76–136.

Towsey, M. R. M., 'Reading the Scottish Enlightenment: Libraries, Readers and Intellectual Culture in Provincial Scotland, c.1750–c.1820' (unpublished PhD thesis, University of St Andrews, 2007).

Treble, J. H., 'The Standard of Living of the Working Class', in Devine and Mitchison (eds), *People and Society in Scotland*, pp. 188–226.

Vincent, E., 'The Responses of Scottish Churchmen to the French Revolution, 1789–1802', *Scottish Historical Review*, 73 (1994), pp. 191–215.

—, 'A City Invincible? Edinburgh and the War against Revolutionary France', *British Journal of Eighteenth Century Studies*, 23 (2000), pp. 153–66.

Vincent Macleod, E., 'Scottish Responses to the Irish Rebellion of 1798', in T. Brotherstone, A. Clark and K. Whelan (eds), *These Fissured Isles: Ireland, Scotland and British History, 1798–1848* (Edinburgh: John Donald, 2005), pp. 123–40.

—, 'The Scottish Opposition Whigs and the French Revolution', in Harris (ed.), *Scotland in the Age of the French Revolution*, pp. 79–98.

Weinstein, B., 'Popular Constitutionalism and the London Corresponding Society', *Albion*, 34 (2002), pp. 37–57.

Wells, R., *Insurrection: The British Experience 1795–1803* (Gloucester: Sutton, 1983).

—, *Wretched Faces: Famine in Wartime England 1763–1803* (Gloucester: Sutton, 1988).

Werkmeister, L., 'Robert Burns and the London Daily Press', *Modern Philology*, 63 (1966), pp. 322–35.

Western, J. R., 'The Formation of the Scottish Militia in 1797', *Scottish Historical Review*, 34 (1955), pp. 1–18.

Whatley, C. A., 'How Tame were the Scottish Lowlanders during the Eighteenth Century?', in Devine (ed.), *Conflict and Stability in Scottish Society*, pp. 1–30.

—, 'Royal Day, People's Day: The Monarch's Birthday in Scotland, c.1660–1860', in R. Mason and N. MacDougall (eds), *People and Power in Scotland: Essays in Honour of T. C. Smout* (Edinburgh: John Donald, 1992), pp. 170–88.

—, '"The Privilege which the Rabble have to be Riotous": Carnivalesque and the Monarch's Birthday in Scotland', in I. Blanchard (ed.), *Labour and Leisure in Historical Perspective: Papers Presented at the 11th International Economic History Congress, Milan 1994* (Stuttgart: Franz Steiner Verlag, 1994), pp. 89–100.

—, *Scottish Society 1707–1830: Beyond Jacobitism, Towards Industrialisation* (Manchester: Manchester University Press, 2000).

—, 'Roots of 1790s Radicalism: Reviewing the Economic and Social Background', in Harris (ed.), *Scotland in the Age of the French Revolution*, pp. 23–48.

—, *The Scots and the Union* (Edinburgh: Edinburgh University Press, 2006).

Whetstone, A. E., *Scottish County Government in the Eighteenth and Nineteenth Centuries* (Edinburgh: John Donald, 1981).

Whyte, I. D., 'Urbanization in Eighteenth-Century Scotland', in Devine and Young (eds), *Eighteenth-Century Scotland*, pp. 176–94.

Winch, D., *Riches and Poverty: An Intellectual History of Political Economy in Britain 1750–1834* (Cambridge: Cambridge University Press, 1996).

Wold, A. L., 'The Scottish Government and the French Threat, 1792–1802' (unpublished PhD thesis, University of Edinburgh, 2003).

INDEX

The Scottish People and the French Revolution